Consensus Building in Group Decision Making

Yucheng Dong · Jiuping Xu

Consensus Building in Group Decision Making

Searching the Consensus Path with Minimum Adjustments

Springer

Yucheng Dong
Business School
Sichuan University
Chengdu, Sichuan
China

Jiuping Xu
Business School
Sichuan University
Chengdu, Sichuan
China

ISBN 978-981-10-1283-9 ISBN 978-981-287-892-2 (eBook)
DOI 10.1007/978-981-287-892-2

Springer Singapore Heidelberg New York Dordrecht London

Softcover re-print of the Hardcover 1st edition 2016

Printed on acid-free paper

Springer Science+Business Media Singapore Pte Ltd. is part of Springer Science+Business Media (www.springer.com)

Preface

The group decision making (GDM) can be seen as a task to find a collective solution to a decision problem in the situations where a group of experts express their opinions regarding multiple alternatives. In essence, the GDM reflects the internal relations between the individuals and group and can be defined as a general model as follows:

$$F(op^1, op^2, \ldots, op^n) = op^c,$$

where $\{op^1, op^2, \ldots, op^n\}$ are the opinions of n individuals, op^c is the opinion of the group, and F is the aggregation function implying the group decision rule to aggregate individual opinions into a collective one.

The GDM is in the important and core position in the economics and management science. From a macro perspective, modern society is essentially a GDM system. In the rational and democratic society, there exit two basic GDM methods: one is "voting", which is usually used in politics, and the other is "market mechanism", which is applied in economic issues. Microscopically, there are numerous GDM problems, and people are often faced with the need to work with others in group settings.

The history of the GDM studies can be tracked back to design of voting method (Lull, 1282, 1287; Borda, 1781; Condorcet, 1785). In the last 60 years, the researches of the GDM have gotten great progresses, and some famous theories have been proposed, e.g., social choice theory (Arrow, 1951) and prospect theory (Kahneman and Tversky, 1979, 1992). The social choice theory dates from Condorcet's formulation of the voting paradox, and provides a theoretical framework for analysis of combining individual opinions, preferences, interests, or welfares to reach a collective decision or social welfare in some sense. The Arrow Impossibility Theorem, the Gibbard-Satterthwaite Strategy-proofness Impossibility Theorem and the Sen Libertarian Impossibility Theorem construct the foot stone of social choice theory. The prospect theory is a descriptive model based on psychology, and tries to model real-life choices, rather than optimal decisions, as normative models do. The prospect theory states that people make decisions based on the potential value of losses and gains rather than the final outcome, and that people evaluate these losses and gains using certain heuristics. The social choice theory and the prospect theory both provide exciting insights for us to better understand and investigate GDM problems.

Consensus is an important area of research in the GDM and is defined as a state of mutual agreement among individuals of a group, where all opinions have been heard and addressed to the satisfaction of the group. A consensus reaching process is a dynamic and an iterative process composed by several rounds where the individuals express, discuss, and modify their opinions until to make a decision. Integrating the consensus reaching process into the GDM offers some advantages: (1) More effective implementation. When individuals' opinions and concerns are taken into account, they are more likely to actively participate in the implementation of the obtained solution, and (2) Building connection among the individuals. Using consensus as a decision tool means taking the time to find unity on how to proceed before moving forward, which promotes communication among individuals.

In the consensus reaching process, individuals often need to adjust their opinions to improve the consensus level among individuals. In this book, we propose a challenge for analysts: how to minimize the adjustment amounts in the consensus reaching process, which can be described as an optimization-based model.

$$\min_{\overline{op^k}} \sum_{k=1}^{n} d(op^k, \overline{op^k}),$$

where $\{op^1, op^2, \ldots, op^n\}$ are the individuals' original opinions, $\{\overline{op^1}, \overline{op^2}, \ldots, \overline{op^n}\}$ are the individuals' adjusted opinions with a consensus, and $d(op^k, \overline{op^k})$ $(k = 1, 2, \ldots, n)$ is to measure the adjustment amounts associated with the individual k. We investigate the optimization-based model to search the consensus path with minimum adjustments under different GDM contexts. Particularly, in Chap. 2 we clarify the basic idea of the consensus with minimum adjustments (or cost), and investigate the consensus model with minimum adjustments (or cost) under the utility preferences and aggregation functions. Then, in Chap. 3 we propose two consensus models for the GDM with preference relations: the iteration-based consensus model and the LP-based consensus model. Next, we investigate the consensus models with minimum adjustments under the 2-tuple linguistic context and the hesitant linguistic context in Chap. 4. Subsequently, in Chap. 5 we propose two consensus models for the GDM with heterogeneous preference representation structures: the direct consensus model and the prospect theory-based consensus model. Finally, Chap. 6 presents two multiple attribute consensus rules with minimum adjustments: the distance-based consensus rule and the count-based consensus rule. Based on the distance-based and count-based consensus rules, we develop an interactive consensus reaching process for multiple attribute group decision making.

We believe that the optimal adjusted opinions, obtained by the methodology presented in the book, can provide a better decision aid which individuals use as a reference to modify their individual opinions.

We want to express special thanks to Professor Yinfeng Xu, Professor Yihua Chen, Professor Zhi-Ping Fan, Professor Wei-Chiang Hong, Professor Enrique Herrera-Viedma, and Professor Francisco Herrera, for their contributions and great support to this book. We also want to express our sincere thanks to the colleagues and students in our group, Hengjie Zhang, Haiming Liang, Cong-Cong Li, Xia Chen, Yuzhu Wu, Nan Luo, Guiqing Zhang, and Bowen Zhang, who have done much work in this field and made a number of corrections. This book is supported by Grants (Nos. 70425005, 71171160, 71571124) from NSF of China, and a Grant (No. skqx201308) from Sichuan University.

Chengdu, China
July 2015

Yucheng Dong
Jiuping Xu

Contents

Chapter 1
Introduction

The basic knowledge regarding the group decision making (GDM) and consensus is introduced in this chapter. In particular, we introduce two key elements in the GDM: *preference representation structure* and *aggregation function*. Subsequently, we conduct a literature review regarding the consensus, present a general consensus framework, and propose the core problem in the consensus reaching process.

1.1 Preference Representation Structure and Aggregation Function

The GDM can be seen as a task to find a collective solution to a decision problem in the situations where a group of experts express their opinions regarding multiple alternatives. Everyday, people are faced with the need to work with others in group settings to make decisions, for example,

(1) In the field of politics, the decision process of United Nations Security Council is a GDM problem. When making decisions, the five permanent members form a group, and they have to find a solution regarding the decision problem collectively.
(2) In the field of economic management, the supplier selection problem is a GDM problem. In the process of the supplier selection, the members from different departments of a company form a decision committee. The decision committee works in collaboration to select a supplier.
(3) In daily life, a family wants to choose a destination to travel. The members of the family need to work together to choose the destination.

The GDM involves multiple disciplines, such as decision science, management, mathematics, economics, social psychology, behavioral science, and political science, etc. In general, a GDM problem can be formally described as follows:

Y. Dong and J. Xu, *Consensus Building in Group Decision Making*,
DOI 10.1007/978-981-287-892-2_1

Let $X = \{X_1, X_2, \ldots, X_m\}(m \geq 2)$ be a set of predefined alternatives. Let $E = \{E_1, E_2, \ldots, E_n\}(n \geq 2)$ be a set of experts. Let $op^k(k = 1, 2, \ldots, n)$ be the individual preference on X provided by expert E_k. The GDM goal is to combine theses individual preferences $op^k(k = 1, 2, \ldots, n)$ using an aggregation function F, to obtain a collective preference op^c on X, i.e.,

$$F(op^1, op^2, \ldots, op^n) = op^c. \tag{1.1}$$

There are two key elements in the GDM model described in Eq. (1.1): *preference representation structure* and *aggregation function*.

(1) Preference representation structure. The preference representation structure is used to represent the opinions of the individuals and the group, i.e., the format of the opinions op^k $(k = 1, 2, \ldots, n)$ and op^c.
(2) Aggregation function. The aggregation function F, which implies the group decision rule, is used to aggregate individual preferences into a collective one.

Using different preference representation structures and aggregation functions in Eq. (1.1) yields different GDM methods.

1.1.1 Preference Representation Structure

There are several widely used preference representation structures: preference ordering [68, 71], utility preference [52, 72], preference relation (e.g., additive preference relation [42, 54, 72], multiplicative preference relation [67]), linguistic preference [32, 33, 86], heterogeneous preference representation structure [8, 14, 15, 18, 34, 40, 75], and multiple attribute preference [17, 74].

(1) Preference ordering

The preference ordering associated with the expert E_k can be described by the vector $R^k = (r_1^k, r_2^k, \ldots, r_m^k)^T$, where r_i^k is the positional index of alternative x_i in the alternatives $\{X_1, X_2, \ldots, X_m\}$. For example, the expert E_k provides his/her preference ordering over $X = \{X_1, X_2, X_3\}$ as $R^k = (3, 1, 2)^T$, then the ranking of X is $X_2 \succ X_3 \succ X_1$.

(2) Utility preference

The utility preference can be described by the vector $U^k = (u_1^k, u_2^k, \ldots, u_m^k)^T$, where $u_i^k \in [0, 1]$ represents the utility evaluation value given by the expert E_k to the alternative X_i. The larger u_i^k value indicates the higher preference degree to the alternative X_i.

(3) Preference relation

When the expert E_k makes pairwise comparisons on X, he/she can construct a preference relation $P^k = (p_{ij}^k)_{m\times m}$, where p_{ij}^k denotes the preference degree or intensity of the alternative X_i over the alternative X_j. According to the domain of p_{ij}^k, two types of preference relations (i.e., the additive preference relations and the multiplicative preference relations) have been proposed, which are defined as Definitions 1.1 and 1.2, respectively.

Definition 1.1 Additive preference relations (also called fuzzy preference relations). The matrix $P^k = (p_{ij}^k)_{m\times m}$ is called an additive preference relation if $p_{ij}^k + p_{ji}^k = 1$ and $p_{ij}^k \in [0, 1]$ for $\forall i, j$, where p_{ij}^k represents the preference degree of the alternative X_i over the alternative X_j.

Definition 1.2 Multiplicative preference relations. The matrix $P^k = (p_{ij}^k)_{m\times m}$ is called a multiplicative preference relation if $p_{ij}^k \times p_{ji}^k = 1$ and $p_{ij}^k > 0$ for $\forall i, j$, where p_{ij}^k indicates a ratio of the preference intensity of alternative X_i to that of the alternative X_j.

(4) Linguistic preference

In some real GDM situations, experts often feel more comfortable providing their preferences in a linguistic way. Let $S = \{s_i | i = 0, 1, \ldots, g\}$ be a linguistic term set with odd cardinality $g + 1$. The term s_i represents a possible value for a linguistic variable. It is required that the linguistic term set should satisfy the following characteristics:

(i) The set is ordered: $s_i > s_j$ if and only if $i > j$;
(ii) There is a negation operator: $Neg(s_i) = s_{g-i}$.

For example, S can be defined as:

$S = \{s_0 = \textit{extremely poor},\ s_1 = \textit{very poor},\ s_2 = \textit{poor},\ s_3 = \textit{slightly poor},\ s_4 = \textit{fair},\ s_5 = \textit{slightly good},\ s_6 = \textit{good},\ s_7 = \textit{very good},\ s_8 = \textit{extremely good}\}$.

When experts use the linguistic term set to express their opinions over X, we call their opinions as linguistic preferences.

(5) Heterogeneous preference representation structure

It is quite natural that different experts may have different experience, cultures and educational backgrounds in GDM problems. As a result, these experts may use heterogeneous preference representation structures to express their individual opinions. For example, in a GDM problem, experts may use one of the following preference representation structures to express their preferences: utility preferences, preference orderings, and preference relations.

(6) Multiple attribute preference

In some GDM problems, experts evaluate alternatives based on multiple attributes. In this situation, an expert expresses his/her preferences using a matrix, which is called multiple attribute decision matrix. Let X be as before, and let $C = \{C_1, C_2, \ldots, C_l\}$ be a set of the attributes. A multiple attribute decision matrix can be denoted as $V^k = (v_{ij}^k)_{m\times l}$, where v_{ij}^k denotes the evaluation value for alternative X_i with respect to attribute C_j provided by expert E_k. This kind of GDM problem is called multiple attribute group decision making (MAGDM) problem.

1.1.2 Aggregation Function

The aggregation function F plays a vital role in the GDM model described as Eq. (1.1). Here, we introduce several widely used aggregation functions.

(1) Aggregation function in cardinal context

In cardinal context, the weighted averaging (WA) operator and the ordered weighted averaging (OWA) operator proposed by Yager [84] are two basic aggregation functions.

Let $\{y_1, y_2, \ldots, y_n\}$ be a set of real numbers, where $y_i \geq 0\,(i = 1, 2, \ldots, n)$. Let $w = (w_1, w_2, \ldots, w_n)^T$ be a weighting vector, where $w_i \in [0, 1]$ and $\sum_{i=1}^{n} w_i = 1$. The *WA* operator, F^{WA}, is defined as

$$F^{WA}(y_1, y_2, \ldots, y_n) = \sum_{i=1}^{n} (w_i \cdot y_i). \tag{1.2}$$

The *OWA* operator, F^{OWA}, is defined as

$$F^{OWA}(y_1, y_2, \ldots, y_n) = \sum_{i=1}^{n} \left(w_i \cdot y_{(i)}\right), \tag{1.3}$$

where $y_{(i)}$ is the ith largest element of $\{y_1, y_2, \ldots, y_n\}$.

When the weighting vector is w, the *WA* operator is denoted as F_w^{WA}, and the *OWA* operator is F_w^{OWA}.

(2) Aggregation function in ordinal context

Let $R^k = (r_1^k, r_2^k, \ldots, r_m^k)^T$ $(k = 1, 2, \ldots, n)$ be the preference ordering on X provided by the expert E_k, and let $R^c = (r_1^c, r_2^c, \ldots, r_m^c)^T$ be the collective preference ordering on X. There are two famous aggregation functions to aggregate $\{R^1, R^2, \ldots, R^n\}$ into R^c: the Condorcet function [19] and the Borda function [85].

(i) Condorcet function

The Condorcet function is based on pairwise voting method, and the Condorcet function over the alternative X_i (i = 1,2,...,m) can be defined as follows:

$$F^{Condorcet}(X_i) = \min_{X_j \in X \backslash X_i} N\{X_i \succ X_j\} \tag{1.4}$$

where $N\{X_i \succ X_j\}$ denotes the number of experts who think the alternative X_i is better than the alternative X_j.

The collective ranking of alternatives, $R^c = (r_1^c, r_2^c, \ldots, r_m^c)^T$, is achieved based on $F^{Condorcet}(X_i)(i = 1, 2, \ldots, m)$, where $r_i^c = j$ if $F^{Condorcet}(X_i)$ is the jth largest value in $\{F^{Condorcet}(X_1), F^{Condorcet}(X_2), \ldots, F^{Condorcet}(X_m)\}$.

(ii) Borda function

The Borda function is a scoring method with the vector of weights $\{m-1, m-2, \ldots, 2, 1, 0\}$. The alternative X_i receives $m-1$ points if it is ranked first by an expert, $m-2$ points if it is ranked second, ..., and 0 points if it is last.

Let

$$f_{ij}^k = \begin{cases} 1, & X_i \succeq X_j \text{ according to } R^k \\ 0, & otherwise \end{cases}. \tag{1.5}$$

For the expert E_k, the Borda value of the alternative X_i is computed by

$$f_i^k = \sum_{j=1, j \neq i}^{m} f_{ij}^k. \tag{1.6}$$

For all experts, the Borda value of the alternative X_i is calculated by

$$F^{Borda}(X_i) = \sum_{k=1}^{n} f_i^k. \tag{1.7}$$

The collective ranking of alternatives, $R^c = (r_1^c, r_2^c, \ldots, r_m^c)^T$, is achieved based on $F^{Borda}(X_i)(i = 1, 2, \ldots, m)$, where $r_i^c = j$ if $F^{Borda}(X_i)$ is the jth largest value in $\{F^{Borda}(X_1), F^{Borda}(X_2), \ldots, F^{Borda}(X_m)\}$.

1.2 Consensus Reaching Process

The GDM model described in Eq. (1.1) cannot guarantee the consensus among experts when obtaining a collective solution to the GDM problem. However, in many real-world GDM problems, obtaining a collective solution which is supported by all or most of experts is crucial. The consensus reaching process is proposed in GDM to achieve a collective solution with a consensus [4, 38, 39, 46, 57, 70]. Integrating consensus reaching process into GDM offers a few key advantages:

(1) More effective implementation. When experts' preferences and concerns are taken into account, they are much more likely to actively participate in the implementation of the obtained solution.
(2) Building connection among the experts. Using consensus as a decision tool means taking the time to find unity on how to proceed before moving forward. It is a synthesizing process, which promotes the communication among experts.

1.2.1 Literature Review Regarding Consensus

To date, numerous of consensus models have been proposed to support the consensus reaching in GDM problems. The first mathematical approaches of consensus model was initiated by French and his collaborators in the late 1940s and early 1950s [12, 20], in which the matrix calculus was employed to model the time evolution and reaching of the consensus process. Utilizing the Markov chain process, Harary [30], and De Groot [28] and French [21] extended the consensus theory into a more general form. Later, many models of consensus reaching have been proposed (e.g., [50, 63]).

In general, the consensus is defined as the full and unanimous agreement of all experts regarding all the feasible alternatives. However, this definition is inconvenient, and a complete agreement is not always necessary in practice. This has led to the use of soft consensus (i.e., consensus measure) [6, 9, 38, 43, 51]. Based on soft consensus, different types of consensus models have been investigated.

(1) Consensus under different preference representation structures

A large number of consensus models for GDM with different preference representation structures have been proposed in the literature. Kacprzyk et al. [44] proposed the consensus models for GDM with additive preference relations. Herrera et al. [35] presented the consensus model for GDM with linguistic preference relations. Moreover, Herrera-Viedma et al. [37] developed the consensus approaches to support consensus reaching with incomplete preference relations. Besides, several approaches [10, 16, 36, 88] have been presented to integrate individual consistency into the consensus models. Furthermore, Herrera-Viedma et al. [40] and Dong and Zhang [15] investigated the consensus models for GDM with heterogeneous preference representation structures.

(2) Consensus in MAGDM

In MAGDM problems, experts provide their preferences using decision matrices over multiple attributes and alternatives. Traditionally, MAGDM models are focused on how to aggregate the decision matrices into a collective one, and to obtain the ranking of alternatives from the collective decision matrix. To achieve a collective decision matrix with a consensus, Kim et al. [49] presented an interactive procedure for solving the MAGDM with incomplete information. Xu and Wu [81] presented a discrete model to support the consensus process for MAGDM problems. Moreover, Fu and Yang [24, 25] investigated the consensus for MAGDM based on evidential reasoning approach.

(3) Consensus under dynamic/Web contexts

In general, the consensus models are assumed that the sets of alternatives and experts are static. However, in some GDM problems, the sets of alternatives and experts can be dynamically changed. Pérez et al. [55, 56] proposed the dynamic consensus models to manage the decision situation that the set of alternatives are dynamically changed. And, Alonso et al. [2] proposed a dynamic consensus model to deal with the decision situation that the participation and contribution rates of experts are dynamically changed.

(4) Consensus considering behaviors/attitudes

There exist a large number of non-cooperative behaviors in the consensus reaching process. For example, some experts will express their opinions dishonestly or refuse to change their opinions to obtain their own interests. Recently, Palomares et al. [58] proposed a novel consensus framework for the GDM with additive preference relations by taking into account non-cooperative behaviors. Further, Palomares et al. [62] extended the consensus framework to detect and manage non-cooperative behaviors under linguistic context.

The related researches regarding different consensus models are listed in Table 1.1.

1.2.2 General Consensus Framework

Analyzing the existing consensus models, we find that most of them follow a general consensus framework. This framework is composed by a three-procedure: (1) using an aggregation function aggregates individual preferences into a collective one, (2) employing a consensus measure method computes the consensus level among experts, and (3) a feedback mechanism is used to help experts modify their individual preferences to improve the consensus level. The general consensus framework is described as Fig. 1.1.

The GDM model described in Eq. (1.1) consists of two key elements: *preference representation structure* and *aggregation function*. Compared with Eq. (1.1), the general consensus framework integrates two new elements: *consensus measure* and *feedback process*.

(1) Consensus measure

Consensus measure indicates how far the preferences of experts are from unanimity. In general, the distance measure is used to measure the consensus level among experts, and the computation of the consensus level is done by two ways [38]: (i)

Table 1.1 Literature review regarding consensus

Consensus models	Related researches	
Consensus under different preference representation structures	Ben-Arieh et al. [3]	
	Cabrerizo et al. [5]	Herrera-Viedma et al. [41]
	Cabrerizo et al. [7]	Kacprzyk et al. [44]
	Chiclana et al. [10]	Kacprzyk et al. [45]
	Choudhury et al. [11]	Kacprzyk et al. [48]
	Dong et al. [16]	Kacprzyk and Fedrizzi [43]
	Dong et al. [13]	Mata et al. [53]
	Dong et al. [14]	Pedrycz and Song [60]
	Dong and Zhang [15]	Pérez et al. [61]
	García et al. [27]	Tapia et al. [73]
	Herrera et al. [35]	Wu and Xu [78]
	Herrera et al. [36]	Wu and Xu [79]
	Herrera-Viedma et al. [37]	Xu and Wu [82]
	Herrera-Viedma et al. [40]	Zhang et al. [89]
Consensus in MAGDM	Fu et al. [22]	
	Fu et al. [26]	Parreiras et al. [59]
	Fu and Yang [23]	Roselló et al. [66]
	Fu and Yang [24]	Sun and Ma [69]
	Fu and Yang [25]	Xu [80]
	Guha and Chakraborty [29]	Xu et al. [83]
	Kim et al. [49]	Xu and Wu [81]
Consensus under dynamic/web contexts	Alonso et al. (2010) [1]	
	Alonso et al. [2]	Pérez et al. [56]
	Kacprzyk and Zadrożny [47]	Wu et al. [77]
	Pérez et al. [55]	Zadrożny and Kacprzyk [87]
Consensus considering behaviors or attitudes	Hartmann et al. [31]	Rega et al. [64]
	Palomares et al. [58]	Rodríguez et al. [65]
	Quesada et al. [62]	Wu and Chiclana [76]

measuring the distances between the individual preferences and the collective preferences, and (ii) measuring the distances among the individual preferences.

(2) Feedback process

In the general consensus framework, the feedback process generates adjustment suggestions to help experts reach a higher consensus level. Most of the existing consensus models are based on the following two rules [6, 40, 41]:

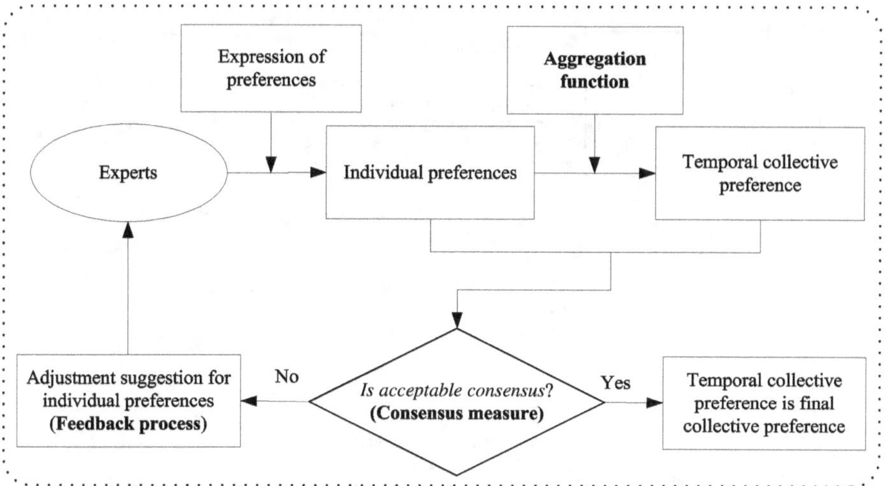

Fig. 1.1 The general consensus framework

(i) Identification rule (IR)

The IR rule identifies the experts contributing less to reach a high level of consensus. Thus, the experts should change their preferences in the feedback process.

(ii) Direction rule (DR)

The DR rule finds out the direction to change experts' preferences. For an expert identified above, he/she should decrease (increase) the assessments for alternatives whose assessments provided by the expert are higher (lower) than the assessments of the group.

1.2.3 The Core Problem in the Consensus Reaching Process

In the general consensus framework described in Fig. 1.1, the feedback process plays a key role. At the beginning of every GDM problem, experts' opinions may differ substantially, and the feedback process provides the adjustment suggestions to help experts adjust their preferences to improve the consensus level. However, The uses of the feedback process based on the IR and DR rules will yield the following consequences:

(1) When experts adjust their preferences based on the IR and DR rules, we often will lose a lot of the experts' original opinions.
(2) This is a very time consuming process, and in some situations the experts are asked to modify their preferences in a dozen rounds to reach a higher consensus level.

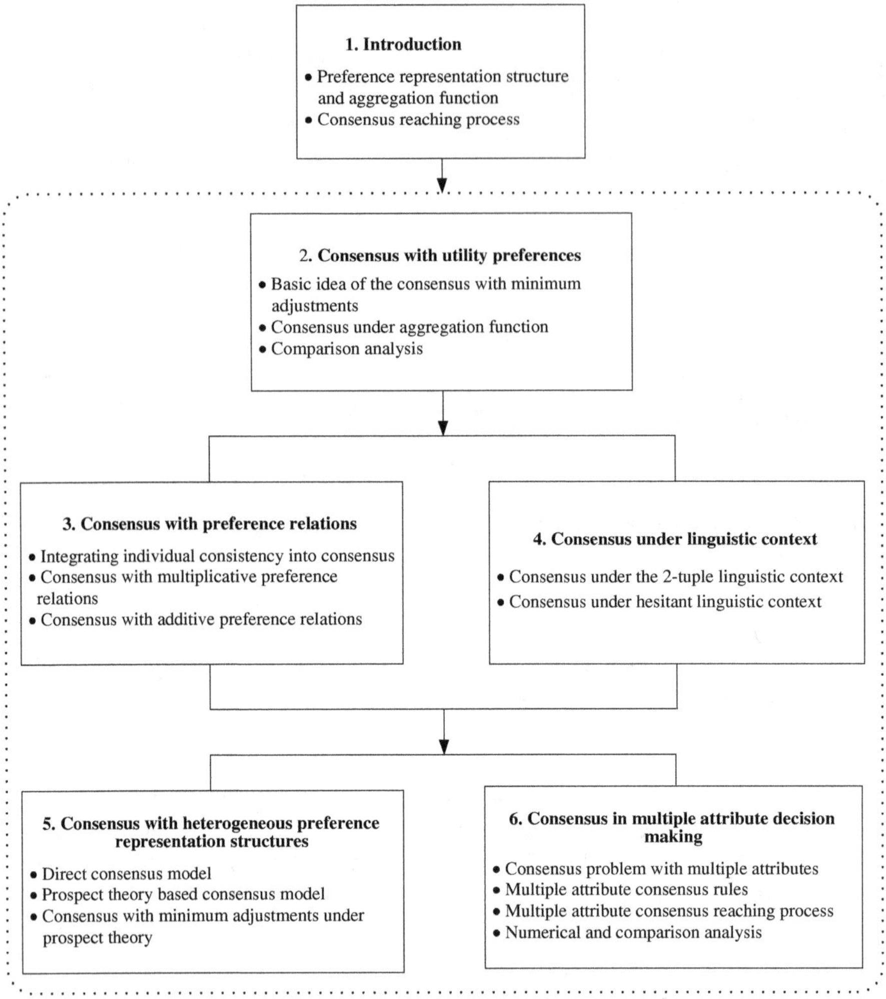

Fig. 1.2 The structure of this book

So, a core problem is naturally proposed for analysts: How to minimize the adjustment amounts in the consensus reaching process, i.e.,

$$\min_{\overline{op^k}} \sum_{k=1}^{n} d(op^k, \overline{op^k}), \tag{1.8}$$

where $\{op^1, op^2, \ldots, op^n\}$ is the experts' original preferences, $\{\overline{op^1}, \overline{op^2}, \ldots, \overline{op^n}\}$ is the experts' adjusted preferences with a consensus, and $d(op^k, \overline{op^k})(k = 1, 2, \ldots, n)$ is used to measure the adjustment amounts associated with the expert E_k $(k =$

$1, 2, \ldots, n$). In Eq. (1.8), the experts' original preference information is preserved as much as possible to support the consensus reaching.

In this book, we investigate Eq. (1.8) to search the consensus path with minimum adjustments under different GDM contexts. Notably, we use two simple aggregation functions: the WA operator and the OWA operator, in the optimization-based consensus model (i.e., Eq. (1.8)). It may be interesting to use other aggregation functions, such as the Condorcet function and the Borda function, in the future research. We organize the rest of this book as follows.

In Chap. 2, we clarify the basic idea of the consensus with minimum adjustments (or cost). Meanwhile, we investigate the consensus with minimum adjustments (or cost) under the utility preferences and aggregation functions.

In Chap. 3, we present two consensus models for the GDM with preference relations: the iteration-based consensus model and the LP-based consensus model. Then, we investigate the use of the iteration-based and LP-based consensus models in managing the individual consistency in the consensus building.

In Chap. 4, we propose the consensus models with minimum adjustments under the 2-tuple linguistic context and the hesitant linguistic context, respectively.

In Chap. 5, we propose two consensus models for the GDM with heterogeneous preference representation structures: the direct consensus model and the prospect theory based consensus model. Furthermore, we develop a minimum adjustments consensus model under prospect theory.

In Chap. 6, we present two multiple attribute consensus rules with minimum adjustments: the distance-based consensus rule and the count-based consensus rule. Based on the distance-based and count-based consensus rules, we develop an interactive consensus reaching process for MAGDM.

The detailed structure of the book is described in Fig. 1.2.

References

1. S. Alonso, E. Herrera-Viedma, F. Chiclana, F. Herrera, A web based consensus support system for group decision making problems and incomplete preferences. Inf. Sci. **180**, 4477–4495 (2010)
2. S. Alonso, I.J. Pérez, F.J. Cabrerizo, E. Herrera-Viedma, A linguistic consensus model for Web 2.0 communities. Appl. Soft Comput. **13**, 149–157 (2013)
3. D. Ben-Arieh, Z.F. Chen, Linguistic-labels aggregation and consensus measure for autocratic decision making using group recommendations. IEEE Trans. Syst. Man Cybern. Part A Syst. Hum. **36**, 558–568 (2006)
4. G. Bordogna, M. Fedrizzi, G. Pasi, A linguistic modeling of consensus in group decision making based on OWA operators. IEEE Trans. Syst. Man Cybern. Part A Syst. Hum. **27**, 126–133 (1997)
5. F.J. Cabrerizo, S. Alonso, E. Herrera-Viedma, A consensus model for group decision making problems with unbalanced fuzzy linguistic information. Int. J. Inf. Technol. Decis. Making **8**, 109–131 (2009)
6. F.J. Cabrerizo, J.M. Moreno, I.J. Pérez, E. Herrera-Viedma, Analyzing consensus approaches in fuzzy group decision making: advantages and drawbacks. Soft. Comput. **14**, 451–463 (2010)

7. F.J. Cabrerizo, I.J. Pérez, E. Herrera-Viedma, Managing the consensus in group decision making in an unbalanced fuzzy linguistic context with incomplete information. Knowl.-Based Syst. **23**, 169–181 (2010)
8. X. Chen, H.J. Zhang, Y.C. Dong, The fusion process with heterogeneous preference structures in group decision making: a survey. Inf. Fusion **24**, 72–83 (2015)
9. F. Chiclana, J.M.T. García, M.J. Del Moral, E. Herrera-Viedma, A statistical comparative study of different similarity measures of consensus in group decision making. Inf. Sci. **221**, 110–123 (2013)
10. F. Chiclana, F. Mata, L. Martínez, E. Herrera-Viedma, S. Alonso, Integration of a consistency control module within a consensus model. Int. J. Uncertainty Fuzziness Knowl. Based Syst. **16**, 35–53 (2008)
11. A.K. Choudhury, R. Shankar, M.K. Tiwari, Consensus-based intelligent group decision-making model for the selection of advanced technology. Decis. Support Syst. **42**, 1776–1799 (2006)
12. L. Coch, J.R.P. French, Overcoming resistance to change. Hum. Relat. **1**, 512–532 (1948)
13. Y.C. Dong, Z.P. Fan, S. Yu, Consensus building in a local context for the AHP-GDM with the individual numerical scale and prioritization method. IEEE Trans. Fuzzy Syst. **23**, 354–368 (2015)
14. Y.C. Dong, N. Luo, H.M. Liang, Consensus building in multiperson decision making with heterogeneous preference representation structures: A perspective based on prospect theory. Appl. Soft Comput. **35**, 898–910 (2015)
15. Y.C. Dong, H.J. Zhang, Multiperson decision making with different preference representation structures: a direct consensus framework and its properties. Knowl.-Based Syst. **58**, 45–57 (2014)
16. Y.C. Dong, G.Q. Zhang, W.C. Hong, Y.F. Xu, Consensus models for AHP group decision making under row geometric mean prioritization method. Decis. Support Syst. **49**, 281–289 (2010)
17. J.S. Dyer, P.C. Fishburn, R.E. Steuer, J. Wallenius, S. Zionts, Multiple criteria decision making, multiattribute utility theory: the next ten years. Manage. Sci. **38**, 645–654 (1992)
18. Z.P. Fan, J. Ma, Y.P. Jiang, Y.H. Sun, L. Ma, A goal programming approach to group decision making based on multiplicative preference relations and fuzzy preference relations. Eur. J. Oper. Res. **174**, 311–321 (2006)
19. P.C. Fishburn, Condorcet social choice functions. SIAM J. Appl. Math. **33**, 469–489 (1977)
20. J.R.P. French, A formal theory of social power. Psychol. Rev. **63**, 181–194 (1956)
21. S. French, Consensus of opinion. Eur. J. Oper. Res. **7**, 332–340 (1981)
22. C. Fu, M. Huhns, S.L. Yang, A consensus framework for multiple attribute group decision analysis in an evidential reasoning context. Inf. Fusion **17**, 22–35 (2014)
23. C. Fu, S.L. Yang, The group consensus based evidential reasoning approach for multiple attributive group decision analysis. Eur. J. Oper. Res. **206**, 601–608 (2010)
24. C. Fu, S.L. Yang, An attribute weight based feedback model for multiple attributive group decision analysis problems with group consensus requirements in evidential reasoning context. Eur. J. Oper. Res. **212**, 179–189 (2011)
25. C. Fu, S.L. Yang, An evidential reasoning based consensus model for multiple attribute group decision analysis problems with interval-valued group consensus requirements. Eur. J. Oper. Res. **223**, 167–176 (2012)
26. C. Fu, J.B. Yang, S.L. Yang, A group evidential reasoning approach based on expert reliability. Eur. J. Oper. Res. **246**, 886–893 (2015)
27. J.M.T. García, M.J.D. Moral, M.A. Martínez, E. Herrera-Viedma, A consensus model for group decision-making problems with interval fuzzy preference relations. Int. J. Inf. Technol. Decis. Making **11**, 709–725 (2012)
28. M.M.D. Groot, Reaching consensus. J. Am. Stat. Assoc. **69**, 118–121 (1974)
29. D. Guha, D. Chakraborty, Fuzzy multi attribute group decision making method to achieve consensus under the consideration of degrees of confidence of experts' opinions. Comput. Ind. Eng. **60**, 493–504 (2011)
30. F. Harary, On the measurement of structural balance. Behav. Sci. **4**, 316–323 (1959)

31. S. Hartmann, C. Martini, J. Sprenger, Consensual decision-making among epistemic peers. Episteme **6**, 110–129 (2009)
32. F. Herrera, S. Alonso, F. Chiclana, E. Herrera-Viedma, Computing with words in decision making: foundations, trends and prospects. Fuzzy Optim. Decis. Making **8**, 337–364 (2009)
33. F. Herrera, E. Herrera-Viedma, Linguistic decision analysis: steps for solving decision problems under linguistic information. Fuzzy Sets Syst. **115**, 67–82 (2000)
34. F. Herrera, E. Herrera-Viedma, L. Martínez, A fusion approach for managing multi-granularity linguistic term sets in decision making. Fuzzy Sets Syst. **114**, 43–58 (2000)
35. F. Herrera, E. Herrera-Viedma, J.L. Verdegay, A model of consensus in group decision making under linguistic assessments. Fuzzy Sets Syst. **78**, 73–87 (1996)
36. F. Herrera, E. Herrera-Viedma, J.L. Verdegay, A rational consensus model in group decision making using linguistic assessments. Fuzzy Sets Syst. **88**, 31–49 (1997)
37. E. Herrera-Viedma, S. Alonso, F. Chiclana, F. Herrera, A consensus model for group decision making with incomplete fuzzy preference relations. IEEE Trans. Fuzzy Syst. **15**, 863–877 (2007)
38. E. Herrera-Viedma, F.J. Cabrerizo, J. Kacprzyk, W. Pedrycz, A review of soft consensus models in a fuzzy environment. Inf. Fusion **17**, 4–13 (2014)
39. E. Herrera-Viedma, J.L. García-Lapresta, J. Kacprzyk, M. Fedrizzi, H. Nurmi, S. Zadrożny (eds.), *Consensual Processes, Studies in Fuzziness and Soft Computing* (Springer, Berlin, 2011)
40. E. Herrera-Viedma, F. Herrera, F. Chiclana, A consensus model for multiperson decision making with different preference structures. IEEE Trans. Syst. Man Cybern. Part A Syst. Hum. **32**, 394–402 (2002)
41. E. Herrera-Viedma, L. Martínez, F. Mata, F. Chiclana, A consensus support system sodel for group decision-making problems with multigranular linguistic preference relations. IEEE Trans. Fuzzy Syst. **13**, 644–658 (2005)
42. J. Kacprzyk, Group decision making with a fuzzy linguistic majority. Fuzzy Sets Syst. **18**, 105–118 (1986)
43. J. Kacprzyk, M. Fedrizzi, A 'soft' measure of consensus in the setting of partial (fuzzy) preferences. Eur. J. Oper. Res. **34**, 316–325 (1988)
44. J. Kacprzyk, M. Fedrizzi, H. Nurmi, Group decision making and consensus under fuzzy preferences and fuzzy majority. Fuzzy Sets Syst. **49**, 21–31 (1992)
45. J. Kacprzyk, M. Fedrizzi, H. Nurmi, Soft degrees of consensus under additive preferences and fuzzy majorities, in *Consensus Under Fuzziness*, ed. by J. Kacprzyk, H. Nurmi, M. Fedrizzi (Kluwer, Boston, 1996), pp. 55–83
46. J. Kacprzyk, H. Nurmi, M. Fedrizzi, *Consensus Under Fuzziness, International Series in Intelligent Technologies* (Springer, US, 1997)
47. J. Kacprzyk, S. Zadrożny, Soft computing and Web intelligence for supporting consensus reaching. Soft Comput. **14**, 833–846 (2010)
48. J. Kacprzyk, S. Zadrożny, Z.W. Ras, How to support consensus reaching using action rules: a novel approach. Int. J. Uncertainty Fuzziness Knowl. Based Syst. **18**, 451–470 (2010)
49. S.H. Kim, S.H. Choi, J.K. Kim, An interactive procedure for multiple attribute group decision making with incomplete information: Range-based approach. Eur. J. Oper. Res. **118**, 139–152 (1999)
50. K. Lehrer, C. Wagner, *Rational Consensus in Science and Society: A Philosophical and Mathematical Study, Philosophical Studies Series in Philosophy*, vol. 24 (Springer, Netherlands, 1981)
51. B. Loewer, Special issue on consensus. Synthese **62**, 1–122
52. R.D. Luce P. Suppes et al. 'Preferences' utility and subject probability, in *Handbook of Mathematical Psychology*, vol. III, eds. by R.D. Luce et al. (Wiley, New York, 1965), pp. 249–410
53. F. Mata, L. Martínez, E. Herrera-Viedma, An adaptive consensus support model for group decision-making problems in a multigranular fuzzy linguistic context. IEEE Trans. Fuzzy Syst. **17**, 279–290 (2009)
54. S.A. Orlovsky, Decision-making with a fuzzy preference relation. Fuzzy Sets Syst. **1**, 155–167 (1978)

55. I.J. Pérez, F.J. Cabrerizo, E. Herrera-Viedma, Group decision making problems in a linguistic and dynamic context. Expert Syst. Appl. **38**, 1675–1688 (2011)
56. I.J. Pérez, F.J. Cabrerizo, E. Herrera-Viedma, A mobile decision support system for dynamic group decision-making problems. IEEE Trans. Syst. Man Cybern. Part A Syst. Hum. **40**, 1244–1256 (2010)
57. I. Palomares, F.J. Estrella, L. Martínez, F. Herrera, Consensus under a fuzzy context: taxonomy, analysis framework AFRYCA and experimental case of study. Inf. Fusion **20**, 252–271 (2014)
58. I. Palomares, L. Martínez, F. Herrera, A consensus model to detect and manage noncooperative behaviors in large-scale group decision making. IEEE Trans. Fuzzy Syst. **22**, 516–530 (2014)
59. R.O. Parreiras, P.Y. Ekel, J.S.C. Martini, R.M. Palhares, A flexible consensus scheme for multicriteria group decision making under linguistic assessments. Inf. Sci. **180**, 1075–1089 (2010)
60. W. Pedrycz, M. Song, Analytic hierarchy process (AHP) in group decision making and its optimization with an allocation of information granularity. IEEE Trans. Fuzzy Syst. **19**, 527–539 (2011)
61. I.J. Pérez, F.J. Cabrerizo, S. Alonso, E. Herrera-Viedma, A new consensus model for group decision making problems with non-homogeneous experts. IEEE Trans. Syst. Man Cybern. Syst. **44**, 494–498 (2014)
62. F. Quesada, I. Palomares, L. Martínez, Using computing with words for managing non-cooperative behaviors in large scale group decision making, in *Granular Computing and Decision-Making. Studies in Big Data. 10* ed. by W. Pedrycz, S-M Chen (Springer International Publishing, 2015) pp.97–121
63. R. Ragade, Fuzzy sets in communication systems and consensus formation systems. J. Cybern. **6**, 21–38 (1976)
64. H.M. Regan, M. Colyvan, L. Markovchick-Nicholls, A formal model for consensus and negotiation in environmental management. J. Environ. Manage. **80**, 167–176 (2006)
65. R.M. Rodríguez, I. Palomares, L. Martínez, Attitude-based consensus model for heterogeneous group decision making, in *Knowledge Engineering and Management, Advances in Intelligent Systems and Computing*, vol. 214, ed. by F. Sun et al. (Springer, 2014)
66. L. Roselló, M. Sánchez, N. Agell, F. Prats, F.A. Mazaira, Using consensus and distances between generalized multi-attribute linguistic assessments for group decision-making. Inf. Fusion **17**, 83–92 (2014)
67. T.L. Saaty, *The Analytic Hierarchy Process* (McGraw-Hill, New York, 1980)
68. F. Seo, M. Sakawa, Fuzzy multiattribute utility analysis for collective choice. IEEE Trans. Syst. Man Cybern. **15**, 45–53 (1985)
69. B.Z. Sun, W.M. Ma, An approach to consensus measurement of linguistic preference relations in multi-attribute group decision making and application. Omega **51**, 83–92 (2015)
70. L. Susskind, S. McKearnen, J. Thomas-Lamar (eds.), *The Consensus Building Handbook: A Comprehensive Guide to Reaching Agreement* (Sage Publications, Thousand Oaks, 1999)
71. T. Tanino, Fuzzy preference orderings in group decision making. Fuzzy Sets Syst. **12**, 117–131 (1984)
72. T. Tanino, On group decision making under fuzzy preferences, in *Multiperson Decision Making Using Fuzzy Sets and Possibility Theory*, ed. by J. Kacprzyk, M. Fedrizzi (Kluwer Academic Publishers, Dordrecht, 1990), pp. 172–185
73. J.M. Tapia, M.J.Del GarćiA, M.A. Moral, E.Herrera-Viedma Martínez,A, consensus model for group decision making problems with linguistic interval fuzzy preference relations. Expert Syst. Appl. **39**, 10022–10030 (2012)
74. J. Wallenius, J.S. Dyer, P.C. Fishburn, R.E. Steuer, S. Zionts, K. Deb, Multiple criteria decision making, multiattribute utility theory: recent accomplishments and what lies ahead. Manage. Sci. **54**, 1336–1349 (2008)
75. Y.M. Wang, Z.P. Fan, Z.S. Hua, A chi-square method for obtaining a priority vector from multiplicative and fuzzy preference relations. Eur. J. Oper. Res. **182**, 356–366 (2007)
76. J. Wu, F. Chiclana, Visual information feedback mechanism and attitudinal prioritisation method for group decision making with triangular fuzzy complementary preference relations. Inf. Sci. **279**, 716–734 (2014)

77. J. Wu, F. Chiclana, E. Herrera-Viedma, Trust based consensus model for social network in an incomplete linguistic information context. Appl. Soft Comput. **35**, 827–839 (2015)
78. Z.B. Wu, J.P. Xu, Consensus reaching models of linguistic preference relations based on distance functions. Soft Comput. **16**, 577–589 (2012)
79. Z.B. Wu, J.P. Xu, A consistency and consensus based decision support model for group decision making with multiplicative preference relations. Decis. Support Syst. **52**, 757–767 (2012)
80. Z.S. Xu, An automatic approach to reaching consensus in multiple attribute group decision making. Comput. Ind. Eng. **56**, 1369–1374 (2009)
81. J.P. Xu, Z.B. Wu, A discrete consensus support model for multiple attribute group decision making. Knowl.-Based Syst. **24**, 1196–1202 (2011)
82. J.P. Xu, Z.B. Wu, A maximizing consensus approach for alternative selection based on uncertain linguistic preference relations. Comput. Ind. Eng. **64**, 999–1008 (2013)
83. J.P. Xu, Z.B. Wu, Y. Zhang, A consensus based method for multi-criteria group decision making under uncertain linguistic setting. Group Decis. Negot. **23**, 127–148 (2014)
84. R.R. Yager, On ordered weighted averaging aggregation operators in multicriteria decision-making. IEEE Trans. Syst. Man Cybern. **18**, 183–190 (1988)
85. H.P. Young, An axiomatization of Borda's rule. J. Econ. Theor. **9**, 43–52 (1974)
86. L.A. Zadeh, The concept of a linguistic variable and its application to approximate reasoning-III. Inf. Sci. **9**, 43–80 (1975)
87. S. Zadrozny, J. Kacprzyk, An internet-based group decision and consensus reaching support system, in *Applied Decision Support with Soft Computing*, ed. by X. Yu, J. Kacprzyk (Springer, Heidelberg, 2003), pp. 263–275
88. G.Q. Zhang, Y.C. Dong, Y.F. Xu, Linear optimization modeling of consistency issues in group decision making based on fuzzy preference relations. Expert Syst. Appl. **39**, 2415–2420 (2012)
89. G.Q. Zhang, Y.C. Dong, Y.F. Xu, Consistency and consensus measures for linguistic preference relations based on distribution assessments. Inf. Fusion **17**, 46–55 (2014)

Chapter 2
Consensus with Utility Preferences

The basic idea of the consensus with minimum adjustments (or cost) is clarified. Meanwhile, the consensus model with minimum adjustments (or cost) is investigated under the utility preferences and aggregation functions.

2.1 Basic Idea of the Consensus with Minimum Adjustments

This section introduces the basic idea of the consensus with minimum adjustments (or cost). As shown in Eq. (1.8), a core problem in consensus building is to search the consensus path with minimum adjustments. In existing researches, Dong et al. [10] proposed the consensus model with minimum adjustments. Meanwhile, Ben-Arieh and Easton [4] presented the consensus model with minimum cost.

2.1.1 Consensus with Minimum Adjustments or Cost

The basic models of the consensus with minimum adjustments or cost are presented below.

(1) Consensus with minimum adjustments

For a GDM problem, let $E = \{E_1, E_2, ..., E_n\}$ denote a set of n experts, and let $o_i \in R$ represent the original opinion of the expert E_i. Furthermore, the original collective opinion is denoted as o.

Several methods exist for measuring the consensus level [3, 7, 8, 13, 16, 17]. The most commonly used method is the Manhattan distance measure [4, 5]. By calculating the Manhattan distance between o_i and o, $|o_i - o|, i = 1, 2..., n$, the *consensus level* of the expert $E_i (i = 1, 2, ..., n)$ can be measured, i.e.,

$$CL(E_i) = |o_i - o|. \tag{2.1}$$

Y. Dong and J. Xu, *Consensus Building in Group Decision Making*,
DOI 10.1007/978-981-287-892-2_2

Let ε denote the established consensus threshold. If $CL(E_i) \leq \varepsilon$, then the expert E_i is of acceptable consensus. Otherwise, we suggest the expert E_i adjust his/her original opinion to reach the established consensus level.

Let $\overline{o_i} \in R$ denote the adjusted individual opinion of expert E_i, and $\overline{o}$ represent the adjusted collective opinion. Naturally, we hope to minimize the adjustment amounts (in the sense of Manhattan distance) in consensus building, i.e.,

$$\min_{\overline{o_i}} \sum_{i=1}^{n} |o_i - \overline{o_i}|. \tag{2.2}$$

Meanwhile, the adjusted individual opinions $\overline{o_i}(i = 1, 2, ..., n)$ are of acceptable consensus, i.e.,

$$CL(E_i) = |\overline{o_i} - \overline{o}| \leq \varepsilon, \quad i = 1, 2, ..., n, \tag{2.3}$$

where, the adjusted collective opinion $\overline{o}$ is obtained by using an aggregation function F, i.e.,

$$\overline{o} = F(o_1, o_2, ..., o_n). \tag{2.4}$$

Based on Eqs. (2.2)–(2.4), the consensus model with minimum adjustments is proposed as follows:

$$\begin{cases} \min\limits_{\overline{o_i}} \sum\limits_{i=1}^{n} |o_i - \overline{o_i}| \\ s.t. \begin{cases} |\overline{o_i} - \overline{o}| \leq \varepsilon, \quad i = 1, ..., n \\ \overline{o} = F\left(\overline{o_1}, \overline{o_2}, ..., \overline{o_n}\right) \end{cases} \end{cases}. \tag{2.5}$$

(2) Consensus with minimum cost

Ben-Arieh and Easton [4], and Ben-Arieh et al. [5] defined c_i as the cost of moving expert E_i's opinion 1 unit. Then, Gong et al. [11, 12] pursued the consensus model with minimum cost. Ben-Arieh and Easton [4] defined the *linear consensus cost* of moving expert E_i's opinion from o_i to $\overline{o_i}$:

$$f_i(o_i, \overline{o_i}) = c_i |\overline{o_i} - o_i|. \tag{2.6}$$

The total consensus cost is computed by

$$\sum_{i=1}^{n} c_i |\overline{o_i} - o_i|. \tag{2.7}$$

The consensus model with minimum cost can be presented using an optimization model, i.e.,

$$\begin{cases} \min \sum_{i=1}^{n} c_i |\overline{o_i} - o_i| \\ s.t. \ |\overline{o_i} - \overline{o}| \le \varepsilon, \ i = 1, 2, ...n \end{cases}. \tag{2.8}$$

Denote model (2.8) as $P_{2.1}$. Let $\Omega_{2.1}$ represent the feasible set corresponding to model $P_{2.1}$. Solving model $P_{2.1}$ yields the optimal adjusted individual opinions $\overline{o_i^*}$ $(i = 1, 2, ..., n)$ and the optimal adjusted collective opinion $\overline{o^*}$.

For $P_{2.1}$, the expert opinion does not need to be changed if it is within ε of $\overline{o^*}$. Furthermore, any original expert opinion that is further than ε from $\overline{o^*}$ should only be adjusted until it is exactly ε from $\overline{o^*}$. Thus Lemma 2.1 is obtained.

Lemma 2.1 *Let* $\left\{\overline{o_1^*}, \overline{o_2^*}, ..., \overline{o_n^*}, \overline{o^*}\right\}$ *denote the optimal solution to* $P_{2.1}$*. Then the following is obtained:*

$$\overline{o_i^*} = \begin{cases} \overline{o^*} - \varepsilon, & i \in \{i : o_i \le \overline{o^*} - \varepsilon\} \\ \overline{o^*} + \varepsilon, & i \in \{i : o_i \ge \overline{o^*} + \varepsilon\} \\ o_i, & i \in \{i : \overline{o^*} - \varepsilon < o_i < \overline{o^*} + \varepsilon\} \end{cases}. \tag{2.9}$$

Proof It is obvious and the proof is omitted.

Based on Lemma 2.1, $P_{2.1}$ can be expressed using an equivalent model when seeking the optimal adjusted collective opinion $\overline{o^*}$:

$$\min_{\overline{o}} \left\{ \sum\nolimits_{i:\ o_i < \overline{o} - \varepsilon} c_i |\overline{o} - \varepsilon - o_i| + \sum\nolimits_{i:\ o_i > \overline{o} + \varepsilon} c_i |\overline{o} + \varepsilon - o_i| \right\}. \tag{2.10}$$

2.1.2 Internal Aggregation Function

In the consensus model, $P_{2.1}$, the aggregation function is not considered. By taking into account the consensus cost and the aggregation function, Zhang et al. [20] proposed a general consensus model to connect model (2.5) and $P_{2.1}$. The consensus model presented in Zhang et al. [20] is described as follows:

$$\begin{cases} \min\limits_{\overline{o_i}} \sum_{i=1}^{n} c_i \ |o_i - \overline{o_i}| \\ s.t. \begin{cases} |\overline{o_i} - \overline{o}| \le \varepsilon, \ i = 1, ..., n \\ \overline{o} = F(\overline{o_1}, \overline{o_2}, ..., \overline{o_n}) \end{cases} \end{cases}. \tag{2.11}$$

Denote model (2.11) as $P_{2.2}$. Let $\Omega_{2.2}$ represent the feasible set corresponding to $P_{2.2}$.

Let $w^* = (\frac{1}{2}, 0, ..., 0, \frac{1}{2})^T$. Using the OWA operator, $F_{w^*}^{OWA}$, to aggregate the expert opinions in $P_{2.2}$ obtains the following model:

$$\begin{cases} \min\limits_{\overline{o_i}} \sum\limits_{i=1}^{n} c_i \left| o_i - \overline{o_i} \right| \\ s.t. \begin{cases} \left| \overline{o_i} - \overline{o} \right| \leq \varepsilon, \ \ i = 1, ..., n \\ \overline{o} = \frac{\max\{\overline{o_i}\} + \min\{\overline{o_i}\}}{2} \end{cases} \end{cases}. \tag{2.12}$$

Denote model (2.12) as $P_{2.3}$. Let $\Omega_{2.3}$ represent the feasible set corresponding to $P_{2.3}$.

Theorem 2.1 *Let* $\overline{o_i^*}$ *(*$i = 1, 2, ..., n$*) and* $\overline{o^*}$ *denote the optimal adjusted individual opinions and adjusted collective opinion obtained using* $P_{2.3}$*, respectively. Then,* $\{\overline{o_1^*}, \overline{o_2^*}, ..., \overline{o_n^*}, \overline{o^*}\}$ *is the optimal solution to* $P_{2.1}$.

Proof Let $\{\overline{\overline{o_1}}, \overline{\overline{o_2}}, ..., \overline{\overline{o_n}}, \overline{\overline{o}}\}$ be the optimal solution to $P_{2.1}$. Since $\{\overline{o_1^*}, \overline{o_2^*}, ..., \overline{o_n^*}, \overline{o^*}\}$ is the optimal solution to $P_{2.3}$ and $\Omega_{2.3} \subseteq \Omega_{2.1}$, the following can be obtained:

$$\begin{aligned} \sum_{i=1}^{n} c_i |o_i - \overline{\overline{o_i}}| &= \min_{\{\overline{o_1}, \overline{o_2}, ..., \overline{o_n}, \overline{o}\} \in \Omega_{2.1}} \sum_{i=1}^{n} c_i |o_i - \overline{o_i}| \\ &\leq \min_{\{\overline{o_1}, \overline{o_2}, ..., \overline{o_n}, \overline{o}\} \in \Omega_{2.3}} \sum_{i=1}^{n} c_i |o_i - \overline{o_i}| \\ &= \sum_{i=1}^{n} c_i |o_i - \overline{o_i^*}|. \end{aligned} \tag{2.13}$$

Moreover, the following relationship between $\overline{\overline{o}}$ and $\overline{\overline{o_i}}$ can be obtained based on Lemma 2.1:

$$\overline{\overline{o_i}} = \begin{cases} \overline{\overline{o}} - \varepsilon, & i \in \{i : o_i \leq \overline{\overline{o}} - \varepsilon\} \\ \overline{\overline{o}} + \varepsilon, & i \in \{i : o_i \geq \overline{\overline{o}} + \varepsilon\} \\ o_i, & i \in \{i : \overline{\overline{o}} - \varepsilon < o_i < \overline{\overline{o}} + \varepsilon\}, \end{cases} \tag{2.14}$$

which satisfies $\max\{\overline{\overline{o_i}}\} - \min\{\overline{\overline{o_i}}\} \leq 2\varepsilon$. Furthermore, we easily obtain

$$|\overline{\overline{o_i}} - \frac{\max\{\overline{\overline{o_i}}\} + \min\{\overline{\overline{o_i}}\}}{2}| \leq \varepsilon, \ \ i = 1, 2, ..., n.$$

Thus, $\{\overline{\overline{o_1}}, \overline{\overline{o_2}}, ..., \overline{\overline{o_n}}, \frac{\max\{\overline{\overline{o_i}}\} + \min\{\overline{\overline{o_i}}\}}{2}\} \in \Omega_{2.3}$. Consequently,

$$\sum_{i=1}^{n} c_i |o_i - \overline{\overline{o_i}}| \geq \min_{\{\overline{o_1}, \overline{o_2}, ..., \overline{o_n}, \overline{o}\} \in \Omega_{2.3}} \sum_{i=1}^{n} c_i |o_i - \overline{o_i}| = \sum_{i=1}^{n} c_i |o_i - \overline{o_i^*}|. \tag{2.15}$$

The following can be obtained based on (2.13) and (2.15)

$$\min_{\{\overline{o_1}, \overline{o_2}, ..., \overline{o_n}, \overline{o}\} \in \Omega_{2.1}} \sum_{i=1}^{n} c_i |o_i - \overline{o_i}| = \sum_{i=1}^{n} c_i |o_i - \overline{o_i^*}|. \tag{2.16}$$

Thus, $\{\overline{o_1^*}, \overline{o_2^*}, ..., \overline{o_n^*}, \overline{o^*}\}$ is the optimal solution to $P_{2.1}$. This completes the proof of Theorem 2.1.

Based on Theorem 2.1, the consensus model, $P_{2.2}$, reduces to $P_{2.1}$, and the internal aggregation function in $P_{2.1}$ is the OWA operator, $F_{w^*}^{OWA}$, where $w^* = (\frac{1}{2}, ..., 0, ..., \frac{1}{2})^T$. In general, $F_{w^*}^{OWA}$ is not employed as the aggregation function in GDM problems.

$P_{2.1}$ and $P_{2.2}$ are called minimum cost consensus models (MCCMs). However, the adjustment cost c_i is difficult to evaluate in practice. So, we only take into account the adjustment cost in the GDM with utility preferences, and in the later chapters the adjustment cost is not considered.

2.2 Consensus Under Aggregation Function

In the section, we investigate the MCCM under the utility preferences and aggregation functions. Moreover, we extend the MCCM into the maximum expert consensus model (MECM).

2.2.1 Minimum Cost Consensus Model

Considering different aggregation functions in $P_{2.2}$ yields different MCCMs. Here, we examine the MCCMs under the WA operator and OWA operator in detail.

(1) Minimum cost consensus model with WA operator

Selecting WA with the weighting vector w as the operator in $P_{2.2}$ yields the following model:

$$\begin{cases} \min\limits_{\overline{o_i}} \sum\limits_{i=1}^{n} c_i \left| o_i - \overline{o_i} \right| \\ s.t. \begin{cases} \left| \overline{o_i} - \overline{o} \right| \leq \varepsilon, \quad i = 1, ..., n \\ \overline{o} = \sum_{i=1}^{n} w_i \overline{o_i} \end{cases} \end{cases}. \tag{2.17}$$

Denote model (2.17) as $P_{2.4}$. Further, let $\Omega_{2.4}$ represent the feasible set corresponding to $P_{2.4}$.

Theorem 2.2 *$P_{2.4}$ can be equivalently transformed into the following linear programming model:*

$$\begin{cases} \min\limits_{\overline{o_i}} \sum\limits_{i=1}^{n} c_i d_i \\ s.t. \begin{cases} \overline{o_i} - \overline{o} \le \varepsilon, \ i = 1, ..., n \\ \overline{o} - \overline{o_i} \le \varepsilon, \ i = 1, ..., n \\ \overline{o} = \sum\limits_{i=1}^{n} w_i \overline{o_i} \\ o_i - \overline{o_i} = x_i, \ i = 1, ..., n \\ x_i \le d_i, \ i = 1, ..., n \\ -x_i \le d_i, \ i = 1, ..., n \end{cases} \end{cases}, \tag{2.18}$$

where $x_i = o_i - \overline{o_i}$ and $d_i \ge |x_i|$.

Proof In the linear programming model (2.18), constraints $\overline{o_i} - \overline{o} \le \varepsilon$ and $\overline{o} - \overline{o_i} \le \varepsilon (i = 1, ..., n)$ guarantee that $|\overline{o_i} - \overline{o}| \le \varepsilon$, and constraints $o_i - \overline{o_i} = x_i$, $x_i \le d_i$ and $-x_i \le d_i$ $(i = 1, ..., n)$ guarantee that $d_i \ge |x_i| = |o_i - \overline{o_i}|$. According to the objective function, $\min\limits_{\overline{o_i}} \sum\limits_{i=1}^{n} c_i d_i$, any feasible solutions with $d_i > |x_i|$ are not the optimal solution to model (2.18). Thus, the six constraints of model (2.18) can guarantee that $d_i = |x_i| = |o_i - \overline{o_i}|$. Therefore, $P_{2.4}$ can be transformed into model (2.18). This completes the proof of Theorem 2.2.

According to Theorem 2.2, the optimal solution to $P_{2.4}$ can be obtained by solving the linear programming model (2.18).

(2) Minimum cost consensus model with OWA operator

Selecting OWA with the weighting vector w as the operator in $P_{2.2}$ yields the following model:

$$\begin{cases} \min\limits_{\overline{o_i}} \sum\limits_{i=1}^{n} c_i |o_i - \overline{o_i}| \\ s.t. \begin{cases} |\overline{o_i} - \overline{o}| \le \varepsilon, \ i = 1, ..., n \\ \overline{o} = F_w^{OWA} (\overline{o_1}, \overline{o_2}, ..., \overline{o_n}) \end{cases} \end{cases} \tag{2.19}$$

Obviously, model (2.19) is a nonlinear optimization model which is difficult to solve. In the following, we consider two cases of model (2.19):

Case A: Homogeneous unit consensus cost. In this case, the cost of adjusting the opinion 1 unit is the same for each expert (i.e., $c_i = c_j$ for $i, j = 1, 2, ..., n$). In this case, the corresponding consensus model (see model (2.20)) has a definite physical implication and can search the consensus path with minimum adjustments (in the sense of Manhattan distance).

Case B: Heterogeneous unit consensus cost. In this case, there exists $c_i \ne c_j$ for $i, j = 1, 2, ..., n$.

These two cases are discussed in more detail below.

(i) Case A

In this case, model (2.19) is transformed into model (2.20):

$$\begin{cases} \min\limits_{\overline{o_i}} \sum\limits_{i=1}^{n} |o_i - \overline{o_i}| \\ s.t. \begin{cases} |\overline{o_i} - \overline{o}| \leq \varepsilon, \ \ i = 1, \ldots, n \\ \overline{o} = F_w^{OWA}(\overline{o_1}, \overline{o_2}, \ldots, \overline{o_n}) \end{cases} \end{cases}. \tag{2.20}$$

Denote $\{\sigma(1), \sigma(2), \ldots, \sigma(n)\}$ as the permutation of $\{1, 2, \ldots, n\}$ such that $o_{\sigma(i-1)} \geq o_{\sigma(i)}$ (i.e., $o_{\sigma(i)}$ is the ith largest variable in $\{o_1, o_2, \ldots, o_n\}$). Similarly, $\{\delta(1), \ldots, \delta(i), \ldots, \delta(n)\}$ is denoted as the permutation of $\{1, 2, \ldots, n\}$ such that $\overline{o_{\delta(i-1)}} \geq \overline{o_{\delta(i)}}$ (i.e., $\overline{o_{\delta(i)}}$ is the ith largest variable in $\{\overline{o_1}, \overline{o_2}, \ldots, \overline{o_n}\}$).

Before presenting the method of solving model (2.20), a new model is introduced, as follows:

$$\begin{cases} \min\limits_{\overline{o_i}} \sum\limits_{i=1}^{n} |o_i - \overline{o_i}| \\ s.t. \begin{cases} |\overline{o_i} - \overline{o}| \leq \varepsilon, \ \ i = 1, \ldots, n \\ \overline{o} = F_w^{OWA}(\overline{o_1}, \overline{o_2}, \ldots, \overline{o_n}) \\ \overline{o_{\sigma(i)}} - \overline{o_{\sigma(i-1)}} \leq 0, \ \ i = 2, \ldots, n \end{cases} \end{cases}. \tag{2.21}$$

The constraint conditions $\overline{o_{\sigma(i)}} - \overline{o_{\sigma(i-1)}} \leq 0$ $(i = 2, \ldots, n)$ guarantee that $\sigma(i) = \delta(i)$ $(i = 1, \ldots, n)$. Consequently,

$$F_w^{OWA}(\overline{o_1}, \ldots, \overline{o_n}) = \sum_{i=1}^{n} w_i \overline{o_{\delta(i)}} = \sum_{i=1}^{n} w_i \overline{o_{\sigma(i)}}. \tag{2.22}$$

Based on (2.22), model (2.21) can be reorganized as follows:

$$\begin{cases} \min\limits_{\overline{o_i}} \sum\limits_{i=1}^{n} |o_i - \overline{o_i}| \\ s.t. \begin{cases} |\overline{o_i} - \overline{o}| \leq \varepsilon, \ \ i = 1, \ldots, n \\ \overline{o} = \sum\limits_{i=1}^{n} w_i \overline{o_{\sigma(i)}} \\ \overline{o_{\sigma(i)}} - \overline{o_{\sigma(i-1)}} \leq 0, \ \ i = 2, \ldots, n \end{cases} \end{cases}. \tag{2.23}$$

Denote models (2.20) and (2.23) as $P_{2.5}$ and $P_{2.6}$, respectively. Moreover, let $\Omega_{2.5}$ and $\Omega_{2.6}$ represent the feasible sets corresponding to $P_{2.5}$ and $P_{2.6}$, respectively. To facilitate the construction of a good linkage of $P_{2.6}$ to $P_{2.5}$, Lemmas 2.2 and 2.3 are introduced.

Lemma 2.2 *For any real numbers x_1, x_2, y_1 and y_2, $|x_1 - y_1| + |x_2 - y_2| \leq |x_2 - y_1| + |x_1 - y_2|$ if $x_1 \leq x_2$ and $y_1 \leq y_2$.*

Proof It is obvious and the proof is omitted.

Lemma 2.3 *Let* $\{\overline{o_1^*}, ..., \overline{o_n^*}, \overline{o^*}\}$ *be the optimal solution to* $P_{2.5}$. *If* $\overline{o_p^*} < \overline{o_q^*}$ *and* $o_p > o_q$, *then* $\{\overline{\overline{o_1}}, ..., \overline{\overline{o_n}}, \overline{o^*}\}$ *is the optimal solution to model* $P_{2.5}$, *where*

$$\overline{\overline{o_i}} = \begin{cases} \overline{o_q^*}\ , \ for\ i = p \\ \overline{o_p^*}\ , \ for\ i = q \\ \overline{o_i^*}\ , \ for\ i \neq p, q \end{cases}.$$

Proof Since

$$\overline{\overline{o_i}} = \begin{cases} \overline{o_q^*}\ , \ for\ i = p \\ \overline{o_p^*}\ , \ for\ i = q \\ \overline{o_i^*}\ , \ for\ i \neq p, q \end{cases}, \tag{2.24}$$

thus

$$\overline{o^*} = F_w^{OWA}(\overline{o_1^*}, ..., \overline{o_n^*}) = F_w^{OWA}(\overline{\overline{o_1}}, ..., \overline{\overline{o_n}}) \tag{2.25}$$

and

$$\max_i |\overline{o_i^*} - \overline{o^*}| = \max_i |\overline{\overline{o_i}} - \overline{o^*}| \leq \varepsilon. \tag{2.26}$$

It is shown by (2.25) and (2.26) that $\{\overline{\overline{o_1}}, ..., \overline{\overline{o_n}}, \overline{o^*}\} \in \Omega_{2.5}$. Consequently,

$$\sum_{i=1}^{n} |o_i - \overline{\overline{o_i}}| \geq \min_{\{\overline{o_1}, ..., \overline{o_n}, \overline{o}\} \in \Omega_{2.5}} \sum_{i=1}^{n} |o_i - \overline{o_i}|. \tag{2.27}$$

Since $\{\overline{o_1^*}, ..., \overline{o_n^*}, \overline{o^*}\}$ is the optimal solution to $P_{2.5}$, thus

$$\sum_{i=1}^{n} |o_i - \overline{o_i^*}| = \min_{\{\overline{o_1}, ..., \overline{o_n}, \overline{o}\} \in \Omega_{2.5}} \sum_{i=1}^{n} |o_i - \overline{o_i}|. \tag{2.28}$$

The following can be obtained based on (2.24) and (2.28):

$$\begin{aligned} &\sum_{i=1}^{n} |o_i - \overline{\overline{o_i}}| - \min_{\{\overline{o_1}, ..., \overline{o_n}, \overline{o}\} \in \Omega_{2.5}} \sum_{i=1}^{n} |o_i - \overline{o_i}| \\ &= \sum_{i=1}^{n} |o_i - \overline{\overline{o_i}}| - \sum_{i=1}^{n} |o_i - \overline{o_i^*}| \\ &= |o_p - \overline{\overline{o_p}}| + |o_q - \overline{\overline{o_q}}| - |o_p - \overline{o_p^*}| - |o_q - \overline{o_q^*}| \\ &= |o_p - \overline{o_q^*}| + |o_q - \overline{o_p^*}| - |o_p - \overline{o_p^*}| - |o_q - \overline{o_q^*}|. \end{aligned} \tag{2.29}$$

Since $\overline{o_p^*} < \overline{o_q^*}$ and $o_q < o_p$, according to Lemma 2.2, the following can be obtained

$$\sum_{i=1}^{n}|o_i - \overline{\overline{o_i}}| - \min_{\{\overline{o_1},\ldots,\overline{o_n},\overline{o}\}\in\Omega_{2.5}} \sum_{i=1}^{n}|o_i - \overline{o_i}| \le 0\,. \tag{2.30}$$

Consequently,

$$\sum_{i=1}^{n}|o_i - \overline{\overline{o_i}}| \le \min_{\{\overline{o_1},\ldots,\overline{o_n},\overline{o}\}\in\Omega_{2.5}} \sum_{i=1}^{n}|o_i - \overline{o_i}|. \tag{2.31}$$

Equations (2.27) and (2.31) show that $\sum_{i=1}^{n}|o_i - \overline{\overline{o_i}}| = \min_{\{\overline{o_1},\overline{o_2},\ldots,\overline{o_n},\overline{o}\}\in\Omega_{2.5}} \sum_{i=1}^{n}|o_i - \overline{o_i}|$. So, $\{\overline{\overline{o_1}}, \ldots, \overline{\overline{o_n}}, \overline{o^*}\}$ is the optimal solution to $P_{2.5}$. This completes the proof of Lemma 2.3.

Theorem 2.3 is obtained based on Lemmas 2.2 and 2.3.

Theorem 2.3 *If $\{\overline{o_1^*}, \ldots, \overline{o_n^*}, \overline{o^*}\}$ is the optimal solution to $P_{2.6}$, then $\{\overline{o_1^*}, \ldots, \overline{o_n^*}, \overline{o^*}\}$ is the optimal solution to $P_{2.5}$.*

Proof Without loss of generality, assume that $o_1 \ge o_2 \ldots \ge o_n$. Let $\{\overline{\overline{o_1}}, \ldots, \overline{\overline{o_n}}, \overline{\overline{o}}\}$ be the optimal solution to $P_{2.5}$. Denote $\{\rho(1), \ldots, \rho(n)\}$ as the permutation of $\{1, 2, \ldots, n\}$ such that $\overline{\overline{o_{\rho(i-1)}}} \ge \overline{\overline{o_{\rho(i)}}}$ (i.e., $\overline{\overline{o_{\rho(i)}}}$ is the ith largest variable in $\{\overline{\overline{o_1}}, \ldots, \overline{\overline{o_n}}\}$). Based on Lemma 2.3, $\{\overline{\overline{o_{\rho(1)}}}, \ldots, \overline{\overline{o_{\rho(n)}}}, \overline{\overline{o}}\}$ is also the optimal solution to $P_{2.5}$. Since $\Omega_{2.6} \subseteq \Omega_{2.5}$, we have that

$$\begin{aligned}\sum_{i=1}^{n}|o_i - \overline{\overline{o_{\rho(i)}}}| &= \min_{\{\overline{o_1},\ldots,\overline{o_n},\overline{o}\}\in\Omega_{2.5}} \sum_{i=1}^{n}|o_i - \overline{o_i}| \\ &\le \min_{\{\overline{o_1},\ldots,\overline{o_n},\overline{o}\}\in\Omega_{2.6}} \sum_{i=1}^{n}|o_i - \overline{o_i}| = \sum_{i=1}^{n}|o_i - \overline{o_i^*}|.\end{aligned} \tag{2.32}$$

Since $\overline{\overline{o_{\rho(i)}}} - \overline{\overline{o_{\rho(i-1)}}} \le 0$, it follows $\{\overline{\overline{o_{\rho(1)}}}, \ldots, \overline{\overline{o_{\rho(n)}}}, \overline{\overline{o}}\} \in \Omega_{2.6}$. Consequently,

$$\sum_{i=1}^{n}|o_i - \overline{\overline{o_{\rho(i)}}}| \ge \min_{\{\overline{o_1},\ldots,\overline{o_n},\overline{o}\}\in\Omega_{2.6}} \sum_{i=1}^{n}|o_i - \overline{o_i}| = \sum_{i=1}^{n}|o_i - \overline{o_i^*}|. \tag{2.33}$$

Equations (2.32) and (2.33) show that

$$\min_{\{\overline{o_1},\ldots,\overline{o_n},\overline{o}\}\in\Omega_{2.5}} \sum_{i=1}^{n}|o_i - \overline{o_i}| = \sum_{i=1}^{n}|o_i - \overline{o_i^*}|. \tag{2.34}$$

Thus, $\{\overline{o_1^*}, \ldots, \overline{o_n^*}, \overline{o^*}\}$ is the optimal solution to $P_{2.5}$. This completes the proof of Theorem 2.3.

Based on Theorem 2.3, the optimal solution to $P_{2.6}$ is the optimal solution to $P_{2.5}$. Similar to Theorem 2.2, when using two transformed decision variables: $x_i = o_i - \overline{o_i}$ and $d_i = |x_i|$, $P_{2.6}$ can be transformed into a linear programming model. Therefore, solving the linear programming model yields the optimal solution to $P_{2.5}$.

(ii) Case B

In this case, to facilitate the solving process of model (2.19), Lemma 2.4 is introduced.

Lemma 2.4 *Let* $\overline{o} = F_w^{OWA}(\overline{o_1}, \overline{o_2}, ..., \overline{o_n})$ *and* $w = (w_1, w_2, ..., w_n)^T$. *Then,* $\overline{o} = \sum_{k=1}^{n} w_k r_k$ *if and only if the following constraints are satisfied.*

$$\begin{cases} r_k \leq \overline{o_i} + MA_{ki}, \quad k, i = 1, 2, ..., n \\ r_k \geq \overline{o_i} - MB_{ki}, \quad k, i = 1, 2, ..., n \\ \sum\limits_{i=1}^{n} A_{ki} \leq k - 1, \quad k = 1, 2, ..., n \\ \sum\limits_{i=1}^{n} B_{ki} \leq n - k, \quad k = 1, 2, ..., n \\ A_{ki}, B_{ki} \in \{0, 1\}, \quad k, i = 1, 2, ..., n \end{cases} \tag{2.35}$$

where M is $+\infty$.

Proof Let $\overline{o_{(k)}}$ be the kth smallest number of $(\overline{o_1}, \overline{o_2}, ..., \overline{o_n})$. Consider two 0-1 mixed programming models:

P_A:

$$\begin{cases} \max r_k \\ s.t. \begin{cases} r_k \leq \overline{o_i} + MA_{ki}, \quad k = 1, ..., n \\ \sum\limits_{i=1}^{n} A_{ki} \leq k - 1, \quad k = 1, ..., n \\ A_{ki} \in \{0, 1\}, \quad k, i = 1, ..., n \end{cases} \end{cases} \tag{2.36}$$

P_B:

$$\begin{cases} \min r_k \\ s.t. \begin{cases} r_k \geq \overline{o_i} - MB_{ki}, \quad k = 1, ..., n \\ \sum\limits_{i=1}^{n} B_{ki} \leq n - k, \quad k = 1, ..., n \\ B_{ki} \in \{0, 1\}, \quad k, i = 1, ..., n \end{cases} \end{cases} \tag{2.37}$$

where M is $+\infty$.

Based on Ogryczak and Śliwiński [18], it is obvious that both of the optimal values of P_A and P_B are $r_k = \overline{o_{(k)}}$, so the solution of constraints of P_A and P_B is $r_k = \overline{o_{(k)}}$. Thus, the constraints in Lemma 2.4 can ensure that $r_k = \overline{o_{(k)}}$. This completes the proof of Lemma 2.4.

Then, based on Lemma 2.4, Theorem 2.4 can be obtained to transform the MCCM under the OWA operator with any weights into mixed 0-1 linear programming problems.

Theorem 2.4 *Model (2.19) can be equivalently transformed into the following mixed 0-1 linear programming model:*

$$\begin{cases} \min \sum_{i=1}^{n} c_i d_i \\ s.t. \begin{cases} \overline{o} - \overline{o_i} \le \varepsilon, \ i = 1, ..., n \\ -\overline{o} + \overline{o_i} \le \varepsilon, \ i = 1, ..., n \\ o_i - \overline{o_i} \le x_i, \ i = 1, ..., n \\ x_i \le d_i, \ i = 1, ..., n \\ -x_i \le d_i, \ i = 1, ..., n \\ \overline{o} = \sum_{i=1}^{n} w_i r_i \\ r_k \le \overline{o_i} + MA_{ki}, \ k, i = 1, ..., n \\ r_k \ge \overline{o_i} - MB_{ki}, \ k, i = 1, ..., n \\ \sum_{i=1}^{n} A_{ki} \le k - 1, \ k, i = 1, ..., n \\ \sum_{i=1}^{n} B_{ki} \le n - k, \ k, i = 1, ..., n \\ A_{ki}, B_{ki} \in \{0, 1\}, \ k, i = 1, ..., n \end{cases} \end{cases}, \tag{2.38}$$

where $x_i = o_i - \overline{o_i}$ and $d_i \ge |x_i|$

Proof In model (2.38), $\overline{o_i} - \overline{o} \le \varepsilon$ and $\overline{o} - \overline{o_i} \le \varepsilon$ can guarantee that $|\overline{o_i} - \overline{o}| \le \varepsilon$. $o_i - \overline{o_i} = x_i$, $x_i \le d_i$ and $-x_i \le d_i$ can guarantee that $d_i \ge |x_i| = |o_i - \overline{o_i}|$. According to the objective function of model (2.38), any feasible solutions with $d_i > |x_i|$ are not the optimal solutions to model (2.38). Thus, $o_i - \overline{o_i} = x_i$, $x_i \le d_i$ and $-x_i \le d_i$ can guarantee that $d_i = |x_i| = |o_i - \overline{o_i}|$. So the following inequalities can guarantee that $|\overline{o_i} - \overline{o}| \le \varepsilon$ and the transformation of objective function from model (2.19) to model (2.38):

$$\begin{cases} \overline{o_i} - \overline{o} \le \varepsilon, \ i = 1, ..., n \\ \overline{o} - \overline{o_i} \le \varepsilon, \ i = 1, ..., n \\ o_i - \overline{o_i} = x_i, \ i = 1, ..., n \\ -x_i \le d_i, \ i = 1, ..., n \\ x_i \le d_i, \ i = 1, ..., n \end{cases}. \tag{2.39}$$

Then, based on Lemma 2.4, other constraints in model (2.38) can guarantee that $\overline{o} = F_w^{OWA}(\overline{o_1}, \overline{o_2}, ..., \overline{o_n})$. Therefore, model (2.19) can be transformed into model (2.38). This completes the proof of Theorem 2.4.

Denote model (2.38) as $P_{2.7}$. Based on Theorem 2.4, the optimal solution to model (2.19) can be obtained by solving the mixed 0-1 linear programming model $P_{2.7}$. Generally, cutting plane is used to solve mixed 0-1 linear programming models [2], and Balas et al. [1] proposed the Specialized Cutting Plane Algorithm to solve mixed 0-1 programs in finitely much iteration. The algorithm is very efficient and valid. Several software packages such as CPLEX and MATLAB also provide efficient algorithm and solver to solve the mixed 0-1 linear programming problems.

(3) Numerical examples

Here, we provide three numerical examples to demonstrate how the MCCMs work in practice.

(i) Example 2.1

Consider the example used in Ben-Arieh and Easton [4]. This example involves a GDM problem evaluated by five experts $\{E_1, E_2, ..., E_5\}$. Let the expert opinions be represented by real numbers, as follows:

$$\{o_1, o_2, o_3, o_4, o_5\} = \{0.5, 1.0, 2.5, 3.0, 6.0\}.$$

Let $\varepsilon = 0.8$, and let the associated weight vector of the weighted averaging operator be $w = (0.375, 0.1875, 0.25, 0.0625, 0.125)^T$. We use model $P_{2.4}$ to reach consensus among $\{o_1, o_2, o_3, o_4, o_5\}$. Table 2.1 lists the optimal adjusted opinions obtained using $P_{2.4}$ when setting different values of c_i $(i = 1, 2, ..., 5)$.

Let the associated weight vector of the selected OWA operator be $w = (0.375, 0.1875, 0.25, 0.0625, 0.125)^T$. Model $P_{2.5}$ is used to aggregate expert opinions. Table 2.2 lists the optimal adjusted opinions when setting different values for parameter ε.

Let the associated weight vector of the selected OWA operator be $w = (0.375, 0.1875, 0.25, 0.0625, 0.125)^T$. Let the consensus threshold $\varepsilon = 0.8$. The consensus model $P_{2.7}$ is used to help experts to reach a consensus. Table 2.3 displays the adjusted individual opinions, the collective group opinion and the total consensus cost under different cost vectors $(c_1, c_2, c_3, c_4, c_5)^T$.

Table 2.1 $P_{2.4}$ under different cost vectors in Example 2.1

$(c_1, c_2, c_3, c_4, c_5)$	$\overline{o_1}$	$\overline{o_2}$	$\overline{o_3}$	$\overline{o_4}$	$\overline{o_5}$	$\overline{o}$
(1, 4, 3, 5, 2)	2	1.4	2.5	3	3	2.2
(6, 3, 4, 1, 2)	0.5	1.0	2.1	2.1	2.1	1.3
(3, 4, 1, 6, 2)	1.6	1.32	2.9	2.92	2.92	2.12

Table 2.2 $P_{2.5}$ under different consensus thresholds in Example 2.1

ε	$\overline{o_1}$	$\overline{o_2}$	$\overline{o_3}$	$\overline{o_4}$	$\overline{o_5}$	$\overline{o}$
0.5	2.43	2.43	2.5	3.0	3.43	2.93
0.6	2.37	2.37	2.5	3.0	3.57	2.97
0.7	2.3	2.3	2.5	3.0	3.7	3.0
0.8	2.25	2.25	2.5	3.0	3.85	3.05

Table 2.3 $P_{2.7}$ under different cost vectors in Example 2.1

$(c_1, c_2, c_3, c_4, c_5)$	$\overline{o_1}$	$\overline{o_2}$	$\overline{o_3}$	$\overline{o_4}$	$\overline{o_5}$	$\overline{o}$	Total cost
(1, 4, 3, 5, 2)	2.575	1.4	2.5	3	3	2.2	9.675
(2, 4, 3, 1, 2.5)	1.078	1.078	2.5	2.5	2.5	1.7	10.72
(4, 1, 4, 2, 5)	1.4	2.575	2.5	3	3	2.2	20.175

Let the associated weight vector of the selected OWA operator be $w = (0.375, 0.1875, 0.25, 0.0625, 0.125)^T$. Then, let the cost vector $(c_1, c_2, c_3, c_4, c_5)^T = (1, 4, 3, 5, 2)^T$. Table 2.4 displays the adjusted individual opinions, the collective group opinion and the total consensus cost under different consensus thresholds ε, using $P_{2.7}$.

(ii) Example 2.2

Consider another example from Ben-Arieh et al. [5]. This example contains four experts $\{E_1, E_2, E_3, E_4\}$, providing the following opinions:

$$\{o_1, o_2, o_3, o_4\} = \{0, 3, 6, 10\}.$$

Let $\varepsilon = 0.8$, and let the associated weight vector of the weighted averaging operator be $w = (0.3, 0.1, 0.4, 0.2)^T$. Model $P_{2.4}$ is used to reach a consensus among $\{o_1, o_2, o_3, o_4\}$. Table 2.5 lists the optimal adjusted opinions obtained using $P_{2.4}$ when setting different values for c_i $(i = 1, 2, ..., 4)$.

Let the associated weight vector of the selected OWA operator be $w = (0.3, 0.1, 0.4, 0.2)^T$. Model $P_{2.5}$ is used to aggregate expert opinions. Table 2.6 lists the optimal adjusted opinions when considering different consensus thresholds ε.

Table 2.4 $P_{2.7}$ under different consensus thresholds in Example 2.1

ε	$\overline{o_1}$	$\overline{o_2}$	$\overline{o_3}$	$\overline{o_4}$	$\overline{o_5}$	$\overline{o}$	Total cost
0.5	2.875	2	2.5	3	3	2.5	12.375
0.6	2.775	1.8	2.5	3	3	2.4	11.475
0.7	2.675	1.6	2.5	3	3	2.3	10.575
0.8	2.575	1.4	2.5	3	3	2.2	9.675

Table 2.5 $P_{2.4}$ under different cost vectors in Example 2.2

(c_1, c_2, c_3, c_4)	$\overline{o_1}$	$\overline{o_2}$	$\overline{o_3}$	$\overline{o_4}$	$\overline{o}$
(1, 4, 3, 5)	4.8	4.8	6	6.4	5.6
(6, 3, 4, 1)	1.4	3	3	1.4	2.2
(3, 6, 4, 1)	3	3	4.4	4.2	3.8

Table 2.6 $P_{2.5}$ under different consensus thresholds in Example 2.2

ε	$\overline{o_1}$	$\overline{o_2}$	$\overline{o_3}$	$\overline{o_4}$	$\overline{o}$
0.5	2.75	3.0	3.75	3.75	3.25
0.6	2.7	3.0	3.9	3.9	3.3
0.7	2.65	3.0	4.05	4.05	3.35
0.8	2.6	3.0	4.2	4.2	3.4

(iii) Example 2.3

Example 2.3 involves an apartment buyer. The family of buyer comprises four members $\{E_1, E_2, E_3, E_4\}$, and five alternative flats $\{X_1, X_2, ..., X_5\}$ are available for consideration. The family members express their opinions regarding the alternatives using real numbers in $[1, 5]$, and o_{ij} estimates the opinion of E_j on X_i. Larger o_{ij} indicates stronger preference of member E_j for alternative X_i. Table 2.7 lists the values of o_{ij}.

Table 2.7 shows that the preferred alternatives of E_1, E_2, E_3 and E_4 are X_3, X_2, X_4 and X_1, respectively. The following uses MCCMs to reach consensus.

Let $\{c_1, c_2, c_3, c_4\} = \{1, 2, 1, 1\}$, and $\varepsilon = 1$. We use $P_{2.1}$ to aggregate the opinions of the family members. Let $\overline{o_{ij}}$ denote the optimal adjusted individual opinions of E_j on X_i. Let $\overline{o_i}$ represent the optimal adjusted collective opinions on X_i. Table 2.8 lists the values of $\overline{o_{ij}}$ and $\overline{o_i}$.

Table 2.8 reveals that $\overline{o_i} = \frac{\min_j\{\overline{o_{ij}}\}+\max_j\{\overline{o_{ij}}\}}{2}$, which is consistent with Theorem 2.1.

Table 2.7 The values of o_{ij} in Example 2.3

	$j = 1$	$j = 2$	$j = 3$	$j = 4$
$i = 1$	1	3	1	5
$i = 2$	3	5	3	2
$i = 3$	4	1	2	1
$i = 4$	2	3	5	1
$i = 5$	2	4	2	3

Table 2.8 The values of $\overline{o_{ij}}$ and $\overline{o_i}$ obtained from $P_{2.1}$ in Example 2.3

	$\overline{o_{i,1}}$	$\overline{o_{i,2}}$	$\overline{o_{i,3}}$	$\overline{o_{i,4}}$	$\overline{o_i}$
$i = 1$	1	3	1	3	2
$i = 2$	3	5	3	3	4
$i = 3$	3	1	2	1	2
$i = 4$	2	3	3	1	2
$i = 5$	2	4	2	3	3

Table 2.9 The values of $\overline{o_{ij}}$ and $\overline{o_i}$ obtained from $P_{2.4}$ in Example 2.3

	$\overline{o_{i,1}}$	$\overline{o_{i,2}}$	$\overline{o_{i,3}}$	$\overline{o_{i,4}}$	$\overline{o_i}$
$i = 1$	1.12	3	1.12	2.86	2.12
$i = 2$	3	4.12	3	2.12	3.12
$i = 3$	2.56	1	2	1	1.56
$i = 4$	2	3	3.59	1.6	2.59
$i = 5$	2	3.8	2	3	2.8

Table 2.10 The values of $\overline{o_{ij}}$ and $\overline{o_i}$ obtained from $P_{2.5}$ in Example 2.3

	$\overline{o_{i,1}}$	$\overline{o_{i,2}}$	$\overline{o_{i,3}}$	$\overline{o_{i,4}}$	$\overline{o_i}$
$i = 1$	1	2.96	1	2.9	1.96
$i = 2$	3	3.9	3	2	2.9
$i = 3$	2.62	1	2	1	1.62
$i = 4$	2	3	3.4	1.5	2.5
$i = 5$	2	3.62	2	3	2.62

Let $\{c_1, c_2, c_3, c_4\} = \{1, 2, 1, 1\}$, and $\varepsilon = 1$. Moreover, let the associated weight vector of the weighted averaging operator be $w = (0.2, 0.3, 0.25, 0.25)^T$. We use model $P_{2.4}$ to aggregate the opinions of the family members. Table 2.9 lists the optimal adjusted opinions.

Let $\varepsilon = 1$, and let the associated weight vector of the selected OWA operator be $w = (0.2, 0.3, 0.25, 0.25)^T$. We use model $P_{2.5}$ to aggregate the opinions of the family members. Table 2.10 lists the optimal adjusted opinions.

Tables 2.8, 2.9 and 2.10 reveal that $\overline{o_2} = \max\{\overline{o_i}\}$. Therefore, $P_{2.1}$, $P_{2.4}$, $P_{2.5}$ and $P_{2.7}$ all indicate that the best alternative is X_2.

2.2.2 Maximum Expert Consensus Model

Zhang et al. [19] further develop the the maximum expert consensus model (MECM) with aggregation functions based on the MCCM.

Given a special cost budget, the MECM seeks to find the maximum number of experts that can fit within the consensus.

Let B denote a specified consensus cost budget. In consensus building, the total consensus cost cannot exceed the cost budget B, i.e.,

$$\sum_{i=1}^{n} c_i \left|\overline{o_i} - o_i\right| \leq B. \tag{2.40}$$

We consider that the adjusted collective opinion $\overline{o}$ is obtained by aggregating the adjusted individual opinions $\overline{o_i}(i = 1, 2, ..., n)$, i.e.,

$$\overline{o} = F(\overline{o_1}, \overline{o_2}, ..., \overline{o_n}). \tag{2.41}$$

Meanwhile, we hope to maximize the number of experts with consensus, i.e.,

$$\max \sum_{i=1}^{n} x_i, \tag{2.42}$$

where, x_i is a 0-1 variable, and x_i is defined as:

$$x_i = \begin{cases} 1, \ if \ |\overline{o_i} - \overline{o}| \leq \varepsilon \\ 0, \ else \end{cases}. \tag{2.43}$$

Based on Eqs. (2.40)–(2.43), the MECM can be presented using an optimization model as follows:

$$\begin{cases} \max \sum\limits_{i=1}^{n} x_i \\ s.t. \begin{cases} \sum\limits_{i=1}^{n} c_i \, |\overline{o_i} - o_i| \leq B \\ \overline{o} = F\,(\overline{o_1}, \overline{o_2}, ..., \overline{o_n}) \\ x_i = \begin{cases} 1, if \ |\overline{o_i} - \overline{o}| \leq \varepsilon \\ 0, else \end{cases}, \quad i = 1, ..., n \end{cases} \end{cases}. \tag{2.44}$$

Denote model (2.44) as $P_{2.8}$. Notably, we use two aggregation functions: the WA operator and the OWA operator, in $P_{2.8}$.

(1) Maximum expert consensus model with WA operator

Selecting the WA operator to aggregate individuals' opinions in $P_{2.8}$ can yield the following model:

$$\begin{cases} \max \sum\limits_{i=1}^{n} x_i \\ s.t. \begin{cases} \sum\limits_{i=1}^{n} c_i \, |\overline{o_i} - o_i| \leq B \\ \overline{o} = F_W^{WA}\,(\overline{o_1}, \overline{o_2}, ..., \overline{o_n}) \\ x_i = \begin{cases} 1, if \ |\overline{o_i} - \overline{o}| \leq \varepsilon \\ 0, else \end{cases}, \quad i = 1, ..., n \end{cases} \end{cases}. \tag{2.45}$$

Denote model (2.45) as $P_{2.9}$. In $P_{2.9}$, $w = (w_1, w_2, ..., w_n)^T$ is the associated weight vector of the WA operator. Let $\Omega_{2.9}$ denote the feasible region of $P_{2.9}$. In order to solve $P_{2.9}$, we propose several equivalent transformations.

Lemma 2.5 *$P_{2.9}$ can be equivalently transformed into the nonlinear mixed 0-1 programming model $P_{2.10}$:*

$$\begin{cases} \max \sum_{i=1}^{n} x_i \\ s.t. \begin{cases} \sum_{i=1}^{n} c_i \left|\overline{o_i} - o_i\right| \le B \\ \overline{o} = \sum_{i=1}^{n} w_i \overline{o_i} \\ x_i \left|\overline{o_i} - \overline{o}\right| \le \varepsilon, \ \ i = 1, ..., n \\ x_i \in \{0, 1\}, \ \ i = 1, ..., n \end{cases} \end{cases}. \tag{2.46}$$

Proof Let $\Omega_{2.10}$ denote the feasible region of $P_{2.10}$. Let $\left\{\overline{o_1^*}, \overline{o_2^*}, ..., \overline{o_n^*}, \overline{o^*}, \overline{x_1^*}, \overline{x_2^*}, ..., \overline{x_n^*}\right\}$ be the optimal solution to $P_{2.9}$ and let $\left\{\overline{\overline{o_1^*}}, \overline{\overline{o_2^*}}, ..., \overline{\overline{o_n^*}}, \overline{\overline{o^*}}, \overline{\overline{x_1^*}}, \overline{\overline{x_2^*}}, ..., \overline{\overline{x_n^*}}\right\}$ be the optimal solution to $P_{2.10}$. For any feasible solution to $P_{2.9}$ $\{\overline{o_1}, \overline{o_2}, ..., \overline{o_n}, \overline{o}, \overline{x_1}, \overline{x_2}, ..., \overline{x_n}\} \in \Omega_{2.9}$, the following two cases can be obtained:

Case 1: $\left|\overline{o_i} - \overline{o}\right| \le \varepsilon$

Based on the constraints of $P_{2.9}$, if $\left|\overline{o_i} - \overline{o}\right| \le \varepsilon$, the following can be obtained: $x_i = 1$;

Consequently

$$x_i \left|\overline{o_i} - \overline{o}\right| = \left|\overline{o_i} - \overline{o}\right| \le \varepsilon\,; \tag{2.47}$$

Case 2: $\left|\overline{o_i} - \overline{o}\right| > \varepsilon$

Based on the constraints of $P_{2.9}$, if $\left|\overline{o_i} - \overline{o}\right| > \varepsilon$, the following can be obtained:

$$x_i = 0;$$

Consequently

$$x_i \left|\overline{o_i} - \overline{o}\right| = 0 \le \varepsilon\,. \tag{2.48}$$

Then, based on Case 1 and Case 2, we can obtain the following inequality:

$$x_i \left|\overline{o_i} - \overline{o}\right| \le \varepsilon. \tag{2.49}$$

Since $\{\overline{o_1}, \overline{o_2}, ..., \overline{o_n}, \overline{o}, \overline{x_1}, \overline{x_2}, ..., \overline{x_n}\} \in \Omega_{2.9}$, we have the following constraints:

$$\sum_{i=1}^{n} c_i \left|\overline{o_i} - o_i\right| \le B, \tag{2.50}$$

$$\overline{o} = F_w^{WA}\left(\overline{o_1}, \overline{o_2} ..., \overline{o_n}\right). \tag{2.51}$$

Based on (2.49)–(2.51), it follows $\{\overline{o_1}, \overline{o_2}, ..., \overline{o_n}, \overline{o}, \overline{x_1}, \overline{x_2}, ..., \overline{x_n}\} \in \Omega_{2.10}$. As a result, we can obtain that $\Omega_{2.9} \subseteq \Omega_{2.10}$. Then, based on the objective functions of $P_{2.9}$ and $P_{2.10}$, we have that

$$\sum_{i=1}^{n} \overline{x_i^*} \leq \sum_{i=1}^{n} \overline{\overline{x_i^*}}. \tag{2.52}$$

Since $\left\{\overline{\overline{o_1^*}}, \overline{\overline{o_2^*}}, ..., \overline{\overline{o_n^*}}, \overline{\overline{o^*}}, \overline{\overline{x_1^*}}, \overline{\overline{x_2^*}}, ..., \overline{\overline{x_n^*}}\right\}$ is the optimal solution to $P_{2.10}$, the following two cases can be obtained:

Case A: $\left|\overline{\overline{o_k^*}} - \overline{\overline{o^*}}\right| \leq \varepsilon$

Based on the constraints of $P_{2.10}$, if $\left|\overline{\overline{o_k^*}} - \overline{\overline{o^*}}\right| \leq \varepsilon$, the following can be obtained: $\overline{\overline{x_k^*}} = 0 \; or \; 1$;

Since $\sum\limits_{i=1, i \neq k}^{n} \overline{\overline{x_i^*}} + 1 \geq \sum\limits_{i=1, i \neq k}^{n} \overline{\overline{x_i^*}} + 0$

Thus $\overline{\overline{x_k^*}} = 1$;

Case B: $\left|\overline{\overline{o_k^*}} - \overline{\overline{o^*}}\right| > \varepsilon$

Based on the constraints of $P_{2.10}$, if $\left|\overline{\overline{o_k^*}} - \overline{\overline{o^*}}\right| > \varepsilon$, we can obtain that: $\overline{\overline{x_k^*}} = 0$;

Based on Case A and Case B, the following can be obtained:

$$\overline{\overline{x_i^*}} = \begin{cases} 1, & if \; \left|\overline{\overline{o_k^*}} - \overline{\overline{o^*}}\right| \leq \varepsilon \\ 0, & else \end{cases}, \; i = 1, 2, ..., n. \tag{2.53}$$

Since $\left\{\overline{\overline{o_1^*}}, \overline{\overline{o_2^*}}, ..., \overline{\overline{o_n^*}}, \overline{\overline{o^*}}, \overline{\overline{x_1^*}}, \overline{\overline{x_2^*}}, ..., \overline{\overline{x_n^*}}\right\} \in \Omega_{2.10}$, we have that:

$$\sum_{i=1}^{n} c_i \left|\overline{\overline{o_i^*}} - o_i\right| \leq B, \tag{2.54}$$

$$\overline{\overline{o^*}} = F_w^{WA}\left(\overline{\overline{o_1^*}}, \overline{\overline{o_2^*}} ..., \overline{\overline{o_n^*}}\right). \tag{2.55}$$

Based on (2.53)–(2.55), the following can be obtained:

$$\left\{\overline{\overline{o_1^*}}, \overline{\overline{o_2^*}}, ..., \overline{\overline{o_n^*}}, \overline{\overline{o^*}}, \overline{\overline{x_1^*}}, \overline{\overline{x_2^*}}, ..., \overline{\overline{x_n^*}}\right\} \in \Omega_{2.9}. \tag{2.56}$$

Then, since $\left\{\overline{o_1^*}, \overline{o_2^*}, ..., \overline{o_n^*}, \overline{o^*}, \overline{x_1^*}, \overline{x_2^*}, ..., \overline{x_n^*}\right\}$ is the optimal solution to $P_{2.9}$, the following can be obtained:

$$\sum_{i=1}^{n} \overline{\overline{x_i^*}} \leq \sum_{i=1}^{n} \overline{x_i^*}. \tag{2.57}$$

Based on (2.52) and (2.57), we have that:

$$\sum_{i=1}^{n} \overline{x_i^*} = \sum_{i=1}^{n} \overline{\overline{x_i^*}}. \tag{2.58}$$

Thus, the optimal solutions to $P_{2.9}$ and $P_{2.10}$ are equal. This completes the proof of Lemma 2.5.

According to Lemma 2.5, the optimal solution to $P_{2.9}$ can be obtained by solving model (2.46). In order to solve model (2.46), Lemma 2.6 is introduced.

Lemma 2.6 (Berthold et al. [6]) *If a constraint in a mixed 0-1 programming contains a product of a binary variable x with a linear term* $\sum_{i=1}^{n} a_i y_i$, *where* $y_i (i = 1, 2, ..., n)$ *are variables with finite bounds, this product can be replaced by a new variable z and the following linear constraints:*

$$\begin{cases} xy^L \le z \le xy^U \\ \sum\limits_{i=1}^{n} a_i y_i - (1-x)y^U \le z \le \sum\limits_{i=1}^{n} a_i y_i - (1-x)y^L \\ y^L = min \sum\limits_{i=1}^{n} a_i y_i, \quad y^U = max \sum\limits_{i=1}^{n} a_i y_i \end{cases}. \tag{2.59}$$

Theorem 2.5 is obtained based on Lemma 2.6.

Theorem 2.5 *$P_{2.9}$ can be equivalently transformed into the mixed 0-1 linear programming model $P_{2.11}$:*

$$\begin{cases} \max \sum\limits_{i=1}^{n} x_i \\ s.t. \begin{cases} \sum\limits_{i=1}^{n} c_i y_i \le B \\ \overline{o_i} - o_i \le y_i, \quad i = 1, ..., n \\ -\overline{o_i} + o_i \le y_i, \quad i = 1, ..., n \\ \overline{o} = \sum\limits_{i=1}^{n} w_i \overline{o_i} \\ z_i \le \varepsilon, \quad i = 1, ..., n \\ -z_i \le \varepsilon, \quad i = 1, ..., n \\ (1-w_i)(a-b)x_i \le z_i \le (1-w_i)(b-a)x_i, \quad i = 1, ..., n \\ \overline{o_i} - \overline{o} - (1-w_i)(b-a)(1-x_i) \le z_i \le \overline{o_i} - \overline{o} - \\ \quad (1-w_i)(a-b)(1-x_i), \quad i = 1, ..., n \\ a \le \overline{o_i} \le b, \quad i = 1, ..., n \\ x_i \in \{0, 1\}, \quad i = 1, ..., n \end{cases} \end{cases}. \tag{2.60}$$

Proof The proof of Theorem 2.5 can be divided into two parts:

Part 1: Proving that constraint $x_i \left|\overline{o_i} - \overline{o}\right| \le \varepsilon$ in $P_{2.9}$ can be transformed into the following constraints in $P_{2.11}$:

$$\begin{cases} z_i \le \varepsilon, \ \ i = 1, ..., n \\ -z_i \le \varepsilon, \ \ i = 1, ..., n \\ (1 - w_i)(a - b)x_i \le z_i \le (1 - w_i)(b - a)x_i, \ \ i = 1, ..., n \,. \\ \overline{o_i} - \overline{o} - (1 - w_i)(b - a)(1 - x_i) \le z_i \le \\ \overline{o_i} - \overline{o} - (1 - w_i)(a - b)(1 - x_i), \ \ i = 1, ..., n \end{cases} \tag{2.61}$$

We can get the following constraints from $x_i \left|\overline{o_i} - \overline{o}\right| \le \varepsilon$:

$$\begin{cases} x_i \left(\overline{o_i} - \overline{o}\right) \le \varepsilon \\ -x_i \left(\overline{o_i} - \overline{o}\right) \le \varepsilon \end{cases}. \tag{2.62}$$

Obviously, $\overline{o_i}$ is bounded in GDM problems. Without loss of generality, assume that $\overline{o_i}$ ranges from a to b. Since $\overline{o} = \sum\limits_{i=1}^{n} w_i \overline{o_i}$, $(\overline{o_i} - \overline{o})$ is a linear term.

$$\begin{cases} \overline{o_i} - \overline{o} = \overline{o_i} - \sum\limits_{j=1}^{n} w_j \overline{o_j} = (1 - w_i)\overline{o_i} - \sum\limits_{j=1, j \ne i}^{n} w_j \overline{o_j} \\ \max \left\{\overline{o_i} - \overline{o}\right\} = (1 - w_i)b - a \sum\limits_{j=1, j \ne i}^{n} w_j = (b - a)(1 - w_i)\,. \\ \min \left\{\overline{o_i} - \overline{o}\right\} = (1 - w_i)a - b \sum\limits_{j=1, j \ne i}^{n} w_j = (a - b)(1 - w_i) \end{cases} \tag{2.63}$$

Since x_i is a binary variable. Then, let

$$z_i = x_i \left(\overline{o_i} - \overline{o}\right). \tag{2.64}$$

The following can be obtained based on Lemma 2.6:

$$\begin{cases} z_i \le \varepsilon, \ \ i = 1, ..., n \\ -z_i \le \varepsilon, \ \ i = 1, ..., n \\ (1 - w_i)(a - b)x_i \le z_i \le (1 - w_i)(b - a)x_i, \ \ i = 1, ..., n \,. \\ \overline{o_i} - \overline{o} - (1 - w_i)(b - a)(1 - x_i) \le z_i \le \\ \quad \overline{o_i} - \overline{o} - (1 - w_i)(a - b)(1 - x_i), \ \ i = 1, ..., n \end{cases} \tag{2.65}$$

So constraint $x_i \left|\overline{o_i} - \overline{o}\right| \le \varepsilon$ in $P_{2.9}$ can be equivalently transformed into these constraints in model $P_{2.11}$.

Part 2: Proving that constraint $\sum\limits_{i=1}^{n} c_i \left|\overline{o_i} - o_i\right| \le B$ in model $P_{2.9}$ can be transformed into the following constraints in model $P_{2.11}$:

$$\begin{cases} \sum\limits_{i=1}^{n} c_i y_i \le B \\ \overline{o_i} - o_i \le y_i \\ -\overline{o_i} + o_i \le y_i \end{cases}. \tag{2.66}$$

Let $\Omega_{2.10}$ denote the feasible region of $P_{2.10}$ and let $\Omega_{2.11}$ denote the feasible region of model $P_{2.11}$.

Let $\left\{\overline{\overline{o_1^*}}, \overline{\overline{o_2^*}}, \ldots, \overline{\overline{o_n^*}}, \overline{\overline{o^*}}, \overline{\overline{x_1^*}}, \overline{\overline{x_2^*}}, \ldots, \overline{\overline{x_n^*}}\right\}$ be the optimal solution to $P_{2.10}$ and let $\left\{\widetilde{o_1^*}, \widetilde{o_2^*}, \ldots, \widetilde{o_n^*}, \widetilde{o^*}, \widetilde{x_1^*}, \widetilde{x_2^*}, \ldots, \widetilde{x_n^*}, \widetilde{y_1^*}, \widetilde{y_2^*}, \ldots, \widetilde{y_n^*}\right\}$ be the optimal solution to $P_{2.11}$.

Since $\left\{\widetilde{o_1^*}, \widetilde{o_2^*}, \ldots, \widetilde{o_n^*}, \widetilde{o^*}, \widetilde{x_1^*}, \widetilde{x_2^*}, \ldots, \widetilde{x_n^*}, \widetilde{y_1^*}, \widetilde{y_2^*}, \ldots, \widetilde{y_n^*}\right\} \in \Omega_{2.11}$, we can obtain that:

$$\begin{cases} \widetilde{o_i^*} - o_i \le \widetilde{y_i^*} \\ -\widetilde{o_i^*} + o_i \le \widetilde{y_i^*} \end{cases}. \tag{2.67}$$

Thus

$$\sum_{i=1}^{n} c_i \left|\widetilde{o_i^*} - o_i\right| \le \sum_{i=1}^{n} c_i \widetilde{y_i^*} \le B. \tag{2.68}$$

Since Part 1 guarantees the transformation of other constraints from $P_{2.10}$ to $P_{2.11}$, we can obtain that:

$$\left\{\widetilde{o_1^*}, \widetilde{o_2^*}, \ldots, \widetilde{o_n^*}, \widetilde{o^*}, \widetilde{x_1^*}, \widetilde{x_2^*}, \ldots, \widetilde{x_n^*}, \widetilde{y_1^*}, \widetilde{y_2^*}, \ldots, \widetilde{y_n^*}\right\} \in \Omega_{2.10}.$$

Then, since $\left\{\overline{\overline{o_1^*}}, \overline{\overline{o_2^*}}, \ldots, \overline{\overline{o_n^*}}, \overline{\overline{o^*}}, \overline{\overline{x_1^*}}, \overline{\overline{x_2^*}}, \ldots, \overline{\overline{x_n^*}}\right\}$ is the optimal solution to $P_{2.10}$, based on the objective functions of $P_{2.10}$ and $P_{2.11}$, the following can be obtained:

$$\sum_{i=1}^{n} \widetilde{x_i^*} \le \sum_{i=1}^{n} \overline{\overline{x_i^*}}. \tag{2.69}$$

Since $\left\{\overline{\overline{o_1^*}}, \overline{\overline{o_2^*}}, \ldots, \overline{\overline{o_n^*}}, \overline{\overline{o^*}}, \overline{\overline{x_1^*}}, \overline{\overline{x_2^*}}, \ldots, \overline{\overline{x_n^*}}\right\}$ is the optimal solution to $P_{2.10}$, the following inequality can be obtained:

$$\sum_{i=1}^{n} c_i \left|\overline{\overline{o_i^*}} - o_i\right| \le B. \tag{2.70}$$

Let

$$y_i = \left|\overline{\overline{o_i^*}} - o_i\right|. \tag{2.71}$$

Then, we have the following inequalities:

$$\overline{\overline{o_i^*}} - o_i \le y_i, \tag{2.72}$$

$$-\overline{\overline{o_i^*}} + o_i \le y_i. \tag{2.73}$$

Thus, since Part 1 guarantees the transformation of other constraints from model $P_{2.10}$ to $P_{2.11}$, the following can be obtained based on (2.70), (2.72) and (2.73):

$$\left\{\overline{\overline{o_1^*}}, \overline{\overline{o_2^*}}, ..., \overline{\overline{o_n^*}}, \overline{\overline{o^*}}, \overline{\overline{x_1^*}}, \overline{\overline{x_2^*}}, ..., \overline{\overline{x_n^*}}, y_1, y_2, ..., y_n\right\} \in \Omega_{2.11}.$$

Since $\left\{\widetilde{o_1^*}, \widetilde{o_2^*}, ..., \widetilde{o_n^*}, \widetilde{o^*}, \widetilde{x_1^*}, \widetilde{x_2^*}, ..., \widetilde{x_n^*}, \widetilde{y_1^*}, \widetilde{y_2^*}, ..., \widetilde{y_n^*}\right\}$ is the optimal solution to $P_{2.11}$, based on the objective functions of $P_{2.10}$ and $P_{2.11}$, we can obtain:

$$\sum_{i=1}^{n} \overline{\overline{x_i^*}} \leq \sum_{i=1}^{n} \widetilde{x_i^*}. \tag{2.74}$$

Then, the following can be obtained based on (2.69) and (2.74):

$$\sum_{i=1}^{n} \overline{\overline{x_i^*}} = \sum_{i=1}^{n} \widetilde{x_i^*}. \tag{2.75}$$

So constraint $\sum_{i=1}^{n} c_i \left|\overline{o_i} - o_i\right| \leq B$ in $P_{2.10}$ can be transformed into the corresponding constraints in $P_{2.11}$.

Thus, based on Part 1 and Part 2, $P_{2.10}$ can be equivalently transformed into $P_{2.11}$. This completes the proof of Theorem 2.5.

From model (2.59) to model (2.60), all nonlinear constraints are transformed into linear constraints. Consequently, the MECM with WA operator is equivalently transformed into a mixed 0-1 linear programming model.

(2) Maximum expert consensus model with OWA operator

Selecting the OWA operator to aggregate individuals' opinions in $P_{2.8}$ can yield the following model:

$$\begin{cases} \max \sum_{i=1}^{n} x_i \\ s.t. \begin{cases} \sum_{i=1}^{n} c_i \left|\overline{o_i} - o_i\right| \leq B \\ \overline{o} = F_w^{OWA}\left(\overline{o_1}, \overline{o_2}, ..., \overline{o_n}\right) \\ x_i = \begin{cases} 1, if \left|\overline{o_i} - \overline{o}\right| \leq \varepsilon \\ 0, else \end{cases}, \quad i = 1, ..., n \end{cases} \end{cases}. \tag{2.76}$$

Denote model (2.76) as $P_{2.12}$.

Then, Theorem 2.6 can be obtained based on Lemma 2.4 and Theorem 2.5.

Theorem 2.6 *$P_{2.12}$ can be equivalently transformed into the mixed 0-1 linear programming model $P_{2.13}$:*

$$\begin{cases} \max \sum_{i=1}^{n} x_i \\ s.t. \begin{cases} \sum_{i=1}^{n} c_i y_i \leq B \\ \overline{o_i} - o_i \leq y_i, \quad i = 1, ..., n \\ -\overline{o_i} + o_i \leq y_i, \quad i = 1, ..., n \\ \overline{o} = \sum_{i=1}^{n} w_i r_i \\ r_k \leq \overline{o_i} + M A_{ki}, \quad k, i = 1, ..., n \\ r_k \geq \overline{o_i} - M B_{ki}, \quad k, i = 1, ..., n \\ \sum_{i=1}^{n} A_{ki} \leq k - 1, \quad k = 1, ..., n \\ \sum_{i=1}^{n} B_{ki} \leq n - k, \quad k = 1, ..., n \\ z_i \leq \varepsilon, \quad i = 1, ..., n \\ -z_i \leq \varepsilon, \quad i = 1, ..., n \\ (1 - w_i)(a - b)x_i \leq z_i \leq (1 - w_i)(b - a)x_i, \quad i = 1, ..., n \\ \overline{o_i} - \overline{o} - (1 - w_i)(b - a)(1 - x_i) \leq z_i \\ \quad \leq \overline{o_i} - \overline{o} - (1 - w_i)(a - b)(1 - x_i), \quad i = 1, ..., n \\ a \leq \overline{o_i} \leq b, \quad i = 1, ..., n \\ x_i, A_{ki}, B_{ki} \in \{0, 1\}, \quad k, i = 1, ..., n \end{cases} \end{cases} . \tag{2.77}$$

Proof Based on the proof of Theorem 2.5, constraint $\sum_{i=1}^{n} c_i \left|\overline{o_i} - o_i\right| \leq B$ in model $P_{2.12}$ can be transformed into the following constraints in $P_{2.13}$:

$$\begin{cases} \sum_{i=1}^{n} c_i y_i \leq B \\ \overline{o_i} - o_i \leq y_i, \quad i = 1, ..., n \\ -\overline{o_i} + o_i \leq y_i, \quad i = 1, ..., n \end{cases} . \tag{2.78}$$

Then, based on Lemma 2.4, constraint $\overline{o} = F_w^{OWA}(\overline{o_1}, \overline{o_2}, ..., \overline{o_n})$ in $P_{2.12}$ can be equivalently transformed into the following constraints in model $P_{2.13}$:

$$\begin{cases} \overline{o} = \sum_{i=1}^{n} w_i r_i \\ r_k \leq \overline{o_i} + M A_{ki}, \quad k, i = 1, ..., n \\ r_k \geq \overline{o_i} - M B_{ki}, \quad k, i = 1, ..., n \\ \sum_{i=1}^{n} A_{ki} \leq k - 1, \quad k = 1, ..., n \\ \sum_{i=1}^{n} B_{ki} \leq n - k, \quad k = 1, ..., n \\ A_{ki}, B_{ki} \in \{0, 1\}, \quad k, i = 1, ..., n \end{cases} . \tag{2.79}$$

Based on the proof of Lemma 2.4, the definition of x_i in model $P_{2.12}$ can be transformed into the following constraints:

$$\begin{cases} x_i \left|\overline{o_i} - \overline{o}\right| \leq \varepsilon, \ \ i = 1, ..., n \\ x_i \in \{0, 1\}, \ \ i = 1, ..., n \end{cases}. \tag{2.80}$$

Then, based on the proof of Theorem 2.5, constraint $x_i|\overline{o_i} - \overline{o}| \leq \varepsilon$ can be transformed into the following constraints in model $P_{2.13}$:

$$\begin{cases} z_i \leq \varepsilon, \ \ i = 1, ..., n \\ -z_i \leq \varepsilon, \ \ i = 1, ..., n \\ (1 - w_i)(a - b)x_i \leq z_i \leq (1 - w_i)(b - a)x_i, \ \ i = 1, ..., n \\ \overline{o_i} - \overline{o} - (1 - w_i)(b - a)(1 - x_i) \leq z_i \leq \overline{o_i} - \overline{o} \\ \quad -(1 - w_i)(a - b)(1 - x_i), \ \ i = 1, ..., n \\ a \leq \overline{o_i} \leq b, \ \ i = 1, ..., n \end{cases}. \tag{2.81}$$

Based on (2.78), (2.79) and (2.81), all the constraints in model $P_{2.12}$ can be equivalently transformed into the constraints in model $P_{2.13}$. This completes the proof of Theorem 2.6.

According to Theorem 2.6, the MECM with OWA operator can be equivalently transformed into a mixed 0-1 linear programming model.

(3) Example 2.4

We continue with Example 2.1, and use MECMs to help experts to reach a consensus.

Let the associated weight vector of the aggregation operator be $w = (0.375, 0.1875, 0.25, 0.0625, 0.125)^T$.

(i) The use of the MECM with WA operator

We use the MECM with WA operator (i.e., $P_{2.11}$) to obtain the adjusted individual opinions, the collective group opinion, the experts within consensus and the total consensus cost.

Let the consensus threshold $\varepsilon = 0.8$, and let the consensus cost budget $B = 5$. Table 2.11 explores the adjusted individual opinions, the collective group opinion, the experts within consensus and the total consensus cost under different cost

Table 2.11 $P_{2.11}$ under different cost vectors in Example 2.4

$(c_1, c_2, c_3, c_4, c_5)$	$\overline{o_1}$	$\overline{o_2}$	$\overline{o_3}$	$\overline{o_4}$	$\overline{o_5}$	$\overline{o}$	Experts within consensus	Total cost
(1, 4, 3, 5, 2)	1.743	1.743	2.5	3	6	2.543	$\{E_1, E_2, E_3, E_4\}$	4.215
(2, 4, 3, 1, 2.5)	1	1	1.3	2.6	6	1.8	$\{E_1, E_2, E_3, E_4\}$	5
(4, 1, 4, 2, 5)	0.5	1.15	2.5	2.75	6	1.95	$\{E_2, E_3, E_4\}$	0.65

Table 2.12 $P_{2.11}$ under different consensus thresholds in Example 2.4

ε	$\overline{o_1}$	$\overline{o_2}$	$\overline{o_3}$	$\overline{o_4}$	$\overline{o_5}$	$\overline{o}$	Experts within consensus	Total cost
0.5	2	1	2.5	3	6	2.5	$\{E_1, E_3, E_4\}$	1.5
0.6	1.84	1	2.5	3	6	2.44	$\{E_1, E_3, E_4\}$	1.34
0.7	1.68	1	2.5	3	6	2.38	$\{E_1, E_3, E_4\}$	1.18
0.8	1.743	1.743	2.5	3	6	2.543	$\{E_1, E_2, E_3, E_4\}$	4.215

Table 2.13 $P_{2.11}$ under different cost budgets in Example 2.4

B	$\overline{o_1}$	$\overline{o_2}$	$\overline{o_3}$	$\overline{o_4}$	$\overline{o_5}$	$\overline{o}$	Experts within consensus	Total cost
5	1.743	1.743	2.5	3	6	2.543	$\{E_1, E_2, E_3, E_4\}$	4.215
4	1.52	1	2.5	3	6	2.32	$\{E_1, E_3, E_4\}$	1.02
3	1.52	1	2.5	3	6	2.32	$\{E_1, E_3, E_4\}$	1.02
2	1.52	1	2.5	3	6	2.32	$\{E_1, E_3, E_4\}$	1.02

vectors $(c_1, c_2, c_3, c_4, c_5)^T$. Moreover, let the cost vector $(c_1, c_2, c_3, c_4, c_5)^T = (1, 4, 3, 5, 2)^T$, and let the consensus cost budget $B = 5$. Table 2.12 displays the adjusted individual opinions, the collective group opinion, the experts within consensus and the total consensus cost under different consensus thresholds ε. Finally, let the consensus threshold $\varepsilon = 0.8$, and let the cost vector $(c_1, c_2, c_3, c_5)^T = (1, 4, 3, 5, 2)^T$. Table 2.13 displays the adjusted individual opinions, the collective group opinion, the experts within consensus and the total consensus cost under different consensus cost budgets B.

(ii) The use of the MECM with OWA operator

We use the MECM with OWA operator (i.e., $P_{2.13}$) to obtain the adjusted individual opinions, the collective group opinion, the experts within consensus and the total consensus cost.

Let the consensus threshold $\varepsilon = 0.8$, and let the consensus cost budget $B = 5$. Table 2.14 displays the adjusted individual opinions, the collective group opinion, the experts within consensus and the total consensus cost under different cost

Table 2.14 $P_{2.13}$ under different cost vectors in Example 2.4

$(c_1, c_2, c_3, c_4, c_5)$	$\overline{o_1}$	$\overline{o_2}$	$\overline{o_3}$	$\overline{o_4}$	$\overline{o_5}$	$\overline{o}$	Experts within consensus	Total cost
(1, 4, 3, 5, 2)	1.743	1.743	2.5	3	6	2.543	$\{E_1, E_2, E_3, E_4\}$	4.215
(2, 4, 3, 1, 2.5)	1	1	2.5	1.325	6	1.8	$\{E_1, E_2, E_3, E_4\}$	2.675
(4, 1, 4, 2, 5)	0.5	1.15	2.5	2.75	6	1.95	$\{E_2, E_3, E_4\}$	0.65

Table 2.15 $P_{2.13}$ under different consensus thresholds in Example 2.4

ε	$\overline{o_1}$	$\overline{o_2}$	$\overline{o_3}$	$\overline{o_4}$	$\overline{o_5}$	$\overline{o}$	Experts within consensus	Total cost
0.5	2.875	1	2.5	3	6	2.5	$\{E_1, E_3, E_4\}$	2.375
0.6	2.467	1	2.5	3	6	2.4	$\{E_1, E_3, E_4\}$	1.967
0.7	1.933	1	2.5	3	6	2.3	$\{E_1, E_3, E_4\}$	1.433
0.8	1.743	1.743	2.5	3	6	2.543	$\{E_1, E_2, E_3, E_4\}$	4.214

Table 2.16 $P_{2.13}$ under different cost budgets in Example 2.4

B	$\overline{o_1}$	$\overline{o_2}$	$\overline{o_3}$	$\overline{o_4}$	$\overline{o_5}$	$\overline{o}$	Experts within consensus	Total cost
5	1.743	1.743	2.5	3	6	2.543	$\{E_1, E_2, E_3, E_4\}$	4.214
4	1.4	1	2.5	3	6	2.2	$\{E_1, E_3, E_4\}$	0.9
3	1.4	1	2.5	3	6	2.2	$\{E_1, E_3, E_4\}$	0.9
2	1.4	1	2.5	3	6	2.2	$\{E_1, E_3, E_4\}$	0.9

vectors $(c_1, c_2, c_3, c_4, c_5)^T$. Moreover, let the cost vector $(c_1, c_2, c_3, c_4, c_5)^T = (1, 4, 3, 5, 2)^T$, and let the consensus cost budget $B = 5$. Table 2.15 displays the adjusted individual opinions, the collective opinion, the experts within consensus and the total consensus cost under different consensus thresholds ε. Finally, let the consensus threshold $\varepsilon = 0.8$, and let the cost vector $(c_1, c_2, c_3, c_4, c_5)^T = (1, 4, 3, 5, 2)^T$. Table 2.16 displays the adjusted individual opinions, the collective group opinion, the experts within consensus and the total consensus cost under different consensus cost budgets B.

2.3 Comparison Analysis

In this section, a comparison analysis is performed to show the advantage of the proposed consensus models. We only compare the MECM with the consensus model based on IR and DR rules (IR-DR consensus model). Without loss of generality, the OWA operator is used to aggregate experts' opinions in the comparison analysis. When using the WA operator, the comparison results are similar. Meanwhile, when comparing the MCCM with the IR-DR consensus model, we can obtain the similar results.

2.3.1 Consensus Based on IR and DR Rules

Based on IR and DR [9, 14, 15] introduced in Chap. 1, we display an IR-DR consensus model. Based on IR, we identify the expert whose opinion has the biggest difference from the collective opinion and should change his/her opinion. Based on DR, we adjust the opinion, which needs to be changed based on IR, to make it reach the given consensus level with minimum cost. Moreover, the OWA operator is used to aggregate individual opinions into a collective opinion. This IR-DR consensus model is described as follows.

IR-DR consensus model

Input: The original opinion of the expert $o_i (i = 1, 2, ..., n)$, the associated weight vector of the aggregation operator $w = (w_1, w_2, ..., w_n)^T$, the consensus threshold ε, the cost vector $c = (c_1, c_2, ..., c_n)^T$, cost budget B, the maximum number of iterations $max\_rounds \geq 1$.

Output: the number of experts within consensus X

Step 1: Set $z = 0$, $o_i^z = o_i (i = 1, 2, ..., n)$ and $B^z = B$.

Step 2: Calculate the collective opinion $o_c^z = F_w^{OWA}(o_1^z, o_2^z, ..., o_n^z)$ and the consensus index $CL^z(E_i) = \left|o_i^z - o_c^z\right|, (i = 1, 2, ..., n)$. $CL^z(E_k) = \max_i \{CL^z(E_i)\}$. Based on IR, the opinion of expert E_k has the biggest difference from the collective opinion. If $CL^z(E_k) \leq \varepsilon$ or $z \geq max\_rounds$, go to Step 4. Otherwise, go to the next step.

Step 3: Based on DR, we adjust the opinion of expert E_k to make it reach the given consensus threshold ε with minimum cost. $B^{z+1} = B^z - c_k \cdot |CL^z(E_k) - \varepsilon|$. If $B^{z+1} < 0$, go to Step 4. Otherwise,

$$o_k^z = \begin{cases} o_c^z + \varepsilon, & if\ o_k^z > o_c^z \\ o_c^z - \varepsilon, & if\ o_k^z \leq o_c^z \end{cases}$$

$o_i^{z+1} = o_i^z$, $z = z + 1$. Go to Step 2.

Step 4: Output the number of experts within consensus X.

2.3.2 Comparison Results

We consider three examples to compare the MECM with the IR-DR consensus model. The three examples are drawn from Examples 2.1–2.3, respectively.

(1) Comparison analysis 2.1

There are five experts in Example 2.1 and their initial opinions are

$$\{o_1, o_2, o_3, o_4, o_5\} = \{0.5, 1, 2.5, 3, 6\}.$$

Let the associated weight vector of the aggregation operator $w = (0.375, 0.1875, 0.25, 0.0625, 0.125)^T$. Firstly, let the cost budget $B = 5$, and let the cost vector $c = (1, 1, 1, 1, 1)^T$. Figure 2.1 shows the comparison results between the MECM and the IR-DR consensus model under different consensus thresholds ε. Then, let the cost vector $c = (1, 4, 3, 5, 2)^T$, and the consensus threshold $\varepsilon = 0.8$. Figure 2.2

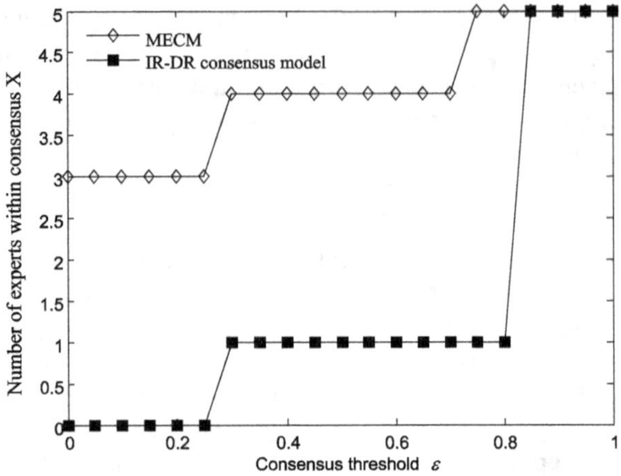

Fig. 2.1 Comparison between the MECM and the IR-DR consensus model under different consensus thresholds in comparison analysis 2.1

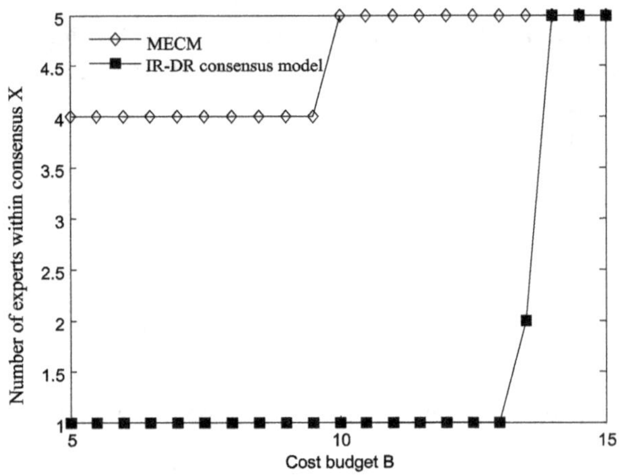

Fig. 2.2 Comparison between the MECM and the IR-DR consensus model under different cost budgets in comparison analysis 2.1

shows the comparison results between the MECM and the IR-DR consensus model under different cost budgets B.

(2) Comparison analysis 2.2

There are four experts in Example 2.2 and their initial opinions are

$$\{o_1, o_2, o_3, o_4\} = \{0, 3, 6, 10\}.$$

Let the associated weight vector of the aggregation operator $w = (0.3, 0.1, 0.4, 0.2)^T$. Firstly, let the cost budget $B = 5$, and let the cost vector $c = (1, 1, 1, 1)^T$. Figure 2.3 shows the comparison results between the MECM and the IR-DR consensus model under different consensus thresholds ε. Then, let the cost vector $c = (1, 4, 3, 5)^T$, and the consensus threshold $\varepsilon = 0.8$. Figure 2.4 shows the com-

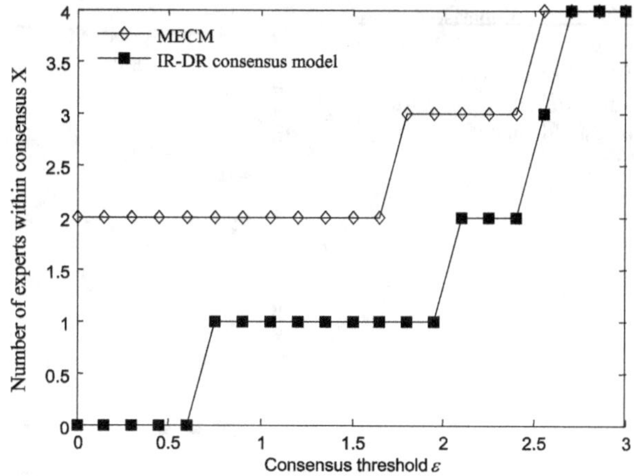

Fig. 2.3 Comparison between the MECM and the IR-DR consensus model under different consensus thresholds in comparison analysis 2.2

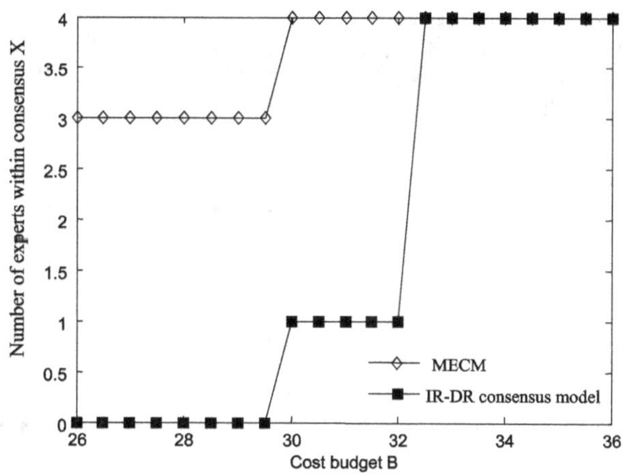

Fig. 2.4 Comparison between the MECM and the IR-DR consensus model under different cost budgets in comparison analysis 2.2

parison results between the MECM and the IR-DR consensus model under different cost budgets B.

(3) Comparison analysis 2.3

There are four experts in Example 2.3 and their initial opinions are

$$\{o_1, o_2, o_3, o_4\} = \{1, 3, 1, 3\}.$$

Let the associated weight vector of the aggregation operator $w = (0.2, 0.3, 0.25, 0.25)^T$. Firstly, let the cost budget $B = 2$, and let the cost vector $c = (1, 1, 1, 1)^T$. Figure 2.5 shows the comparison results between the MECM and the IR-DR consensus model under different consensus thresholds ε. Then, let the cost vector $c = (1, 2, 1, 1)^T$, and the consensus threshold $\varepsilon = 0.8$, and Fig. 2.6 shows the com-

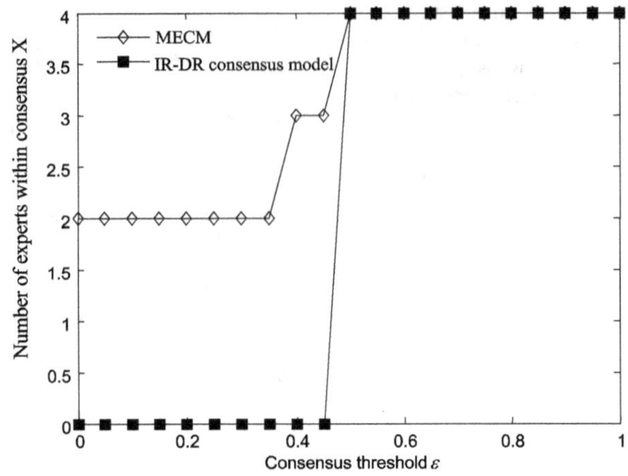

Fig. 2.5 Comparison between the MECM and the IR-DR consensus model under different consensus thresholds in comparison analysis 2.3

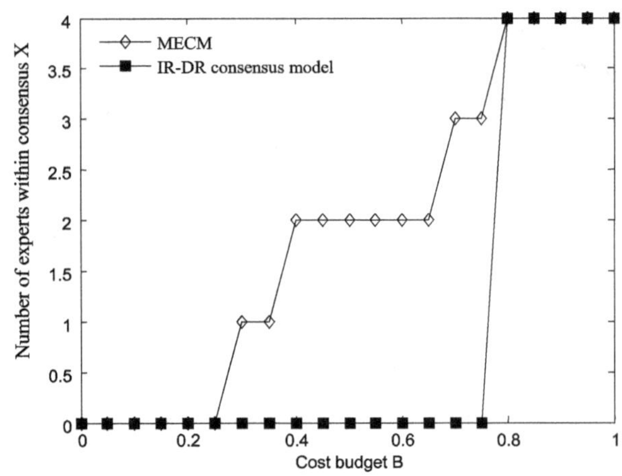

Fig. 2.6 Comparison between the MECM and the IR-DR consensus model under different cost budgets in comparison analysis 2.3

parison result between the MECM and the IR-DR consensus model under different cost budgets B.

In the above three comparison examples, the MECM can make more experts reach the consensus level under the given cost budget. As a result, when the cost budget is not enough to make all the experts reach the consensus level, the MECM can give a more effective aid for GDM problems.

References

1. E. Balas, S. Ceria, G. Cornuéjols, A lift-and-project cutting plane algorithm for mixed 0–1 programs. Math. Program. **58**, 295–324 (1993)
2. E. Balas, S. Ceria, G. Cornuéjols, Mixed 0–1 programming by lift-and-project in a branch-and-cut framework. Manage. Sci. **42**, 1229–1246 (1996)

3. D. Ben-Arieh, Z.F. Chen, Linguistic-labels aggregation and consensus measure for autocratic decision making using group recommendations. IEEE Trans. Syst. Man Cybern. Part A Syst. Hum. **36**, 558–568 (2006)
4. D. Ben-Arieh, T. Easton, Multi-criteria group consensus under linear cost opinion elasticity. Decis. Support Syst. **43**, 713–721 (2007)
5. D. Ben-Arieh, T. Easton, B. Evans, Minimum cost consensus with quadratic cost functions. IEEE Trans. Syst. Man Cybern. Part A **39**, 210–217 (2009)
6. T. Berthold, S. Heinz, S. Vigerske, *Extending a cip Framework to Solve MIQCPS*. ZIB-Report 09-23, (Zuse Institute, Berlin, 2009)
7. G. Bordogna, M. Fedrizzi, G. Pasi, A linguistic modeling of consensus in group decision making based on OWA operators. IEEE Trans. Syst. Man Cybern. Part A Syst. Hum. **27**, 126–133 (1997)
8. N. Bryson, Group decision-making and the analytic hierarchy process: exploring the consensus-relevant information content. Comput. Oper. Res. **23**, 27–35 (1996)
9. F.J. Cabrerizo, J.M. Moreno, I.J. Pérez, E. Herrera-Viedma, Analyzing consensus approaches in fuzzy group decision making: advantages and drawbacks. Soft Comput. **14**, 451–463 (2010)
10. Y.C. Dong, Y.F. Xu, H.Y. Li, B. Feng, The OWA-based consensus operator under linguistic representation models using position indexes. Eur. J. Oper. Res. **203**, 455–463 (2010)
11. Z.W. Gong, X.X. Xu, H.H. Zhang, U.A. Ozturk, E. Herrera-Viedma, C. Xu, The consensus models with interval preference opinions and their economic interpretation. Omega **55**, 81–90 (2015)
12. Z.W. Gong, H.H. Zhang, J. Forrest, L.S. Li, X.X. Xu, Two consensus models based on the minimum cost and maximum return regarding either all individuals or one individual. Eur. J. Oper. Res. **240**, 183–192 (2015)
13. F. Herrera, E. Herrera-Viedma, J.L. Verdegay, A model of consensus in group decision making under linguistic assessments. Fuzzy Sets Syst. **78**, 73–87 (1996)
14. E. Herrera-Viedma, F. Herrera, F. Chiclana, A consensus model for multiperson decision making with different preference structures. IEEE Trans. Syst. Man Cybern. Part A Syst. Hum. **32**, 394–402 (2002)
15. E. Herrera-Viedma, L. Martínez, F. Mata, F. Chiclana, A consensus support system model for group decision-making problems with multigranular linguistic preference relations. IEEE Trans. Fuzzy Syst. **13**, 644–658 (2005)
16. J. Kacprzyk, M. Fedrizzi, A soft measure of consensus in the setting of partial (fuzzy) preferences. Eur. J. Oper. Res. **34**, 316–325 (1988)
17. J. Kacprzyk, M. Fedrizzi, H. Nurmi, Group decision making and consensus under fuzzy preferences and fuzzy majority. Fuzzy Sets Syst. **49**, 21–31 (1992)
18. W. Ogryczak, T. Śliwiński, On solving linear programs with the ordered weighted averaging objective. Eur. J. Oper. Res. **148**, 80–91 (2003)
19. B.W. Zhang, Y.C. Dong, Y.F. Xu, Maximum expert consensus models with linear cost function and aggregation operators. Comput. Ind. Eng. **66**, 147–157 (2013)
20. G.Q. Zhang, Y.C. Dong, Y.F. Xu, H.Y. Li, Minimum-cost consensus models under aggregation operators. IEEE Trans. Syst. Man Cybern. Part A Syst. Hum. **41**, 1253–1261 (2011)

Chapter 3
Consensus with Preference Relations

The iteration-based consensus model and *the LP-based consensus model* for the GDM with preference relations are proposed to deal with the individual consistency in the consensus building.

3.1 Integrating Individual Consistency into Consensus

In the GDM with preference relations, two kinds of measures are widely studied (1) *individual consistency*, and (2) *consensus*. The individual consistency and the consensus are related but different concepts in the GDM with preference relations. The individual consistency is performed to ensure the expert is being neither random nor illogical in his/her pairwise comparisons, and the consensus means the preferences among a group of experts are similar. Chiclana et al. [9] and Herrera et al. [27] investigated the consensus framework to integrate individual consistency, and their consensus framework is described as Fig. 3.1. The implementation of the framework presented in Chiclana et al. and Herrera et al. deals with a two-step procedure.

(1) Consistency improving process. Before each round of consensus reaching process, the consistency control method is used to help the experts obtain the preference relations with acceptably consistency.
(2) Consensus improving process. Once all preference relations are of acceptably individual consistency, the consensus improving process is applied to help the experts modify their preference relations to improve the consensus level.

Repeat these two processes, until the adjusted preference relations with acceptably consistency and acceptable consensus are achieved.

In the consensus framework described in Fig. 3.1, the individual consistency may be destroyed in the consensus improving process. Thus, the individual consistency improving process is needed before each round of the consensus improving process. Clearly, this consensus framework described is very time-consuming.

Y. Dong and J. Xu, *Consensus Building in Group Decision Making*,
DOI 10.1007/978-981-287-892-2_3

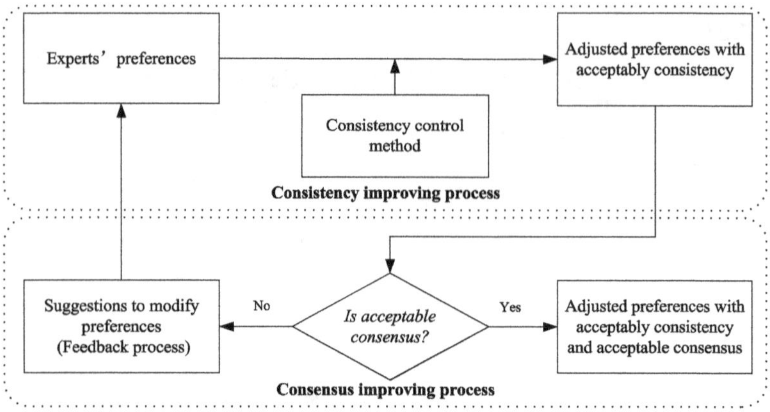

Fig. 3.1 Consensus framework presented in [9, 27]

By incorporating the consistency improving process and the consensus improving process into one phase, we proposed two novel consensus models: *the iteration-based consensus model* and *the LP-based consensus model.* Specifically, Dong et al. [18] proposed the iteration-based consensus model to address the GDM with multiplicative preference relations, and Zhang et al. [34] presented the LP-based consensus model to address the GDM with additive preference relations. When using the iteration-based consensus model, the individual consistency is maintained and the Pareto principle of social choice theory is satisfied in the consensus building. In the LP-based consensus model, both the acceptable individual consistency and consensus are obtained simultaneously in a linear programming model.

The transformation functions among different kinds of preference relations have been presented (e.g., [8, 17, 23]), so both the iteration-based consensus model and the LP-based consensus model can be exported to other kinds of preference relations.

3.2 Consensus with Multiplicative Preference Relations

In the analytic hierarchy process (AHP), experts express their preferences using multiplicative preference relations (i.e., judgement matrices) [12, 14, 16]. In this section, we investigate the consensus in the GDM with multiplicative preference relations.

3.2.1 Prioritization and Aggregation Methods

The basic knowledge regarding the prioritization and aggregation methods in multiplicative preference relations is introduced below.

(1) Prioritization method

Let $A = (a_{ij})_{m\times m}$, where $a_{ij} > 0$ and $a_{ij} \times a_{ji} = 1$, be a multiplicative preference relation. The prioritization method refers to the process of deriving a priority vector $pv = (pv_1, pv_2, \ldots, pv_m)^T$, where $pv_i \geq 0$ and $\sum_{i=1}^{m} pv_i = 1$, from A. Two most commonly used prioritization methods (EM [29, 30] and RGMM [11]) are listed below.

(i) The Eigenvalue Method

Saaty proposes the principal eigenvector of A as the desired priority vector pv, which can be obtained by solving the linear system:

$$A \cdot pv = \lambda \cdot pv, \ \ e^T \cdot pv = 1, \tag{3.1}$$

where λ is the principal eigenvalue of A.

(ii) Row Geometric Mean Method

The RGMM uses the L^2 metric in defining an objective function of the following optimization problem:

$$\begin{cases} min \sum_{i=1}^{m} \sum_{j>i} [ln(a_{ij}) - (ln(pv_i) - ln(pv_j))]^2 \\ \ \ s.t. \ \ pv_i \geq 0, \sum_{i=1}^{m} pv_i = 1 \end{cases}. \tag{3.2}$$

Crawford and Williams [11] have shown that the solution to the above problem is unique and can be simply found as the geometric means of the rows of matrix A:

$$pv_i = \frac{\sqrt[1/m]{\prod_{j=1}^{m} a_{ij}}}{\sum_{i=1}^{m} \left(\sqrt[1/m]{\prod_{j=1}^{m} a_{ij}} \right)}. \tag{3.3}$$

The RGMM is also called the logarithmic least square method.

Dong et al. [15] and Herman and Koczkodaj [26] showed that the effects of these two prioritization methods are very similar. Moreover, the computational times of EM and RGMM are $o(m^2)$ and $o(m)$, respectively. Thus, RGMM has a less computational time than EM, and we select RGMM as the prioritization method in this book.

(2) AIJ and AIP

Consider an AHP group decision making problem. Let $E = \{E_1, E_2, \ldots, E_n\}$ be the set of experts, and $w = (w_1, w_2, \ldots, w_n)^T$ be the weight vector of experts, where $w_k \geq 0$ and $\sum_{k=1}^{n} w_k = 1$. Let $A^k = (a_{ij}^k)_{m \times m}$ be the multiplicative preference relation provided by the expert E_k $(k = 1, 2, \ldots, n)$. As mentioned above, two of the methods that have been found to be the most useful in AHP group decision making are AIJ and AIP. In AIJ and AIP, the weighted geometric mean method is generally used as the aggregation procedure.

(i) The aggregation of individual judgments

For AIJ, the experts use the weighted geometric mean method to aggregate individual multiplicative preference relations to obtain a collective multiplicative preference relation, $A^c = (a_{ij}^c)_{m \times m}$, where

$$a_{ij}^c = \prod_{k=1}^{n} (a_{ij}^k)^{w_k}. \tag{3.4}$$

Then, we use certain prioritization method to derive a collective priority vector $pv^c = (pv_1^c, pv_2^c, \ldots, pv_m^c)^T$ from A^c to order the alternatives.

(ii) The aggregation of individual priorities

Let $pv^k = (pv_1^k, pv_2^k, \ldots, pv_m^k)^T$ be the individual priority vector derived from A^k using certain prioritization method. Then, the collective priority vector obtained using AIP is $pv^c = (pv_1^c, pv_2^c, \ldots, pv_m^c)^T$ from A^c, where,

$$pv_i^c = \frac{\prod_{k=1}^{n} (pv_i^k)^{w_k}}{\sum_{i=1}^{m} \prod_{k=1}^{n} (pv_i^k)^{w_k}}. \tag{3.5}$$

When selecting EM as the prioritization method, some researchers have some disputes on the use of the AIJ and the AIP. Ramanathan and Ganesh [28] observed that AIJ violates the Pareto principle of social choice theory [2], and suggested using AIP in AHP group decision making. Forman and Peniwati [21] argued that AIJ and AIP are philosophically different circumstances [6], and whether AIJ or AIP should be used depended on whether the group intends to behave as a synergistic unit or as collection of individuals. However, when selecting RGMM as the prioritization method, Barzilai and Golany [3] have shown the equivalence between AIJ and AIP (see Lemma 3.1)

Lemma 3.1 *Let* $pv^c = (pv_1^c, pv_2^c, \ldots, pv_m^c)^T$ *and* $\widetilde{pv^c} = (\widetilde{pv_1^c}, \widetilde{pv_2^c}, \ldots, \widetilde{pv_m^c})^T$ *be two collective priority vectors, derived using AIJ and AIP under RGMM, respectively. Then* $pv_i^c = \widetilde{pv_i^c}$, *for* $i = 1, 2, \ldots, m$.

The AIP doesn't violate the Pareto principle of social choice theory, so, based on Lemma 3.1, we have that AIJ satisfies the Pareto principle of social choice theory under RGMM (see Corollary 3.1).

Corollary 3.1 *Let* $pv^k = (pv_1^k, \ldots, pv_m^k)^T$ *and* $pv^c = (pv_1^c, \ldots, pv_m^c)^T$ *be as before. Then, if* $pv_i^k \geq pv_j^k$ *for* $k = 1, 2, \ldots, n$, $pv_i^c \geq pv_j^c$.

3.2.2 Consistency and Consensus in Multiplicative Preference Relations

The consistency and consensus measures in multiplicative preference relations are presented as follows.

(1) Consistency measure

For the RGMM, Crawford and Williams [11] and Aguarón et al. [1] have developed a consistency index to measure individual consistency, namely the geometric individual consistency level (GICL) (see Definition 3.1).

Definition 3.1 (Crawford and Williams [11]). Let $A = (a_{ij})_{m\times m}$ be a multiplicative preference relation, and let $pv = (pv_1, pv_2, \ldots, pv_m)^T$ be the priority vector derived from A using the RGMM. The geometric individual consistency level (GICL) is given by

$$GICL(A) = \frac{2}{(m-1)(m-2)} \sum_{i<j} \left(log(a_{ij}) - log(pv_i) + log(pv_j)\right)^2. \quad (3.6)$$

When $GICL(A) = 0$, we consider A is fully consistent. Aguarón et al. [1] provided the thresholds ($\overline{GICL}$) for $GICL$: $\overline{GICL} = 0.31$ for $m = 3$; $\overline{GICL} = 0.35$ for $m = 4$ and $\overline{GICL} = 0.37$ for $m > 4$. When $GICL(A) < \overline{GICL}$, we consider that the matrix A is of acceptably individual consistency.

(2) Consensus measure

In general, the computation of the consensus indexes for group decision making using preference relations is done by measuring the distance between individual preference values and collective preference values [9]. Inspired by this idea, we define the geometric cardinal consensus level for AHP group decision making using RGMM (see Definition 3.2).

Definition 3.2 Let $A^k = (a^k_{ij})_{m\times m}$ be the multiplicative preference relation provided by the expert E_k, and $pv^c = (pv^c_1, pv^c_2, \ldots, pv^c_m)^T$ be the collective priority vector, derived from $\{A^1, A^2, \ldots, A^n\}$ using AIJ under RGMM. Then, the geometric cardinal consensus level (GCCL) of A^k is defined by

$$GCCL(A^k) = \frac{2}{(m-1)(m-2)} \sum_{i<j} \left(log(a^k_{ij}) - log(pv^c_i) + log(pv^c_j)\right)^2. \quad (3.7)$$

If $GCCL(A^k) = 0$, then the kth expert is of fully cardinal consensus with the collective preference. Otherwise, the smaller the value of $GCCL(A^k)$, the more the cardinal consensus. According to the actual situation, the experts establish the thresholds $\overline{GCCL}$ for $GCCL(A^k)$. If $\forall k$ $GCCL(A^k) \le \overline{GCCL}$, we conclude that the acceptably cardinal consensus are reached among the experts.

Let $pv^k = (pv_1^k, \ldots, pv_m^k)^T$ be the individual priority vector derived from the multiplicative preference relation A^k using RGMM, and let $R^k = (r_1^k, \ldots, r_m^k)^T$, where r_i^k is the position of the alternative X_i in pv^k. For example, if $pv^k = (0.3,\ 0.2,\ 0.5)^T$, then $R^k = (2,\ 3,\ 1)^T$. Let $pv^c = (pv_1^c, pv_2^c, \ldots, pv_m^c)^T$ be the collective priority vector, derived from $\{A^1, A^2, \ldots, A^n\}$ using AIJ under RGMM, and let $R^c = (r_1^c, \ldots, r_m^c)^T$, where r_i^c is the position of alternative X_i in pv^c. Herrera-Viedma et al. [23] proposed the comparison approach of positions of alternatives between two preference vectors to measure the consensus degree. Inspired by this idea, we define the geometric ordinal consensus level for AHP GDM using RGMM (see Definition 3.3).

Definition 3.3 Let pv^k, pv^c, R^k and R^c be as before. The geometric ordinal consensus level (GOCL) of A^k is defined by

$$GOCL(A^k) = \frac{1}{m}\sum_{i=1}^{m} |r_i^k - r_i^c|. \tag{3.8}$$

If $GOCL(A^k) = 0$, then the kth expert is of fully ordinal consensus with the collective preference. Otherwise, the smaller the value of $GOCL(A^k)$, the more the ordinal consensus. According to the actual situation, the experts also may establish the thresholds $\overline{GOCL}$ for $GOCL(A^k)$. If $\forall k\ GOCL(A^k) \leq \overline{GOCL}$, we conclude that the acceptably ordinal consensus are reached among the experts.

Note 3.1 Let $Q = \{(pv_1, pv_2, \ldots, pv_m)^T | 0 \leq pv_i \leq 1, \sum_{i=1}^{m} pv_i = 1\}$. According to Definitions 3.1 and 3.2, we have that $GICL(A) = \frac{2}{(m-1)(m-2)} \min_{w \in Q} \sum_{i<j} (log(a_{ij}) - log(pv_i) + log(pv_j))^2 \leq GCCL(A)$. Thus, we suggest $\overline{GCCL} \geq \overline{GICL}$. Moreover, if $GOCL(A) \neq 0$, then $GOCL(A) \geq \frac{2}{m}$. So, we also suggest $\overline{GOCL} \geq \frac{2}{m}$. It may be an interesting future research issue to investigate the thresholds of $\overline{GCCL}$ and $\overline{GOCL}$ in details.

3.2.3 Iteration-Based Consensus Model

In this subsection, we present the iteration-based consensus model to deal with the individual consistency and consensus in the GDM with multiplicative preference relations. Then, the individual consistency improving method and the consensus model are proposed, respectively. Finally, several properties of the proposed consensus reaching model are analyzed.

(1) Consensus framework

The implementation of the iteration-based consensus model deals with a two-step procedure (see Fig. 3.2).

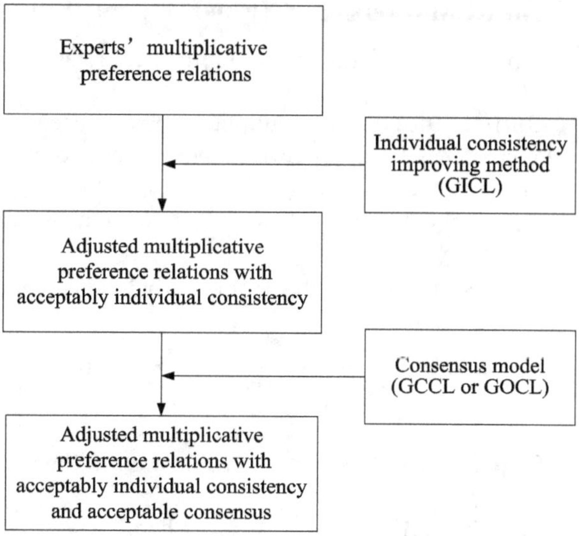

Fig. 3.2 The Iteration-based consensus framework with the multiplicative preference relations

(i) Individual consistency improving method

The individual consistency improving method firstly uses GICL to measure the individual consistency degree of multiplicative preference relations $A^k,\ k = 1, 2, \ldots, n$. If $GICL(A^k) \leq \overline{GICL}$, it doesn't adjust A^k. Otherwise, it helps the expert E_k improve the GICL values of A^k.

(ii) Consensus model

Once all multiplicative preference relations are of acceptably individual consistency, we apply a consensus model to reach the acceptable consensus. The consensus model firstly uses GCCL (or GOCL) to measure the consensus degree of multiplicative preference relations $A^k,\ k = 1, 2, \ldots, n$. If $GCCL(A^k) \leq \overline{GCCL}$ (or $GOCL(A^k) \leq \overline{GOCL}$), $k = 1, 2, \ldots, n$, it doesn't adjust $A^k,\ k = 1, 2, \ldots, n$. Otherwise, it helps the experts reach the acceptable consensus. Finally, all multiplicative preference relations $A^k,\ k = 1, 2, \ldots, n$, are of acceptably individual consistency and are of acceptable consensus.

(2) Individual consistency improving method

In the AHP discipline, individual consistency improving methods are very widely investigated [6, 13, 20, 22, 30, 32]. In particular, Xu and Wei [32] proposed an individual consistency improving method based on the EM and Saaty's consistency index. In Xu and Wei's method, we replace EM by RGMM, and replace Saaty's consistency index by the geometric consistency index. In this way, we obtain the RGMM version of this method.

Let z be the number of iterations, and $0 < \theta < 1$. The steps of the RGMM version of Xu and Wei's method are described as follows:

The RGMM version of Xu and Wei's method

Input: The multiplicative preference relation A, the threshold $\overline{GICL}$ and $0 < \theta < 1$.

Output: The adjusted multiplicative preference relation $\overline{A}$, its geometric individual consistency level $GICL(\overline{A})$ and the number of iterations z.

Step 1: Let $z = 0$ and $A^z = (a_{ij}^z)_{m\times m} = (a_{ij})_{m\times m}$.

Step 2: Let $pv^z = (pv_1^z, pv_2^z, \ldots, pv_m^z)^T$ be the priority vector derived from A^z using RGMM.

Step 3: We calculate the geometric individual consistency level:

$$GICL(A^z) = \frac{2}{(m-1)(m-2)}\sum_{i<j}(log(a_{ij}^z) - log(pv_i^z) + log(pv_j^z))^2.$$

Step 4: If $GICL(A^z) \le \overline{GICL}$, then go to Step 6; otherwise, continue with the next step;

Step 5: Let $A^{z+1} = (a_{ij}^{z+1})_{m\times m}$, where

$$a_{ij}^{z+1} = (a_{ij}^z)^\theta \left(\frac{pv_i^z}{pv_j^z}\right)^{(1-\theta)}.$$

Step 6: Let $\overline{A} = A^z$. Output the adjusted multiplicative preference relation $\overline{A}$, its geometric individual consistency level $GICL(\overline{A})$ and the number of iterations z.

(3) Consensus models

Let $A = \{A^1, A^2, \ldots, A^n\}$ and $w = (w_1, \ldots, w_n)^T$ be as before. Let $pv^k = (pv_1^k, \ldots, pv_m^k)^T$ be the individual priority vector derived from the multiplicative preference relation A^k using RGMM. Let $pv^c = (pv_1^c, pv_2^c, \ldots, pv_m^c)^T$ be the collective priority vector, derived from $\{A^1, \ldots, A^n\}$ using AIJ under RGMM.

In the following, we respectively propose two consensus models, based on $GCCL$ and $GOCL$. Without loss of generality, suppose that the multiplicative preference relation A^τ has the largest cardinal (or ordinal) consensus level. The main step of the proposed consensus models is to construct a new multiplicative preference relation $\overline{A^\tau}$ according to original multiplicative preference relation A^τ. When structuring $\overline{A^\tau} = (\overline{a_{ij}^\tau})$, we suggest that

$$\overline{a_{ij}^\tau} = \left(a_{ij}^\tau\right)^\theta \left(\frac{pv_i^c}{pv_j^c}\right)^{(1-\theta)}, \tag{3.9}$$

where $0 < \theta < 1$. Follow this procedure until multiplicative preference relations with acceptable consensus are obtained or the established maximum number of iterations is obtained. The consensus model based on GCCL is called cardinal consensus model, and the cardinal consensus model is described as Algorithm 3.1.

Algorithm 3.1

Input: Multiplicative preference relations $\{A^1, A^2, \ldots, A^n\}$, the weight vector of experts $(w_1, w_2, \ldots, w_n)^T$, the threshold $\overline{GCCL}$, the established maximum number of iterations $z_{max} \geq 1$ and $0 < \theta < 1$.

Output: Adjusted multiplicative preference relations $\{\overline{A^1}, \overline{A^2}, \ldots, \overline{A^n}\}$, the cardinal consensus level $GCCL(\overline{A^k})$ $(k = 1, 2, \ldots, n)$, the collective priority vector $\overline{pv^c} = (\overline{pv_1^c}, \overline{pv_2^c}, \ldots, \overline{pv_m^c})^T$, and the number of iterations z.

Step 1: Let $z = 0$ and $A_z^k = (a_{ijz}^k)_{m\times m} = (a_{ij}^k)_{m\times m}$;

Step 2: Let $pv_z^c = (pv_{1,z}^c, pv_{2,z}^c, \ldots, pv_{m,z}^c)^T$ be the collective priority vector, derived from the collective multiplicative preference relation $A_z^c = (a_{ijz}^c)$, where $a_{ijz}^c = \prod_{k=1}^n (a_{ijz}^k)^{w_k}$, using RGMM.

Step 3: Calculate the cardinal consensus level of A_z^k:

$$GCCL(A_z^k) = \frac{2}{(m-1)(m-2)} \sum_{i<j} \left(log(a_{ijz}^k) - log(pv_{i,z}^c) + log(pv_{j,z}^c) \right)^2 .$$

If $\forall k$, $GCCL(A_z^k) \leq \overline{GCCL}$ or $z \geq z_{max}$, then go to Step 5; otherwise, continue with the next step;

Step 4: Without loss of generality, suppose that

$$GCCL(A_z^\tau) = \max_k \{GCCL(A_z^k\}.$$

Let $A_{z+1}^k = (a_{ij,z+1}^k)_{m\times m}$, where

$$a_{ij,z+1}^k = \begin{cases} \left(a_{ij,z}^k\right)^\theta \left(\frac{pv_{i,z}^c}{pv_{j,z}^c}\right)^{(1-\theta)}, & k = \tau \\ a_{ij,z}^k, & k \neq \tau \end{cases},$$

and $z = z + 1$. Then, go to Step 2.

Step 5: Let $\overline{A^k} = A_z^k$ and $\overline{pv^c} = pv_z^c$. Output the adjusted multiplicative preference relation $\overline{A^k}$, its cardinal consensus level $GCCL(\overline{A^k})$, the collective priority vector $\overline{pv^c}$ and the number of iterations z.

Moreover, the consensus model based on $GOCL$ is called ordinal consensus model, and the ordinal consensus model is described as Algorithm 3.2.

Algorithm 3.2

Input: Multiplicative preference relations $\{A^1, A^2, \ldots, A^n\}$, the weight vector of experts $(w_1, w_2, \ldots, w_n)^T$, the threshold $\overline{GOCL}$, and the established maximum number of iterations $z_{max} \geq 1$ and $0 < \theta < 1$.

Output: Adjusted multiplicative preference relations $\{\overline{\overline{A^1}}, \overline{\overline{A^2}}, \ldots, \overline{\overline{A^n}}\}$, the ordinal consensus level $GOCL(\overline{\overline{A^k}})$ $(k = 1, 2, \ldots, n)$, the collective priority vector $\overline{\overline{pv^c}} = (\overline{\overline{pv_1^c}}, \overline{\overline{pv_2^c}}, \ldots, \overline{\overline{pv_m^c}})^T$, and the number of iterations z.

Step 1: Let $z = 0$ and $A_z^k = (a_{ijz}^k)_{m\times m} = (a_{ij}^k)_{m\times m}$;

Step 2: Let $pv_z^k = (pv_{1,z}^k, \ldots, pv_{m,z}^k)^T$ be the individual priority vector derived from multiplicative preference relation A_z^k using RGMM, and $R_z^k = (r_{1,z}^k, \ldots, r_{m,z}^k)^T$, where $r_{i,z}^k$ is the position of the ith alternative in pv_z^k. Let $pv_z^c = (pv_{1,z}^c, pv_{2,z}^c, \ldots, pv_{m,z}^c)^T$ be the collective priority vector, derived from the collective multiplicative preference relation A_z^c, where $a_{ijz}^c = \prod_{k=1}^n (a_{ijz}^k)^{w_k}$, using RGMM, and $r_z^c = (r_{1,z}^c, \ldots, r_{m,z}^c)^T$, where $r_{i,z}^c$ is the position of alternative X_i in pv_z^c.

Step 3: Calculate the ordinal consensus level

$$GOCL(A_z^k) = \frac{1}{m}\sum_{i=1}^{m} |r_{i,z}^k - r_{i,z}^c|,$$

for $k = 1, 2, \ldots, n$. If $\forall k$, $GOCL(A_z^k) \leq \overline{GOCL}$ or $z \geq z_{max}$, then go to Step 5; otherwise, continue with the next step;

Step 4: Without loss of generality, suppose that

$$GOCL(A_z^\tau) = \max_k\{GOCL(A_z^k)\}.$$

Let $A_{z+1}^k = (a_{ij,z+1}^k)_{m\times m}$, where

$$a_{ij,z+1}^k = \begin{cases} (a_{ij,z}^k)^\theta (\frac{pv_{i,z}^c}{pv_{j,z}^c})^{(1-\theta)}, & k = \tau \\ a_{ij,z}^c, & k \neq \tau \end{cases},$$

and $z = z + 1$. Then, go to Step 2.

Step 5: Let $\overline{\overline{A^k}} = A_z^k$, and $\overline{\overline{pv^c}} = pv_z^c$. Output the adjusted multiplicative preference relation $\overline{\overline{A^k}}$, its ordinal consensus level $GOCL(\overline{\overline{A^k}})$, the collective priority vector $\overline{\overline{pv^c}}$ and the number of iterations z.

Note 3.2 The ordinal consensus model and the cardinal consensus model have similarity with each other. The main difference between these two consensus models are using different consensus indexes.

(4) Properties of consensus models

Here, we discuss some desired properties of the proposed consensus models.

(i) The individual consistencies can be improved

We first introduce Lemma 3.2, presented in Escobar et al. [19].

Lemma 3.2 (Escobar et al. [19]). *Let* $\{A^1, A^2, \ldots, A^n\}$, $\{w_1, w_2, \ldots, w_n\}$, *and* A^c *be as before. Then,* $GICL(A^c) \leq \max_k\{GICL(A^k)\}$.

Theorem 3.1 *Let* $\{A^1, A^2, \ldots, A^n\}$, $\{w_1, w_2, \ldots, w_n\}$, $\{\overline{A^1}, \overline{A^2}, \ldots, \overline{A^n}\}$ *and* $\{\overline{\overline{A^1}}, \overline{\overline{A^2}}, \ldots, \overline{\overline{A^n}}\}$ *be as before. Then,* $GICL(\overline{A^k}) \leq GICL(A^k)$ *and* $GICL(\overline{\overline{A^k}}) \leq GICL(A^k)$, *for* $k = 1, 2, \ldots, n$.

Proof We first prove $GICL(\overline{A^k}) \leq GICL(A^k)$. Let $A_z^k = (a_{ijz}^k)_{m\times m}$ $(k = 1, 2, \ldots, n)$ be the adjusted multiplicative preference relations in the zth iteration using the cardinal consensus model. Let $pv_z^c = (pv_{1,z}^c, pv_{2,z}^c, \ldots, pv_{m,z}^c)^T$ be the collective priority vector, derived from the collective multiplicative preference relation $A_z^c = (a_{ijz}^c)_{m\times m}$, where $a_{ijz}^c = \prod_{k=1}^n (a_{ijz}^k)^{w_k}$, using RGMM. Without loss of generality, suppose that $GCCL(A_z^\tau) = \max_k\{GCCL(A_z^k\}$. We consider two cases.

Case A: $k = \tau$. In this case, according to the cardinal consensus model, we have that $A_{z+1}^k = (a_{ij,z+1}^k)_{m\times m}$, where $a_{ij,z+1}^k = (a_{ij,z}^k)^\theta (\frac{pv_{i,z}^c}{pv_{j,z}^c})^{(1-\theta)}$. Let $PV_z = (pv_{ij,z}) = (\frac{pv_{i,z}^c}{pv_{j,z}^c})$. From Lemma 3.2, we have that $GICL(A_{z+1}^k) \leq max\{GICL(A_z^k), GICL(PV_z)\} = GICL(A_z^k)$.

Case B: $k \neq \tau$. In this case, $A_{z+1}^k = A_z^k$. So, $GICL(A_{z+1}^k) = GICL(A_z^k)$.

Summarizing Case A and Case B, we have that $GICL(A_{z+1}^k) \leq GICL(A_z^k)$ for $k = 1, 2, \ldots, n$.

Consequently, $GICL(\overline{A^k}) \leq GICL(A_0^k) = GICL(A^k)$ for $k = 1, 2, \ldots, n$.

Similarly, we can prove $GICL(\overline{\overline{A^k}}) \leq GICL(A^k)$. This completes the proof of Theorem 3.1.

Based on Theorem 3.1, the adjusted multiplicative preference relation has a better individual consistency index (i.e., GICL) than the corresponding original multiplicative preference relation, when using the proposed consensus models.

From Theorem 3.1, we have Corollary 3.2.

Corollary 3.2 *Let* $\overline{A^c}$ *and* $\overline{\overline{A^c}}$ *be the collective judgement matrices of* $\{\overline{A^1}, \overline{A^2}, \ldots, \overline{A^n}\}$ *and* $\{\overline{\overline{A^1}}, \overline{\overline{A^2}}, \ldots, \overline{\overline{A^n}}\}$, *respectively. Then,* $GICL(\overline{A^c}) \leq \overline{GICL}$ *and* $GICL(\overline{\overline{A^c}}) \leq \overline{GICL}$ *under the condition that* $GICL(A^k) \leq \overline{GICL}$ *for* $k = 1, 2, \ldots, n$.

(ii) Pareto principle of social choice theory can be satisfied

Theorem 3.2 *Let* $\{A^1, A^2, \ldots, A^n\}$, $pv^k = \{pv_1^k, pv_2^k, \ldots, pv_m^k\}$ $(k = 1, 2, \ldots, n)$, $\overline{pv^c} = \{\overline{pv_1^c}, \overline{pv_2^c}, \ldots, \overline{pv_m^c}\}$ *and* $\overline{\overline{pv^c}} = \{\overline{\overline{pv_1^c}}, \overline{\overline{pv_2^c}}, \ldots, \overline{\overline{pv_m^c}}\}$ *be as before. Then, if* $pv_i^k > pv_j^k$, *for* $k = 1, 2, \ldots, n$, *we have that* $\overline{pv_i^c} > \overline{pv_j^c}$ *and* $\overline{\overline{pv_i^c}} > \overline{\overline{pv_j^c}}$.

Proof We first prove $\overline{pv_i^c} > \overline{pv_j^c}$. Let $A_z^k = (a_{ijz}^k)_{m\times m}$ $(k = 1, 2, \ldots, n)$ be adjusted multiplicative preference relations in the zth iteration using the cardinal consensus model. Let $pv_z^k = (pv_{1,z}^k, \ldots, pv_{m,z}^k)^T$ be individual priority vector derived from multiplicative preference relation A_z^k using RGMM. Let $pv_z^c = (pv_{1,z}^c, pv_{2,z}^c, \ldots, pv_{m,z}^c)^T$ be the collective priority vector, derived from the collective multiplicative preference relation $A_z^c = (a_{ijz}^c)_{m\times m}$, where $a_{ijz}^c = \prod_{k=1}^n (a_{ijz}^k)^{w_k}$, using RGMM.

By induction over z, the proof can be completed. For $z = 0$, we have that $pv_z^k = pv^k$. Since $pv_i^k > pv_j^k$ $(k = 1, 2, \ldots, n)$, we have that $pv_{i,0}^k > pv_{j,0}^k$ for $k = 1, 2, \ldots, n$. According to Corollary 3.1, we have that $pv_{i,0}^c > pv_{j,0}^c$. Suppose that it is true for z, i.e., $pv_{i,z}^k > pv_{j,z}^k$ for $k = 1, 2, \ldots, n$, and $pv_{i,z}^c > pv_{j,z}^c$.

Without loss of generality, suppose that $GCCL(A_{z+1}^\tau) = \max_k\{GCCL(A_{z+1}^k\}$. For $z + 1$, we consider two cases.

Case A: $k = \tau$. In this case, according to the cardinal consensus model, we have that $A_{z+1}^k = (a_{ij,z+1}^k)_{m\times m}$, where $a_{ij,z+1}^k = (a_{ij,z}^k)^\theta (\frac{pv_{i,z}^c}{pv_{j,z}^c})^{(1-\theta)}$. Since $pv_{i,z}^k > pv_{j,z}^k$ and $pv_{i,z}^c > pv_{j,z}^c$, according to Corollary 3.1, we have that $pv_{i,z+1}^k > pv_{j,z+1}^k$.

Case B: $k \neq \tau$. In this case, $A_{z+1}^k = A_z^k$ and $pv_{z+1}^k = pv_z^k$. Since $pv_{i,z}^k > pv_{j,z}^k$, we have $pv_{i,z+1}^k > pv_{j,z+1}^k$.

Summarizing Case A and Case B, we have that $pv_{i,z+1}^k > pv_{j,z+1}^k$ for $k = 1, 2, \ldots, n$. From Corollary 3.1, we have that $pv_{i,z+1}^c > pv_{j,z+1}^c$.

Consequently, $\overline{pv_i^c} > \overline{pv_j^c}$.

Similarly, we can prove $\overline{\overline{pv_i^c}} > \overline{\overline{pv_j^c}}$. This completes the proof of Theorem 3.2.

Based on Theorem 3.2, the proposed consensus models satisfy the Pareto principle of social choice theory.

(iii) The convergence of the consensus models

Naturally, we hope that the proposed consensus models can improve the consensus indexes (i.e., GCCL and GOCL) of multiplicative preference relations to help the experts reach consensus. In the following, we use simulation methods to study this issue. The main idea of the simulation methods is to randomly generate experts' multiplicative preference relations and the corresponding weights of the experts. Using the individual consistency improving method, we transform these multiplicative preference relations into ones with acceptably individual consistency. Then, we take these multiplicative preference relations with acceptably individual consistency as the inputs of the proposed consensus models to study the convergence of the proposed consensus models.

Next, we describe the simulation methods in detail.

Simulation method 3.1

Input: $n, m, \overline{GCCL}, z_{max}$ and $0 < \theta < 1$.

Output: z and p

Step 1: We randomly generate n $m \times m$ multiplicative preference relations $\{A^1, \ldots, A^n\}$, whose entries are uniformly randomly selected from $\{1/9, 1/8, \ldots, 1, \ldots, 8, 9\}$.

Step 2: We randomly generate a weight vector, $w = \{w_1, w_2, \ldots, w_n\}$, where w_i $(i = 1, 2, \ldots n)$ is uniformly distributed on $[0, 1]$. Then we normalize $w = \{w_1, w_2, \ldots, w_n\}$, that is $w_i = \frac{w_i}{\sum_{i=1}^{n} w_i}$.

Step 3: Using the RGMM version of Xu and Wei's individual consistency improving method, we transform $\{A^1, \ldots, A^n\}$ into the multiplicative preference relations with acceptably individual consistency. For simplicity, we still denote these multiplicative preference relations with acceptably individual consistency as $\{A^1, \ldots, A^n\}$.

Step 4: We take $\{A^1, \ldots, A^n\}, w = \{w_1, w_2, \ldots, w_n\}, \overline{GCCL}, z_{max}$ and $0 < \theta < 1$ as the inputs of the cardinal consensus model. Applying the cardinal consensus model, we obtain the adjusted multiplicative preference relations $\overline{A^k}$ $(k = 1, 2, \ldots, n)$, and the cardinal consensus levels $GCCL(\overline{A^k})$ $(k = 1, 2, \ldots, n)$, and the number of iterations z.

Step 5: If $\max_k(GCCL(\overline{A^k})) \leq \overline{GCCL}$, then $p = 1$. Otherwise $p = 0$. Output z and p.

In simulation method 3.1, we replace the cardinal consensus model, $GCCL$, $\overline{GCCL}$ by the ordinal consensus model, $GOCL$ and $\overline{GOCL}$, respectively. We call the modified simulation method, simulation method 3.2.

When setting different input parameters of simulation method 3.1, we run this simulation method 1000 times, obtaining the average values of z and p. We also set different input parameters for simulation method 3.2, and run it 1000 times to obtain the average values of z and p. Tables 3.1 and 3.2 respectively show the corresponding average values of z and p, under the different input parameters for simulation method 3.1 and simulation method 3.2.

Note 3.3 The average value of p has a definite physical implication, and reflects the success ratio of reaching a consensus in the simulation experiments. Moreover, in running the simulation experiments, we set $z_{max} = 300$, and approximatively consider that the experts are of fully cardinal consensus when $GCCL(A^k) \leq 0.01$ for $k = 1, 2, \ldots, n$.

From Tables 3.1 and 3.2, we have the following observations:

(a) Simulation method 3.1 and Simulation method 3.2 definitely help experts reach cardinal and ordinal consensus, under the established input parameters, respectively.
(b) With the increase of n and m, the number of the iterations z is increasing. Moreover, the smaller the parameter θ, the smaller the number of the iterations z.

Table 3.1 Average values of z and p for simulation method 3.1 under the different input parameters

m	n	$\overline{GCCL}$	$\theta = 0.1$		$\theta = 0.3$		$\theta = 0.5$		$\theta = 0.8$	
			p	z	p	z	p	z	p	z
3	3	0.01	1	5.49	1	7.67	1	11.76	1	31.09
		0.31	1	2.02	1	2.76	1	3.55	1	9.07
3	7	0.01	1	12.42	1	17.96	1	27.6	1	76.59
		0.31	1	5.68	1	6.9	1	9.2	1	22.63
4	5	0.01	1	9.35	1	13.05	1	19.53	1	54.16
		0.35	1	4.08	1	4.61	1	6.33	1	14.88
4	9	0.01	1	15.7	1	22.63	1	35.19	1	98.13
		0.35	1	7.73	1	8.65	1	11.81	1	28.11
7	7	0.01	1	12.11	1	16.35	1	25.45	1	70.62
		0.37	1	6.03	1	6.2	1	7.21	1	15.53
7	9	0.01	1	15.25	1	20.96	1	32.66	1	91.01
		0.37	1	7.98	1	8.19	1	9.68	1	20.77
9	20	0.37	1	18.58	1	19.14	1	19.62	1	39.6

Table 3.2 Average values of z and p for simulation method 3.2 under the different input parameters

m	n	$\overline{GOCL}$	$\theta = 0.1$		$\theta = 0.3$		$\theta = 0.5$		$\theta = 0.8$	
			p	z	p	z	p	z	p	z
3	3	0	1	2.28	1	2.90	1	3.76	1	9.73
		2/3	1	0.83	1	0.94	1	1.07	1	2.33
3	7	0	1	6.58	1	8.43	1	11.96	1	31.47
		2/3	1	2.64	1	3.24	1	3.93	1	9.33
4	5	0	1	6.22	1	8.16	1	11.54	1	28.47
		1/2	1	3.72	1	4.68	1	5.98	1	14.42
4	9	0	1	11.94	1	15.44	1	22.44	1	60.43
		1/2	1	6.98	1	9.12	1	13.11	1	30.95
7	7	0	1	14.09	1	19.47	1	28.74	1	56.22
		2/7	1	11.35	1	14.95	1	21.77	1	54.9
7	9	0	1	18.82	1	24.69	1	37.88	1	99.95
		2/7	1	14.56	1	19.46	1	28.69	1	75.55
9	20	2/9	1	38.44	1	54.7	1	84.54	1	235.93

Based on Theorems 3.1, 3.2 and the above simulation analysis, we find that these two consensus models satisfy the following three properties:

(a) The consensus levels (i.e., GCCL and GOCL) of multiplicative preference relations can be improved.

(b) In reaching consensus, the adjusted multiplicative preference relation has a better individual consistency level (i.e., GICL) than the corresponding original multiplicative preference relation.
(c) The Pareto principle of social choice theory can be satisfied.

(5) Example 3.1

In order to show how the consensus models work in practice, let us consider the following example. Suppose we have a set of five experts providing the following multiplicative preference relations $\{A^1, \ldots, A^5\}$ on a set of four alternatives. Let $pv^k = (pv_1^k, \ldots, pv_4^k)^T$ be the individual priority vector derived from multiplicative preference relation A^k using RGMM. A^k and pv^k ($k = 1, 2, \ldots, 5$) are listed below.

$$A^1 = \begin{pmatrix} 1 & 4 & 6 & 7 \\ 1/4 & 1 & 3 & 4 \\ 1/6 & 1/3 & 1 & 2 \\ 1/7 & 1/4 & 1/2 & 1 \end{pmatrix},$$

$$pv^1 = (0.6145, 0.2246, 0.0985, 0.0624)^T.$$

$$A^2 = \begin{pmatrix} 1 & 5 & 7 & 9 \\ 1/5 & 1 & 4 & 6 \\ 1/7 & 1/4 & 1 & 2 \\ 1/9 & 1/6 & 1/2 & 1 \end{pmatrix},$$

$$pv^2 = (0.6461, 0.227, 0.0793, 0.0476)^T.$$

$$A^3 = \begin{pmatrix} 1 & 3 & 5 & 8 \\ 1/3 & 1 & 4 & 5 \\ 1/5 & 1/4 & 1 & 2 \\ 1/8 & 1/5 & 1/2 & 1 \end{pmatrix},$$

$$pv^3 = (0.5693, 0.2764, 0.0967, 0.0575)^T.$$

$$A^4 = \begin{pmatrix} 1 & 4 & 5 & 6 \\ 1/4 & 1 & 3 & 3 \\ 1/5 & 1/3 & 1 & 2 \\ 1/6 & 1/3 & 1/2 & 1 \end{pmatrix},$$

$$pv^4 = (0.5967, 0.2208, 0.1089, 0.0736)^T.$$

Table 3.3 The *GICL*, *GCCL* and *GOCL* values of A^k $(k = 1, 2, \ldots, 5)$ and A^c

	A^1	A^2	A^3	A^4	A^5	A^c
GICL	0.1349	0.2358	0.1194	0.1657	0.2208	0.056
GCCL	0.4285	0.8707	0.4113	0.3774	2.1944	Undefined
GOCL	0	0	0	0	1	Undefined

$$A^5 = \begin{pmatrix} 1 & 1/2 & 1 & 2 \\ 2 & 1 & 1/2 & 3 \\ 1 & 1/2 & 1 & 4 \\ 1/2 & 1/3 & 1/4 & 1 \end{pmatrix},$$

$$pv^5 = (0.2247, 0.2958, 0.378, 0.1015)^T.$$

Let $w = (0.1,\ 0.3,\ 0.1,\ 0.2,\ 0.3)^T$ be the weights of experts. Let A^c be the collective multiplicative preference relation derived from $\{A^1, \ldots, A^5\}$ using AIJ. Let $pv^c = (pv_1^c, pv_2^c, \ldots, pv_m^c)^T$ be the collective priority vector, derived from A^c using RGMM. A^c and pv^c are listed below.

$$A^c = \begin{pmatrix} 1 & 2.227 & 3.4756 & 5.0937 \\ 0.4490 & 1 & 1.9663 & 4.0005 \\ 0.2877 & 0.5086 & 1 & 2.4623 \\ 0.1963 & 0.2500 & 0.4061 & 1 \end{pmatrix},$$

$$pv^c = (0.4984, 0.2727, 0.1541, 0.0747)^T.$$

We compute the *GICL*, *GCCL* and *GOCL* values of A^k $(k = 1, 2, \ldots, 5)$ and A^c. These values are listed in Table 3.3.

Table 3.3 shows that $GICL(A^k) < \overline{GICL} = 0.35$ $(k = 1, 2, \ldots, 5)$, so $A^1, \ldots, A^5$ are of acceptably individual consistency.

When setting $\overline{GCCL} = 0.35$ and $\theta = 0.8$, we apply the cardinal consensus model to adjust multiplicative preference relations. The adjusted multiplicative preference relations and the collective multiplicative preference relation are $\overline{A^k}$, $(k = 1, 2, \ldots, 5)$ and $\overline{A^c}$, respectively. The corresponding priority vectors are $\overline{pv^k} = (\overline{pv_1^k}, \ldots, \overline{pv_4^k})^T$ $(k = 1, 2, \ldots, 5)$ and $\overline{pv^c} = (\overline{pv_1^c}, \ldots, \overline{pv_4^c})^T$, respectively. The cardinal consensus model ends in the 4th iteration. We find that $\overline{A^k} = A^k$ and $\overline{pv^k} = pv^k$ for $k = 1, 2, \ldots, 4$. And, $\overline{A^5}$, $\overline{A^c}$, $\overline{pv^5}$, and $\overline{pv^c}$ are listed below.

Table 3.4 The *GICL* and *GCCL* values of $\overline{A^k}$ $(k = 1, 2, \ldots, 5)$ and $\overline{A^c}$

	$\overline{A^1}$	$\overline{A^2}$	$\overline{A^3}$	$\overline{A^4}$	$\overline{A^5}$	$\overline{A^c}$
GICL	0.1349	0.2358	0.1194	0.1657	0.037	0.0688
GCCL	0.1054	0.2579	0.1051	0.1150	0.3138	Undefined

$$\overline{A^5} = \begin{pmatrix} 1.0000 & 1.1297 & 2.2014 & 4.3352 \\ 0.8852 & 1.0000 & 1.1044 & 3.4108 \\ 0.4543 & 0.9055 & 1.0000 & 2.6158 \\ 0.2307 & 0.2932 & 0.3823 & 1.0000 \end{pmatrix},$$

$$\overline{pv^5} = \{0.3954, 0.2949, 0.2222, 0.0875\}^T.$$

$$\overline{A^c} = \begin{pmatrix} 1.0000 & 2.8439 & 4.4040 & 6.4243 \\ 0.3516 & 1.0000 & 2.4940 & 4.1575 \\ 0.2271 & 0.4010 & 1.0000 & 2.1677 \\ 0.1557 & 0.2405 & 0.4613 & 1.0000 \end{pmatrix},$$

$$\overline{pv^c} = \{0.5540, 0.2556, 0.1233, 0.0671\}^T.$$

We compute the *GICL* and *GCCL* values of $\overline{A^k}$ $(k = 1, 2, \ldots, 5)$ and $\overline{A^c}$. These values are listed in Table 3.4.

When setting $\overline{GOCL} = 0$ and $\theta = 0.5$, we apply the ordinal consensus model to adjust multiplicative preference relations. The adjusted multiplicative preference relations and the collective multiplicative preference relation are $\overline{\overline{A^k}}$, $(k = 1, 2, \ldots, 5)$ and $\overline{\overline{A^c}}$, respectively. The corresponding priority vectors are $\overline{\overline{pv^k}} = (\overline{\overline{pv_1^k}}, \ldots, \overline{\overline{pv_4^k}})^T$ $(k = 1, 2, \ldots, 5)$ and $\overline{\overline{pv^c}} = (\overline{\overline{pv_1^c}}, \ldots, \overline{\overline{pv_4^c}})^T$, respectively. The ordinal consensus model ends in the 2th iteration. We find that $\overline{\overline{A^k}} = A^k$ and $\overline{\overline{pv^k}} = pv^k$ for $k = 1, 2, \ldots, 4$. And, $\overline{\overline{A^5}}$, $\overline{\overline{A^c}}$, $\overline{\overline{pv^5}}$, and $\overline{\overline{pv^c}}$ are listed below.

$$\overline{\overline{A^5}} = \begin{pmatrix} 1 & 0.9560 & 1.7984 & 3.6521 \\ 1.0460 & 1 & 0.9406 & 3.3085 \\ 0.5560 & 1.0631 & 1 & 2.8719 \\ 0.2738 & 0.3023 & 0.3482 & 1 \end{pmatrix},$$

$$\overline{\overline{pv^5}} = (0.3028, 0.3021, 0.2985, 0.0966)^T.$$

Table 3.5 The *GICL* and *GOCL* values of $\overline{\overline{A^k}}$ $(k = 1, 2, \ldots, 5)$ and $\overline{\overline{A^c}}$

	$\overline{\overline{A^1}}$	$\overline{\overline{A^2}}$	$\overline{\overline{A^3}}$	$\overline{\overline{A^4}}$	$\overline{\overline{A^5}}$	$\overline{\overline{A^c}}$
GICL	0.1349	0.2358	0.1194	0.1657	0.1077	0.0659
GOCL	0	0	0	0	0	Undefined

$$\overline{\overline{A^c}} = \begin{pmatrix} 1.0000 & 2.7049 & 4.1448 & 6.1022 \\ 0.3697 & 1.0000 & 2.3767 & 4.1197 \\ 0.2413 & 0.4207 & 1.0000 & 2.2293 \\ 0.1639 & 0.2427 & 0.4486 & 1.0000 \end{pmatrix},$$

$$\overline{\overline{pv^c}} = (0.5416, 0.2597, 0.1299, 0.0688)^T.$$

We compute the *GICL* and *GOCL* values of $\overline{\overline{A^k}}$ $(k = 1, 2, \ldots, 5)$ and $\overline{\overline{A^c}}$. These values are listed in Table 3.5.

The results in this example are in accordance with Theorems 3.1 and 3.2.

3.3 Consensus with Additive Preference Relations

In this section, we investigate the consensus in the GDM with additive preference relations.

3.3.1 Consistency and Consensus in Additive Preference Relations

The consistency and consensus measures in additive preference relations are presented below.

(1) Consistency measure

Let $X = \{X_1, X_2, \ldots, X_m\}$ be as before. When an expert makes pairwise comparisons using the values in [0, 1], he/she can construct an additive preference relation $D = (d_{ij})_{m\times m}$, where $d_{ij} + d_{ji} = 1$ and $0 \le d_{ij} \le 1$, to represent his/her own opinion on X. Transitive properties are very important concept to character consistent additive preference relations. Some transitive properties of additive preference relations can be described as follows (see [4, 5, 7, 10, 31]):

(i) Weak stochastic transitivity. $d_{ij} \ge 0.5, d_{jk} \ge 0.5 \Rightarrow d_{ik} \ge 0.5\ \forall i, j, k$.
(ii) Strong stochastic transitivity (or restricted maximum transitivity). $d_{ij} \ge 0.5, d_{jk} \ge 0.5 \Rightarrow d_{ik} \ge max(d_{ij}, d_{ik})\ \forall i, j, k$.

(iii) Additive transitivity. $d_{ij} + d_{jk} - d_{ik} = 0.5\ \forall i, j, k$.
(iv) Multiplicative transitivity (or product rule). $\forall i, j, k : d_{ij}, d_{jk}, d_{ki} \notin \{0, 1\} \Rightarrow d_{ij}d_{jk}d_{ki} = d_{ik}d_{kj}d_{ji}$.

Additive transitivity is most commonly used to character consistency of additive preference relations in the existing literatures. Herrera-Viedma et al. [25] proposed the consistency index based on additive transitivity to evaluate the individual consistency level of an additive preference relation D:

$$ICL(D) = \frac{2}{3m(m-1)(m-2)} \sum_{i,k=1;i\neq k}^{m} \sum_{j=1;j\neq i,k}^{m} \left|d_{ij} + d_{jk} - d_{ik} - 0.5\right|. \quad (3.10)$$

If $ICL(D) = 0$, then the preference relation D is consistent, otherwise, the smaller $ICL(D)$ the more consistent. According to the actual situation, the experts may establish the consistency threshold ($\overline{ICL}$) for $ICL(D)$. If $ICL(D) \leq \overline{ICL}$, we conclude that D is of acceptable consistency; otherwise, we conclude that D is of unacceptable consistency.

(2) Consensus measure

Consider a GDM problem using additive preference relations. Let $E = \{E_1, E_2, \ldots, E_n\}$ be as before, and $\{D^1, D^2, \ldots, D^n\}$ be the additive preference relations provided by n experts E_k $(k = 1, 2, \ldots, n)$, where $D^k = (d_{ij}^k)_{m\times m}$, $(k = 1, 2, \ldots, n; i, j = 1, 2, \ldots, m)$. In general, the computation of the consensus level among the experts is done by measuring the distance between their preference values. Chiclana et al. [9] proposed the following approach to measure consensus lelvel:

(i) For each pair of experts E_r and E_t $(r \leq t)$, a deviation matrix is calculated $DM^{rt} = (dm_{ij}^{rt})_{m\times m}$, where

$$dm_{ij}^{rt} = |d_{ij}^r - d_{ij}^t|, \quad i, j = 1, \ldots, m. \quad (3.11)$$

(ii) A consensus matrix, $CM = (cm_{ij})_{m\times m}$, is obtained by aggregating all deviation matrices using arithmetic mean:

$$cm_{ij} = \frac{2}{n(n-1)} \sum_{t\geq r}^{n} \sum_{r=1}^{n} dm_{ij}^{rt}. \quad (3.12)$$

Obviously, $cm_{ij} = cm_{ji} (\forall i, j)$.
(iii) Consensus level among $\{D^1, \ldots., D^n\}$ is defined as follows:

$$\begin{aligned} CL\{D^1, \ldots., D^n\} &= \tfrac{1}{m(m-1)} \sum_{i=1}^{m} \sum_{j=1,j\neq i}^{m} cm_{ij} \\ &= \tfrac{2}{mn(n-1)(m-1)} \sum_{i=1}^{m} \sum_{j=1,j\neq i}^{m} \sum_{t\geq r}^{n} \sum_{r=1}^{n} |d_{ij}^r - d_{ij}^t|. \end{aligned} \quad (3.13)$$

If $CL\{D^1, \ldots, D^n\} = 0$, then the experts are of full consensus, otherwise, the smaller $CL\{D^1, \ldots, D^n\}$ the more consensus. According to the actual situation, the experts also may establish the threshold (ε) for $CL\{D^1, \ldots, D^n\}$. If $CL\{D^1, \ldots, D^n\} \leq \varepsilon$, we conclude that $\{D^1, \ldots, D^n\}$ are of acceptable consensus; otherwise, we conclude that $\{D^1, \ldots, D^n\}$ are of unacceptable consensus.

3.3.2 LP-Based Consensus Model

The LP-based consensus model is proposed to manage the individual consistency and consensus in the GDM with additive preference relations.

(1) Consensus framework

The proposed LP-based consensus framework is described as Fig. 3.3, and the consensus framework can optimally preserve original preference information in constructing individual consistency and reaching consensus (in Manhattan distance sense).

(2) Linear programming model

(i) Constructing consistency of individual additive preference relations

Let $D^u = (d_{ij}^u)_{m\times m}$ and $D^v = (d_{ij}^v)_{m\times m}$ be two additive preference relations. The Manhattan distance between D^u and D^v is

$$d(D^u, D^v) = \frac{1}{m^2}\sum_{i=1}^{m}\sum_{j=1}^{m}|d_{ij}^u - d_{ij}^v|. \tag{3.14}$$

Consistency construction issue of individual additive preference relations is presented in Herrera-Viedma et al. [24]. We denote $K_{D_m} = \{D = (d_{ij})_{m\times m} : d_{ij} \geq 0; d_{ij}+d_{ji} = 1; i, j = 1, 2, \ldots, m\}$ as the set of $m \times m$ additive preference relations,

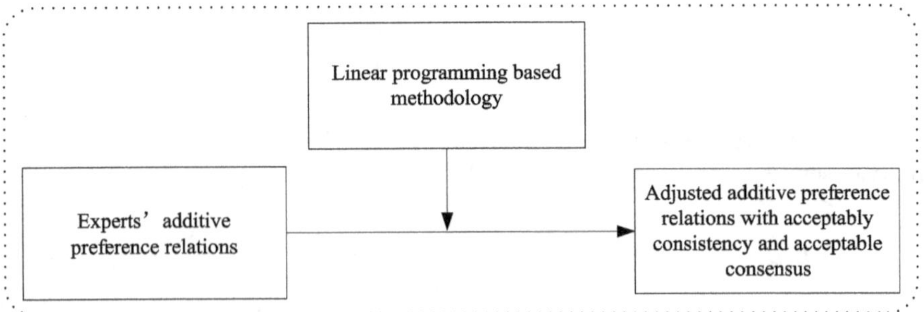

Fig. 3.3 Linear programming based consensus framework

and $M_{D_m} = \{D = (d_{ij})_{m\times m} : d_{ij} \geq 0, d_{ij}+d_{ji} = 1, d_{ij}+d_{jc}-d_{ic} = 0.5; i, j, c = 1, 2, \ldots, m\}$ as the set of $m \times m$ individual consistent additive preference relations. Let $D = (d_{ij})_{m\times m}$ be an additive preference relation. The main task of constructing the individual consistent additive preference relation of $D = (d_{ij})_{m\times m}$ is to find an additive preference relation $\overline{D} = (\overline{d_{ij}})_{m\times m} \in M_{D_m}$. In order to minimize the adjustments in D, we hope that the distance measure between D and $\overline{D}$ is minimal, namely

$$\min_{\overline{D}\in M_{D_m}} d(D, \overline{D}). \tag{3.15}$$

We use two transformed decision variables: $y_{ij} = d_{ij} - \overline{d_{ij}}$ and $z_{ij} = |y_{ij}|$. In this way, model (3.15) is transformed into a linear programming model $P_{3.1}$:

$$\left\{\begin{array}{ll} \min \frac{1}{m^2} \sum\limits_{j=1}^{m} \sum\limits_{i=1}^{m} z_{ij} & (a) \\ s.t. \left\{\begin{array}{l} \overline{d_{ij}} \geq 0,\ i, j = 1, \ldots, m \\ \overline{d_{ij}} + \overline{d_{ji}} = 1,\ i, j = 1, \ldots, m \\ \overline{d_{ij}} + \overline{d_{jk}} - \overline{d_{ik}} = 0.5,\ i, j, k = 1, \ldots, m \\ y_{ij} = d_{ij} - \overline{d_{ij}},\ i, j = 1, \ldots, m \\ y_{ij} \leq z_{ij},\ i, j = 1, \ldots, m \\ -y_{ij} \leq z_{ij},\ i, j = 1, \ldots, m \end{array}\right. & \begin{array}{l} (b) \\ (c) \\ (d) \\ (e) \\ (f) \\ (g) \end{array} \end{array}\right. . \tag{3.16}$$

In (3.16), constraints (*b*)–(*d*) guarantee that $\overline{D} \in M_{D_n}$ and constraints (*e*)–(*g*) enforce that $z_{ij} \geq |y_{ij}| = |d_{ij} - \overline{d_{ij}}|$. According to the objective function (i.e., Eq. 3.16(*a*)), we find that any feasible solutions with $z_{ij} > |y_{ij}|$ are not the optimal solution to $P_{3.1}$. Thus, constraints (*e*)–(*g*) guarantee that $z_{ij} \geq |y_{ij}| = |d_{ij} - \overline{d_{ij}}|$.

Clearly, any $m \times m$ consistent additive preference relations satisfy all the constraints of $P_{3.1}$, and therefore represent feasible solutions. A closed bounded feasible region for $P_{3.1}$ would satisfy the assumption of Weierstrass theorem. This could be achieved, for instance, by introducing an upper bound for z_{ij}. Since $y_{ij} = d_{ij} - \overline{d_{ij}}$, a suitable inequality that doesn't affect the optimal solution could be $z_{ij} \leq 2$, $i, j = 1, 2, \ldots, m$. According to Weierstrass theorem, the optimal solution to $P_{3.1}$ exists.

In general, it is hard to obtain consistency of additive preference relations, especially when the number of alternatives is large. Let $N_{D_m} = \{D : D \in K_{D_m}, ICL(D) \leq \overline{ICL}\}$ be the set of $m \times m$ additive preference relations with acceptably individual consistency. Furthermore, we present an optimization-based model to construct the acceptable consistency additive preference relation of $D = (d_{ij})_{m\times m}$. The main task of the proposed model is to find an additive preference relation $\overline{\overline{D}} = (\overline{\overline{d_{ij}}})_{m\times m} \in N_{D_m}$. In order to minimize the adjustments in D, we hope that the distance measure between D and $\overline{\overline{D}}$ is minimal, namely

$$\min_{\overline{\overline{D}}\in N_{D_m}} d(D, \overline{\overline{D}}). \tag{3.17}$$

We use four transformed decision variables: $a_{ijc} = \overline{\overline{d_{ij}}} + \overline{\overline{d_{jc}}} - \overline{\overline{d_{ic}}} - 0.5$, $b_{ijc} = |a_{ijc}|$, $c_{ij} = \overline{\overline{d_{ij}}} - d_{ij}$ and $e_{ij} = |c_{ij}|$. In this way, model (3.17) is transformed into a linear programming model $P_{3.2}$:

$$\begin{cases} \min \frac{1}{m^2} \sum\limits_{j=1}^{m} \sum\limits_{i=1}^{m} e_{ij} & (a) \\ s.t. \begin{cases} \overline{\overline{d_{ij}}} \geq 0, \ i, j = 1, \ldots, m & (b) \\ \overline{\overline{d_{ij}}} + \overline{\overline{d_{ji}}} = 1, \ i, j = 1, \ldots, m & (c) \\ a_{ijk} = \overline{\overline{d_{ij}}} + \overline{\overline{d_{jk}}} - \overline{\overline{d_{ik}}} = 0.5, \ i, j, k = 1, \ldots, m & (d) \\ a_{ijk} \leq b_{ijk}, \ i, j, k = 1, \ldots, m & (e) \\ -a_{ijk} \leq b_{ijk}, \ i, j, k = 1, \ldots, m & (f) \\ \frac{2}{3m(m-1)(m-2)} \sum\limits_{i,k=1; i \neq k}^{m} \sum\limits_{j=1; j \neq i,k}^{m} b_{ijk} \leq \overline{ICL} & (g) \\ c_{ij} = \overline{\overline{d_{ij}}} - d_{ij}, \ i, j = 1, \ldots, m & (h) \\ c_{ij} \leq e_{ij}, \ i, j = 1, \ldots, m & (i) \\ -c_{ij} \leq e_{ij}, \ i, j = 1, \ldots, m & (j) \end{cases} \end{cases} . \quad (3.18)$$

In model (3.18), constraints (d)–(f) guarantee that $b_{ijc} = |a_{ijc}| = |\overline{\overline{d_{ij}}} + \overline{\overline{d_{jc}}} - \overline{\overline{d_{ic}}} - 0.5|$, constraints $(b)(c)(g)$ guarantee that $\overline{\overline{D}} \in N_{D_m}$, and constraints (h)–(j) guarantee that $e_{ij} = |c_{ij}| = |\overline{\overline{d_{ij}}} - d_{ij}|$.

Similar to $P_{3.1}$, $P_{3.2}$ has optimum solutions. Obviously, when setting $\overline{ICL} = 0$, $P_{3.2}$ reduces to $P_{3.1}$.

(ii) Consensus model

Let $\{D^1, D^2, \ldots, D^n\}$ be a group of additive preference relations with unacceptable consensus. The key task of reaching consensus among $D^k = (d_{ij}^k)_{m \times m}$ $(k = 1, 2, \ldots, n)$ is to find a group of individual additive preference relations $\{\overline{D^1}, \overline{D^2}, \ldots, \overline{D^n}\}$ with acceptable consensus and acceptably individual consistency. In order to minimize the adjustments in $D^k = (d_{ij}^k)_{m \times m}$ $(k = 1, 2, \ldots, n)$, we hope that the distance measure between D^k and $\overline{D^k}$ $(k = 1, 2, \ldots, n)$ is minimal, namely

$$\min_{\overline{D^{(k)}}} \sum_{k=1}^{n} d(D^k, \overline{D^k}), \quad (3.19)$$

i.e.,

$$\min_{\overline{d_{ij}^k}} \frac{1}{m^2 n} \sum_{k=1}^{n} \sum_{i=1}^{m} \sum_{j=1}^{m} |d_{ij}^k - \overline{d_{ij}^k}|. \quad (3.20)$$

At the same time, $\overline{D^k} = \left(\overline{d_{ij}^k}\right)_{m\times m}$ $(k = 1, 2, \ldots, n)$ has acceptably individual consistency level,

$$ICL(\overline{D^k}) \leq \overline{ICL}, \;\; k = 1, 2, \ldots n. \tag{3.21}$$

i.e.,

$$\frac{2}{3m(m-1)(m-2)} \sum_{i,c=1;i\neq c}^{m} \sum_{j=1;j\neq i,c}^{m} \left|\overline{d_{ij}^k} + \overline{d_{jc}^k} - \overline{d_{ic}^k} - 0.5\right| \leq \overline{ICL}, \;\; k = 1, 2, \ldots n. \tag{3.22}$$

and has the acceptable consensus level, that is

$$CL\{\overline{D^1}, \ldots., \overline{D^n}\} \leq \varepsilon. \tag{3.23}$$

i.e.,

$$\frac{2}{mn(n-1)(m-1)} \sum_{i=1}^{m} \sum_{j=1,j\neq i}^{m} \sum_{t\geq r}^{n} \sum_{r=1}^{n} |\overline{d_{ij}^r} - \overline{d_{ij}^t}| \leq \varepsilon. \tag{3.24}$$

In this way, an optimization-based model to reaching consensus is constructed as follows:

$$\begin{cases} \min\limits_{\overline{d_{ij}^k}} \frac{1}{m^2 n} \sum\limits_{k=1}^{n} \sum\limits_{i=1}^{m} \sum\limits_{j=1}^{m} \left|d_{ij}^k - \overline{d_{ij}^k}\right| \\ s.t. \begin{cases} \frac{2}{3m(m-1)(m-2)} \sum\limits_{i,c=1,i\neq c}^{m} \sum\limits_{j=1;j\neq i,c}^{m} \left|\overline{d_{ij}^k} + \overline{d_{jc}^k} - \overline{d_{ic}^k} - 0.5\right| \leq \overline{ICL}, \;\; k = 1, \ldots, n \\ \frac{2}{mn(n-1)(m-1)} \sum\limits_{i=1}^{m} \sum\limits_{j=1,j\neq i}^{m} \sum\limits_{t\geq r}^{n} \sum\limits_{r=1}^{n} \left|\overline{d_{ij}^r} - \overline{d_{ij}^t}\right| \leq \varepsilon \end{cases} \end{cases} . \tag{3.25}$$

We use six transformed decision variables: $a_{ijck} = \overline{d_{ij}^k} + \overline{d_{jc}^k} - \overline{d_{ic}^k} - 0.5$, $b_{ijck} = |a_{ijck}|$, $c_{ijrt} = \overline{d_{ij}^r} - \overline{d_{ij}^t}$, $dd_{ijrt} = |c_{ijrt}|$, $e_{ijk} = d_{ij}^k - \overline{d_{ij}^k}$ and $g_{ijk} = |e_{ijk}|$. In this way, model (3.25) is transformed into the following linear programming model $P_{3.3}$:

$$\begin{cases} \min \frac{1}{m^2 n} \sum_{k=1}^{n} \sum_{i=1}^{m} \sum_{j=1}^{m} g_{ijk} & (a) \\ s.t. \begin{cases} \overline{d_{ij}^k} \geq 0,\ i,j = 1,\ldots,m; k = 1,\ldots,n & (b) \\ \overline{d_{ij}^k} + \overline{d_{ji}^k} = 1,\ i,j = 1,\ldots,m; k = 1,\ldots,n & (c) \\ a_{ijck} = \overline{d_{ij}^k} + \overline{d_{jc}^k} - \overline{d_{ic}^k} - 0.5,\ i,j = 1,\ldots,m; k = 1,\ldots,n & (d) \\ a_{ijck} \leq b_{ijck},\ i,j = 1,\ldots,m; k = 1,\ldots,n & (e) \\ -a_{ijck} \leq b_{ijck},\ i,j = 1,\ldots,m; k = 1,\ldots,n & (f) \\ \frac{2}{3m(m-1)(m-2)} \sum_{i,c=1;i\neq c}^{m} \sum_{j=1;j\neq i,c}^{m} b_{ijck} \leq \overline{ICL},\ k = 1,\ldots,n & (g) \\ c_{ijrt} = \overline{d_{ij}^r} - \overline{d_{ij}^t},\ i,j = 1,\ldots,m; r,t = 1,\ldots,n & (h) \\ c_{ijrt} \leq dd_{ijrt},\ i,j = 1,\ldots,m; r,t = 1,\ldots,n & (i) \\ -c_{ijrt} \leq dd_{ijrt},\ i,j = 1,\ldots,m; r,t = 1,\ldots,n & (j) \\ \frac{2}{mn(n-1)(m-1)} \sum_{i=1}^{m} \sum_{j=1,j\neq i}^{m} \sum_{t\geq r}^{n} \sum_{r=1}^{n} dd_{ijrt} \leq \varepsilon & (k) \\ e_{ijk} = d_{ij}^k - \overline{d_{ij}^k},\ i,j = 1,\ldots,m; k = 1,\ldots,n & (l) \\ e_{ijk} \leq g_{ijk},\ i,j = 1,\ldots,m; k = 1,\ldots,n & (m) \\ -e_{ijk} \leq g_{ijk},\ i,j = 1,\ldots,m; k = 1,\ldots,n & (n) \end{cases} \end{cases} \quad (3.26)$$

In (3.26), constraints (b)–(c) guarantee that $\overline{D^k} \in K_{D_m}$, constraints ($d$)–($f$) guarantee that $b_{ijck} = |a_{ijck}| = |\overline{d_{ij}^k} + \overline{d_{jc}^k} - \overline{d_{ic}^k} - 0.5|$, constraint ($g$) guarantees $\overline{D^k} \in N_{D_m}$, constraints ($h$)–($j$) guarantee that $dd_{ijrt} = |c_{ijrt}| = |\overline{d_{ij}^r} - \overline{d_{ij}^t}|$, constraint ($k$) guarantees $CL\{\overline{D^1}, \ldots, \overline{D^n}\} \leq \varepsilon$, and constraints ($l$)–($n$) guarantee that $g_{ijk} = |e_{ijk}| = |d_{ij}^k - \overline{d_{ij}^k}|$.

Similar to $P_{3.1}$, $P_{3.3}$ has optimum solutions. Obviously, when setting $n = 1$, $P_{3.3}$ reduces to $P_{3.2}$.

(3) Numerical examples

Here, two numerical examples are provided to demonstrate the proposed models ($P_{3.1}$, $P_{3.2}$ and $P_{3.3}$).

(i) Example 3.2

We consider the following additive preference relation:

$$D = \begin{pmatrix} 0.5 & 0.59 & 0.67 & 0.93 \\ 0.41 & 0.5 & 0.59 & 0.62 \\ 0.33 & 0.41 & 0.5 & 0.61 \\ 0.07 & 0.38 & 0.39 & 0.5 \end{pmatrix}.$$

We use model $P_{3.1}$ to construct a consistent additive preference relation of D. The corresponding consistent additive preference relation is

$$\overline{D} = \begin{pmatrix} 0.5 & 0.59 & 0.6754 & 0.7854 \\ 0.41 & 0.5 & 0.5854 & 0.6954 \\ 0.3246 & 0.4146 & 0.5 & 0.61 \\ 0.2146 & 0.3046 & 0.39 & 0.5 \end{pmatrix},$$

where $d(D, \overline{D}) = 0.0288$.

When setting $\overline{ICL} = 0.05$, we use model $P_{3.2}$ to construct the additive preference relations with acceptable consistency:

$$\overline{\overline{D}} = \begin{pmatrix} 0.5 & 0.59 & 0.6736 & 0.8776 \\ 0.41 & 0.5 & 0.5847 & 0.6387 \\ 0.3264 & 0.4153 & 0.5 & 0.61 \\ 0.1224 & 0.3613 & 0.39 & 0.5 \end{pmatrix},$$

where $d(D, \overline{\overline{D}}) = 0.01$.

We also set $\overline{ICL} = 0.02$ and construct the additive preference relations with acceptable consistency:

$$\overline{\overline{D'}} = \begin{pmatrix} 0.5 & 0.59 & 0.6732 & 0.8159 \\ 0.41 & 0.5 & 0.5854 & 0.6682 \\ 0.3268 & 0.4146 & 0.5 & 0.61 \\ 0.1841 & 0.3318 & 0.39 & 0.5 \end{pmatrix},$$

where $d(D, \overline{\overline{D'}}) = 0.0213$.

(ii) Example 3.3

We consider the example presented in Chiclana et al. [9]. In Chiclana et al.'s example, there are four experts providing the following additive preference relations on a set of four alternatives:

$$D^1 = \begin{pmatrix} 0.5 & 0.2 & 0.6 & 0.4 \\ 0.8 & 0.5 & 0.9 & 0.7 \\ 0.4 & 0.1 & 0.5 & 0.3 \\ 0.6 & 0.3 & 0.7 & 0.5 \end{pmatrix},$$

$$D^2 = \begin{pmatrix} 0.5 & 0.7 & 0.9 & 0.5 \\ 0.3 & 0.5 & 0.6 & 0.7 \\ 0.1 & 0.4 & 0.5 & 0.8 \\ 0.5 & 0.3 & 0.2 & 0.5 \end{pmatrix},$$

$$D^3 = \begin{pmatrix} 0.5 & 0.3 & 0.5 & 0.7 \\ 0.7 & 0.5 & 0.1 & 0.3 \\ 0.5 & 0.9 & 0.5 & 0.25 \\ 0.3 & 0.7 & 0.75 & 0.5 \end{pmatrix},$$

$$D^4 = \begin{pmatrix} 0.5 & 0.25 & 0.15 & 0.65 \\ 0.75 & 0.5 & 0.6 & 0.8 \\ 0.85 & 0.4 & 0.5 & 0.5 \\ 0.35 & 0.2 & 0.5 & 0.5 \end{pmatrix}.$$

where $ICL(D^1) = 0$, $ICL(D^2) = 0.2333$, $ICL(D^3) = 0.35$, $ICL(D^4) = 0.1667$ and $CL\{D^1, D^2, D^3, D^4\} = 0.25$.

When respectively setting $\overline{ICL} = 0.05$ and $\varepsilon = 0.15$, we use model $P_{3.3}$ to reach consensus among $\{D^1, D^2, D^3, D^4\}$. The adjusted additive preference relations with acceptable consensus and acceptably individual consistency are

$$\overline{D^1} = \begin{pmatrix} 0.5 & 0.2 & 0.6 & 0.4 \\ 0.8 & 0.5 & 0.9 & 0.7 \\ 0.4 & 0.1 & 0.5 & 0.3 \\ 0.6 & 0.3 & 0.7 & 0.5 \end{pmatrix},$$

$$\overline{D^2} = \begin{pmatrix} 0.5 & 0.475 & 0.575 & 0.525 \\ 0.525 & 0.5 & 0.6 & 0.7 \\ 0.425 & 0.4 & 0.5 & 0.6 \\ 0.475 & 0.3 & 0.4 & 0.5 \end{pmatrix},$$

$$\overline{D^3} = \begin{pmatrix} 0.5 & 0.37 & 0.5 & 0.42 \\ 0.63 & 0.5 & 0.6 & 0.4 \\ 0.5 & 0.4 & 0.5 & 0.3 \\ 0.58 & 0.6 & 0.7 & 0.5 \end{pmatrix},$$

$$\overline{D^4} = \begin{pmatrix} 0.5 & 0.25 & 0.35 & 0.525 \\ 0.75 & 0.5 & 0.6 & 0.775 \\ 0.65 & 0.4 & 0.5 & 0.525 \\ 0.475 & 0.225 & 0.475 & 0.5 \end{pmatrix},$$

where $ICL\left(\overline{D^1}\right) = 0$, $ICL\left(\overline{D^2}\right) = 0.05$, $ICL\left(\overline{D^3}\right) = 0.05$, $ICL\left(\overline{D^4}\right) = 0.05$ and $CL\left\{\overline{D^1}, \overline{D^2}, \overline{D^3}, \overline{D^4}\right\} = 0.15$.

References

1. J. Aguarón, J.M. Moreno-Jiménez, The geometric consistency index: approximated thresholds. Eur. J. Oper. Res. **147**, 137–145 (2003)
2. K.J. Arrow, *Social Choice and Individual Values*, 2nd edn. (Wiley, New York, 1963)
3. J. Barzilai, B. Golany, AHP rank reversal normalization and aggregation rules. Infor **32**, 57–64 (1994)
4. B. De Baets, H. De Meyer, Transitivity frameworks for reciprocal relations: cycle-transitivity versus FG-transitivity. Fuzzy Sets Syst. **152**, 249–270 (2005)

5. B. De Baets, H. De Meyer, B. De Schuymer, S. Jenei, Cyclic evaluation of transitivity of reciprocal relations. Soc. Choice Welfare **26**, 217–238 (2006)
6. D. Cao, L.C. Leung, J.S. Law, Modifying inconsistent comparison matrix in analytic hierarchy process: a heuristic approach. Decis. Support Syst. **44**, 944–953 (2008)
7. B. Cavallo, L. D'Apuzzo, A general unified framework for pairwise comparison matrices in multicriterial methods. Int. J. Intell. Syst. **24**, 377–398 (2009)
8. F. Chiclana, F. Herrera, E. Herrera-Viedma, Integrating multiplicative preference relations in a multipurpose decision-making model based on fuzzy preference relations. Fuzzy Sets Syst. **122**, 277–291 (2001)
9. F. Chiclana, F. Mata, L. Martínez, E. Herrera-Viedma, S. Alonso, Integration of a consistency control module within a consensus model. Int. J. Uncertainty Fuzziness Knowl. Based Syst. **16**, 35–53 (2008)
10. F. Chiclana, E. Herrera-Viedma, S. Alonso, F. Herrera, Cardinal consistency of reciprocal preference relations: an characterization of multiplicative transitivity. IEEE Trans. Fuzzy Syst. **17**, 14–23 (2009)
11. G. Crawford, C. Williams, A note on the analysis of subjective judgement matrices. J. Math. Psychol. **29**, 387–405 (1985)
12. Y.C. Dong, Z.P. Fan, S. Yu, Consensus building in a local context for the AHP-GDM with the individual numerical scale and prioritization method. IEEE Trans. Fuzzy Syst. **23**, 354–368 (2015)
13. Y.C. Dong, E. Herrera-Viedma, Consistency-driven automatic methodology to set interval numerical scales of 2-tuple linguistic term sets and its use in the linguistic GDM with preference relation. IEEE Trans. Cybern. **45**, 780–792 (2015)
14. Y.C. Dong, W.C. Hong, Y.F. Xu, S. Yu, Numerical scales generated individually for analytic hierarchy process. Eur. J. Oper. Res. **229**, 654–662 (2013)
15. Y.C. Dong, Y.F. Xu, H.Y. Li, M. Dai, A comparative study of the numerical scales and the prioritizationmethods in AHP. Eur. J. Oper. Res. **186**, 229–242 (2008)
16. Y.C. Dong, W.J. Xu, W.D. Xu, An automatic method to reach consensus in a local context for AHP group decision making. Eur. J. Ind. Eng. **7**, 456–474 (2013)
17. Y.C. Dong, Y.F. Xu, S. Yu, Linguistic multiperson decision making based on the use of multiple preference relations. Fuzzy Sets Syst. **160**, 603–623 (2009)
18. Y.C. Dong, G.Q. Zhang, W.C. Hong, Y.F. Xu, Consensus models for AHP group decision making under row geometric mean prioritization method. Decis. Support Syst. **49**, 281–289 (2010)
19. M.T. Escobar, J. Aguarón, J.M. Moreno-Jiménez, A note on AHP group consistency for the row geometric mean priorization procedure. Eur. J. Oper. Res. **153**, 318–322 (2004)
20. J.S. Fiana, W.J. Hurley, The analytic hierarchy process: does adjusting a pairwise comparison matrix to improve the consistency ratio help? Comput. Oper. Res. **24**, 749–755 (1997)
21. E. Forman, K. Peniwati, Aggregating individual judgments and priorities with the analytic hierarchy process. Eur. J. Oper. Res. **108**, 165–169 (1998)
22. P.T. Harker, Derivatives of the Perron root of a positive reciprocal matrix: with application to the analytic hierarchy process. Appl. Math. Comput. **22**, 217–232 (1987)
23. E. Herrera-Viedma, F. Herrera, F. Chiclana, A consensus model for multiperson decision making with different preference structures. IEEE Trans. Syst. Man Cybern. Part A Syst. Hum. **32**, 394–402 (2002)
24. E. Herrera-Viedma, F. Herrera, F. Chiclana, M. Luque, Some issues on consistency of fuzzy preference relations. Eur. J. Oper. Res. **154**, 98–109 (2004)
25. E. Herrera-Viedma, F. Chiclana, F. Herrera, S. Alonso, Group decision making model with incomplete fuzzy preference eelations based on additive consistency. IEEE Trans. Syst. Man Cybern. Part B Cybern. **37**, 176–189 (2007)
26. M.W. Herman, W.W. Koczkodaj, A Monte Carlo study of pairwise comparison. Inf. Process. Lett. **57**, 25–29 (1996)
27. F. Herrera, E. Herrera-Viedma, J.L. Verdegay, A rational consensus model in group decision making using linguistic assessments. Fuzzy Sets Syst. **88**, 31–49 (1997)

28. R. Ramanathan, L.S. Ganesh, Group preference aggregation methods employed in AHP: an evaluation and intrinsic process for deriving members' weightages. Eur. J. Oper. Res. **79**, 249–265 (1994)
29. T.L. Saaty, *The Analytic Hierarchy Process* (McGraw-Hill, New York, 1980)
30. T.L. Saaty, Decision-making with the AHP: why is the principal eigenvector necessary. Eur. J. Oper. Res. **145**, 85–91 (2003)
31. T. Tanino, Fuzzy preference orderings in group decision making. Fuzzy Sets Syst. **12**, 117–131 (1994)
32. Z.S. Xu, C.P. Wei, A consistency improving method in analytic hierarchy process. Eur. J. Oper. Res. **116**, 443–449 (1999)
33. Z.S. Xu, On consistency of the weighted geometricmean complex judgementmatrix in AHP. Eur. J. Oper. Res. **126**, 683–687 (2000)
34. G.Q. Zhang, Y.C. Dong, Y.F. Xu, Linear optimization modeling of consistency issues in group decision making based on fuzzy preference relations. Expert Syst. Appl. **39**, 2415–2420 (2012)

Chapter 4
Consensus Under Linguistic Context

We investigate the consensus in linguistic GDM problems. Specifically, we develop a consensus operator with minimum adjustments under the 2-tuple linguistic context. Furthermore, we propose an optimization-based two-stage model to minimize the adjusted simple terms in the consensus reaching under the hesitant linguistic context.

4.1 Consensus Under the 2-tuple Linguistic Context

We introduce several symbolic linguistic computational models, and propose a consensus operator under the 2-tuple linguistic representation model (or the continuous linguistic model).

4.1.1 Several Symbolic Linguistic Computational Models

The 2-tuple linguistic representation model and several symbol OWA-based linguistic aggregation functions are introduced below.

(1) The 2-tuple linguistic representation model

The basic knowledge regarding the linguistic variables [6, 7, 10–12, 15, 16, 24] has been introduced in Chap. 1. Here, we introduce a notable symbol linguistic model: the 2-tuple linguistic representation model initiated by Herrera and Martínez [11].

Let $S = \{s_0, s_1, \ldots, s_g\}$ be a linguistic term set with the granularity $[0, g]$. Then the 2-tuple that expresses the equivalent information to $y \in [0, g]$ is obtained with the following function:

$$\Delta : [0, g] \rightarrow S \times [-0.5, 0.5)$$
$$\Delta(y) = (s_i, \alpha), \; with \begin{cases} s_i, & i = round(y) \\ \alpha = y - i, & \alpha \in [-0.5, 0.5). \end{cases} \tag{4.1}$$

Y. Dong and J. Xu, *Consensus Building in Group Decision Making*,
DOI 10.1007/978-981-287-892-2_4

where Δ is an one to one mapping function. For convenience, its range is denoted as $\overline{S}$. Then, Δ has an inverse function:

$$\Delta^{-1} : \overline{S} \rightarrow [0, g] \tag{4.2}$$

with $\Delta^{-1}((s_i, \alpha)) = i + \alpha$.

Let $(r_i, \alpha_i), (r_j, \alpha_j) \in \overline{S}$ be two linguistic 2-tuples.

If $\Delta^{-1}((r_i, \alpha_i)) < \Delta^{-1}((r_j, \alpha_j))$, then (r_i, α_i) is smaller than (r_j, α_j).

If $\Delta^{-1}((r_i, \alpha_i)) = \Delta^{-1}((r_j, \alpha_j))$, then (r_i, α_i) and (r_j, α_j) represent the same information.

The negation operator over 2-tuples is defined as

$$Neg((s_i, \alpha)) = \Delta(g - \Delta^{-1}((s_i, \alpha))). \tag{4.3}$$

Let $s_i, s_j \in S$ be two linguistic terms. The deviation measure between s_i and s_j is defined as follows:

$$d(s_i, s_j) = \frac{|i - j|}{T}, \tag{4.4}$$

where T is the number of linguistic terms in the set S.

The deviation measure between two linguistic 2-tuples (r_i, α_i) and (r_j, α_j) is defined as follows:

$$d((r_i, \alpha_i), (r_j, \alpha_j)) = \frac{|\Delta^{-1}((r_i, \alpha_i)) - \Delta^{-1}((r_j, \alpha_j))|}{T}. \tag{4.5}$$

Let $a = \{a_1, \ldots, a_n\}$ and $b = \{b_1, \ldots, b_n\}$ be two sets of linguistic 2-tuples, where $a_i, b_i \in \overline{S}(i = 1, 2, \ldots, n)$. Dong et al. [4] defined the deviation measure between a and b as follows:

$$d(a, b) = \sqrt{\frac{1}{n}\sum_{i=1}^{n} (d\,(a_i, b_i))^2}. \tag{4.6}$$

(2) Linguistic aggregation functions

Here, we introduce several symbol OWA-based linguistic aggregation functions, i.e., the LOWA, TOWA and EOWA operators, and analyze the internal relationship among them.

(i) LOWA operator

The LOWA operator, presented in Herrera et al. [14], is based on the OWA operator and the convex combination of linguistic terms defined by Delgado et al. [3]. Let $w = (w_1, w_2, \ldots, w_n)^T$ be as before. Let $\{a_1, \ldots, a_n\}$ be a set of linguistic terms to aggregate, where $a_i \in S$, and then the LOWA operator with w, F_w^{LOWA}, is defined as follows:

$$F_w^{LOWA}(a_1, \ldots, a_n) = C^n\{w_k, s_{\beta_k}, k = 1, 2, \ldots, n\}$$
$$= w_1 \odot s_{\beta_1} \overline{\oplus} (1 - w_1) \odot C^{n-1}\{\lambda_h, s_{\beta_h}, h = 2, \ldots, n\}. \quad (4.7)$$

where $\lambda_h = w_h / \sum_{k=2}^{n} w_k, h = 2, \ldots, n$ and s_{β_k} is the kth largest term in $\{a_1, \ldots, a_n\}$. C^n is the convex combination operator of n terms and if $n = 2$, then it is defined as

$$C^2\{w_i, b_i, i = 1, 2\} = w_1 \odot s_j \overline{\oplus} (1 - w_1) \odot s_i = s_k, \quad s_j, s_i \in S \ (j \geq i) \quad (4.8)$$

such that $k = min\{t, i + round(w_1(j - i))\}$, where *round* is the usual round operation, and $b_1 = s_j,\ b_2 = s_i$.

(ii) TOWA operator

In order to avoid information loss in aggregating the linguistic variables, Herrera and Martínez [11] presented the TOWA operator, which is based on the 2-tuple linguistic representation model.

Let $a = \{a_1, \ldots, a_n\}$, where $a_i = (r_i, \alpha_i) \in \overline{S}$, be a set of 2-tuples to aggregate. The TOWA operator with w, F_w^{TOWA}, is defined by

$$F_w^{TOWA}(a_1, a_2, \ldots, a_n) = \Delta\left(\sum_{i=1}^{n} w_i y_{(i)}\right), \quad (4.9)$$

where $y_{(i)}$ is the ith largest of $\{y_1, y_2, \ldots, y_n\}$, and $y_i = \Delta^{-1}(a_i)$.

(iii) EOWA operator

Xu [26] extended the discrete linguistic term set S to a continuous linguistic term set $\widetilde{S} = \{s_\alpha | \alpha \in [0, q]\}$, where q $(q \geq g)$ is a sufficiently large positive integer. If $s_\alpha \in S$, then s_α is called the original linguistic term; otherwise, it is called the virtual linguistic term. In general, expert uses the original linguistic terms to evaluate alternatives, and the virtual linguistic terms can only appear in operations.

Considering any two linguistic terms $s_\alpha, s_\beta \in \widetilde{S}$, and $\mu, \mu_1, \mu_2 \in [0, 1]$, Xu [26] introduced some new operational laws as follows:

(a) $s_\alpha \oplus s_\beta = s_{\alpha+\beta}$;
(b) $s_\alpha \oplus s_\beta = s_\beta \oplus s_\alpha$;
(c) $\mu s_\alpha = s_{\mu\alpha}$;
(d) $(\mu_1 + \mu_2)s_\alpha = \mu_1 s_\alpha \oplus \mu_2 s_\alpha$;
(e) $\mu(s_\alpha \oplus s_\beta) = \mu s_\alpha \oplus \mu s_\beta$.

Let $\{a_1, a_2, \ldots, a_n\}$ be a set of linguistic terms to aggregate, where $a_i \in \widetilde{S}$, then the EOWA operator with w, F_w^{EOWA}, is defined as follows:

$$F_w^{EOWA}(a_1, a_2, \ldots, a_n) = w_1 s_{\beta_1} \oplus w_2 s_{\beta_2} \oplus \cdots \oplus w_n s_{\beta_n} = s_{\overline{\beta}}, \quad (4.10)$$

where $\overline{\beta} = \sum_{k=1}^{n} w_k \beta_k$, and s_{β_k} is the kth largest term in $\{a_1, a_2, \ldots, a_n\}$.

(iv) The internal relationship between the TOWA and EOWA operators

Let $\{a_1, a_2, \ldots, a_n\}$ be a set of linguistic terms to aggregate, where $a_i \in S$. Let s^c be the result of aggregating $\{a_1, a_2, \ldots, a_n\}$ using F_w^{EOWA}, and (r^c, α^c) be the result of aggregating $\{(a_1, 0), \ldots, (a_n, 0)\}$ using F_w^{TOWA}. Dong et al. [5, 6] showed that

$$\Delta^{-1}((r^c, \alpha^c)) = I(s^c). \tag{4.11}$$

Furthermore, let (s_i, x), where $s_i \in S$, be a 2-tuple linguistic term, then the corresponding continuous linguistic term is $s_{i+x} \in \widetilde{S}$. In this way,

$$\Delta^{-1}((s_i, x)) = I(s_{i+x}). \tag{4.12}$$

Theorem 4.1 *Let $\{a_1, a_2, \ldots, a_n\}$ be a set of linguistic terms to aggregate, where $a_i \in \widetilde{S}$, and let (r_i, α_i) be the 2-tuples corresponding to a_i. Let $\{w_1, w_2, \ldots, w_n\}$ be an associated weighting vector that satisfies $w_i \geq 0$ and $\sum_{i=1}^{n} w_i = 1$. Then*

$$\Delta^{-1}(F_w^{TOWA}((r_1, \alpha_1), (r_2, \alpha_2), \ldots, (r_n, \alpha_n))) = I(F_w^{EOWA}(a_1, a_2, \ldots, a_n)). \tag{4.13}$$

Proof Since (r_i, α_i) is the 2-tuple corresponding to a_i, we have that $\Delta^{-1}(r_i, \alpha_i) = I(a_i)$. Let $y_{(i)}$ be the ith largest of the y_i values, where $y_i = \Delta^{-1}((r_i, \alpha_i)) = I(a_i)$, then we have that

$$\Delta^{-1}(F_w^{TOWA}((r_1, \alpha_1), (r_2, \alpha_2), \ldots, (r_n, \alpha_n))) = \sum_{i=1}^{n} w_i y_{(i)} \tag{4.14}$$

and

$$I(F_w^{EOWA}(a_1, a_2, \ldots, a_n)) = \sum_{i=1}^{n} w_i y_{(i)}. \tag{4.15}$$

Consequently, $\Delta^{-1}(F_w^{TOWA}((r_1, \alpha_1), (r_2, \alpha_2), \ldots, (r_n, \alpha_n))) = I(F_w^{EOWA}(a_1, a_2, \ldots, a_n))$. This completes the proof of Theorem 4.1.

Theorem 4.1 is a generalization of the result presented in Dong et al. [5]. It further shows that the EOWA operator has similarity to the TOWA operator. The main difference between these two operators is using different representation formats. In the rest of sections of this chapter, we adopt the TOWA operator and the 2-tuple linguistic representation model.

Yager [27] suggested a notable way to compute the weights (i.e., $w_k, k = 1, 2, \ldots, n$) of the OWA-based operators using linguistic quantifiers (Zadeh [28]), which, in the case of a non-decreasing proportional quantifier Q, is given by

$$w_k = Q(k/n) - Q((k-1)/n), \ \forall k \tag{4.16}$$

where the membership function of a non-decreasing proportional quantifier Q is given as follows:

$$Q(x) = \begin{cases} 0, & 0 \le x < c \\ \frac{x-c}{d-c}, & c \le x \le d \\ 1, & d < x \le 1 \end{cases} \tag{4.17}$$

with $c, d \in [0, 1]$.

In general, we denote $[c, d]$ a relative linguistic quantifier. When a relative linguistic quantifier Q is used to compute the weights of the EOWA operator, it is symbolized by F_Q^{EOWA}.

(v) The information loss of the LOWA operator

Herrera and Martínez [11], and Ben-Arieh and Chen [2] pointed out that the LOWA operator loses some useful information in the aggregation process. When using the deviation measure between $F_w^{LOWA}(a_1, a_2, \ldots, a_n)$ and $F_w^{TOWA}(a_1, a_2, \ldots, a_n)$, that is $d(F_w^{LOWA}(a_1, a_2, \ldots, a_n), F_w^{TOWA}(a_1, a_2, \ldots, a_n))$, to measure the information loss of the LOWA operator, we can provide an upper bound for this information loss.

Theorem 4.2 *Let* $\{a_1, a_2, \ldots, a_n\}$ *be a set of linguistic terms to aggregate and* $w = (w_1, w_2, \ldots, w_n)^T$ *be a weighting vector, such that* $w_i \ge 0$ *and* $\sum_{i=1}^n w_i = 1$, *then we have*

$$d(F_w^{LOWA}(a_1, a_2, \ldots, a_n), F_w^{TOWA}(a_1, a_2, \ldots, a_n)) \le \frac{n-1}{2T}. \tag{4.18}$$

Proof By induction over the number of arguments to aggregate, the proof can be completed. Without loss of generality, suppose that $a_i \ge a_j$ for $i > j$. For $n = 2$, let s_p, s_q be the terms corresponding to $F_w^{LOWA}(a_1, a_2)$ and $F_w^{TOWA}(a_1, a_2)$, then we have

$$p = min\{t, \Delta^{-1}(a_1) + round(w_1(\Delta^{-1}(a_2) - \Delta^{-1}(a_1)))\}, \tag{4.19}$$

and

$$q = w_1\Delta^{-1}(a_2) + (1 - w_1)\Delta^{-1}(a_1). \tag{4.20}$$

Consequently,

$$d(F_w^{LOWA}(a_1, a_2), F_w^{TOWA}(a_1, a_2)) = \frac{1}{T}|p - q| \le \frac{1}{2T}. \tag{4.21}$$

Suppose that it is true for $n - 1$, i.e.,

$$d(F_w^{LOWA}(a_1, a_2, \ldots, a_{n-1}), F_w^{TOWA}(a_1, a_2, \ldots, a_{n-1})) \le \frac{n-2}{2T}. \tag{4.22}$$

For n, $F_w^{LOWA}(a_1, a_2, \ldots, a_n) = w_1 \odot a_1 \overline{\oplus} (1-w_1) \odot C^{n-1}\{\lambda_h, a_h, h = 2, \ldots, n\}$. Let $s_x = C^{n-1}\{\lambda_h, a_h, h = 2, \ldots, n\}$ and $s_y = \lambda_2 a_2 \oplus \cdots \oplus \lambda_h a_h \oplus \cdots \lambda_n a_n$. Using induction hypothesis, we obtain

$$d(s_x, s_y) = \frac{1}{T}|y - x| \leq \frac{n-2}{2T}. \tag{4.23}$$

Since

$$F_w^{LOWA}(a_1, a_2, \ldots, a_n) = w_1 \odot a_1 \overline{\oplus} (1 - w_1) \odot s_x \tag{4.24}$$

and

$$F_w^{TOWA}(a_1, a_2, \ldots, a_n) = \Delta(w_1 \Delta^{-1}(a_1) + (1 - w_1)\Delta^{-1}(s_y)), \tag{4.25}$$

we have that

$$\begin{aligned}
&d(F_w^{LOWA}(a_1, a_2, \ldots, a_n), F_w^{TOWA}(a_1, \ldots, a_n)) \\
&= d(w_1 \odot a_1 \overline{\oplus} (1 - w_1) \odot s_x, \Delta(w_1 \Delta^{-1}(a_1) + (1 - w_1)\Delta^{-1}(s_x) \\
&\quad +(1 - w_1)\Delta^{-1}(s_{y-x}))) \\
&= \tfrac{1}{T}|\Delta^{-1}((w_1 \odot a_1 \overline{\oplus} (1 - w_1) \odot s_x) - (w_1 \Delta^{-1}(a_1) + (1 - w_1)\Delta^{-1}(s_x) \\
&\quad +(1 - w_1)\Delta^{-1}(s_{y-x}))| \\
&\leq \tfrac{1}{T}(|\Delta^{-1}(w_1 \odot a_1 \overline{\oplus} (1 - w_1) \odot s_x) - (w_1 \Delta^{-1}(a_1) + (1 - w_1)\Delta^{-1}(s_x))| + |y - x|).
\end{aligned} \tag{4.26}$$

Based on (4.21) and (4.23), we have that

$$d(F_w^{LOWA}(a_1, a_2, \ldots, a_n), F_w^{TOWA}(a_1, a_2, \ldots, a_n)) \leq \frac{n-1}{2T}. \tag{4.27}$$

This completes the proof of Theorem 4.2.

4.1.2 The Consensus Operator

In this section, we develop a consensus operator with minimum adjustments to support the consensus reaching under the 2-tuple linguistic representation model.

(1) Modeling the OWA-based consensus operator

Let $E = \{E_1, E_2, \ldots, E_n\}$ be as before. In GDM under the 2-tuple linguistic representation model, experts provide a set of linguistic 2-tuples $a = \{a_1, a_2, \ldots, a_n\}$ to represent their own opinions on an alternative, where $a_k = (r_k, \alpha_k) \in \overline{S}$ is provided by expert E_k. Using the TOWA operator to aggregate the linguistic 2-tuples $\{a_1, a_2, \ldots, a_n\}$, we obtain the collective linguistic 2-tuple $a^c = (r^c, \alpha^c) \in \overline{S}$. By calculating $d(a_i, a^c)$, $i = 1, 2, \ldots, n$, we can measure the deviation degree between the individual opinions and the collective opinion. When $d(a_k, a^c) > \varepsilon$, where ε is the established threshold, we argue that the expert E_k has the unacceptable consensus degree, and suggest to adjust the original linguistic preferences to reach a consensus.

The core problem of reaching consensus is to find a set of adjusted linguistic 2-tuples with the acceptable consensus level, $\overline{a} = \{\overline{a_1}, \overline{a_2}, \ldots, \overline{a_n}\}$, where $\overline{a_i} = (\overline{r_i}, \overline{\alpha_i}) \in \overline{S}$. In order to minimize the adjustments in $a = \{a_1, a_2, \ldots, a_n\}$, we hope that the deviation degree between a and $\overline{a}$ is minimal, namely,

$$\min_{\overline{a}} d(a, \overline{a}). \tag{4.28}$$

Here, we define $d(a, \overline{a}) = \frac{1}{nT^2} \sum_{i=1}^{n} (\Delta^{-1}(a_i) - \Delta^{-1}(\overline{a_i}))^2$. Then, Eq. (4.28) can be rewritten as

$$\min_{\overline{a}} (\frac{1}{nT^2} \sum_{i=1}^{n} (\Delta^{-1}(a_i) - \Delta^{-1}(\overline{a_i}))^2). \tag{4.29}$$

The adjusted collective linguistic references, $\overline{a^c} = (\overline{r^c}, \overline{\alpha^c})$, is obtained by using the aggregation function, F_w^{TOWA}, i.e.,

$$\overline{a^c} = F_w^{TOWA}(\overline{a_1}, \overline{a_2}, \ldots, \overline{a_n}). \tag{4.30}$$

At the same time, $\overline{a} = \{\overline{a_1}, \ldots, \overline{a_n}\}$ has the acceptable consensus level, that is

$$d(\overline{a_i}, \overline{a^c}) \leq \varepsilon, \; i = 1, 2, \ldots, n \tag{4.31}$$

i.e.,

$$d(\overline{a_i}, F_w^{TOWA}(\overline{a_1}, \overline{a_2}, \ldots, \overline{a_n})) \leq \varepsilon, \; i = 1, 2, \ldots, n. \tag{4.32}$$

Based on Eqs. (4.28)–(4.32), an optimization-based model to reach consensus can be constructed as follows:

$$\begin{cases} \min_{\overline{a}} (\frac{1}{nT^2} \sum_{i=1}^{n} (\Delta^{-1}(a_i) - \Delta^{-1}(\overline{a_i}))^2) \\ s.t. \; d(\overline{a_i}, F_w^{TOWA}(\overline{a_1}, \overline{a_2}, \ldots, \overline{a_n})) \leq \varepsilon, \; i = 1, 2, \ldots, n \end{cases}. \tag{4.33}$$

Let $x_i = \Delta^{-1}(\overline{a_i})$. We denote $\{\sigma_a(1), \sigma_a(2), \ldots, \sigma_a(n)\}$ as a permutation of $\{1, 2, \ldots, n\}$ such that $a_{\sigma_a(i-1)} \geq a_{\sigma_a(i)}$ for $i = 2, \ldots, n$. (i.e., $a_{\sigma_a(i)}$ is the ith largest variable in a). Let $\{\sigma_x(1), \sigma_x(2), \ldots, \sigma_x(n)\}$ be another permutation of $\{1, 2, \ldots, n\}$ such that $x_{\sigma_x(i-1)} \geq x_{\sigma_x(i)}$ for $i = 2, \ldots, n$. Model (4.33) can be redescribed as follows:

$$\begin{cases} \min_{x} (\frac{1}{nT^2} \sum_{i=1}^{n} (\Delta^{-1}(a_i) - x_i)^2) \\ s.t. \; \frac{1}{T} |x_i - \sum_{i=1}^{n} w_i x_{\sigma_x(i)}| \leq \varepsilon, \; i = 1, 2, \ldots, n \end{cases}. \tag{4.34}$$

We denote model (4.34) as $P_{4.1}$. Solving $P_{4.1}$, we obtain $\overline{a_i} = \Delta(x_i), i = 0, 1, \ldots, n$. Before presenting the approach to solve $P_{4.1}$, we introduce a new model:

$$\begin{cases} \min\limits_{x} \frac{1}{nT^2} \sum\limits_{i=1}^{n} \left(\Delta^{-1}(a_i) - x_i\right)^2 \\ s.t. \begin{cases} \frac{1}{T}\left| x_i - \sum\limits_{i=1}^{n} w_i x_{\sigma_x(i)} \right| \leq \varepsilon, \ i = 1, \ldots, n \\ x_{\sigma_a(i)} - x_{\sigma_a(i-1)} \leq 0, \ i = 2, \ldots, n \end{cases} \end{cases} \tag{4.35}$$

Denote model (4.35) as $P_{4.2}$.

Lemma 4.1 *$P_{4.2}$ is a strictly convex quadratic programming.*

Proof The constraint condition $x_{\sigma_a(i)} - x_{\sigma_a(i-1)} \leq 0$ $(i = 2, \ldots, n)$ guarantees that $\sigma_x(i) = \sigma_a(i)$. Consequently,

$$\frac{1}{T}|x_i - \sum_{i=1}^{n} w_i x_{\sigma_x(i)}| = \frac{1}{T}|x_i - \sum_{i=1}^{n} w_i x_{\sigma_a(i)}|. \tag{4.36}$$

Based on (4.36), $P_{4.2}$ can be redescribed as follows:

$$\begin{cases} \min\limits_{x}(\frac{1}{nT^2} \sum_{i=1}^{n}(\Delta^{-1}(a_i) - x_i)^2) \\ s.t. \begin{cases} x_i - \sum_{i=1}^{n} w_i x_{\sigma_a(i)} \leq T\varepsilon, \ i = 1, 2, \ldots, n \\ \sum_{i=1}^{n} w_i x_{\sigma_a(i)} - x_i \leq T\varepsilon, \ i = 1, 2, \ldots, n \\ x_{\sigma_a(i)} - x_{\sigma_a(i-1)} \leq 0, \ i = 2, \ldots, n \end{cases} \end{cases} \tag{4.37}$$

Let $f(x) = \frac{1}{nT^2} \sum_{i=1}^{n}(\Delta^{-1}(a_i) - x_i)^2$. We prove that $f(x)$ is a strictly convex function. Moreover, $\sigma_a(i)$ completely depends on a, so the constraint conditions of $P_{4.2}$ are linear. Hence, $P_{4.2}$ is a strictly convex quadratic programming. This completes the proof of Lemma 4.1.

It is well known that the optimal solution to the strictly convex quadratic programming exists and is unique, and can be effectively solved by some classical methods such as Lemke algorithm, etc. In the following, we present a good linkage of $P_{4.2}$ to $P_{4.1}$. Let $\Omega_{4.1}$ and $\Omega_{4.2}$ be the feasible sets corresponding to $P_{4.1}$ and $P_{4.2}$, respectively. Naturally,

$$\Omega_{4.1} \supseteq \Omega_{4.2}. \tag{4.38}$$

Lemma 4.2 *Let a_p, $a_q \in a$, and $\overline{a} = \{\overline{a_1}, \overline{a_2}, \ldots, \overline{a_n}\}$ be the optimal solution to $P_{4.1}$. Then, $\overline{a_p} \geq \overline{a_q}$ for $a_p > a_q$.*

Proof Using reduction to absurdity, we assume that there exist p and q, such that $a_p > a_q$ and $\overline{a_p} < \overline{a_q}$. Let $\overline{\overline{a}} = \{\overline{\overline{a_1}}, \overline{\overline{a_2}} \ldots, \overline{\overline{a_n}}\}$, where

$$\overline{\overline{a_i}} = \begin{cases} \overline{a_q}, \ for\ i = p \\ \overline{a_p}, \ for\ i = q \\ \overline{a_i}, \ for\ i \neq p, q \end{cases}.$$

Since $d(\overline{a_i}, F_w^{TOWA}(\overline{a_1}, \overline{a_2}, \ldots, \overline{a_n})) \leq \varepsilon$, we find that $d(\overline{\overline{a_i}}, F_w^{TOWA}(\overline{\overline{a_1}}, \overline{\overline{a_2}}, \ldots, \overline{\overline{a_n}})) \leq \varepsilon$. So, $\overline{\overline{a}} \in \Omega_{4.1}$. Moreover, we have that

$$(d(a, \overline{a}))^2 - (d(a, \overline{\overline{a}}))^2 = \frac{1}{nT^2}((\Delta^{-1}(a_p) - \Delta^{-1}(\overline{a_p}))^2 + (\Delta^{-1}(a_q) - \Delta^{-1}(\overline{a_q}))^2 - (\Delta^{-1}(a_p) - \Delta^{-1}(\overline{\overline{a_p}}))^2 - (\Delta^{-1}(a_q) - \Delta^{-1}(\overline{\overline{a_q}}))^2). \tag{4.39}$$

Since $\overline{a_p} = \overline{\overline{a_q}}$ and $\overline{a_q} = \overline{\overline{a_p}}$, from (4.39), we obtain that

$$(d(a, \overline{a}))^2 - (d(a, \overline{\overline{a}}))^2 = \frac{1}{nT^2}(\Delta^{-1}(a_q) - \Delta^{-1}(a_p))(\Delta^{-1}(\overline{a_p}) - \Delta^{-1}(\overline{a_q})) > 0. \tag{4.40}$$

Consequently,

$$d(a, \overline{a}) > d(a, \overline{\overline{a}}), \tag{4.41}$$

which contradicts the fact that $\overline{a}$ is the optimal solution to $P_{4.1}$. This completes the proof of Lemma 4.2.

Lemma 4.3 *Let a_p, $a_q \in a$ and $a_p = a_q$. If $\overline{a} = \{\overline{a_1}, \overline{a_2}, \ldots, \overline{a_n}\}$ is the optimal solution to $P_{4.1}$, then $\overline{\overline{a}} = \{\overline{\overline{a_1}}, \overline{\overline{a_2}}, \ldots, \overline{\overline{a_n}}\}$ is the optimal solution to $P_{4.1}$, where*

$$\overline{\overline{a_i}} = \begin{cases} \overline{a_q}, \ for\ i = p \\ \overline{a_p}, \ for\ i = q \\ \overline{a_i}, \ for\ i \neq p, q \end{cases}.$$

Proof Since $F_w^{TOWA}(\overline{a_1}, \overline{a_2}, \ldots, \overline{a_n}) = F_w^{TOWA}(\overline{\overline{a_1}}, \overline{\overline{a_2}}, \ldots, \overline{\overline{a_n}})$, we have that

$$d(\overline{\overline{a_i}}, F_w^{TOWA}(\overline{\overline{a_1}}, \overline{\overline{a_2}}, \ldots, \overline{\overline{a_n}})) = d(\overline{a_i}, F_w^{TOWA}(\overline{a_1}, \overline{a_2}, \ldots, \overline{a_n})) \leq \varepsilon. \tag{4.42}$$

Therefore, $\overline{\overline{a}} \in \Omega_{4.1}$. Moreover, when $a_p = a_q$, we have that $d(a, \overline{\overline{a}}) = d(a, \overline{a}) = \min_{x \in \Omega_{4.1}} d(a, x)$. Consequently, $\overline{\overline{a}} = \{\overline{\overline{a_1}}, \overline{\overline{a_2}}, \ldots, \overline{\overline{a_n}}\}$ is the optimal solution to $P_{4.1}$. This completes the proof of Lemma 4.3.

Theorem 4.3 *If $\overline{a} = \{\overline{a_1}, \overline{a_2}, \ldots, \overline{a_n}\}$ is the optimal solution to $P_{4.2}$, then $\overline{a} = \{\overline{a_1}, \overline{a_2}, \ldots, \overline{a_n}\}$ is the optimal solution to $P_{4.1}$.*

Proof Let $\overline{a^*} = \{\overline{a_1^*}, \overline{a_2^*}, \ldots, \overline{a_n^*}\}$ be an optimal solution to $P_{4.1}$. From (4.38), we have that

$$d(a, \overline{a^*}) = \min_{x \in \Omega_{4.1}} d(a, x) \leq \min_{x \in \Omega_{4.2}} d(a, x) = d(a, \overline{a}). \tag{4.43}$$

Here, we consider two cases:

Case A: $a_p \neq a_q$ for any $a_p,\ a_q \in a$. In this case, based on Lemma 4.2, we have $\overline{a^*_{\sigma_a(i)}} - \overline{a^*_{\sigma_a(i-1)}} \leq 0$, so $\overline{a^*} \in \Omega_{4.2}$. Consequently,

$$d(a, \overline{a^*}) \geq \min_{x \in \Omega_{4.2}} d(a, x) = d(a, \overline{a}). \tag{4.44}$$

From (4.43) and (4.44), we obtain that $d(a, \overline{a^*}) = d(a, \overline{a})$. The optimal solution of $P_{4.2}$ exists and is unique, so $\overline{a} = \overline{a^*}$.

Case B: There exists $a_p, a_q \in a$ and $a_p = a_q$. Without loss of generality, we suppose that $a_i \neq a_j$ for any $a_i, a_j \in a/\{a_p\}$. In this case, based on Lemma 4.3, $\overline{\overline{a^*}} = \{\overline{\overline{a^*_1}}, \overline{\overline{a^*_2}}, \ldots, \overline{\overline{a^*_n}}\}$ is also the optimal solution to $P_{4.1}$, where

$$\overline{\overline{a^*_i}} = \begin{cases} \overline{a^*_q}, \text{ for } i = p \\ \overline{a^*_p}, \text{ for } i = q \\ \overline{a^*_i}, \text{ for } i \neq p, q \end{cases}.$$

From Lemma 4.2, we also know that if $a_i \in a/\{a_p, a_q\}$ is the kth largest variable in a, then $\overline{a^*_i}/\overline{\overline{a^*_i}}$ is the kth largest variable in $\overline{a^*}/\overline{\overline{a^*}}$. Thus, $\overline{a^*} \in \Omega_{4.2}$ or $\overline{\overline{a^*}} \in \Omega_{4.2}$. Without loss of generality, we suppose that $\overline{a^*} \in \Omega_{4.2}$. Similar to Case A, we have that $\overline{a} = \overline{a^*}$. This completes the proof of Theorem 4.3.

Theorem 4.4 *Let* $\overline{a^1} = \left\{\overline{a^1_1}, \overline{a^1_2}, \ldots, \overline{a^1_n}\right\}$, $\overline{a^2} = \left\{\overline{a^2_1}, \overline{a^2_2}, \ldots, \overline{a^2_n}\right\}$ *be two optimal solutions to* $P_{4.1}$, *and let* $\overline{a} = \{\overline{a_1}, \overline{a_2}, \ldots, \overline{a_n}\}$ *be the optimal solution to* $P_{4.2}$. *Then,*

$$F_w^{TOWA}\left(\overline{a^1_1}, \overline{a^1_2}, \ldots, \overline{a^1_n}\right) = F_w^{TOWA}\left(\overline{a^2_1}, \overline{a^2_2}, \ldots, \overline{a^2_n}\right) = F_w^{TOWA}\left(\overline{a_1}, \overline{a_2}, \ldots, \overline{a_n}\right).$$

Proof We consider two cases:

Case A: $a_p \neq a_q$ for any $a_p,\ a_q \in a$. In this case, from the proof of Theorem 4.3, we can find that $\overline{a} = \overline{a^1}$ and $\overline{a} = \overline{a^2}$. This means that $F_w^{TOWA}\left(\overline{a^1_1}, \overline{a^1_2}, \ldots, \overline{a^1_n}\right) = F_w^{TOWA}\left(\overline{a^2_1}, \overline{a^2_2}, \ldots, \overline{a^2_n}\right) = F_w^{TOWA}\left(\overline{a_1}, \overline{a_2}, \ldots, \overline{a_n}\right)$.

Case B: There exists $a_p, a_q \in a$ and $a_p = a_q$. In this case, according to Lemma 4.3, we can construct two optimal solutions $\overline{a^{1,*}}, \overline{a^{2,*}}$ to $P_{4.1}$, satisfying the following conditions:

$$F_w^{TOWA}\left(\overline{a^{k,*}_1}, \overline{a^{k,*}_2}, \ldots, \overline{a^{k,*}_n}\right) = F_w^{TOWA}\left(\overline{a^k_1}, \overline{a^k_2}, \ldots, \overline{a^k_n}\right), \quad k = 1, 2. \tag{4.45}$$

$$\overline{a^{k,*}_{\sigma_a(i)}} - \overline{a^{k,*}_{\sigma_a(i-1)}} \leq 0, \quad k = 1, 2. \tag{4.46}$$

The Eq. (4.46) guarantees that $\overline{a^{1,*}}, \overline{a^{2,*}} \in \Omega_{4.2}$. Similar to the proof of Theorem 4.3, we have that $\overline{a^{(1,*)}} = \overline{a^{(2,*)}} = \overline{a}$. Consequently,

$$F_w^{TOWA}\left(\overline{a_1^{1,*}}, \overline{a_2^{1,*}}, \ldots, \overline{a_n^{1,*}}\right) = F_w^{TOWA}\left(\overline{a_1^{2,*}}, \overline{a_2^{2,*}}, \ldots, \overline{a_n^{2,*}}\right)$$
$$= F_w^{TOWA}(\overline{a_1}, \overline{a_2}, \ldots, \overline{a_n}). \quad (4.47)$$

From (4.45), we obtain that

$$F_w^{TOWA}\left(\overline{a_1^1}, \overline{a_2^1}, \ldots, \overline{a_n^1}\right) = F_w^{TOWA}\left(\overline{a_1^2}, \overline{a_2^2}, \ldots, \overline{a_n^2}\right) = F_w^{TOWA}\left(\overline{a_1}, \overline{a_2}, \ldots, \overline{a_n}\right). \quad (4.48)$$

This completes the proof of Theorem 4.4.

The implementation of the proposed consensus reaching model requires the following two-step procedure.

Step 1: Solve the optimization model $P_{4.1}$ to obtain $\overline{a} = \{\overline{a_1}, \overline{a_2}, \ldots, \overline{a_n}\}$.
Step 2: Obtain the collective linguistic term a^c, by aggregating $\overline{a}$ using the TOWA operator.

Note 4.1 Let S be a linguistic term set. Theorem 4.4 shows that the proposed consensus reaching model is a mapping: $S^n \to S$, in essence. Thus, we call the proposed consensus reaching model as the OWA-based consensus operator. When the weighting vector is w and the established deviation threshold is ε, we denote the OWA-based consensus operator as $F_{w,\varepsilon}^{TOWA}$.

Note 4.2 Based on Theorem 4.3, the optimal solution to $P_{4.2}$ is also one to $P_{4.1}$. Therefore, in the rest of this chapter, we replace $P_{4.1}$ with $P_{4.2}$ in the implementation of the consensus operator.

Theorem 4.5 $F_{w,\varepsilon}^{TOWA}(a_1, a_2, \ldots, a_n) = F_w^{TOWA}(a_1, a_2, \ldots, a_n)$ *under the condition that* $d(a_i, F^{TOWA}(a_1, a_2, \ldots, a_n)) \leq \varepsilon (i = 1, 2, \ldots, n)$.

Proof When $d(a_i, F^{TOWA}(a_1, a_2, \ldots, a_n)) \leq \varepsilon (i = 1, 2, \ldots, n)$, the optimal solution to $P_{4.1}$ (or $P_{4.2}$) is a. Thus, $F_{w,\varepsilon}^{TOWA}(a_1, a_2, \ldots, a_n) = F_w^{TOWA}(a_1, a_2, \ldots, a_n)$. This completes the proof of Theorem 4.5.

(2) Numerical examples

In order to show how the OWA-based consensus operator (i.e., $F_{w,\varepsilon}^{TOWA}$) work in practice, let us consider the following three examples.

(i) Example 4.1

Let $T = 9$, $w = (1/2, 1/4, 1/4)^T$ and $a = (s_8, s_6, s_7)^T$, then we have

$$F_w^{LOWA}(a_1, a_2, a_3) = \frac{1}{2} \odot s_8 \overline{\oplus} \frac{1}{2} \odot C^2\{\lambda_h, a_h, h = 2, 3\},$$

where $\lambda_h = 1/2,\ h = 2, 3$. Since $C^2\{\lambda_h, a_h, h = 2, 3\} = s_7$, we have that

$$F_w^{LOWA}(a_1, a_2, a_3) = s_8.$$

Moreover, we have that

$$F_w^{EOWA}(a_1, a_2, a_3) = s_{\frac{29}{4}},$$

and

$$F_w^{TOWA}((s_8, 0), (s_6, 0), (s_7, 0)) = (s_7, 0.25).$$

Consequently,

$$I(F_w^{EOWA}(a_1, a_2, a_3)) = \Delta^{-1}(F_w^{TOWA}((s_8, 0), (s_6, 0), (s_7, 0))) = \frac{29}{4},$$

and

$$d(F_w^{LOWA}(a_1, a_2, a_3), F_w^{EOWA}(a_1, a_2, a_3)) = \frac{1}{12} < \frac{n-1}{2T} = \frac{1}{9}.$$

The above results are consistent with Theorems 4.1 and 4.2. Let $\varepsilon = \frac{1}{12}$, we consider using $F_{w,\varepsilon}^{TOWA}$ to aggregate linguistic terms in a.

Step 1: Computing the adjusted preference values $\overline{a} = \{\overline{a_1}, \overline{a_2}, \overline{a_3}\}$. According to $P_{4.2}$, we have that

$$\begin{cases} \min\limits_{x} \frac{1}{243} \sum\limits_{i=1}^{3} \left(\Delta^{-1}(a_i) - x_i\right)^2 \\ s.t. \begin{cases} \frac{1}{9}\left| x_i - \sum\limits_{i=1}^{3} w_i x_{\sigma_x(i)} \right| \leq \frac{1}{12}, i = 1, 2, 3 \\ x_{\sigma_a(i)} - x_{\sigma_a(i-1)} \leq 0, i = 2, 3 \end{cases} \end{cases}. \tag{4.49}$$

The constraint condition $x_{\sigma_a(i)} - x_{\sigma_a(i-1)} \leq 0$, $(i = 2, 3)$ guarantees that $\sigma_a(i) = \sigma_x(i)$ $(i = 1, 2, 3)$. Since $\sigma_a(1) = 1$, $\sigma_a(2) = 3$ and $\sigma_a(3) = 2$, we can transform model (4.49) into model (4.50):

$$\begin{cases} \min\limits_{x} \frac{1}{243} \left((8 - x_1)^2 + (6 - x_2)^2 + (7 - x_3)^2\right) \\ s.t. \begin{cases} 2x_1 - x_2 - x_3 - 3 \leq 0 \\ -2x_1 + x_2 + x_3 - 3 \leq 0 \\ -2x_1 + 3x_2 - x_3 - 3 \leq 0 \\ 2x_1 - 3x_2 + x_3 - 3 \leq 0 \\ -2x_1 - x_2 + 3x_3 - 3 \leq 0 \\ 2x_1 + x_2 - 3x_3 - 3 \leq 0 \\ x_3 - x_1 \leq 0 \\ x_2 - x_3 \leq 0 \end{cases} \end{cases}. \tag{4.50}$$

Solving model (4.50), we can obtain $x_1 = 7.72$, $x_2 = 6.43$ and $x_3 = 6.85$. Since $\overline{a_i} = \Delta(x_i)$, $i = 0, 1, \ldots, n$, we have that $\overline{a} = \{(s_8, -0.28), (s_6, 0.43), (s_7, -0.15)\}$.

Table 4.1 The results of Example 4.2

	UNIX	WIN-NT	AS/400	VMS
p_1	s_3	s_3	s_2	s_3
p_2	$s_{3.2}$	$s_{2.7}$	$s_{2.4}$	$s_{2.9}$
p_3	$(s_3, 0.1)$	$(s_3, -0.4)$	$(s_2, 0.35)$	$(s_3, -0.2)$

Step 2: Obtain the collective linguistic variable a^c. By aggregating $\overline{a}$ using F_w^{TOWA}, we have that $a^c = (s_7, 0.18)$.

(ii) Example 4.2

Let us consider the example used in Herrera and Martínez [11]. In the example, there is a linguistic pre-established term set:

$$S^{Example\ 4.2} = \{s_0 = N, s_1 = VL, s_2 = L, s_3 = M, s_4 = H, s_5 = VH, s_6 = P\}.$$

A distribution company needs to renew its computing system, so it contracts a consulting company to carry out a survey of the different possibilities existing on the market, to decide which is the best option for its needs. There are four alternatives: X_1 = UNIX, X_2 = WINDOWS-NT, X_3 = AS/400 and X_4 = VMS. The consulting company has a group of four consultancy departments $\{E_1, E_2, E_3, E_4\}$. They supply a linguistic decision matrix LDM:

$$LDM = (LDM_{ij})_{4\times 4} = \begin{pmatrix} s_1 & s_3 & s_3 & s_2 \\ s_3 & s_2 & s_1 & s_4 \\ s_4 & s_1 & s_3 & s_3 \\ s_4 & s_4 & s_2 & s_2 \end{pmatrix},$$

where $LDM_{i,j}$ denotes the preference degree of the expert E_i over X_j.

Without loss of generality, we set $w = (0.3, 0.3, 0.2, 0.2)^T$. Applying the F_w^{LOWA} operator and the F_w^{EOWA} operator, respectively, we obtain the corresponding collective preference vectors p_1 and p_2. Let $\varepsilon = 0.1$, we also consider using the consensus operator $F_{w,\varepsilon}^{TOWA}$ to aggregate individual preferences. Then the adjusted individual preferences and the collective preference vector are $\overline{LDM}$ and p_3, respectively. $\overline{LDM}$ is listed as follows:

$$\overline{LDM} = \begin{pmatrix} (s_3, -0.5) & (s_3, -0.2) & (s_3, -0.25) & (s_2, 0.2) \\ (s_3, -0.35) & (s_2, 0) & (s_2, 0.25) & (s_3, 0.4) \\ (s_3, 0.45) & (s_2, 0) & (s_3, -0.25) & (s_3, 0) \\ (s_3, 0.45) & (s_3, 0.2) & (s_2, -0.25) & (s_2, 0.2) \end{pmatrix}.$$

The values of p_1, p_2 and p_3 are listed in Table 4.1. p_1 shows that {UNIX, WIN-NT, VMS} are the best options for the distribution company. p_2 and p_3 show that UNIX is the best option for the distribution company.

(iii) Example 4.3

Let us also consider the example used in Xu [26]. In the example, there are four experts E_k ($k = 1, 2, \ldots, 4$). The experts compare five alternatives with respect to certain criterion by using $S^{Example\ 4.3}$

$$S^{Example\ 4.3} = \left\{ \begin{array}{l} s_0 = extremely\ poor, s_1 = very\ \ poor, s_2 = poor \\ s_3 = slightly\ poor, s_4 = fair, s_5 = slightly\ good \\ s_6 = good, s_7 = very\ good, s_8 = extremely\ good \end{array} \right\},$$

and construct, respectively, the linguistic preference relations L^1, L^2, L^3 and L^4. They are listed as follows:

$$L^1 = \begin{pmatrix} s_4 & s_3 & s_7 & s_3 & s_7 \\ s_5 & s_4 & s_5 & s_4 & s_6 \\ s_2 & s_3 & s_4 & s_3 & s_6 \\ s_5 & s_4 & s_5 & s_4 & s_4 \\ s_1 & s_2 & s_2 & s_4 & s_4 \end{pmatrix}, L^2 = \begin{pmatrix} s_4 & s_5 & s_6 & s_4 & s_8 \\ s_3 & s_4 & s_3 & s_4 & s_4 \\ s_2 & s_5 & s_4 & s_3 & s_7 \\ s_4 & s_4 & s_5 & s_4 & s_5 \\ s_0 & s_4 & s_1 & s_3 & s_4 \end{pmatrix},$$

$$L^3 = \begin{pmatrix} s_4 & s_4 & s_7 & s_5 & s_7 \\ s_4 & s_4 & s_2 & s_6 & s_6 \\ s_1 & s_6 & s_4 & s_5 & s_5 \\ s_3 & s_2 & s_3 & s_4 & s_3 \\ s_1 & s_2 & s_3 & s_5 & s_4 \end{pmatrix}, L^4 = \begin{pmatrix} s_4 & s_6 & s_4 & s_3 & s_6 \\ s_2 & s_4 & s_3 & s_5 & s_4 \\ s_4 & s_5 & s_4 & s_3 & s_6 \\ s_5 & s_3 & s_5 & s_4 & s_5 \\ s_2 & s_4 & s_2 & s_3 & s_4 \end{pmatrix}.$$

When applying the fuzzy quantifier $Q = [0.2, 0.8]$ to compute the weights of $F^{TOWA}_{w,\varepsilon}$, we have that $w = (0.0833, 0.4167, 0.4167, 0.0833)^T$. Let $\varepsilon = 1$, we consider using the consensus operator $F^{TOWA}_{w,\varepsilon}$ to aggregate L^1, L^2, L^3 and L^4. In this case, the consensus operator $F^{TOWA}_{w,\varepsilon}$ reduces to the TOWA operator. The obtained collective linguistic preference relation is L^c:

$$L^c = \begin{pmatrix} (s_4, 0) & (s_5, 0.1668) & (s_7, -0.3332) & (s_4, 0.2501) & (s_7, 0.3334) \\ (s_3, -0.1668) & (s_4, 0) & (s_4, -0.2499) & (s_5, 0.2501) & (s_6, -0.3332) \\ (s_1, 0.3332) & (s_4, 0.2499) & (s_4, 0) & (s_4, -0.1666) & (s_6, 0.3334) \\ (s_4, -0.2501) & (s_3, -0.2501) & (s_4, 0.1666) & (s_4, 0) & (s_5, -0.2499) \\ (s_1, -0.3334) & (s_2, 0.3332) & (s_2, -0.3334) & (s_3, 0.2499) & (s_4, 0) \end{pmatrix}$$

Without loss of generality, we also set $\varepsilon = 0.08$. Using the consensus operator $F^{TOWA}_{w,\varepsilon}$ to aggregate L^1, L^2, L^3 and L^4, we obtain the adjusted preference relations $\overline{L^1}, \overline{L^2}, \overline{L^3}, \overline{L^4}$, and the collective linguistic preference relation $\overline{L^c}$. They are listed as follows:

$$\overline{L^1} = \begin{pmatrix} (s_4, 0) & (s_4, -0.2) & (s_7, -0.5) & (s_3, 0.2) & (s_7, 0) \\ (s_4, 0.2) & (s_4, 0) & (s_4, -0.1) & (s_4, 0.2) & (s_6, -0.3) \\ (s_2, -0.5) & (s_4, 0.1) & (s_4, 0) & (s_3, 0.3) & (s_6, 0) \\ (s_5, -0.2) & (s_4, -0.2) & (s_5, -0.3) & (s_4, 0) & (s_4, -0.3) \\ (s_1, 0) & (s_2, 0.3) & (s_2, 0) & (s_4, 0.3) & (s_4, 0) \end{pmatrix},$$

$$\overline{L^2} = \begin{pmatrix} (s_4, 0) & (s_5, 0) & (s_6, -0.5) & (s_4, 0.2) & (s_8, -0.3) \\ (s_3, 0) & (s_4, 0) & (s_3, 0.2) & (s_4, 0.2) & (s_4, 0.3) \\ (s_3, -0.5) & (s_5, -0.2) & (s_4, 0) & (s_3, 0.3) & (s_7, -0.3) \\ (s_4, -0.2) & (s_4, -0.2) & (s_5, -0.3) & (s_4, 0) & (s_5, -0.3) \\ (s_0, 0.3) & (s_4, -0.3) & (s_1, 0.3) & (s_3, 0.3) & (s_4, 0) \end{pmatrix},$$

$$\overline{L^3} = \begin{pmatrix} (s_4, 0) & (s_4, 0) & (s_7, -0.5) & (s_4, 0.4) & (s_7, 0) \\ (s_4, 0) & (s_4, 0) & (s_3, -0.5) & (s_5, 0.4) & (s_6, -0.3) \\ (s_2, -0.5) & (s_6, -0.5) & (s_4, 0) & (s_4, 0.1) & (s_5, 0.3) \\ (s_4, -0.4) & (s_3, -0.4) & (s_4, -0.1) & (s_4, 0) & (s_4, -0.5) \\ (s_1, 0) & (s_2, 0.3) & (s_3, -0.3) & (s_5, -0.5) & (s_4, 0) \end{pmatrix},$$

$$\overline{L^4} = \begin{pmatrix} (s_4, 0) & (s_5, 0.2) & (s_5, 0.3) & (s_3, 0.2) & (s_6, 0.3) \\ (s_3, -0.2) & (s_4, 0) & (s_3, 0.2) & (s_5, 0.2) & (s_4, 0.3) \\ (s_3, -0.3) & (s_5, -0.2) & (s_4, 0) & (s_3, 0.3) & (s_6, 0) \\ (s_5, -0.2) & (s_3, -0.2) & (s_5, -0.3) & (s_4, 0) & (s_5, -0.3) \\ (s_2, -0.3) & (s_4, 0.3) & (s_2, 0) & (s_3, 0.3) & (s_4, 0) \end{pmatrix},$$

$$\overline{L^c} = \begin{pmatrix} (s_4, 0) & (s_5, -0.5) & (s_5, -0.0167) & (s_4, -0.2833) & (s_7, 0) \\ (s_4, -0.5) & (s_4, 0) & (s_3, 0.2) & (s_5, -0.2833) & (s_5, 0) \\ (s_2, 0.0167) & (s_5, -0.2) & (s_4, 0) & (s_3, 0.3667) & (s_6, 0) \\ (s_4, 0.2833) & (s_4, 0.2833) & (s_5, -0.3667) & (s_4, 0) & (s_4, 0.1833) \\ (s_1, 0) & (s_3, 0) & (s_2, 0) & (s_4, -0.1833) & (s_4, 0) \end{pmatrix}.$$

4.1.3 Properties of the Operator

When using $F_{w,\varepsilon}^{TOWA}$ to respectively aggregate $a = \{a_1, a_2, \ldots, a_n\}$ and $b = \{b_1, b_2, \ldots, b_n\}$, let $\overline{a} = \{\overline{a_1}, \overline{a_2}, \ldots, \overline{a_n}\}$ and $\overline{b} = \{\overline{b_1}, \overline{b_2}, \ldots, \overline{b_n}\}$ be two sets of the corresponding linguistic 2-tuples to be adjusted. Before proposing some desired properties of the consensus operator $F_{w,\varepsilon}^{TOWA}$, we first introduce Lemmas 4.4 and 4.5.

Lemma 4.4 *$min\{\overline{a_i}\} \geq min\{a_i\}$ and $max\{\overline{a_i}\} \leq max\{a_i\}$.*

Proof We first prove that $min\{\overline{a_i}\} \geq min\{a_i\}$. Using reduction to absurdity, we assume that $min\{\overline{a_i}\} < min\{a_i\}$. Without loss of generality, we also assume that $P \subset \{1, 2, \ldots, n\}$ and $\overline{a_p} < min\{a_i\}$ for $p \in P$. Let $\overline{\overline{a}} = \{\overline{\overline{a_1}}, \ldots, \overline{\overline{a_n}}\}$, where

$$\overline{\overline{a_i}} = \begin{cases} min\{a_i\}\ ,\ for\ i \in P \\ \overline{a_i}\ ,\ for\ i \overline{\in} P \end{cases}, \tag{4.51}$$

We find that

$$d(F_w^{TOWA}(\overline{\overline{a_1}}, \ldots, \overline{\overline{a_n}}), max(\overline{\overline{a_i}})) \leq \beta, \tag{4.52}$$

and

$$d(F_w^{TOWA}(\overline{\overline{a_1}}, \ldots, \overline{\overline{a_n}}), min(\overline{\overline{a_i}})) \leq \beta. \tag{4.53}$$

Thus, $\overline{\overline{a}}$ is a feasible solution to $P_{4.1}$. Since

$$(d(a, \overline{\overline{a}}))^2 - (d(a, \overline{a}))^2$$

$$= \frac{1}{T^2 n} \sum_{i \in P} (\Delta^{-1}(\overline{\overline{a_i}}) - \Delta^{-1}(\overline{a_i}))(\Delta^{-1}(\overline{\overline{a_i}}) + \Delta^{-1}(\overline{a_i}) - 2\Delta^{-1}(a_i)) < 0, \tag{4.54}$$

we have that $d(a, \overline{\overline{a}}) - d(a, \overline{a}) < 0$, which contradicts the fact that $\overline{a}$ is the optimal solution to $P_{4.1}$. Similarly, we prove that $max\{\overline{a_i}\} \leq max\{a_i\}$. This completes the proof of Lemma 4.4.

From Lemma 4.4, we can obtain Corollary 4.1.

Corollary 4.1 $d(min\{\overline{a_i}\}, max\{\overline{a_i}\}) \leq d(min\{a_i\}, max\{a_i\})$.

Lemma 4.5 *If* $\Delta^{-1}(a_i) + \Delta^{-1}(b_i) = g/2$ *and* $w_i = w_{n+1-i}$ *for* $i = 1, \ldots, n$, *then* $\Delta^{-1}(\overline{a_i}) + \Delta^{-1}(\overline{b_i}) = g/2$.

Proof When using $F_{w,\varepsilon}^{TOWA}$ to aggregate $\{a_1, a_2, \ldots, a_n\}$ (or $\{b_1, b_2, \ldots, b_n\}$), let Ω_a (or Ω_b) be the feasible sets corresponding to $P_{4.2}$. When

$$\overline{a} \in \Omega_a, \tag{4.55}$$

we find that

$$Neg(\overline{a}) \in \Omega_b \tag{4.56}$$

under condition that $w_i = w_{i+n-1}$.

Since

$$d(a, \overline{a}) = \min_{x \in \Omega_a} d(a, x). \tag{4.57}$$

we have that

$$d(b, Neg(\overline{a})) = \min_{x \in \Omega_b} d(b, x). \tag{4.58}$$

under the condition $w_i = w_{i+n-1}$.

Based on Eqs. (4.56) and (4.58), we have that $\overline{b_i} = Neg(\overline{a_i})$, that is $\Delta^{-1}(\overline{a_i}) + \Delta^{-1}(\overline{b_i}) = g/2$. This completes the proof of Lemma 4.5.

In the following, we introduce some desired properties of the consensus operator $F_{w,\varepsilon}^{TOWA}$.

Property 4.1 *For any consensus operator* $F_{w,\varepsilon}^{TOWA}$

$$min\{a_i\} \leq F_{w,\varepsilon}^{TOWA}(a_1, a_2, \ldots, a_n) \leq max\{a_i\}.$$

Proof From the implementation of the consensus operator, we have that

$$min\{\overline{a_i}\} \leq F_{w,\varepsilon}^{TOWA}(a_1, a_2, \ldots, a_n) = F_{w}^{TOWA}(\overline{a_1}, \overline{a_2}, \ldots, \overline{a_n}) \leq max\{\overline{a_i}\}. \quad (4.59)$$

By Lemma 4.4, we obtain that $min\{a_i\} \leq F_{w,\varepsilon}^{TOWA}(a_1, a_2, \ldots, a_n) \leq max\{a_i\}$. This completes the proof of Property 4.1.

Property 4.2 *Commutativity. Let* $\{a_1, a_2, \ldots, a_n\}$ *be a set of linguistic 2-tuples and* $\{d_1, d_2, \ldots, d_n\}$ *be a permutation of the* $\{a_1, a_2, \ldots, a_n\}$*. Then, for any consensus operator* $F_{w,\varepsilon}^{TOWA}$,

$$F_{w,\varepsilon}^{TOWA}(a_1, a_2, \ldots, a_n) = F_{w,\varepsilon}^{TOWA}(d_1, d_2, \ldots, d_n).$$

Property 4.3 *Monotonicity. Let* $\{a_1, a_2, \ldots, a_n\}$ *be a set of linguistic 2-tuples, let* $\{c_1, c_2, \ldots, c_n\}$ *be another set of linguistic 2-tuples, such that* $\forall i,\ a_i \geq c_i$*. Then, when* $n \leq 2$,

$$F_{w,\varepsilon}^{TOWA}(c_1, c_2, \ldots, c_n) \leq F_{w,\varepsilon}^{TOWA}(a_1, a_2, \ldots, a_n),$$

for any consensus operator $F_{w,\varepsilon}^{TOWA}$.

Proof Without loss of generality, we first suppose that $a_i > a_j$ and $c_i > c_j$ for $i > j$. Property 4.3 can be obtained by showing $\overline{a_i} \geq \overline{c_i}$ for $i = 1, 2, \ldots, n$. When $n = 1$, it is obvious that $\overline{a_1} \geq \overline{c_1}$. When $n = 2$, using reduction to absurdity, we assume that $\overline{a_1} < \overline{c_1}$ or $\overline{a_2} < \overline{c_2}$. We consider three cases:

Case A: $\overline{a_1} < \overline{c_1}$ and $\overline{a_2} < \overline{c_2}$. In this case,

$$\begin{aligned}(d(a,\overline{a}))^2 - (d(a,\overline{c}))^2 &= \frac{1}{nT^2}(\overline{a_1}^2 + \overline{a_2}^2 - \overline{c_1}^2 - \overline{c_2}^2 + 2a_1(\overline{c_1} - \overline{a_1}) + 2a_2(\overline{c_2} - \overline{a_2})) \\ &> \frac{1}{nT^2}(\overline{a_1}^2 + \overline{a_2}^2 - \overline{c_1}^2 - \overline{c_2}^2 + 2c_1(\overline{c_1} - \overline{a_1}) + 2c_2(\overline{c_2} - \overline{a_2})) \\ &= (d(c,\overline{a}))^2 - (d(c,\overline{c}))^2 \geq 0. \qquad (4.60)\end{aligned}$$

Thus, we have that $d(a, \overline{a}) > d(a, \overline{c})$, which contradicts the fact that $\overline{a}$ is the adjusted preference values in using $F_{w,\varepsilon}^{TOWA}$ to aggregate $\{a_1, a_2, \ldots, a_n\}$.

Case B: $\overline{a_1} < \overline{c_1}$ and $\overline{a_2} \geq \overline{c_2}$. In this case, let $\overline{\overline{c}} = \{\overline{\overline{c_1}}, \overline{\overline{c_2}}\}$, where $\overline{\overline{c_1}} = \overline{a_1}$ and $\overline{\overline{c_2}} = min\{\overline{a_2}, c_2\}$, we have that

$$d(\overline{\overline{c_i}}, F_w^{EOWA}(\overline{\overline{c_1}}, \overline{\overline{c_2}})) \leq \varepsilon, \quad i = 1, 2 \tag{4.61}$$

and

$$d(c, \overline{\overline{c}}) < d(c, \overline{c}). \tag{4.62}$$

This contradicts the fact that $\overline{c}$ is the adjusted preference values in using $F_{w,\varepsilon}^{TOWA}$ to aggregate $\{c_1, c_2, \ldots, c_m\}$.

Case C: $\overline{a_1} \geq \overline{c_1}$ and $\overline{a_2} < \overline{c_2}$. In this case, let $\overline{\overline{a}} = \{\overline{\overline{a_1}}, \overline{\overline{a_2}}\}$, where $\overline{\overline{a_1}} = max\{\overline{c_1}, a_1\}$ and $\overline{\overline{a_2}} = \overline{c_2}$, similarly, we have that

$$d(\overline{\overline{a_i}}, F_w^{TOWA}(\overline{\overline{a_1}}, \overline{\overline{a_2}})) \leq \varepsilon, \quad i = 1, 2 \tag{4.63}$$

and

$$d(a, \overline{\overline{a}}) < d(a, \overline{a}). \tag{4.64}$$

This contradicts the fact that $\overline{a}$ is the adjusted preference values in using $F_{w,\varepsilon}^{TOWA}$ to aggregate $\{a_1, a_2, \ldots, a_n\}$.

Based on the three cases, we have $\overline{a_1} \geq \overline{c_1}$ and $\overline{a_2} \geq \overline{c_2}$. Consequently, $F_{w,\varepsilon}^{TOWA}$ $(c_1, c_2) \leq F_{w,\varepsilon}^{TOWA}$ (a_1, a_2), which completes this proof of Property 4.3.

Property 4.4 *Idempotency. If* $a_i = a$ *for* $i = 1, \ldots, n$*, then for any consensus operator* $F_{w,\varepsilon}^{TOWA}(a_1, a_2, \ldots, a_n) = a$.

Property 4.5 *Let* $\{a_1, a_2, \ldots, a_n\}$ *be a set of linguistic 2-tuples. If* $w_i = w_{n+1-i}$ *for* $i = 1, \ldots, n$*, then,*

$$\Delta^{-1}(F_{w,\varepsilon}^{TOWA}(a_1, a_2, \ldots, a_n)) + \Delta^{-1}(F_{w,\varepsilon}^{TOWA}(Neg(a_1), Neg(a_2), \ldots, Neg(a_n))) = g/2.$$

for any consensus operator $F_{w,\varepsilon}^{TOWA}$.

Proof Let $F_{w,\varepsilon}^{TOWA}(a_1, a_2, \ldots, a_n) = F_w^{TOWA}(\overline{a_1}, \overline{a_2}, \ldots, \overline{a_n})$. By Lemma 4.5, we have that

$$F_{w,\varepsilon}^{TOWA}(Neg(a_1), Neg(a_2), \ldots, Neg(a_n)) = F_w^{TOWA}(Neg(\overline{a_1}), Neg(\overline{a_2}), \ldots, Neg(\overline{a_n})).$$

Since $w_i = w_{n+1-i}$, we have that

$$F_w^{TOWA}(\overline{a_1}, \overline{a_2}, \ldots, \overline{a_n}) = Neg(F_w^{TOWA}(Neg(\overline{a_1}), Neg(\overline{a_2}), \ldots, Neg(\overline{a_n}))). \tag{4.65}$$

Consequently, Δ^{-1} $(F_{w,\varepsilon}^{TOWA}$ $(a_1, a_2, \ldots, a_n))+\Delta^{-1}$ $(F_{w,\varepsilon}^{TOWA}$ $(Neg(a_1), Neg(a_2), \ldots, Neg(a_n))) = g/2$. This completes the proof of Property 4.5.

There are a set of alternatives $X = \{X_1, \ldots, X_m\}$, and a set of linguistic preference relations $\{L^1, \ldots, L^n\}$, where $L^k = (l_{ij}^k)_{m\times m}$, and $l_{ij}^k \in S$ represents the preference degree or intensity of alternative X_i over alternative X_j for expert E_k. In general, we assume that L^k is reciprocal in the sense that $l_{ij}^k \oplus l_{ji}^k = s_{g/2}$ ($s_{g/2}$ is the median term in S). Using the consensus operator $F_{w,\varepsilon}^{TOWA}$, we derive a collective preference relation, $L^c = (l_{ij}^c)_{m\times m}$ indicating the global preference between every pair of alternatives. In this case,

$$l_{ij}^c = F_{w,\varepsilon}^{TOWA}\left((l_{ij}^1, 0), \ldots, (l_{ij}^k, 0), \ldots, (l_{ij}^n, 0)\right) = F_w^{TOWA}\left(\overline{l_{ij}^1}, \ldots, \overline{l_{ij}^k}, \ldots, \overline{l_{ij}^n}\right). \quad (4.66)$$

Theorem 4.6 *When $w_i = w_{n+1-i}$ for $i = 1, \ldots, n$, we have that*

(1) $\overline{L^k}$ $(k = 1, 2, \ldots, n)$ and L^c are reciprocal linguistic preference relations,

(2) Let $d(L^c, \overline{L^k}) = \sqrt{\frac{2}{m(m-1)} \sum\limits_{j=i+1}^{m} \sum\limits_{i=1}^{m} \left(\frac{\Delta^{-1}(l_{ij}^c) - \Delta^{-1}(\overline{l_{ij}^k})}{T}\right)^2}$, then $d(L^c, \overline{L^k}) \leq \varepsilon$.

Proof From Lemma 4.5, we have that $\overline{L^k} (k = 1, 2, \ldots, n)$ are reciprocal linguistic preference relations under the condition that $w_i = w_{n+1-i}$ for $i = 1, \ldots, n$. By Property 4.5, we have that L^c is also a reciprocal linguistic preference relation. Then, we obtain that $d(L^c, \overline{L^k}) \leq \varepsilon$.

This completes the proof of Theorem 4.6.

4.2 Consensus Under Hesitant Linguistic Context

In this section, we propose an optimization-based two-stage model to support the consensus reaching in the GDM with hesitant linguistic assessments, and analyze the desirable properties of the hesitant consensus model.

4.2.1 Hesitant Consensus Problem

Here, we review the concept and related operation laws of the hesitant fuzzy linguistic term set (HFLTS), and propose the consensus problem in the GDM with the HFLTS.

(1) HFLTS

Torra [22] introduced the hesitant fuzzy set. Similar to the situations that are described and managed by hesitant fuzzy sets in [22], experts may hesitate among several linguistic terms to assess an alternative. Bearing this idea in mind, Rodríguez et al. [19] gave the concepts regarding HFLTSs as follows:

Definition 4.1 ([19]) Let $S = \{s_j | j = 0, 1, \ldots, g\}$ be a linguistic term set, where $g + 1$ is odd. A hesitant fuzzy linguistic term set (HFLTS), M^s, is an ordered finite subset of consecutive linguistic terms of S.

In this section, if $s_j \in M^s$, we define that s_j is a simple term in M^s. For example, s_2 is a simple term in $M^s = \{s_2, s_3, s_4\}$.

Once the concept of HFLTS has been introduced, some operation laws can be performed on HFLTSs.

Let $S = \{s_j | j = 0, 1, \ldots, g\}$ be as before. Let M^s, M_1^s and M_2^s be three HFLTSs of S.

Definition 4.2 The upper bound M^{s+} and lower bound M^{s-} of the HFLTS M^s are defined as:

(i) $M^{s+} = max(s_i) = s_j$ where $s_i \in M^s$;
(ii) $M^{s-} = min(s_i) = s_j$ where $s_i \in M^s$.

Definition 4.3 The envelope of the HFLTS M^s, denoted as $env(M^s)$, is a linguistic interval whose limits are obtained by means of lower bound M^{s-} and upper bound M^{s+}, i.e.,

$$env(M^s) = [M^{s-}, M^{s+}]. \tag{4.67}$$

Based on the concept of the envelope of the HFLTS, $env(M^s)$, the definition of the comparison between two HFLTSs is defined as Definition 4.4.

Definition 4.4 The comparison between M_1^s and M_2^s is defined as follows:

(i) $M_1^s > M_2^s$ if $env(M_1^s) > env(M_2^s)$,
(ii) $M_1^s = M_2^s$ if $env(M_1^s) = env(M_2^s)$.

The latest proposals regarding the HFLTSs include the formulas for comparing HFLTSs [25], the aggregation operators on HFLTSs [1, 23, 25] and the consistency measures for hesitant fuzzy linguistic preference relations, etc. Rodríguez et al. [20] provided an overview to present a clear view about the different concepts, tools and trends related to the use of hesitant fuzzy sets in decision making.

(2) Proposed problem in the hesitant linguistic GDM

Let $E = \{E_1, E_2, \ldots, E_n\} (n \geq 2)$ and $S = \{s_0, s_1, \ldots, s_g\}$ be as before. In some situations, it is more appropriate for experts to provide their preferences using HFLTSs instead of single linguistic term set. Here, we consider the experts provide their original preferences by HFLTSs of S, denoted by $H_i (i = 1, 2, \ldots, n)$.

Then, the decision problem is how to obtain a collective opinion with an acceptable consensus level in the hesitant linguistic GDM. In order to deal with this open decision problem, we must tackle the following two challenges [8]:

(i) How to measure the consensus level among experts in hesitant linguistic GDM problems.
(ii) How to design a procedure to provide adjustment suggestions, which help the experts reach a consensus in the hesitant linguistic GDM context. Particularly, we hope to minimize the adjustments between original and adjusted hesitant linguistic opinions in the consensus building.

These two challenges will be tackled in the rest of the chapter.

4.2.2 Hesitant Consensus Measure

Here, we develop a novel distance-based approach for measuring the consensus level in the hesitant linguistic GDM.

Let M^s be a HFLTS of S, and let $\#(M^s)$ denote the number of simple linguistic terms in M^s. For example, if $M^s = \{s_2, s_3, s_4, s_5\}$, then $\#(M^s) = 4$. For two arbitrary HFLTSs, N_1 and N_2, here we propose the following equation to measure the difference between N_1 and N_2, as Eq. (4.68):

$$d(N_1, N_2) = \#(N_1 \cup N_2) - \#(N_1 \cap N_2). \tag{4.68}$$

The value of $d(N_1, N_2)$ has a definite implication, and measures the number of different simple terms between N_1 and N_2. For example, $N_1 = \{s_1, s_2, s_3\}$ and $N_2 = \{s_3, s_4\}$, the number of different simple terms between N_1 and N_2 is $\#(N_1 \cup N_2) - \#(N_1 \cap N_2) = 3$. Then, we use $d(N_1, N_2) = 3$ to measure the difference between N_1 and N_2.

Furthermore, we prove this difference measure between two HFLTSs is a distance metric as Theorem 4.7.

Theorem 4.7 *Let N_1, N_2 and N_3 be three HFLTSs. Then, the following conditions are satisfied:*

(1) $d(N_1, N_2) = 0$ if and only if $N_1 = N_2$;
(2) $d(N_1, N_2) = d(N_2, N_1)$;
(3) $d(N_1, N_3) + d(N_3, N_2) \geq d(N_1, N_2)$;
(4) $0 \leq d(N_1, N_2) \leq \#(N_1 \cup N_2)$.

Proof Obviously, $d(N_1, N_2)$ satisfies conditions (1), (2) and (4). Here we only have to prove that $d(N_1, N_2)$ satisfies the condition (3).

Because

$$\begin{aligned} d(N_1, N_3) + d(N_3, N_2) &= \#(N_1 \cup N_3) - \#(N_1 \cap N_3) + \#(N_3 \cup N_2) - \#(N_3 \cap N_2) \\ &= \#(N_1) + \#(N_3) - 2\#(N_1 \cap N_3) + \#(N_3) + \#(N_2) - 2\#(N_3 \cap N_2) \end{aligned} \tag{4.69}$$

and

$$d(N_1, N_2) = \#(N_1) + \#(N_2) - 2\#(N_1 \cap N_2) \tag{4.70}$$

Based on Eqs. (4.69) and (4.70), then

$$d(N_1, N_3) + d(N_3, N_2) - d(N_1, N_2) = 2(\#(N_3) + \#(N_1 \cap N_2) - \#(N_1 \cap N_3) - \#(N_3 \cap N_2)). \tag{4.71}$$

To discuss the Eq. (4.71), we consider three cases:

Case 1: if $\#(N_1 \cap N_3) + \#(N_3 \cap N_2) < \#(N_3)$, then $d(N_1, N_3) + d(N_3, N_2) - d(N_1, N_2) > 0$.

Case 2: if $\#(N_1 \cap N_3) + \#(N_3 \cap N_2) = \#(N_3)$, then $d(N_1, N_3) + d(N_3, N_2) - d(N_1, N_2) \geq 0$.

Case 3: if $\#(N_1 \cap N_3) + \#(N_3 \cap N_2) > \#(N_3)$, we have $\#(N_1 \cap N_3) + \#(N_3 \cap N_2) = \#(N_3) + \#(N_1 \cap N_2 \cap N_3)$, then $d(N_1, N_3) + d(N_3, N_2) - d(N_1, N_2) \geq 0$.

This completes the proof of Theorem 4.7.

Note 4.3 To our knowledge, Falc et al. [9] proposed a distance measure for sets of consecutive terms, which is based on the computing with position indexes (see Definition 4.6). The distance measure proposed in [9] can guarantee the accuracy when the linguistic term set distributes uniform and symmetrical. The new distance measure for HFLTSs has a definite implication, which measures the number of different simple terms between two HFLTSs. The new proposed distance measure for HFLTSs not only can be used in the hesitant linguistic GDM with uniformly and symmetrically distributed term set, but also in the hesitant linguistic GDM with the linguistic term set that are not uniformly and symmetrically distributed.

Usually, distance based approaches are used to measure the consensus level among experts' opinions. Based on Eq. (4.68), an approach for measuring consensus level in the hesitant linguistic GDM can be proposed as Definition 4.5.

Definition 4.5 Let H_i represent the individual opinion of E_i and let H^c represent the collective opinion. Here, we define the consensus level of E_i as Eq. (4.72):

$$CL(E_i) = \frac{d(H_i, H^c)}{\#(H_i \cup H^c)}, \tag{4.72}$$

i.e.,

$$CL(E_i) = 1 - \frac{\#(H_i \cap H^c)}{\#(H_i \cup H^c)}. \tag{4.73}$$

Clearly, $CL(E_i) \in [0, 1]$. The value of $CL(E_i)$ has a definite implication, and measures the proportion of the different simple terms between H_i and H^c. The smaller $CL(E_i)$ value indicates the higher consensus level associated with E_i. When $CL(E_i) = 0$, the expert E_i achieves full agreement with the collective opinion.

4.2.3 *Minimizing the Adjusted Simple Terms*

Using the novel distance-based consensus measure, we develop an optimization-based two-stage procedure to obtain the optimal adjusted suggestions in the hesitant linguistic GDM context, which minimizes the number of adjusted simple terms in the consensus building.

(1) Minimum adjusted simple terms model

Usually, distance-based approaches are used to measure the adjustments between original and adjusted individual opinions. Here, we use the distance defined by Eq. (4.68) to measure the adjustments between H_i and $\overline{H_i}(i = 1, 2, \ldots, n)$, i.e.,

$$d(H_i, \overline{H_i}) = \#(H_i \cup \overline{H_i}) - \#(H_i \cap \overline{H_i}). \tag{4.74}$$

In order to preserve the original preference information as much as possible, we hope to minimize the adjustments between the original and adjusted individual opinions of all experts. Namely,

$$\min_{\overline{H_i}} \sum_{i=1}^{n} d(H_i, \overline{H_i}) = \min_{\overline{H_i}} \sum_{i=1}^{n} (\#(H_i \cup \overline{H_i}) - \#(H_i \cap \overline{H_i})). \tag{4.75}$$

Here, in the sense of the distance defined by Eq. (4.68), the value of $\min_{\overline{H_i}} \sum_{i=1}^{n} d(H_i, \overline{H_i})$ has a definite implication, and measures the minimum number of adjusted simple terms of all experts in the consensus building.

Meanwhile, the adjusted individual opinions $\overline{H_i}$ are of acceptable consensus, i.e.,

$$CL(E_i) = 1 - \frac{\#(\overline{H_i} \cap \overline{H^c})}{\#(\overline{H_i} \cup \overline{H^c})} \leq \varepsilon, \quad i = 1, 2, \ldots, n. \tag{4.76}$$

Furthermore, $\overline{H_i}(i = 1, 2, \ldots, n)$ and $\overline{H^c}$ are HFLTSs, i.e.,

$$\overline{H_i} \in H^s(i = 1, 2, \ldots, n), \tag{4.77}$$

and

$$\overline{H^c} \in H^s \tag{4.78}$$

where H^s is the set of the HFLTSs of S, and $H^s = \{M^s | M^s \textit{ is a HFLTS of } S\}$.

Additionally, in order to get relatively precise collective opinion $\overline{H^c}$, the upper bound of $\#(\overline{H^c})$ is limited as β, i.e.,

$$\#(\overline{H^c}) \leq \beta. \tag{4.79}$$

Generally, we suggest $\beta \leq 3$.

According to Eqs. (4.75)–(4.79), an optimization-based consensus model in the hesitant linguistic GDM is constructed as:

$$\begin{cases} \min\limits_{\overline{H_i}} \sum\limits_{i=1}^{n} \left(\#\left(H_i \cup \overline{H_i}\right) - \#\left(H_i \cap \overline{H_i}\right)\right) \\ s.t. \begin{cases} 1 - \frac{\#(H_i \cap \overline{H_i})}{\#(H_i \cup \overline{H_i})} \le \varepsilon,\ i = 1, \ldots, n \\ \overline{H_i} \in H^s,\ i = 1, \ldots, n \\ \overline{H^c} \in H^s \\ \#\left(\overline{H^c}\right) \le \beta \end{cases} \end{cases} \tag{4.80}$$

In model (4.80), the constraint condition $1 - \frac{\#(\overline{H_i} \cap \overline{H^c})}{\#(\overline{H_i} \cup \overline{H^c})} \le \varepsilon$ $(i = 1, 2, \ldots, n)$ guarantees all the experts can reach the established consensus threshold ε. Meanwhile, the constraint conditions $\overline{H_i} \in H^s (i = 1, 2, \ldots, n)$ and $\overline{H^c} \in H^s$ guarantee the adjusted opinions are HFLTSs. Denote model (4.80) as $P_{4.3}$, which we call minimum adjusted simple terms model (MASTM).

(2) Procedure to solve minimum adjusted simple terms model

We present a mixed 0-1 linear programming to obtain the optimal solutions to minimum adjusted simple terms model (i.e., $P_{4.3}$).

In order to transform $P_{4.3}$ into a mixed 0-1 linear programming model, three binary variables x_i^j, y_i^j and z^j are introduced, i.e.,

$$x_i^j = \begin{cases} 1, & s_j \in H_i \\ 0, & s_j \notin H_i \end{cases},\ i = 1, 2, \ldots, n;\ j = 0, 1, \ldots, g, \tag{4.81}$$

$$y_i^j = \begin{cases} 1, & s_j \in \overline{H_i} \\ 0, & s_j \notin \overline{H_i} \end{cases},\ i = 1, 2, \ldots, n;\ j = 0, 1, \ldots, g, \tag{4.82}$$

and let

$$z^j = \begin{cases} 1, & s_j \in \overline{H^c} \\ 0, & s_j \notin \overline{H^c} \end{cases},\ j = 0, 1, \ldots, g. \tag{4.83}$$

Let H_i and $\overline{H_i}$ be the original and adjusted opinions associated with the expert E_i, respectively. Let H^c and $\overline{H^c}$ be the original and adjusted collective opinions, respectively. Then, Lemmas 4.6–4.8 are proposed.

Lemma 4.6 $\#(H_i \cup \overline{H_i}) - \#(H_i \cap \overline{H_i}) = \sum_{j=1}^{g} |x_i^j - y_i^j| (i = 1, 2, \ldots, n)$.

Proof Based on Eqs. (4.81) and (4.82), we introduce $\Phi_{H_i}(x)$ to denote $\#(H_i)$, i.e., $\Phi_{H_i}(x) = \sum\limits_{j=0}^{g} x_i^j$ and introduce $\Phi_{\overline{H_i}}(y)$ to denote $\#(\overline{H_i})$, i.e., $\Phi_{\overline{H_i}}(y) = \sum\limits_{j=0}^{g} y_i^j$. Hence,

$$\begin{aligned}\#(H_i \cup \overline{H_i}) - \#(H_i \cap \overline{H_i}) &= \Phi_{H_i}(x) + \Phi_{\overline{H_i}}(y) - 2\sum_{j=0}^{g} x_i^j \cdot y_i^j \\ &= \sum_{j=0}^{g} x_i^j + \sum_{j=0}^{g} y_i^j - 2\sum_{j=0}^{g} x_i^j \cdot y_i^j \\ &= \sum_{j=0}^{g} (x_i^j)^2 + \sum_{j=0}^{g} (y_i^j)^2 - 2\sum_{j=0}^{g} x_i^j \cdot y_i^j \\ &= \sum_{j=0}^{g} (x_i^j - y_i^j)^2\end{aligned}$$

Due to x_i^j, y_i^j are binary variables, Thus $\#(H_i \cup \overline{H_i}) - \#(H_i \cap \overline{H_i}) = \sum_{j=0}^{g} \left| x_i^j - y_i^j \right|$. This completes the proof of Lemma 4.6.

Lemma 4.7 $\frac{\#(\overline{H_i} \cap \overline{H^c})}{\#(\overline{H_i} \cup \overline{H^c})} = \frac{\sum_{j=0}^{g} y_i^j + \sum_{j=0}^{g} z^j - \sum_{j=0}^{g} |y_i^j - z^j|}{\sum_{j=0}^{g} y_i^j + \sum_{j=0}^{g} z^j + \sum_{j=0}^{g} |y_i^j - z^j|} (i = 1, 2, \ldots, n)$.

Proof According to the Lemma 4.6, we can easily obtain:

$$\#(\overline{H_i} \cup \overline{H^c}) - \#(\overline{H_i} \cap \overline{H^c}) = \sum_{j=0}^{g} \left| y_i^j - z^j \right| \tag{4.84}$$

while

$$\#(\overline{H_i} \cup \overline{H^c}) = \sum_{j=0}^{g} y_i^j + \sum_{j=0}^{g} z^j - \#(\overline{H_i} \cap \overline{H^c}) \tag{4.85}$$

Based on Eqs. (4.84) and (4.85), then

$$\#(\overline{H_i} \cap \overline{H^c}) = \frac{\sum_{j=0}^{g} y_i^j + \sum_{j=0}^{g} z^j - \sum_{j=0}^{g} \left| y_i^j - z^j \right|}{2}, \tag{4.86}$$

and

$$\#(\overline{H_i} \cup \overline{H^c}) = \frac{\sum_{j=0}^{g} y_i^j + \sum_{j=0}^{g} z^j + \sum_{j=0}^{g} \left| y_i^j - z^j \right|}{2} \tag{4.87}$$

According to Eqs. (4.86) and (4.87), $\frac{\#(\overline{H_i} \cap \overline{H^c})}{\#(\overline{H_i} \cup \overline{H^c})} = \frac{\sum_{j=0}^{g} y_i^j + \sum_{j=0}^{g} z^j - \sum_{j=0}^{g} \left| y_i^j - z^j \right|}{\sum_{j=0}^{g} y_i^j + \sum_{j=0}^{g} z^j + \sum_{j=0}^{g} \left| y_i^j - z^j \right|}$. This completes the proof of Lemma 4.7.

Lemma 4.8 *(i)* $\overline{H_i}(i = 1, 2, \ldots, n)$ *is a HFLTS if and only if the following conditions are satisfied:*

(a) $\sum_{j=0}^{g-1} |y_i^{j+1} - y_i^j| \le 2, \quad i = 1, 2, \ldots, n;$
(b) $y_i^0 + y_i^g \le 1, \quad i = 1, 2, \ldots, n.$

(ii) $\overline{H^c}$ *is a HFLTS if and only if the following conditions are satisfied:*

(a) $\sum_{j=0}^{g-1} |z^{j+1} - z^j| \le 2;$
(b) $z^0 + z^g \le 1.$

Proof **Part 1**: Proving that $\overline{H_i}(i = 1, 2, \ldots, n)$ is a HFLTS if and only if the following conditions are satisfied:
(i) $\sum\limits_{j=0}^{g-1} \left|y_i^{j+1} - y_i^j\right| \le 2 \ (i = 1, 2, \ldots, n)$
(ii) $y_i^0 + y_i^g \le 1 \ (i = 1, 2, \ldots, n)$.

Necessity: If $\overline{H_i}(i = 1, 2, \ldots, n)$ is a HFLTS, then there are three distribution cases in $\overline{H_i}$:

Case 1: $\overline{H_i} = \{s_0, \ldots, s_k\} \ (0 \le k < g)$, then $\sum\limits_{j=0}^{g-1} \left|y_i^{j+1} - y_i^j\right| = 1$ and $y_i^0 + y_i^g = 1$;

Case 2: $\overline{H_i} = \left\{s_k, \ldots, s_g\right\} \ (0 \le k < g)$, then $\sum\limits_{j=0}^{g-1} \left|y_i^{j+1} - y_i^j\right| = 1$ and $y_i^0 + y_i^g = 1$;

Case 3: $\overline{H_i} = \left\{s_k, \ldots, s_{k+q}\right\} \ (k > 0, q \ge 0 \ and \ k + q < g)$, then $\sum\limits_{j=0}^{g-1} \left|y_i^{j+1} - y_i^j\right| = 2$ and $y_i^0 + y_i^g = 0$.

Therefore, if $\overline{H_i}(i = 1, 2, \ldots, n)$ is a HFLTS, it satisfies $\sum\limits_{j=0}^{g-1} \left|y_i^{j+1} - y_i^j\right| \le 2(i = 1, 2, \ldots, n)$ and $y_i^0 + y_i^g \le 1(i = 1, 2, \ldots, n)$.

Sufficiency: If $\sum\limits_{j=0}^{g-1} \left|y_i^{j+1} - y_i^j\right| \le 2(i = 1, 2, \ldots, n)$, then there are four distribution cases in $\overline{H_i}(i = 1, 2, \ldots, n)$:

Case 1: $\overline{H_i} = \{s_0, \ldots s_k\} \ (0 \le k < g)$, then $\sum\limits_{j=0}^{g-1} \left|y_i^{j+1} - y_i^j\right| = 1$.

Case 2: $\overline{H_i} = \left\{s_k, \ldots s_g\right\} \ (0 < k \le g)$, then $\sum\limits_{j=0}^{g-1} \left|y_i^{j+1} - y_i^j\right| = 1$.

Case 3: $\overline{H_i} = \left\{s_k, \ldots s_{k+q}\right\} \ (k > 0, q \ge 0 \ and \ k + q < g)$, then $\sum\limits_{j=0}^{g-1} \left|y_i^{j+1} - y_i^j\right| = 2$.

Case 4: $\overline{H_i} = \left\{s_0, \ldots s_k, s_{k+p}, \ldots s_g\right\} \ (k \ge 0, p \ge 2 \ and \ k + p \le g)$, then $\sum\limits_{j=0}^{g-1} |y_i^{j+1} - y_i^j| = 2$.

Requiring $y_i^0 + y_i^g \leq 1$ for $\overline{H_i}$, Case 4 is excluded. In Cases 1–3, simple terms in $\overline{H_i}$ are consecutive, i.e., $\overline{H_i}(i = 1, 2, \ldots, n)$ is a HFLTS.

Part 2: Proving that $\overline{H^c}$ is a HFLTS if and only if the following conditions are satisfied:

(i) $\sum_{j=0}^{g-1} \left| z^{j+1} - z_i^j \right| \leq 2$

(ii) $z^0 + z^g \leq 1$.

The proof of Part 2 is the same as the proof of Part 1. This completes the proof of Lemma 4.8.

Based on Lemmas 4.6–4.8, we can obtain Lemma 4.9.

Lemma 4.9 *$P_{4.3}$ can be transformed into model (4.88):*

$$\begin{cases} \min \sum_{i=1}^{n} \sum_{j=0}^{g} \left| x_i^j - y_i^j \right| \\ s.t. \begin{cases} 1 - \dfrac{\sum_{j=0}^{g} y_i^j + \sum_{j=0}^{g} z^j - \sum_{j=0}^{g} \left| y_i^j - z^j \right|}{\sum_{j=0}^{g} y_i^j + \sum_{j=0}^{g} z^j + \sum_{j=0}^{g} \left| y_i^j - z^j \right|} \leq \varepsilon, \ i = 1, \ldots, n \\ \sum_{j=0}^{g-1} \left| y_i^{j+1} - y_i^j \right| \leq 2, \ i = 1, \ldots, n \\ y_i^0 + y_i^g \leq 1, \ i = 1, \ldots, n \\ \sum_{j=0}^{g-1} \left| z^{j+1} - z^j \right| \leq 2 \\ z^0 + z^g \leq 1, \\ \sum_{j=0}^{g} z^j \leq \beta, \\ y_i^j \in \{0, 1\}, \ i = 1, \ldots, n; \ j = 0, 1, \ldots, g \\ z^j \in \{0, 1\}, \ j = 0, 1, \ldots, g \end{cases} \end{cases} \tag{4.88}$$

Based on Lemma 4.9, the optimal solution to $P_{4.3}$ can be obtained by solving model (4.88). In order to solve model (4.88), Theorem 4.8 is provided to transform model (4.88) into a mixed 0-1 linear programming model.

Theorem 4.8 *By introducing eight transformed decision variables: $b_i^j = x_i^j - y_i^j$, $c_i^j = |b_i^j|$, $e_i^j = y_i^j - z^j$, $f_i^j = |e_i^j|$, $h_i^j = y_i^{j+1} - y_i^j$, $o_i^j = |h_i^j|$, $u^j = z^{j+1} - z^j$ and $v^j = |u^j|$. Model (4.88) can be transformed into a mixed 0-1 linear programming model (4.89):*

$$
\begin{cases}
\min \sum_{i=1}^{n} \sum_{j=0}^{g} c_i^j \\
s.t. \begin{cases}
b_i^j = x_i^j - y_i^j, \ \ i = 1, 2, \ldots, n;\ j = 0, 1, \ldots, g \\
b_i^j \le c_i^j, \ \ i = 1, 2, \ldots, n;\ j = 0, 1, \ldots, g \\
-b_i^j \le c_i^j, \ \ i = 1, 2, \ldots, n;\ j = 0, 1, \ldots, g \\
\varepsilon \sum_{j=0}^{g} y_i^j + \varepsilon \sum_{j=0}^{g} z^j - (2-\varepsilon) \sum_{j=0}^{g} f_i^j \ge 0, \ \ i = 1, 2, \ldots, n \\
e_i^j = y_i^j - z^j, \ \ i = 1, 2, \ldots, n;\ j = 0, 1, \ldots, g \\
e_i^j \le f_i^j, \ \ i = 1, 2, \ldots, n;\ j = 0, 1, \ldots, g \\
-e_i^j \le f_i^j, \ \ i = 1, 2, \ldots, n;\ j = 0, 1, \ldots, g \\
\sum_{j=0}^{g-1} o_i^j \le 2, \ \ i = 1, 2, \ldots, n \\
h_i^j = y_i^{j+1} - y_i^j, \ \ i = 1, 2, \ldots, n;\ j = 0, 1, \ldots, g-1 \\
h_i^j \le o_i^j, \ \ i = 1, 2, \ldots, n;\ j = 0, 1, \ldots, g-1 \\
-h_i^j \le o_i^j, \ \ i = 1, 2, \ldots, n;\ j = 0, 1, \ldots, g-1 \\
y_i^0 + y_i^g \le 1, \ \ i = 1, 2, \ldots, n \\
\sum_{j=0}^{g-1} v^j \le 2 \\
u^j = z^{j+1} - z^j, \ \ j = 0, 1, \ldots, g-1 \\
u^j \le v^j, \ \ j = 0, 1, \ldots, g-1 \\
-u^j \le v^j, \ \ j = 0, 1, \ldots, g-1 \\
z^0 + z^g \le 1 \\
\sum_{j=0}^{g} z^j \le \beta \\
y_i^j = 0 \ or \ 1, \ \ i = 1, 2, \ldots, n;\ j = 0, 1, 2, \ldots, g \\
z^j = 0 \ or \ 1, \ \ j = 0, 1, \ldots, g
\end{cases}
\end{cases}
\tag{4.89}
$$

Proof Eight transformed decision variables are introduced as: $b_i^j = x_i^j - y_i^j$, $c_i^j = \left|b_i^j\right|$, $e_i^j = y_i^j - z^j$, $f_i^j = \left|e_i^j\right|$, $h_i^j = y_i^{j+1} - y_i^j$, $o_i^j = \left|h_i^j\right|$, $u^j = z^{j+1} - z^j$ and $v^j = \left|u^j\right|$. Then

(i) $b_i^j = x_i^j - y_i^j$, $b_i^j \le c_i^j$ and $-b_i^j \le c_i^j$ guarantee $c_i^j \ge \left|b_i^j\right| = \left|x_i^j - y_i^j\right|$.
(ii) $e_i^j = y_i^j - z^j$, $e_i^j \le f_i^j$ and $-e_i^j \le f_i^j$ guarantee $f_i^j \ge \left|e_i^j\right| = \left|y_i^j - z^j\right|$.
(iii) $h_i^j = y_i^{j+1} - y_i^j$, $h_i^j \le o_i^j$ and $-h_i^j \le o_i^j$ guarantee $o_i^j \ge \left|h_i^j\right| = \left|y_i^{j+1} - y_i^j\right|$.
(iv) $u^j = z^{j+1} - z^j$, $u^j \le v^j$, and $-u^j \le v^j$ guarantee $v^j \ge \left|u^j\right| = \left|z^{j+1} - z^j\right|$.

Therefore, $P_{4.3}$ can be equivalently transformed into the mixed 0-1 linear programming model $P'_{4.3}$. This completes the proof of Theorem 4.8.

Denote model (4.89) as $P'_{4.3}$. Theorem 4.8 guarantees the equivalence between $P_{4.3}$ and $P'_{4.3}$. So, to simplify the notation, models $P_{4.3}$ and $P'_{4.3}$ are called $P_{4.3}$ in this book.

(3) Optimizing the optimal solutions to minimum adjusted simple terms model

In some situations, the optimal solution(s) to $P_{4.3}$ is not unique. Particularly, some of the optimal solutions are not reasonable enough (in some sense). For illustrating this idea, an example is shown as follows:

Example 4.4. Let $S^1 = \{s_0^1, s_2^1, \ldots, s_6^1\}$ be the established linguistic term set. The five experts $E = \{E_1, E_2, E_3, E_4, E_5\}$ provide their preferences by HFLTSs of S^1 to assess an alternative. We assume that the original individual opinions of these five experts are $H = (H_1, H_2, H_3, H_4, H_5) = (\{s_3^1, s_4^1\}, \{s_4^1, s_5^1, s_6^1\}, \{s_0^1, s_1^1\}, \{s_6^1\}, \{s_2^1, s_3^1, s_4^1\})$. Then we use $P_{4.3}$ to obtain the optimal solution, i.e., $\overline{H} = (\overline{H_1}, \overline{H_2}, \overline{H_3}, \overline{H_4}, \overline{H_5}) = (\{s_3^1, s_4^1\}, \{s_2^1, s_3^1, s_4^1, s_5^1, s_6^1\}, \{s_0^1, s_1^1, s_2^1, s_3^1, s_4^1\}, \{s_2^1, s_3^1\}, \{s_2^1, s_3^1, s_4^1\})$, and $\overline{H^c} = \{s_2^1, s_3^1, s_4^1\}$. Here, we can construct another set of HFLTSs, $\overline{\overline{H}} = (\overline{\overline{H_1}}, \overline{\overline{H_2}}, \overline{\overline{H_3}}, \overline{\overline{H_4}}, \overline{\overline{H_5}})$ and $\overline{\overline{H^c}}$, where $\overline{\overline{H_i}} = \begin{cases} \overline{H_i}, \ i = 1, 2, 3, 5 \\ \{s_3^1, s_4^1\}, \ i = 4 \end{cases}$ and $\overline{\overline{H^c}} = \{s_2^1, s_3^1, s_4^1\}$. $\overline{\overline{H_i}}(i = 1, 2, 3, 4, 5)$ satisfies $1 - \frac{\#(\overline{\overline{H_i}} \cap \overline{\overline{H^c}})}{\#(\overline{\overline{H_i}} \cup \overline{\overline{H^c}})} \leq \varepsilon$ and $\sum_{i=1}^{5} d(H_i, \overline{\overline{H_i}}) = \sum_{i=1}^{5} d(H_i, \overline{H_i})$. As a result, $\overline{\overline{H}}$ is also an optimal solution to $P_{4.3}$.

Through Example 4.4, we present two issues of $P_{4.3}$:

(i) In some situations, the optimal solution(s) to $P_{4.3}$ is not unique.
(ii) s is an ordered linguistic term set, intuitively, the deviation between H_4 (i.e., $\{s_6^1\}$) and $\overline{H_4}$ (i.e., $\{s_2^1, s_3^1\}$) is larger than the deviation between H_4 and $\overline{\overline{H_4}}$ (i.e., $\{s_3^1, s_4^1\}$), which implies some of the optimal solutions to $P_{4.3}$ are not reasonable enough.

So, it is necessary to further optimize the optimal solutions to $P_{4.3}$. In order to do this, we introduce another approach for measuring the distance between two HFLTSs. Let $s \in S$, we denote $I(s)$ be the position index (or lower index) of s in S. For example, if $s = s_j$, then $I(s_j) = j$. According to the Manhattan distance, a natural distance between two HFLTSs is defined as Definition 4.6.

Definition 4.6 For two HFLTSs N_1 and N_2, the distance between N_1 and N_2 can be defined as

$$d(N_1, N_2) = |I(N_1^+) - I(N_2^+)| + |I(N_1^-) - I(N_2^-)|, \tag{4.90}$$

where N_1^+ and N_1^- respectively denote the upper bound and the lower bound of N_1, and N_2^+ and N_2^- respectively denote the upper bound and the lower bound of N_2.

Then, we optimize the optimal solutions to $P_{4.3}$ by minimizing the Manhattan distance between H_i and $\overline{OH_i}$, defined by Definition 4.6, i.e.,

$$\min_{\overline{OH_i}} \sum_{i=1}^{n} l(H_i, \overline{OH_i}) = \min_{\overline{OH_i}} \sum_{i=1}^{n} (|I(\overline{OH_i}^{+}) - I(H_i^{+}))| + |I(\overline{OH_i}^{-}) - I(H_i^{-})|) \quad (4.91)$$

where $(\overline{OH_1}, \ldots, \overline{OH_n}, \overline{OH^c})$ is the optimal solution to $P_{4.3}$, and thus must satisfy the Conditions (4.92)–(4.96)

$$\sum_{i=1}^{n} d(H_i, \overline{OH_i}) = \sum_{i=1}^{n} (\#(H_i \cup \overline{OH_i}) - \#(H_i \cap \overline{OH_i})) = OM, \quad (4.92)$$

where OM is the optimal objective function value of $P_{4.3}$,

$$1 - \frac{\#(\overline{OH_i} \cap \overline{OH^c})}{\#(\overline{OH_i} \cup \overline{OH^c})} \leq \varepsilon \; i = 1, 2, \ldots, n \quad (4.93)$$

$$\overline{OH_i} \in H^s \; (i = 1, 2, \ldots, n) \quad (4.94)$$

$$\overline{OH^c} \in H^s \quad (4.95)$$

and

$$\#(\overline{OH^c}) \leq \beta \quad (4.96)$$

Then, based on Eqs. (4.91)–(4.96), a two-stage model can be constructed as:

$$\begin{cases} \min_{\overline{OH_i}} \sum_{k=1}^{n} (|I(\overline{OH_i}^{+}) - I(H_i^{+})| + |I(\overline{OH_i}^{-}) - I(H_i^{-})|) \\ s.t. \begin{cases} \sum_{i=1}^{n} (\#(H_i \cup \overline{OH_i}) - \#(H_i \cap \overline{OH_i})) = OM \\ 1 - \frac{\#(\overline{OH_i} \cap \overline{OH^c})}{\#(\overline{OH_i} \cup \overline{OH^c})} \leq \varepsilon, \quad i = 1, 2, \ldots, n \\ \overline{OH_i} \in H^s, \quad i = 1, 2, \ldots, n \\ \overline{OH^c} \in H^s \\ \#(\overline{OH^c}) \leq \beta \end{cases} \end{cases} \quad (4.97)$$

In model (4.97), the constraint condition $1 - \frac{\#(\overline{OH_i} \cap \overline{OH^c})}{\#(\overline{OH_i} \cup \overline{OH^c})} \leq \varepsilon \; (i = 1, \ldots, n)$ guarantees all the experts can reach the established consensus threshold ε. Meanwhile, the constraint condition $\sum_{i=1}^{n} (\#(H_i \cup \overline{OH_i}) - \#(H_i \cap \overline{OH_i})) = OM$ guarantees the adjusted simple terms between original and adjusted individual opinions are minimum. The constraint conditions $\overline{OH_i} \in H^s(i = 1, \ldots, n)$ and $\overline{OH^c} \in H^s$ guarantee the adjusted opinions are HFLTSs. Denote model (4.97) as $P_{4.4}$.

Subsequently, we show that $P_{4.4}$ can be transformed into a mixed 0-1 linear programming model. In order to do so, Lemma 4.10 is proposed.

Lemma 4.10 *For* $i = 1, 2, \ldots, n$, *the following equations can be obtained*

(i) $I(\overline{OH_i}^-) = \max\limits_{j=0,\ldots,g} \sum\limits_{k=0}^{j} (y_i^j - y_i^k)$

(ii) $I(\overline{OH_i}^+) = \max\limits_{j=0,\ldots,g} \sum\limits_{k=0}^{j} (y_i^j - y_i^k) + \sum\limits_{j=0}^{g} y_i^j - 1$

(iii) $I(H_i^-) = \max\limits_{j=0,\ldots,g} \sum\limits_{k=0}^{j} (x_i^j - x_i^k)$

(iv) $I(H_i^+) = \max\limits_{j=0,\ldots,g} \sum\limits_{k=0}^{j} (x_i^j - x_i^k) + \sum\limits_{j=0}^{g} x_i^j - 1$

Proof For $i = 1, 2, \ldots, n$, we assume $\overline{OH_i} = \{s_p, \ldots, s_{p+q}\} (p \geq 0, 0 \leq q = \sum\limits_{j=0}^{g} y_i^j - 1 \leq g)$. Based on Eq. (4.82), the values $y_i^j (j = 0, 1, \ldots, g)$ of $\overline{OH_i}$ can be denoted as $\{y_i^0, y_i^1, \ldots, y_i^g\} = \{\underbrace{0, \ldots 0}_{p-1}, \underbrace{1, \ldots 1}_{\sum_{j=0}^{g} y_i^j}, 0, \ldots 0\}$.

For all $j \in [0, g]$, we have

$$\sum_{k=0}^{j} (y_i^j - y_i^k) = \begin{cases} 0, & j \in [0, p-1] \\ p, & j \in [p, p + \sum\limits_{j=0}^{g} y_i^j - 1] \\ -\sum\limits_{j=0}^{g} y_i^j, & j \in [p + \sum\limits_{j=0}^{g} y_i^j, g] \end{cases}. \tag{4.98}$$

According to (4.98), thus

$$I(\overline{OH_i}^-) = p = \max_{j=0,\ldots,g} \sum_{k=0}^{j} (y_i^j - y_i^k)$$

and

$$I(\overline{OH_i}^+) = \max_{j=0,\ldots,g} \sum_{k=0}^{j} (y_i^j - y_i^k) + \sum_{j=0}^{g} y_i^j - 1$$

In the same way, we can obtain

$$I(H_i^-) = \max_{j=0,\ldots,g} \sum_{k=0}^{j} (x_i^j - x_i^k)$$

and

$$I(H_i^+) = \max_{j=0,\ldots,g} \sum_{k=0}^{j} (x_i^j - x_i^k) + \sum_{j=0}^{g} x_i^j - 1$$

This completes the proof of Lemma 4.10.

Let

$$\max_{j=0,\ldots,g} \sum_{k=0}^{j} (x_i^j - x_i^k) + \sum_{j=0}^{g} x_i^j = X_i \quad i = 1, 2, \ldots, n; \tag{4.99}$$

$$\left| \max_{j=0,\ldots,g} \sum_{k=0}^{j} (y_i^j - y_i^k) + \sum_{j=0}^{g} y_i^j - X_i \right| \leq r_i \quad i = 1, 2, \ldots, n \tag{4.100}$$

and let

$$\left| \max_{j=0,\ldots,g} \sum_{k=0}^{j} (y_i^j - y_i^k) + \sum_{j=0}^{g} x_i^j - X_i \right| \leq t_i \quad i = 1, 2, \ldots, n \tag{4.101}$$

Based on Lemmas 4.6–4.10, we can obtain Theorem 4.9.

Theorem 4.9 *$P_{4.4}$ can be transformed into model (4.102):*

$$\begin{cases} \min \sum_{i=1}^{n} (r_i + t_i) \\ s.t. \begin{cases} \max_{j=0,\ldots,g} \sum_{k=0}^{j} (x_i^j - x_i^k) + \sum_{j=0}^{g} x_i^j = X_i, & i = 1, \ldots, n \\ \sum_{k=0}^{j} (y_i^j - y_i^k) - X_i + \sum_{j=0}^{g} y_i^j \leq r_i, & i = 1, \ldots, n;\ j = 0, \ldots, g \\ X_i - \sum_{k=0}^{j} (y_i^j - y_i^k) - \sum_{j=0}^{g} y_i^j \leq r_i + M(1 - w_{ij}), & i = 1, \ldots, n;\ j = 0, \ldots, g \\ \sum_{j=0}^{g} w_{ij} \geq 1, & i = 1, \ldots, n \\ \sum_{k=0}^{j} (y_i^j - y_i^k) - X_i + \sum_{j=0}^{g} x_i^j \leq t_i, & i = 1, \ldots, n;\ j = 0, \ldots, g \\ X_i - \sum_{k=0}^{j} (y_i^j - y_i^k) - \sum_{j=0}^{g} x_i^j \leq t_i + M(1 - h_{ij}), & i = 1, \ldots, n;\ j = 0, \ldots, g \\ \sum_{j=0}^{g} h_{ij} \geq 1, & i = 1, \ldots, n \\ \sum_{i=1}^{n} \sum_{j=0}^{g} \left| x_i^j - y_i^j \right| = OM \\ 1 - \dfrac{\sum_{j=0}^{g} y_i^j + \sum_{j=0}^{g} z^j - \sum_{j=0}^{g} \left| y_i^j - z^j \right|}{\sum_{j=0}^{g} y_i^j + \sum_{j=0}^{g} z^j + \sum_{j=0}^{g} \left| y_i^j - z^j \right|} \leq \varepsilon, & i = 1, \ldots, n \\ \sum_{j=0}^{g-1} \left| y_i^{j+1} - y_i^j \right| \leq 2, & i = 1, \ldots, n \\ y_i^0 + y_i^g \leq 1, & i = 1, \ldots, n \\ \sum_{j=0}^{g-1} \left| z^{j+1} - z^j \right| \leq 2, & i = 1, \ldots, n \\ z^0 + z^g \leq 1 \\ \sum_{j=0}^{g} z^j \leq \beta \\ y_i^j, w_{ij}, h_{ij} = 0 \text{ or } 1, & i = 1, \ldots, n;\ j = 0, \ldots, g \\ z^j = 0 \text{ or } 1, & j = 0, \ldots, g \end{cases} \end{cases} \tag{4.102}$$

where M is a very large number.

Proof The process of obtaining Theorem 4.9 can be divided into four steps:

Step 1: The constraint conditions in $P_{4.4}$, i.e.,

$$\begin{cases} \sum_{i=1}^{n} (\#(H_i \cup \overline{OH_i}) - \#(H_i \cap \overline{OH_i})) = OM \\ 1 - \frac{\#(\overline{OH_i} \cap \overline{OH^c})}{\#(\overline{OH_i} \cup \overline{OH^c})} \leq \varepsilon, \qquad i = 1, \ldots, n \\ \overline{OH_i} \in H^s \qquad i = 1, \ldots, n \\ \overline{OH^c} \in H^s, \\ \#(\overline{OH^c}) \leq \beta \end{cases} \tag{4.103}$$

can be transformed into the following mixed 0-1 constraint conditions in model (4.102):

$$\begin{cases} \sum_{i=1}^{n} \sum_{j=0}^{g} \left| x_i^j - y_i^j \right| = OM \\ 1 - \frac{\sum_{j=0}^{g} y_i^j + \sum_{j=0}^{g} z^j - \sum_{j=0}^{g} \left| y_i^j - z^j \right|}{\sum_{j=0}^{g} y_i^j + \sum_{j=0}^{g} z^j + \sum_{j=0}^{g} \left| y_i^j - z^j \right|} \leq \varepsilon, \qquad i = 1, \ldots, n \\ \sum_{j=0}^{g-1} \left| y_i^{j+1} - y_i^j \right| \leq 2, \qquad i = 1, \ldots, n \\ y_i^0 + y_i^g \leq 1, \qquad i = 1, \ldots, n \\ \sum_{j=0}^{g-1} \left| z^{j+1} - z^j \right| \leq 2, \\ z^0 + z^g \leq 1 \\ \sum_{j=0}^{g} z^j \leq \beta \end{cases} \tag{4.104}$$

Step 2: Let $\max_{j=0,\ldots,g} \sum_{k=0}^{j} (x_i^j - x_i^k) + \sum_{j=0}^{g} x_i^j = X_i (i = 1, \ldots, n)$, and based on Lemma 4.10, the objective function $\min_{\overline{OH_i}} \sum_{i=1}^{n} (|I(\overline{OH_i}^+) - I(H_i^+)| + |I(\overline{OH_i}^-) - I(H_i^-)|)$ in $P_{4.4}$ can be transformed as

$$\min \sum_{i=1}^{n} (|\max_{j=0,\ldots,g} \sum_{k=0}^{j} (y_i^j - y_i^k) + \sum_{j=0}^{g} y_i^j - X_i| + |\max_{j=0,\ldots,g} \sum_{k=0}^{j} (y_i^j - y_i^k) + \sum_{j=0}^{g} x_i^j - X_i|). \tag{4.105}$$

Step 3: Introducing two transformed decision variables: r_i and $t_i (i = 1, 2, \ldots, n)$.

Similar to the proof of Theorem 4.8, let $|\max_{j=0,\ldots,g}\sum_{k=0}^{j}(y_i^j-y_i^k)+\sum_{j=0}^{g}y_i^j-X_i|\leq r_i$ and $|\max_{j=0,\ldots,g}\sum_{k=0}^{j}(y_i^j-y_i^k)+\sum_{j=0}^{g}x_i^j-X_i|\leq t_i$, then Eq. (4.105) can be further transformed as

$$\min\sum_{i=1}^{n}(r_i+t_i). \tag{4.106}$$

Meanwhile, several new constraint conditions are produced as:

$$\max_{j=0,\ldots,g}\sum_{k=0}^{j}(y_i^j-y_i^k)+\sum_{j=0}^{g}y_i^j-X_i\leq r_i \tag{4.107}$$

$$X_i-\sum_{j=0}^{g}y_i^j-\max_{j=0,\ldots,g}\sum_{k=0}^{j}(y_i^j-y_i^k)\leq r_i \tag{4.108}$$

$$\max_{j=0,\ldots,g}\sum_{k=0}^{j}(y_i^j-y_i^k)+\sum_{j=0}^{g}x_i^j-X_i\leq t_i \tag{4.109}$$

$$X_i-\sum_{j=0}^{g}x_i^j-\max_{j=0,\ldots,g}\sum_{k=0}^{j}(y_i^j-y_i^k)\leq t_i \tag{4.110}$$

Step 4: Transforming Eqs. (4.107)–(4.110) into linear constraint conditions in model (4.102).

(i) For $i=1,2,\ldots,n$, $\max_{j=0,\ldots,g}\sum_{k=0}^{j}(y_i^j-y_i^k)+\sum_{j=0}^{g}y_i^j-X_i\leq r_i$ if and only if the following constraints are satisfied:

$$\sum_{k=0}^{j}(y_i^j-y_i^k)-X_i+\sum_{j=0}^{g}y_i^j\leq r_i,\ \ j=0,1,\ldots,g. \tag{4.111}$$

(ii) For $i=1,2,\ldots,n$, $\max_{j=0,\ldots,g}\sum_{k=0}^{j}(y_i^j-y_i^k)+\sum_{j=0}^{g}x_i^j-X_i\leq t_i$ if and only if the following constraints are satisfied:

$$\sum_{k=0}^{j}(y_i^j-y_i^k)-X_i+\sum_{j=o}^{g}x_i^j\leq t_i,\ j=0,1,\ldots,g. \tag{4.112}$$

(iii) For $i = 1, 2, \ldots, n$, $X_i - \sum_{j=0}^{g} y_i^j - r_i \leq \max_{j=0,\ldots,g} \sum_{k=0}^{j} (y_i^j - y_i^k)$ if and only if the following constraints are satisfied:

$$X_i - \sum_{j=0}^{g} y_i^j - r_i \leq \sum_{k=0}^{j} (y_i^j - y_i^k) + M(1 - w_{ij}) \tag{4.113}$$

and

$$\sum_{j=0}^{g} w_{ij} \geq 1, \tag{4.114}$$

where M is a very large number, $w_{ij} \in \{0, 1\}$.

(iv) For $i = 1, 2, \ldots, n$, $X_i - \sum_{j=0}^{g} x_i^j - t_i \leq \max_{j=0,\ldots,g} \sum_{k=0}^{j} (y_i^j - y_i^k)$ if and only if the following constraints are satisfied:

$$X_i - \sum_{j=0}^{g} x_i^j - t_i \leq \sum_{k=1}^{j} (y_i^j - y_i^k) + M(1 - h_{ij})(j = 0, 1, \ldots, g) \tag{4.115}$$

and

$$\sum_{j=0}^{g} h_{ij} \geq 1, \tag{4.116}$$

where M is a very large number, $h_{ij} \in \{0, 1\}$.

Therefore, based on Eqs. (4.104), (4.106) and (4.111)–(4.116), all the constraint conditions in $P_{4.4}$ can be equivalently transformed into the constraint conditions in model (4.102). This completes the proof of Theorem 4.9.

Similar to Theorem 4.8, model (4.102) can be equivalently transformed into a mixed 0-1 linear programming model.

Note 4.4 Solving models $P_{4.3}$ and $P_{4.4}$ obtains the optimal adjusted individual opinions, which should only be considered as a decision aid that experts use as a reference to modify their individual opinions.

Table 4.2 The values of x_i^j

x_i^j	$j=0$	$j=1$	$j=2$	$j=3$	$j=4$	$j=5$	$j=6$
$i=1$	0	0	0	1	1	0	0
$i=2$	0	0	0	0	1	1	1
$i=3$	1	1	0	0	0	0	0
$i=4$	0	0	0	0	0	0	1
$i=5$	0	0	1	1	1	0	0

Note 4.5 In classical GDM studies, the number of experts in the most effective GDM context is less than 7 (see Thomas and Fink [21]). Meanwhile, the granularity of a linguistic term set used by experts without confusion is less than 9 (see Miller [17]). As a result, the proposed mixed 0-1 linear programming models usually are small-scale optimization problems, except in the case of the large-scale GDM recently proposed in [13]. Generally, mixed 0-1 linear programming models with a few hundred binary variables can be effectively solved by several software packages (e.g., Lingo and CEPLEX).

(2) Numerical examples

In order to show how these theoretical results work in practice, let us consider the following two examples.

(i) Example 4.5

We suppose that five experts, $E = \{E_1, E_2, \ldots, E_5\}$, want to assess an alternative using HFLTSs of the linguistic term set $S^{Example\ 4.5}$, where $S^{Example\ 4.5} = \{s_0 = neither,\ s_1 = very\ low,\ s_2 = low,\ s_3 = medium,\ s_4 = high,\ s_5 = very\ high,\ s_6 = absolute\}$.

Experts provide their original individual preferences using HFLTSs of $S^{Example\ 4.5}$, i.e., $H = (H_1, H_2, H_3, H_4, H_5) = (\{s_3, s_4\}, \{s_4, s_5, s_6\}, \{s_0, s_1\}, \{s_6\}, \{s_2, s_3, s_4\})$.

According to these original individual opinions, using Eq. (4.81) obtains the values of $x_i^j (i = 1, 2, \ldots, 5;\ j = 0, 1, \ldots, 6)$, which are listed in Table 4.2.

We set $\varepsilon = 0.4$ and $\beta = 3$. After determining the values of $x_i^j (i = 1, \ldots, 5;\ j = 0, \ldots, 6)$, ε and β, we use the mixed 0-1 linear programming model $P'_{4.3}$ to obtain model (4.117):

$$
\begin{cases}
\min \sum_{i=1}^{5}\sum_{j=0}^{6} c_i^j \\
s.t. \begin{cases}
x_i^j - y_i^j \le c_i^j, & i=1,2,3,4,5;\ j=0,1,2,3,4,5,6 \\
y_i^j - x_i^j \le c_i^j, & i=1,2,3,4,5;\ j=0,1,2,3,4,5,6 \\
0.4\sum_{j=0}^{6} y_i^j + 0.4\sum_{j=0}^{6} z^j - 1.6\sum_{j=0}^{6} f_i^j \ge 0, & i=1,2,3,4,5 \\
y_i^j - z^j \le f_i^j, & i=1,2,3,4,5;\ j=0,1,2,3,4,5,6 \\
z^j - y_i^j \le f_i^j, & i=1,2,3,4,5;\ j=0,1,2,3,4,5,6 \\
\sum_{j=0}^{5} o_i^j \le 2, & i=1,2,3,4,5 \\
y_i^{j+1} - y_i^j \le o_i^j, & i=1,2,3,4,5;\ j=0,1,2,3,4,5 \\
y_i^j - y_i^{j+1} \le o_i^j, & i=1,2,3,4,5;\ j=0,1,2,3,4,5 \\
y_i^0 + y_i^6 \le 1, & i=1,2,3,4,5 \\
\sum_{j=0}^{5} v^j \le 2 \\
z^{j+1} - z^j \le v^j, & j=0,1,2,3,4,5 \\
z^j - z^{j+1} \le v^j, & j=0,1,2,3,4,5 \\
z^0 + z^6 \le 1 \\
\sum_{j=0}^{6} z^j \le 3 \\
y_i^j = 0 \text{ or } 1, & i=1,2,3,4,5;\ j=0,1,2,3,4,5,6 \\
z^j = 0 \text{ or } 1, & j=0,1,2,3,4,5,6
\end{cases}
\end{cases}
\tag{4.117}
$$

Solving model (4.117) by the software package LINGO, we obtain the values of $y_i^j (i=1,\ldots,5;\ j=0,\ldots,6)$ and $z^j\ (j=0,1,\ldots,6)$, which are listed in Tables 4.3 and 4.4, respectively.

Subsequently, based on Eqs. (4.82) and (4.83), we can obtain the adjusted individual opinions, i.e., $\overline{H} = (\overline{H_1}, \overline{H_2}, \overline{H_3}, \overline{H_4}, \overline{H_5}) = (\{s_3, s_4\}, \{s_2, s_3, s_4, s_5, s_6\}, \{s_0, s_1, s_2, s_3, s_4\}, \{s_2, s_3\}, \{s_2, s_3, s_4\})$ and the adjusted collective opinion $\overline{H^c} = \{s_2, s_3, s_4\}$.

Table 4.3 The values of y_i^j

y_i^j	$j=0$	$j=1$	$j=2$	$j=3$	$j=4$	$j=5$	$j=6$
$i=1$	0	0	0	1	1	0	0
$i=2$	0	0	1	1	1	1	1
$i=3$	1	1	1	1	1	0	0
$i=4$	0	0	1	1	0	0	1
$i=5$	0	0	1	1	1	0	0

Table 4.4 The values of z^j

	$j=0$	$j=1$	$j=2$	$j=3$	$j=4$	$j=5$	$j=6$
z^j	0	0	0	1	1	0	0

Let $OM = \sum_{i=1}^{5} d(H_i, \overline{H_i}) = 8$ be the optimal objective function value of $P_{4.3}$. After determining the value of OM, we use $P_{4.4}$ further to optimize the optimal solutions to model (4.117). Finally, we can obtain the optimal adjusted individual opinions, i.e., $\overline{OH} = (\overline{OH_1}, \overline{OH_2}, \overline{OH_3}, \overline{OH_4}, \overline{OH_5}) = (\{s_3, s_4\}, \{s_2, s_3, s_4, s_5, s_6\}, \{s_0, s_1, s_2, s_3, s_4\}, \{s_3, s_4\}, \{s_2, s_3, s_4\})$ and the optimal adjusted collective opinion $\overline{OH^c} = \{s_2, s_3, s_4\}$.

Clearly, $\sum_{i=1}^{5} d(H_i, \overline{H_i}) = 8$, $\sum_{i=1}^{5} l(H_i, \overline{H_i}) = 12$, $\sum_{i=1}^{5} d(H_i, \overline{OH_i}) = 8$ and $\sum_{i=1}^{5} l(H_i, \overline{OH_i}) = 10$. In other words, $\overline{OH}$ is also the optimal solution to $P_{4.3}$, however, the Manhattan distance between H_i and $\overline{OH_i} (i = 1, 2, \ldots, n)$ is smaller than the Manhattan distance between H_i and $\overline{H_i} (i = 1, 2, \ldots, n)$.

(ii) Example 4.6

We suppose that a committee composed of seven experts, $E = \{E_1, E_2, \ldots, E_7\}$, want to compare five alternatives $X = \{X_1, X_2, \ldots, X_5\}$ by using HFLTSs of the linguistic term set $S^{Example\ 4.6}$, where $S^{Example\ 4.6} = \{s_0 = neither,\ s_1 = very\ low,\ s_2 = low,\ s_3 = slightly\ low,\ s_4 = medium,\ s_5 = slightly\ high,\ s_6 = high,\ s_7 = very\ high,\ s_8 = absolute\}$, and construct, respectively, the linguistic preference relations $L^k = \left(l_{ij}^k\right)_{5\times 5} (k = 1, 2, \ldots, 7;\ i, j = 1, 2, \ldots, 5)$, where l_{ij}^k denotes the linguistic preference degree of the alternative X_i over X_j for the expert E_k. They are listed as follows:

$$L^1 = \begin{pmatrix} - & \{s_1, s_2\} & \{s_7\} & \{s_2, s_3\} & \{s_5, s_6\} \\ \{s_5, s_6\} & - & \{s_4, s_5\} & \{s_1, s_2, s_3\} & \{s_2\} \\ \{s_2\} & \{s_3, s_4\} & - & \{s_6, s_7\} & \{s_4, s_5, s_6\} \\ \{s_6, s_7\} & \{s_5, s_6, s_7\} & \{s_1, s_2\} & - & \{s_4, s_5, s_6\} \\ \{s_1, s_2\} & \{s_5\} & \{s_1, s_2\} & \{s_1, s_2, s_3\} & - \end{pmatrix},$$

$$L^2 = \begin{pmatrix} - & \{s_1, s_2\} & \{s_4, s_5, s_6\} & \{s_2, s_3, s_4\} & \{s_4, s_5, s_6\} \\ \{s_4, s_5, s_6\} & - & \{s_6\} & \{s_3\} & \{s_0, s_1\} \\ \{s_0, s_1\} & \{s_4\} & - & \{s_7, s_8\} & \{s_4, s_5\} \\ \{s_6, s_7\} & \{s_7\} & \{s_0, s_1, s_2\} & - & \{s_5\} \\ \{s_1, s_2\} & \{s_4, s_5, s_6\} & \{s_1, s_2, s_3\} & \{s_3\} & - \end{pmatrix},$$

$$L^3 = \begin{pmatrix} - & \{s_3, s_4\} & \{s_4, s_5\} & \{s_4\} & \{s_0, s_1, s_2\} \\ \{s_0, s_1, s_2\} & - & \{s_5, s_6\} & \{s_6, s_7\} & \{s_0, s_1, s_2\} \\ \{s_1, s_2\} & \{s_2\} & - & \{s_5\} & \{s_4\} \\ \{s_3\} & \{s_1, s_2\} & \{s_2\} & - & \{s_3, s_4, s_5\} \\ \{s_3, s_4\} & \{s_4, s_5\} & \{s_2\} & \{s_4, s_5, s_6\} & - \end{pmatrix},$$

$$L^4 = \begin{pmatrix} - & \{s_3, s_4\} & \{s_5, s_6\} & \{s_1, s_2\} & \{s_0, s_1\} \\ \{s_4, s_5\} & - & \{s_6, s_7\} & \{s_2, s_3\} & \{s_0, s_1, s_2\} \\ \{s_1, s_2\} & \{s_2, s_3\} & - & \{s_5, s_6\} & \{s_4, s_5, s_6\} \\ \{s_7, s_8\} & \{s_6, s_7\} & \{s_4, s_5\} & - & \{s_4, s_5, s_6\} \\ \{s_3, s_4\} & \{s_4, s_5\} & \{s_1, s_2, s_3\} & \{s_3, s_4\} & - \end{pmatrix},$$

$$L^5 = \begin{pmatrix} - & \{s_1, s_2\} & \{s_6, s_7\} & \{s_1, s_2\} & \{s_4, s_5, s_6\} \\ \{s_5, s_6\} & - & \{s_4, s_5, s_6\} & \{s_1, s_2\} & \{s_0, s_1, s_2\} \\ \{s_0, s_1\} & \{s_3\} & - & \{s_5, s_6, s_7\} & \{s_3, s_4\} \\ \{s_5, s_6, s_7\} & \{s_5, s_6\} & \{s_0, s_1, s_2\} & - & \{s_3, s_4\} \\ \{s_2\} & \{s_4, s_5, s_6\} & \{s_3, s_4\} & \{s_5\} & - \end{pmatrix},$$

$$L^6 = \begin{pmatrix} - & \{s_2, s_3, s_4\} & \{s_7, s_8\} & \{s_3, s_4\} & \{s_4, s_5, s_6\} \\ \{s_5, s_6\} & - & \{s_5, s_6\} & \{s_0, s_1\} & \{s_0, s_1, s_2\} \\ \{s_0, s_1\} & \{s_3, s_4\} & - & \{s_7, s_8\} & \{s_3, s_4, s_5\} \\ \{s_4, s_5\} & \{s_7\} & \{s_0, s_1\} & - & \{s_3, s_4\} \\ \{s_1, s_2\} & \{s_4, s_5, s_6\} & \{s_2, s_3, s_4\} & \{s_5\} & - \end{pmatrix},$$

$$L^7 = \begin{pmatrix} - & \{s_2, s_3\} & \{s_6, s_7, s_8\} & \{s_2, s_3\} & \{s_5\} \\ \{s_6, s_7\} & - & \{s_6, s_7\} & \{s_1, s_2\} & \{s_4, s_5\} \\ \{s_0, s_1, s_2\} & \{s_3, s_4\} & - & \{s_5, s_6\} & \{s_3, s_4\} \\ \{s_5, s_6\} & \{s_7, s_8\} & \{s_4, s_5\} & - & \{s_5, s_6\} \\ \{s_2\} & \{s_0, s_1, s_2\} & \{s_4, s_5\} & \{s_3, s_4\} & - \end{pmatrix}.$$

Here, we set $\beta = 3$ and $\varepsilon = 0.6$. Then, we use models $P_{4.3}$ and $P_{4.4}$ to obtain the optimal adjusted individual preferences $\overline{l_{ij}^1}, \overline{l_{ij}^2}, \ldots, \overline{l_{ij}^7}$ and the adjusted collective preference $\overline{l_{ij}^c}$, associated with $l_{ij}^1, l_{ij}^2, \ldots, l_{ij}^7$, respectively. Let $\overline{L^k} = \left(\overline{l_{ij}^k}\right)_{5\times 5} (k = 1, 2, \ldots, 7)$ and $\overline{L^c} = (\overline{l_{ij}^c})_{5\times 5}$, which are listed as follows:

$$\overline{L^1} = \begin{pmatrix} - & \{s_1, s_2, s_3\} & \{s_6, s_7\} & \{s_2, s_3\} & \{s_5, s_6\} \\ \{s_5, s_6\} & - & \{s_5, s_6\} & \{s_1, s_2, s_3\} & \{s_1, s_2\} \\ \{s_1, s_2\} & \{s_3, s_4\} & - & \{s_6, s_7\} & \{s_4, s_5, s_6\} \\ \{s_6, s_7\} & \{s_5, s_6, s_7\} & \{s_1, s_2\} & - & \{s_4, s_5, s_6\} \\ \{s_1, s_2\} & \{s_5, s_6\} & \{s_1, s_2, s_3\} & \{s_2, s_3, s_4, s_5\} & - \end{pmatrix},$$

$$\overline{L^2} = \begin{pmatrix} - & \{s_1, s_2, s_3\} & \{s_4, s_5, s_6, s_7\} & \{s_2, s_3, s_4\} & \{s_4, s_5, s_6\} \\ \{s_4, s_5, s_6\} & - & \{s_6, s_7\} & \{s_2, s_3\} & \{s_0, s_1\} \\ \{s_0, s_1\} & \{s_3, s_4\} & - & \{s_5, s_6, s_7, s_8\} & \{s_4, s_5\} \\ \{s_6, s_7\} & \{s_6, s_7\} & \{s_0, s_1, s_2\} & - & \{s_4, s_5\} \\ \{s_1, s_2\} & \{s_4, s_5, s_6\} & \{s_1, s_2, s_3\} & \{s_3, s_4\} & - \end{pmatrix},$$

$$\overline{L^3} = \begin{pmatrix} - & \{s_2, s_3, s_4\} & \{s_4, s_5, s_6, s_7\} & \{s_3, s_4\} & \{s_4, s_5\} \\ \{s_4, s_5\} & - & \{s_5, s_6\} & \{s_2, s_3\} & \{s_0, s_1, s_2\} \\ \{s_1, s_2\} & \{s_2, s_3\} & - & \{s_5, s_6\} & \{s_4, s_5\} \\ \{s_5, s_6\} & \{s_5, s_6\} & \{s_1, s_2\} & - & \{s_3, s_4, s_5\} \\ \{s_2, s_3\} & \{s_4, s_5\} & \{s_2, s_3\} & \{s_3, s_4, s_5, s_6\} & - \end{pmatrix},$$

$$\overline{L^4} = \begin{pmatrix} - & \{s_2, s_3, s_4\} & \{s_5, s_6\} & \{s_2, s_3\} & \{s_4, s_5\} \\ \{s_4, s_5\} & - & \{s_6, s_7\} & \{s_2, s_3\} & \{s_0, s_1, s_2\} \\ \{s_1, s_2\} & \{s_2, s_3\} & - & \{s_5, s_6\} & \{s_4, s_5, s_6\} \\ \{s_5, s_6, s_7, s_8\} & \{s_6, s_7\} & \{s_1, s_2\} & - & \{s_4, s_5, s_6\} \\ \{s_2, s_3\} & \{s_4, s_5\} & \{s_1, s_2, s_3\} & \{s_3, s_4\} & - \end{pmatrix},$$

$$\overline{L^5} = \begin{pmatrix} - & \{s_1, s_2, s_3\} & \{s_6, s_7\} & \{s_2, s_3\} & \{s_4, s_5, s_6\} \\ \{s_5, s_6\} & - & \{s_5, s_6\} & \{s_1, s_2\} & \{s_0, s_1, s_2\} \\ \{s_0, s_1\} & \{s_3, s_4\} & - & \{s_5, s_6\} & \{s_3, s_4, s_5\} \\ \{s_5, s_6, s_7\} & \{s_5, s_6\} & \{s_0, s_1, s_2\} & - & \{s_3, s_4, s_5\} \\ \{s_2, s_3\} & \{s_4, s_5, s_6\} & \{s_2, s_3, s_4\} & \{s_4, s_5\} & - \end{pmatrix},$$

$$\overline{L^6} = \begin{pmatrix} - & \{s_2, s_3, s_4\} & \{s_6, s_7\} & \{s_3, s_4\} & \{s_4, s_5, s_6\} \\ \{s_5, s_6\} & - & \{s_5, s_6\} & \{s_1, s_2\} & \{s_0, s_1, s_2\} \\ \{s_0, s_1\} & \{s_3, s_4\} & - & \{s_5, s_6, s_7, s_8\} & \{s_3, s_4, s_5\} \\ \{s_5, s_6\} & \{s_6, s_7\} & \{s_0, s_1\} & - & \{s_3, s_4, s_5\} \\ \{s_1, s_2\} & \{s_4, s_5, s_6\} & \{s_2, s_3, s_4\} & \{s_4, s_5\} & - \end{pmatrix},$$

$$\overline{L^7} = \begin{pmatrix} - & \{s_2, s_3\} & \{s_6, s_7\} & \{s_2, s_3\} & \{s_5, s_6\} \\ \{s_4, s_5, s_6, s_7\} & - & \{s_6, s_7\} & \{s_1, s_2\} & \{s_1, s_2\} \\ \{s_0, s_1, s_2\} & \{s_3, s_4\} & - & \{s_5, s_6\} & \{s_3, s_4, s_5\} \\ \{s_5, s_6\} & \{s_5, s_6, s_7, s_8\} & \{s_1, s_2\} & - & \{s_4, s_5, s_6\} \\ \{s_2, s_3\} & \{s_5, s_6\} & \{s_2, s_3, s_4\} & \{s_3, s_4\} & - \end{pmatrix},$$

$$\overline{L^c} = \begin{pmatrix} - & \{s_2, s_3\} & \{s_5, s_6, s_7\} & \{s_2, s_3, s_4\} & \{s_4, s_5, s_6\} \\ \{s_4, s_5, s_6\} & - & \{s_5, s_6, s_7\} & \{s_1, s_2, s_3\} & \{s_0, s_1, s_2\} \\ \{s_0, s_1, s_2\} & \{s_2, s_3, s_4\} & - & \{s_5, s_6, s_7\} & \{s_4, s_5\} \\ \{s_5, s_6, s_7\} & \{s_5, s_6, s_7\} & \{s_0, s_1, s_2\} & - & \{s_4, s_5\} \\ \{s_0, s_1, s_2\} & \{s_4, s_5, s_6\} & \{s_2, s_3\} & \{s_3, s_4, s_5\} & - \end{pmatrix}.$$

In this way, the experts $E = \{E_1, E_2, \ldots, E_7\}$ can adjust their individual preference relations with the established consensus level.

4.2.4 Properties of the Hesitant Model

Here, we analyze some properties of the hesitant consensus model.

(1) Desirable properties of model $P_{4.3}$

Let S, H_i, $\overline{H_i}$ and $\overline{H^c}$ be as before, then the following properties of $P_{4.3}$ (i.e., Properties 4.6–4.11) are satisfied:

Property 4.6 *Idempotency. If* $H_i = H_{i+1}$ *for* $i = 1, 2, \ldots, n-1$, *then* $\overline{H^c} = H_i$.

Proof The original individual opinions $H_i = H_{i+1}$ for $i = 1, 2, \ldots, n-1$, i.e., $H_1 = H_2 = \cdots = H_n$. We use model $P_{4.3}$ to obtain the adjusted opinions $\overline{H_i} = H_i (i = 1, 2, \ldots, n)$ and $\overline{H^c} = H_i$, which guarantee the consensus level $CL(E_i) = 1 - \frac{\#(\overline{H_i} \cap \overline{H^c})}{\#(\overline{H_i} \cup \overline{H^c})} = 0 (i = 1, \ldots, n)$ (i.e., there is a full and unanimous consensus among experts) and the number of adjusted simple terms $\sum_{i=1}^{n} d(H_i, \overline{H_i}) = 0$. This completes the proof of Property 4.6.

Property 4.7 $\min\limits_{i=1,\ldots,n} (H_i) \leq \overline{H^c} \leq \max\limits_{i=1,\ldots,n} (H_i)$.

Proof From the implementation of the adjusted collective opinion, we have $\min\limits_{i=1,\ldots,n} (\overline{H_i}) \leq \overline{H^c} \leq \max\limits_{i=1,\ldots,n} (\overline{H_i})$. We first prove that $\min\limits_{i=1,\ldots,n} (\overline{H_i}) \geq \min\limits_{i=1,\ldots,n} (H_i)$. Using reduction to absurdity, we assume that $\min\limits_{i=1,\ldots,n} (\overline{H_i}) < \min\limits_{i=1,\ldots,n} (H_i)$. Afterward, we assume that $P \subset \{1, 2, \ldots n\}$ and $\overline{H_p} < \min\limits_{i=1,\ldots,n} (H_i)$ for $p \in P$. Let $\overline{\overline{H}} = (\overline{\overline{H_1}}, \ldots, \overline{\overline{H_n}})$, where

$$\overline{\overline{H_i}} = \begin{cases} \min\limits_{i=1,\ldots,n} (H_i), \ i \in P \\ \overline{H_i}, \ i \notin P \end{cases}$$

We find that

$$1 - \frac{\#(\overline{\overline{H^c}} \cap \max(\overline{\overline{H_i}}))}{\#(\overline{\overline{H^c}} \cup \max(\overline{\overline{H_i}}))} \leq \varepsilon$$

and

$$1 - \frac{\#(\overline{\overline{H^c}} \cap \min\limits_{i=1,\ldots,n} (\overline{\overline{H_i}}))}{\#(\overline{\overline{H^c}} \cup \min\limits_{i=1,\ldots,n} (\overline{\overline{H_i}}))} \leq \varepsilon$$

Thus, $\overline{\overline{H}}$ is a feasible solution to $P_{4.3}$. Since

$$\sum_{i=1}^{n} d(H_i, \overline{\overline{H_i}}) - \sum_{i=1}^{n} d(H_i, \overline{H_i})$$

$$= \sum_{i \in P} (((\#(H_i \cup \overline{\overline{H_i}}) - \#(H_i \cap \overline{\overline{H_i}})) - (\#(H_i \cup \overline{H_i}) - \#(H_i \cap \overline{H_i}))) < 0,$$

we have that $\sum_{i=1}^{n} d(H_i, \overline{\overline{OH_i}}) < \sum_{i=1}^{n} d(H_i, \overline{H_i})$, which contradicts the fact that $(\overline{H_1}, \ldots, \overline{H_n})$ is the optimal solution to $P_{4.3}$. Similarly, we can prove that $\max_{i=1,\ldots,n} \{\overline{H_i}\} \leq \max_{i=1,\ldots,n} \{H_i\}$. This completes the proof of Property 4.7.

Based on Property 4.7, we can obtain that the adjusted collective opinion obtained by $P_{4.3}$ ranges from the minimum original individual opinion to the maximum original individual opinion.

Note 4.6 In [18], $M_1^S > M_2^S$ if $env(M_1^S) > env(M_2^S)$. Furthermore, in this book we define $env(M_1^S) > env(M_2^S)$ if $\frac{I(M_1^{S-})+I(M_1^{S+})}{2} > \frac{I(M_2^{S-})+I(M_2^{S+})}{2}$.

Property 4.8 *Commutativity. Let* $(Q_1, Q_2, \ldots, Q_n)$ *be a permutation of* $(H_1, H_2, \ldots, H_n)$, *and let* $\overline{Q^c}$ *be the adjusted collective opinion that obtained by* $P_{4.3}$, *associated with* $(Q_1, Q_2, \ldots, Q_n)$. *Then,* $\overline{H^c} = \overline{Q^c}$.

Proof Let $\{\sigma(1), \ldots, \sigma(n)\}$ be a permutation of $\{1, \ldots, n\}$ such that $H_{\sigma(i-1)} \geq H_{\sigma(i)}$ for $i = 2, 3, \ldots, n$ and $\{\rho(1), \ldots, \rho(n)\}$ be a permutation of $\{1, \ldots, n\}$ such that $Q_{\sigma(i-1)} \geq Q_{\sigma(i)}$ for $i = 2, 3, \ldots, n$.

Since $(Q_1, Q_2, \ldots, Q_n)$ is a permutation of $(H_1, H_2, \ldots, H_n)$, we have $\sigma(i) = \rho(i)$, $i = 1, 2, \ldots, n$. Applying model $P_{4.3}$, we can obtain $\overline{H^c} = \overline{Q^c}$. This completes the proof of Property 4.8.

Property 4.9 *Monotonicity. Let* $H' = (H_1', H_2', \ldots, H_n')$ *be another set of HFLTSs of S, where* $H_i \leq H_i'$ *for* $i = 1, 2, \ldots, n$. *Let* $\overline{H'^c}$ *be the adjusted collective opinion that obtained by* $P_{4.3}$, *associated with* $(H_1', H_2', \ldots, H_n')$. *Then, when* $n \leq 2$, $\overline{H^c} \leq \overline{H'^c}$.

Proof Without loss of generality, we first suppose that for $i < j$, $H_i < H_j$ and $H_i' < H_j'$.

When $n = 1$, it is obvious that $\overline{H^c} = \overline{H_1} = H_1 \leq H_1' = \overline{H_1'} = \overline{H'^c}$.

When $n = 2$, using reduction to absurdity, we assume that $\overline{H_1'} < \overline{H_1}$ or $\overline{H_2'} < \overline{H_2}$. Here, we consider three cases:

Case 1: $\overline{H_1'} < \overline{H_1}$ and $\overline{H_2'} \geq \overline{H_2}$.

In this case, let $\overline{\overline{H}} = (\overline{\overline{H_1}}, \overline{\overline{H_2}})$, where $\overline{\overline{H_1}} = \overline{H_1'}, \overline{\overline{H_2}} = \min(\overline{H_2'}, H_2)$, we have that $1 - \frac{\#(\overline{\overline{H_i}} \cap \overline{\overline{H^c}})}{\#(\overline{\overline{H_i}} \cup \overline{\overline{H^c}})} \leq \varepsilon$ for $i = 1, 2$ and

$$\sum_{i=1}^{2} d(H_i, \overline{\overline{H_i}}) \leq \sum_{i=1}^{2} d(H_i, \overline{H_i}).$$

This contradicts the fact that $(\overline{H_1}, \ldots, \overline{H_n})$ is the optimal adjusted opinion of $(H_1, H_2, \ldots, H_n)$.

Case 2: $\overline{H_1'} \geq \overline{H_1}$ and $\overline{H_2'} < \overline{H_2}$.

In this case, let $\overline{\overline{H'}} = (\overline{\overline{H_1'}}, \overline{\overline{H_2'}})$, where $\overline{\overline{H_1'}} = \max(H_1', \overline{H_1}), \overline{\overline{H_2'}} = \overline{H_2}$, we have that $1 - \frac{\#(\overline{\overline{H_i'}} \cap \overline{\overline{H'^c}})}{\#(\overline{\overline{H_i'}} \cup \overline{\overline{H'^c}})} \leq \varepsilon$ for $i = 1, 2$ and

$$\sum_{i=1}^{2} d(H_i', \overline{\overline{H_i'}}) \leq \sum_{i=1}^{2} d(H_i', \overline{H_i'})$$

This contradicts the fact that $(\overline{H_1'}, \ldots, \overline{H_n'})$ is the optimal adjusted opinion of $(H_1', \ldots, H_n')$.

Case 3: $\overline{H_1'} < \overline{H_1}$ and $\overline{H_2'} < \overline{H_2}$.

In this case, $H_1 < H_1' \leq \overline{H_1'} < \overline{H_1}$ and $\overline{H_2'} < \overline{H_2} \leq H_2 < H_2'$. Thus, it cannot absolutely guarantee the value of $\sum_{i=1}^{2} d(H_i', \overline{H_i'})$ is smaller than $\sum_{i=1}^{2} d(H_i', \overline{H_i})$, which contradicts the fact that $(\overline{H_1'}, \ldots, \overline{H_n'})$ is the optimal adjusted opinion of $(H_1', H_2', \ldots, H_n')$.

Based on the three cases, we have $\overline{H_1} \leq \overline{H_1'}$ and $\overline{H_2} \leq \overline{H_2'}$. Consequently, $\overline{H^c} \leq \overline{H'^c}$. This completes the proof of Property 4.9.

Property 4.10

$$\#[\min\{\min_{i=1,\ldots,n}(\overline{H_i})\}, \max\{\max_{i=1,\ldots,n}(\overline{H_i})\}] \leq \#[\min\{\min_{i=1,\ldots,n}(H_i)\}, \max\{\max_{i=1,\ldots,n}(H_i)\}]$$

Proof Because $\min_{i=1,\ldots,n}(H_i) \leq \min_{i=1,\ldots,n}(\overline{H_i})$ and $\max_{i=1,\ldots,n}(\overline{H_i}) \leq \max_{i=1,\ldots,n}(H_i)$, then

$$\min\{\min_{i=1,\ldots,n}(H_i)\} \leq \min\{\min_{i=1,\ldots,n}(\overline{H_i})\}$$

and

$$\max\{\max_{i=1,\ldots,n}(\overline{H_i})\} \leq \max\{\max_{i=1,\ldots,n}(H_i)\}.$$

Therefore,

$$\#[\min\{\min_{i=1,\ldots,n}(\overline{H_i})\}, \max\{\max_{i=1,\ldots,n}(\overline{H_i})\}] \leq \#[\min\{\min_{i=1,\ldots,n}(H_i)\}, \max\{\max_{i=1,\ldots,n}(H_i)\}].$$

This completes the proof of Property 4.10.

Property 4.10 shows that the adjusted individual opinions obtained by $P_{4.3}$ concentrate into a smaller domain than original individual opinions.

Property 4.11 $\overline{H_1} \cap \ldots \cap \overline{H_n} \subseteq \overline{H^c}$

Proof There are two cases:

(i) If $\overline{H_1} \cap \ldots \cap \overline{H_n} = \emptyset$, then $\overline{H_1} \cap \ldots \cap \overline{H_n} \subseteq \overline{H^c}$.
(ii) If $\overline{H_1} \cap \ldots \cap \overline{H_n} \neq \emptyset$, then using reduction to absurdity, we assume that $\overline{H_1} \cap \ldots \cap \overline{H_n} \not\subset \overline{H^c}$, thus we can construct another HFLTSs of S: $\overline{\overline{H}} = (\overline{\overline{H_1}}, \ldots, \overline{\overline{H_n}})$ and $\overline{\overline{H^c}}$, where $\overline{\overline{H_i}} = \overline{H_i}(i = 1, 2, \ldots, n)$ and $\overline{\overline{H^c}} = (\overline{H_1} \cap \ldots \cap \overline{H_n}) \cup \overline{H^c}$.

Then, we can find that

$$\sum_{i=1}^{n} d(H_i, \overline{\overline{H_i}}) = \sum_{i=1}^{n} d(H_i, \overline{H_i})$$

and for $i = 1, 2, \ldots, n$,

$$\frac{\#(\overline{\overline{H_i}} \cap \overline{\overline{H^c}})}{\#(\overline{\overline{H_i}} \cup \overline{\overline{H^c}})} = \frac{\#(\overline{H_i} \cap \overline{\overline{H^c}})}{\#(\overline{H_i} \cup \overline{\overline{H^c}})} > \frac{\#(\overline{H_i} \cap \overline{H^c})}{\#(\overline{H_i} \cup \overline{H^c})}$$

which contradicts the fact that $\overline{H^c}$ is the optimal solution to $P_{4.3}$.

Therefore, $\overline{H_1} \cap \ldots \cap \overline{H_n} \subseteq \overline{H^c}$.

This completes the proof of Property 4.11.

Based on Property 4.11, the intersection of the adjusted individual opinions is a subset of the adjusted collective opinion. In other words, if $s_j \in S$ is used by all experts to assess an alternative, then the collective will be in favor of using s_j to assess the alternative.

(2) Uniqueness of solution to model $P_{4.4}$

Before proposing the uniqueness of the solution to model $P_{4.4}$, we introduce Lemmas 4.11–4.12.

Lemma 4.11 *If* $(\overline{H_1}, \ldots, \overline{H_n}, \overline{H^c})$ *is an optimal solution to* $P_{4.3}$ *and* $\exists p \in \{1, \ldots, n\}$, $\overline{H_p} \subset \overline{H^c}$ *and* $H_p \cap \overline{H^c} = \emptyset$, *then* $\overline{\overline{H}} = (\overline{\overline{H_1}}, \ldots, \overline{\overline{H_n}}, \overline{\overline{H^c}})$, *where* $\overline{\overline{H_i}} = \overline{H_i}(i \neq p)$ *and* $\overline{\overline{H^c}} = \overline{H^c}$, *is an optimal solution to* $P_{4.3}$ *if and only if* $\overline{\overline{H_p}}$ *satisfies the following conditions:*

(i) $\overline{\overline{\overline{H_p}}} \subset \overline{H^c}$;
(ii) $\#(\overline{\overline{\overline{H_p}}}) = \#(\overline{H_p})$.

Proof (i) **Sufficiency**. For $i \neq p$, it satisfies

$$1 - \frac{\#(\overline{\overline{\overline{H_i}}} \cap \overline{\overline{\overline{H^c}}})}{\#(\overline{\overline{\overline{H_i}}} \cup \overline{\overline{\overline{H^c}}})} = 1 - \frac{\#(\overline{H_i} \cap \overline{H^c})}{\#(\overline{H_i} \cup \overline{H^c})} \leq \varepsilon.$$

For $i = p$, since $\overline{\overline{\overline{H^c}}} = \overline{H^c}$, $\overline{\overline{\overline{H_p}}} \subset \overline{H^c}$, $\#(\overline{\overline{\overline{H_p}}}) = \#(\overline{H_p})$ and $\overline{H_p} \subset \overline{H^c}$, it satisfies

$$1 - \frac{\#(\overline{\overline{\overline{H_p}}} \cap \overline{\overline{\overline{H^c}}})}{\#(\overline{\overline{\overline{H_p}}} \cup \overline{\overline{\overline{H^c}}})} = 1 - \frac{\#(\overline{H_p})}{\#(\overline{H^c})} = 1 - \frac{\#(\overline{H_p} \cap \overline{H^c})}{\#(\overline{H_p} \cup \overline{H^c})} \leq \varepsilon.$$

Furthermore, $\sum_{i=1}^{n} d(H_i, \overline{\overline{\overline{H_i}}}) = \sum_{i=1, i\neq p}^{n} d(H_i, \overline{H_i}) + d(H_p, \overline{\overline{\overline{H_p}}})$,
since $\#(\overline{\overline{\overline{H_p}}}) = \#(\overline{H_p})$ and $\overline{\overline{\overline{H_p}}} \cap H_p = \emptyset$, then

$$d(H_p, \overline{\overline{\overline{H_p}}}) = \#(H_p \cup \overline{\overline{\overline{H_p}}}) - \#(H_p \cap \overline{\overline{\overline{H_p}}}) = \#(H_p) + \#(\overline{H_p}) = d(H_p, \overline{H_p}).$$

Thus it satisfies $\sum_{i=1}^{n} d(H_i, \overline{\overline{\overline{H_i}}}) = \sum_{i=1}^{n} d(H_i, \overline{H_i})$.
Therefore, $\overline{\overline{H}} = (\overline{\overline{\overline{H_1}}}, \overline{\overline{\overline{H_2}}}, \ldots, \overline{\overline{\overline{H_n}}}, \overline{\overline{\overline{H^c}}})$ is the optimal solution to $P_{4.3}$.
(ii) **Necessity**. For $i = p$, Since $\overline{\overline{\overline{H^c}}} = \overline{H^c}$,

$$\frac{\#(\overline{\overline{\overline{H_p}}} \cap \overline{\overline{\overline{H^c}}})}{\#(\overline{\overline{\overline{H_p}}} \cup \overline{\overline{\overline{H^c}}})} = \frac{\#(\overline{\overline{\overline{H_p}}} \cap \overline{H^c})}{\#(\overline{\overline{\overline{H_p}}} \cup \overline{H^c})}.$$

There are three cases between $\overline{\overline{\overline{H_p}}}$ and $\overline{H^c}$:
(a) If $\overline{\overline{\overline{H_p}}} \cap \overline{H^c} = \emptyset$, then $\frac{\#(\overline{\overline{\overline{H_p}}} \cap \overline{H^c})}{\#(\overline{\overline{\overline{H_p}}} \cup \overline{H^c})} = 0$. Therefore, $\overline{\overline{H}} = (\overline{\overline{\overline{H_1}}}, \overline{\overline{\overline{H_2}}}, \ldots, \overline{\overline{\overline{H_n}}}, \overline{\overline{\overline{H^c}}})$ is not an optimal solution to $P_{4.3}$.
(b) If $\overline{\overline{\overline{H_p}}} \cap \overline{H^c} \neq \emptyset$ and $\overline{\overline{\overline{H_p}}} \not\subset \overline{H^c}$, since $\overline{H_p} \subset \overline{H^c}$ and $H_p \cap \overline{H^c} = \emptyset$, then $d(H_p, \overline{\overline{\overline{H_p}}}) \neq d(H_p, \overline{H_p})$.
As a result, $\sum_{i=1}^{n} d(H_i, \overline{\overline{\overline{H_i}}}) \neq \sum_{i=1}^{n} d(H_i, \overline{H_i})$.
Therefore, $\overline{\overline{H}} = (\overline{\overline{\overline{H_1}}}, \ldots, \overline{\overline{\overline{H_n}}}, \overline{\overline{\overline{H^c}}})$ is not an optimal solution to $P_{4.3}$.
(c) If $\overline{\overline{\overline{H_p}}} \subset \overline{H^c}$, then

$$\frac{\#(\overline{\overline{\overline{H_p}}} \cap \overline{H^c})}{\#(\overline{\overline{\overline{H_p}}} \cup \overline{H^c})} = \frac{\#(\overline{\overline{\overline{H_p}}})}{\#(\overline{H^c})}.$$

When $\#(\overline{\overline{H_p}}) = \#(\overline{H_p})$, $d(H_p, \overline{\overline{H_p}}) = d(H_p, \overline{H_p})$, then it guarantees

$$\sum_{i=1}^{n} d(H_i, \overline{\overline{H_i}}) = \sum_{i=1}^{n} d(H_i, \overline{H_i})$$

and

$$1 - \frac{\#(\overline{\overline{H_p}} \cap \overline{H^c})}{\#(\overline{\overline{H_p}} \cup \overline{H^c})} = 1 - \frac{\#(\overline{H_p} \cap \overline{H^c})}{\#(\overline{H_p} \cup \overline{H^c})} \leq \varepsilon.$$

Therefore, if $\overline{\overline{H}} = (\overline{\overline{H_1}}, \ldots, \overline{\overline{H_n}}, \overline{\overline{H^c}})$, where $\overline{\overline{H_i}} = \overline{H_i}(i \neq p)$ and $\overline{\overline{H^c}} = \overline{H^c}$, is an optimal solution to $P_{4.3}$, then $\overline{\overline{H_p}}$ satisfies $\overline{\overline{H_p}} \subset \overline{H^c}$ and $\#(\overline{\overline{H_p}}) = \#(\overline{H_p})$. This completes the proof of Lemma 4.11.

Lemma 4.12 *Let $[a, b]$ and $[c, d]$ be two real number intervals, and $[a, b] \cap [c, d] = \emptyset$.*

Let k be a constant and $0 \leq k < d - c$. Then, the mathematical programming

$$\begin{cases} \min\limits_{x,y}(|x-a| + |y-b|) \\ s.t. \begin{cases} [x, y] \subset [c, d] \\ y - x = k \end{cases} \end{cases} \tag{4.118}$$

where x and y are decision variables, has a unique solution.

Proof It is obvious and the proof is omitted.

Based on Lemmas 4.11–4.12, the uniqueness of the solution to model $P_{4.4}$ is presented as Theorem 4.10.

Theorem 4.10 *The optimal solution to $P_{4.4}$ is unique.*

Proof Based on Lemma 4.11, we prove the uniqueness of solution to model $P_{4.4}$ as follows:

(i) For $i \neq p$, $\overline{OH_i} = \overline{H_i}$ is the unique optimal solution to $P_{4.4}$.
(ii) For $i = p$, $\overline{H_p}$ can be further optimized to $\overline{OH_p}$ by applying model $P_{4.4}$ to minimize the Manhattan distance between H_p and $\overline{OH_p}$.

$$\begin{cases} \min\limits_{\overline{OH_p}}(|I(\overline{OH_p}^{-}) - I(H_p^{-})| + |I(\overline{OH_p}^{+}) - I(H_p^{+})|) \\ s.t. \begin{cases} [I(\overline{OH_p}^{-}), I(\overline{OH_p}^{+})] \subset [I(\overline{H^c}^{-}), I(\overline{H^c}^{+})] \\ I(\overline{OH_p}^{+}) - I(\overline{OH_p}^{-}) = \#(\overline{H_p}) \end{cases} \end{cases} \cdot \tag{4.119}$$

According to Lemma 4.12, the above mathematical programming (4.119) has a unique solution.

Therefore, $\overline{OH} = (\overline{OH_1}, \ldots, \overline{OH_n})$ is the unique optimal solution to $P_{4.4}$. This completes the proof of Theorem 4.10.

Based on Theorem 4.10, we can obtain that the solution to model $P_{4.4}$ is unique, through which we obtain the optimal adjustment suggestions to support the consensus reaching process in the hesitant linguistic GDM.

References

1. I. Beg, T. Rashid, TOPSIS for hesitant fuzzy linguistic term sets. Int. J. Intell. Syst. **28**(12), 1162–1171 (2013)
2. D. Ben-Arieh, Z. Chen, Linguistic-labels aggregation and consensus measure for autocratic decision making using group recommendations. IEEE Trans. Syst. Man Cybern.-Part A: Syst. Hum. 36, 558–568 (2006)
3. M. Delgado, J.L. Verdegay, M.A. Vila, On aggregation operations of linguistic labels. Int. J. Intell. Syst. **8**, 351–370 (1993)
4. Y.C. Dong, Y.F. Xu, H.Y. Li, On consistency measures of linguistic preference relations. Eur. J. Oper. Res. **189**, 430–444 (2008)
5. Y.C. Dong, Y.F. Xu, S. Yu, Linguistic multiperson decision making based on the use of multiple preference relations. Fuzzy Sets Syst. **160**, 603–623 (2009)
6. Y.C. Dong, Y.F. Xu, H.Y. Li, B. Feng, The OWA-based consensus operator under linguistic representation models using position indexes. Eur. J. Oper. Res. **203**, 455–463 (2010)
7. Y.C. Dong, C.C. Li, Y.F. Xu, X. Gu, Consensus-based group decision making under multi-granular unbalanced 2-tuple linguistic preference relations. Group Decis. Negot. **24**, 217–242 (2015)
8. Y.C. Dong, X. Chen, F. Herrera, Minimizing adjusted simple terms in the consensus reaching process with hesitant linguistic assessments in group decision making. Inf. Sci. **297**, 95–117 (2015)
9. E. Falcó, J.L. García-Lapresta, L. Roselló, Allowing agents to be imprecise: A proposal using multiple linguistic terms. Inf. Sci. **258**, 249–265 (2014)
10. F. Herrera, E. Herrera-Viedma, Linguistic decision analysis: Steps for solving decision problems under linguistic information. Fuzzy Sets Syst. **115**, 67–82 (2000)
11. F. Herrera, L. Martínez, A 2-tuple fuzzy linguistic representation model for computing with words. IEEE Trans. Fuzzy Syst. **8**(6), 746–752 (2000)
12. F. Herrera, L. Martínez, A model based on linguistic 2-tuples for dealing with multigranularity hierarchical linguistic contexts in multi-expert decision making. IEEE Trans. Syst. Man Cybern.-Part B: Cybern. 31, 227–234 (2001)
13. I. Palomares, L. Martínez, F. Herrera, A consensus model to detect and manage non-cooperative behaviors in large scale group decision making. IEEE Trans. Fuzzy Syst. **22**, 516–530 (2014)
14. F. Herrera, E. Herrera-Viedma, J.L. Verdegay, Direct approach processes in group decision making using linguistic OWA operators. Fuzzy Sets Syst. **79**, 175–190 (1996)
15. F. Herrera, F. Herrera-Viedma, L. Martínez, A fuzzy linguistic methodology to deal with unbalanced linguistic term sets. IEEE Trans. Fuzzy Syst. **16**, 354–370 (2008)
16. F. Herrera, S. Alonso, F. Chiclana, E. Herrera-Viedma, Computing with words in decision making: foundations, trends and prospects. Fuzzy Optim. Decis. Making **8**, 337–64 (2009)
17. G.A. Miller, The magical number seven plus or minus two: Some limits on our capacity of processing information. Psychol. Rev. **63**, 81–97 (1956)
18. I. Palomares, F.J. Estrella, L. Martínez, F. Herrera, Consensus under a fuzzy context: taxonomy, analysis framework AFRYCA and experimental case of study. Inf. Fusion **20**, 252–271 (2014)
19. R.M. Rodríguez, L. Martínez, F. Herrera, Hesitant fuzzy linguistic term set for decision making. Fuzzy Sets Syst. **20**(1), 109–119 (2012)

20. R.M. Rodríguez, L. Martínez, V. Torra, Z.S. Xu, F. Herrera, Hesitant fuzzy sets: state of the art and future directions. Int. J. Intell. Syst. **29**, 495–524 (2014)
21. E.G. Thomas, C.F. Fink, Effects of group size. Psychol. Bull. **60**(4), 371–384 (1963)
22. V. Torra, Hesitant fuzzy sets. Int. J. Intell. Syst. **25**(6), 529–539 (2010)
23. J.Q. Wang, J. Wang, Q.H. Chen, H.Y. Zhang, X.H. Chen, An outranking approach for multi-criteria decision-making with hesitant fuzzy linguistic term sets. Inf. Sci. **280**, 338–351 (2014)
24. J.H. Wang, J.Y. Hao, A new version of 2-tuple fuzzy linguistic representation model for computing with words. IEEE Trans. Fuzzy Syst. **14**, 435–445 (2006)
25. C.P. Wei, N. Zhao, X.J. Tang, Operators and comparisons of hesitant fuzzy linguistic term sets. IEEE Trans. Fuzzy Syst. **22**(3), 575–585 (2014)
26. Z.S. Xu, Deviation measures of linguistic preference relations in group decision making. Omega **33**, 249–254 (2005)
27. R.R. Yager, Quantifer guided aggregation using OWA operators. Int. J. Intell. Syst. **11**, 49–73 (1996)
28. L.A. Zadeh, A computational approach to fuzzy quantifers in natural languages. Comput. Math. Appl. **9**, 149–184 (1983)

Chapter 5
Consensus with Heterogeneous Preference Representation Structures

The direct consensus model and the prospect theory based consensus model are proposed for the GDM with heterogeneous preference representation structures. Furthermore, a minimum adjustments consensus model under the prospect theory is presented.

5.1 Direct Consensus Model

This section proposes the direct consensus model for the GDM with heterogeneous preference representation structures. The direct consensus model can avoid the internal inconsistency issue when using the transformation functions among different preference representation structures, and also satisfy the Pareto principle of social choice theory.

5.1.1 Direct Consensus Framework

Let $X = \{X_1, X_2, \ldots, X_m\}$ and $E = \{E_1, E_2, \ldots, E_n\}$ be as before. Suppose that the experts' preference information over the set of alternatives X may be represented in one of the four formats: preference orderings, utility preferences, multiplicative preference relations, and additive preference relations. The decision problem is how to obtain the collective solution with a consensus.

Let E^U, E^R, E^A and E^D be four subsets of E, representing experts whose preference information on X are expressed by utility preferences, preference orderings, multiplicative preference relations, and additive preference relations, respectively. Without loss of generality, we assume that $E^U = \{E_1, E_2, \ldots, E_{n_1}\}$, $E^R = \{E_{n_1+1}, E_{n_1+2}, \ldots, E_{n_2}\}$, $E^A = \{E_{n_2+1}, E_{n_2+2}, \ldots, E_{n_3}\}$ and $E^D = \{E_{n_3+1}, E_{n_3+2}, \ldots, E_n\}$. To solve the GDM problem with heterogeneous preference

Y. Dong and J. Xu, *Consensus Building in Group Decision Making*,
DOI 10.1007/978-981-287-892-2_5

representation structures, several approaches have been proposed (e.g., [6, 12–16, 21, 23]). In the following, we present the direct consensus framework.

(1) Consensus framework

In GDM models (e.g., [20]), there are two processes to implement before obtaining a final solution, namely: (i) the selection process, and (ii) the consensus process. Inspired by these two processes, we propose a direct consensus framework for GDM problems with four kinds of preference representation structures. This consensus framework is presented in Fig. 5.1. In this framework, the selection process and the consensus process are used.

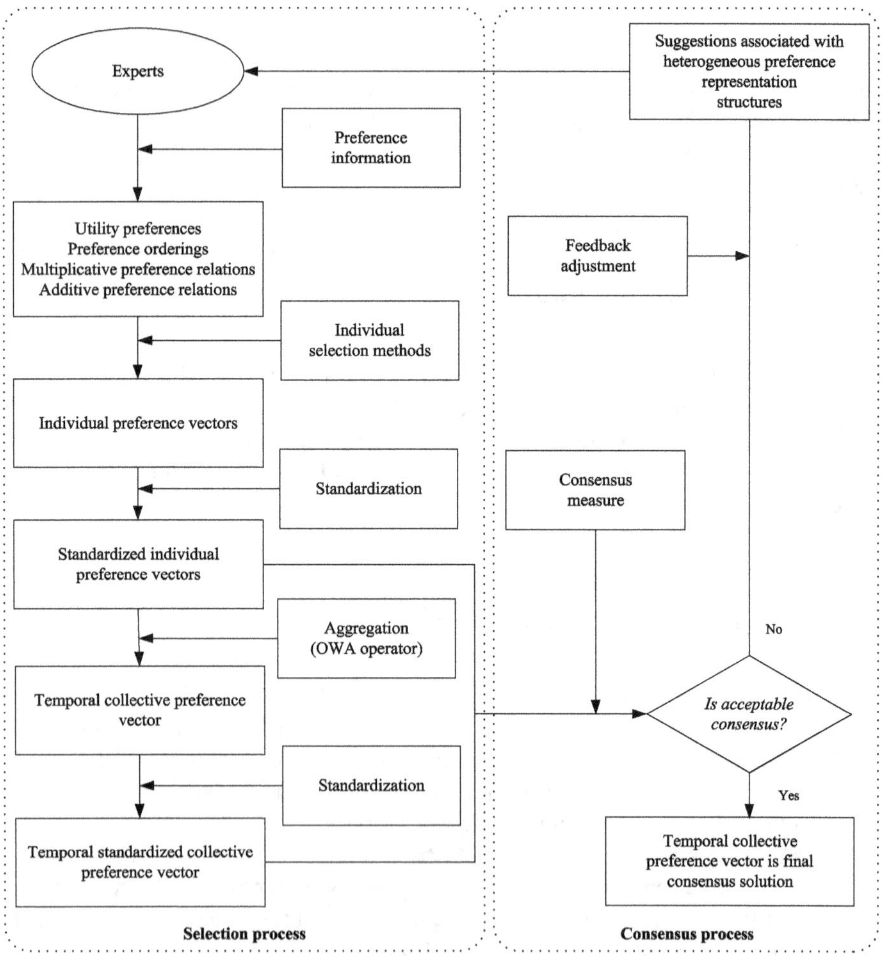

Fig. 5.1 The direct consensus framework

(i) Selection process

In this process, we obtain the standardized individual preference vectors and the standardized collective preference vector. The implementation of this selection process deals with a two-step procedure.

(a) Obtaining individual preference vectors

In this step, the individual selection methods, associated with different preference representation structures, are used to obtain individual preference vectors.

(b) Obtaining a collective preference vector

In this step, the individual preference vectors are transformed into standardized individual preference vectors. Then, a collective preference vector is obtained from the standardized individual preference vectors, using an OWA operator. Finally, the collective preference vector is transformed into the standardized collective preference vector.

(ii) Consensus process

The aim of the consensus process is to improve the consensus level among the experts. The implementation of this consensus process deals with a two-step procedure.

(a) Consensus measure

In this step, two consensus measure methods are introduced to measure the consensus levels among the experts.

(b) Feedback adjustment

Based on the standardized collective preference vector, the novel feedback adjustment rules, associated with different preference representation structures, are presented to help the experts modify their preference information.

Note 5.1 Herrera et al. [19] argued that two basic selection models may be considered. They are the direct approach and indirect approach. The proposed framework is based on the direct approach, so this framework is called the direct consensus framework. The selection process and consensus process under the direct consensus framework are called the direct selection process and direct consensus process, respectively.

(2) Differences between the direct consensus framework and the models presented in [7, 8, 20]

The direct consensus framework is inspired by the GDM model initiated by Chiclana et al. [7] and the corresponding consensus model presented in Herrera-Viedma et al. [20]. However, there are some differences between the direct consensus framework and the models presented in [7, 8, 20]. Specifically, the differences are shown from three aspects:

(i) Process of selection

The process of selection consists of three steps in models presented in [7, 8, 20], namely: (a) making the information uniform through transformation functions, in order to carry out the next step of aggregation. In [7, 8, 20], preference orderings, utility preferences and multiplicative preference relations are transformed into additive preference relations employing the corresponding transformation functions; (b) aggregating all the uniformed individual preferences into a collective one via an aggregation operator. In [7, 8, 20], a collective additive preference relation is obtained in this step, and in [11], the reciprocity of the obtained collective additive preference relation is discussed; and (c) ranking alternatives or selecting the best alternative(s) according to the *quantifier-guided dominance degree* (QGDD) and the *quantifier-guided nondominance degree* (QGNDD).

In the direct consensus model, the implementation of the process of selection contains two steps: (a) obtaining individual preference vectors by using the corresponding individual selection methods; and (b) obtaining a collective preference vector by aggregating all the standardized individual preference vectors.

(ii) Process of consensus

Compared with the model presented in Herrera-Viedma et al. [20], we propose the novel feedback adjustment rules. The proposed feedback adjustment rules are associated with the individual preference representation structures, and consist of two steps: (a) the collective preference vector is transformed into the preference information that is described by the preference representation structure used by the expert; and (b) experts revise their preferences, according to the original individual preference information and the transformed collective preference information.

(iii) Internal consistency and Pareto principle

The direct consensus framework can avoid internal inconsistency issue when using the transformation functions among different preference representation structures, and satisfy Pareto principle of social choice theory.

5.1.2 Direct Selection Process

The direct selection process consists of two steps: *obtaining the individual preference vectors* and *obtaining a collective preference vector*.

(1) Obtaining the individual preference vectors

The individual selection methods, associated with different preference representation structures, are used to obtain individual preference vectors $pv^k = (pv_1^k, pv_2^k, \ldots, pv_m^k)^T (k = 1, 2, \ldots, n)$. According to the formats of preference representation structures, four cases are considered.

Case A: $E_k \in E^U$

In this case, expert E_k provides his/her preference information on X using the utility preference $U^k = (u_1^k, u_2^k, \ldots, u_m^k)^T$. Considering that larger u_i^k values indicate larger preference values, pv_i^k. Therefore, pv_i^k is given as follows:

$$pv_i^k = u_i^k. \tag{5.1}$$

Case B: $E_k \in E^R$

In this case, expert E_k provides his/her preference information on X by means of the preference ordering $R^k = (r_1^k, r_2^k, \ldots, r_m^k)^T$. Considering that smaller r_i^k values indicate larger preference values, pv_i^k. So, pv_i^k is given as follows:

$$pv_i^k = \frac{m - r_i^k}{m - 1}. \tag{5.2}$$

Case C: $E_k \in E^A$

In this case, expert E_k provides his/her preference information on X by means of the multiplicative preference relation $A^k = (a_{ij}^k)_{m \times m}$. The pv_i^k value is given by

$$pv_i^k = \frac{\left(\prod_{j=1}^{m} a_{ij}^k\right)^{1/m}}{\sum_{i=1}^{m} \left(\prod_{j=1}^{m} a_{ij}^k\right)^{1/m}}. \tag{5.3}$$

Case D: $E_k \in E^D$

In this case, expert E_k provides his/her preference information on X by means of the additive preference relation $D^k = (d_{ij}^k)_{m \times m}$. For the alternative X_i, the quantifier-guided dominance degree $QGDD_i^k$, presented in [7], is used to quantify the dominance that the alternative X_i has over all the others in a fuzzy majority sense Q^k as follows:

$$QGDD_i^k = F_{Q^k}^{OWA}(d_{i1}^k, d_{i2}^k, \ldots, d_{im}^k). \tag{5.4}$$

Let

$$pv_i^k = QGDD_i^k. \tag{5.5}$$

(2) Obtaining a collective preference vector

In this phase, the individual preference vector $pv^k = (pv_1^k, pv_2^k, \ldots, pv_m^k)^T (k = 1, 2, \ldots, n)$ is transformed into the standardized individual preference vector $pv^{k*} = (pv_1^{k*}, pv_2^{k*}, \ldots, pv_m^{k*})^T$, where

$$pv_i^{k*} = \frac{pv_i^k}{\sum_{i=1}^m pv_i^k}. \tag{5.6}$$

Once the standardized individual preference vectors are achieved, the OWA operator and the fuzzy majority Q^c are applied to obtain the collective preference vector, $pv^c = \left(pv_1^c, pv_2^c, \ldots, pv_m^c\right)^T$, where

$$pv_i^c = F_{Q^c}^{OWA}\left(pv_i^{1*}, pv_i^{2*}, \ldots, pv_i^{m*}\right). \tag{5.7}$$

Normalizing $pv^c = \left(pv_1^c, pv_2^c, \ldots, pv_m^c\right)^T$ yields the standardized collective preference vector $pv^{c*} = (pv_1^{c*}, pv_2^{c*}, \ldots, pv_m^{c*})^T$, where

$$pv_i^{c*} = \frac{pv_i^c}{\sum_{i=1}^m pv_i^c}. \tag{5.8}$$

(3) Example 5.1

In the following, we provide an example to demonstrate the direct selection process.

Let us consider the example presented in Herrera-Viedma et al. [20]. In this example, there are a set of eight experts $E = \{E_1, E_2, \ldots, E_8\}$ and a set of six alternatives $X = \{X_1, \ldots, X_6\}$. The experts E_1 and E_2 provide their opinions using the utility preferences U^1 and U^2. The experts E_3 and E_4 provide their opinions using the preference orderings R^3 and R^4. The experts E_5 and E_6 provide their opinions using the multiplicative preference relations A^5 and A^6. And, the experts E_7 and E_8 provide their opinions using the additive preference relations D^7 and D^8. These preferences are as follows:

$$U^1 = (0.3, 0.2, 0.8, 0.6, 0.4, 0.1)^T,\ U^2 = (0.3, 0.9, 0.4, 0.2, 0.7, 0.5)^T,$$

$$R^3 = (2, 1, 3, 6, 4, 5)^T,\ R^4 = (1, 3, 4, 2, 6, 5)^T,$$

$$A^5 = \begin{pmatrix} 1 & 1/2 & 1/3 & 4 & 3 & 5 \\ 2 & 1 & 1/3 & 1/4 & 4 & 6 \\ 3 & 3 & 1 & 7 & 6 & 9 \\ 1/4 & 4 & 1/7 & 1 & 1/2 & 3 \\ 1/3 & 1/4 & 1/6 & 2 & 1 & 4 \\ 1/5 & 1/6 & 1/9 & 1/3 & 1/4 & 1 \end{pmatrix},\ A^6 = \begin{bmatrix} 1 & 1/5 & 1/4 & 1/2 & 3 & 1/6 \\ 5 & 1 & 2 & 4 & 6 & 1/3 \\ 4 & 1/2 & 1 & 3 & 5 & 4 \\ 2 & 1/4 & 1/3 & 1 & 3 & 6 \\ 1/3 & 1/6 & 1/5 & 1/3 & 1 & 8 \\ 6 & 3 & 1/4 & 1/6 & 1/8 & 1 \end{bmatrix},$$

$$D^7 = \begin{pmatrix} 0.5 & 0.55 & 0.45 & 0.25 & 0.7 & 0.3 \\ 0.45 & 0.5 & 0.7 & 0.85 & 0.4 & 0.8 \\ 0.55 & 0.3 & 0.5 & 0.65 & 0.7 & 0.6 \\ 0.75 & 0.15 & 0.35 & 0.5 & 0.95 & 0.6 \\ 0.3 & 0.6 & 0.3 & 0.05 & 0.5 & 0.85 \\ 0.7 & 0.2 & 0.4 & 0.4 & 0.15 & 0.5 \end{pmatrix}, D^8 = \begin{pmatrix} 0.5 & 0.7 & 0.75 & 0.95 & 0.6 & 0.85 \\ 0.3 & 0.5 & 0.55 & 0.8 & 0.4 & 0.65 \\ 0.25 & 0.45 & 0.5 & 0.7 & 0.6 & 0.45 \\ 0.05 & 0.2 & 0.3 & 0.5 & 0.85 & 0.4 \\ 0.4 & 0.6 & 0.4 & 0.15 & 0.5 & 0.75 \\ 0.15 & 0.35 & 0.55 & 0.6 & 0.25 & 0.5 \end{pmatrix}.$$

(i) Obtaining individual preference vectors

According to the formats of preference representation structures, the individual preference vectors are respectively derived.

Since $E_1, E_2 \in E^U$, using Eq. (5.1) obtains pv^1 and pv^2 from U^1 and U^2, i.e.,

$$pv^1 = (0.3, 0.2, 0.8, 0.6, 0.4, 0.1)^T, \ pv^2 = (0.3, 0.9, 0.4, 0.2, 0.7, 0.5)^T.$$

Since E_3, $E_4 \in E^R$, using Eq. (5.2) obtains pv^3 and pv^4 from R^3 and R^4, i.e.,

$$pv^3 = (0.8, 1, 0.6, 0, 0.4, 0.2)^T, \ pv^4 = (1, 0.6, 0.4, 0.8, 0, 0.2)^T.$$

Since E_5, $E_6 \in E^A$, using Eq. (5.3) obtains pv^5 and pv^6 from A^5 and A^6, i.e.,

$$pv^5 = (0.1762, 0.1512, 0.4654, 0.0928, 0.0832, 0.0312)^T,$$

$$pv^6 = (0.0668, 0.2879, 0.308, 0.1666, 0.0772, 0.0935)^T.$$

Since E_7, $E_8 \in E^D$, according to Eq. (5.4), using the fuzzy quantifier *as many as possible* (i.e., the OWA operator with the weighting vector $(0, 0, 0, 1/3, 1/3, 1/3)^T$) obtains the *QGDD* values from D^7 and D^8. Then, using Eq. (5.5) obtains pv^7 and pv^8:

$$pv^7 = (0.3333, 0.45, 0.45, 0.3333, 0.2167, 0.25)^T,$$

$$pv^8 = (0.6, 0.4, 0.3833, 0.1833, 0.3167, 0.25)^T.$$

(ii) Obtaining a collective preference vector

Firstly, the individual preference vector $pv^k = (pv_1^k, pv_2^k, \ldots, pv_6^k)^T (k = 1, 2, \ldots, 8)$ is transformed into the standardized individual preference vector $pv^{k*} = (pv_1^{k*}, pv_2^{k*}, \ldots, pv_6^{k*})^T$ based on Eq. (5.6). The standardized individual preference vectors are:

$$pv^{1*} = (0.1250, 0.0833, 0.3333, 0.2500, 0.1667, 0.0417)^T,$$

$$pv^{2*} = (0.1000, 0.3000, 0.1333, 0.0667, 0.2333, 0.1667)^T,$$

$$pv^{3*} = (0.2667, 0.3333, 0.2000, 0.0000, 0.1333, 0.0667)^T,$$

$$pv^{4*} = (0.3333, 0.2000, 0.1333, 0.2667, 0.0000, 0.0667)^T,$$

$$pv^{5*} = (0.1762, 0.1512, 0.4654, 0.0928, 0.0832, 0.0312)^T,$$

$$pv^{6*} = (0.0668, 0.2879, 0.308, 0.1666, 0.0772, 0.0935)^T,$$

$$pv^{7*} = (0.1639, 0.2213, 0.2213, 0.1639, 0.1066, 0.123)^T,$$

$$pv^{8*} = (0.2813, 0.1875, 0.1797, 0.0859, 0.1484, 0.1172)^T.$$

Then, according to Eq. (5.7), using the fuzzy quantifier *most* (i.e., the OWA operator with the weighting vector $(0, 0, 0.15, 0.25, 0.25, 0.25, 0.1, 0)^T$) obtains a collective preference vector, i.e., pv^c:

$$pv^c = (0.1663, 0.2105, 0.2098, 0.1173, 0.1108, 0.0785)^T.$$

Finally, based on Eq. (5.8), $pv^c = \left(pv_1^c, pv_2^c, \ldots, pv_6^c\right)^T$ is transformed into the standardized collective preference vector, i.e., pv^{c*}:

$$pv^{c*} = (0.1862, 0.2357, 0.2349, 0.1314, 0.1240, 0.0878)^T.$$

5.1.3 Direct Consensus Process

The direct consensus process deals with a two-step procedure: *consensus measure* and *feedback adjustment*.

(1) Consensus measure

By measuring the distance between individual preference values and collective preference values, we define the cardinal consensus level (CCL) as Definition 5.1.

Definition 5.1 Let pv^{k*} and pv^{c*} be as earlier. The cardinal consensus level for E_k is defined by

$$CCL(E_k) = \sqrt{\frac{1}{m}\sum_{i=1}^{m}(pv_i^{k*} - pv_i^{c*})^2}. \tag{5.9}$$

The cardinal consensus level among all the experts is defined by

$$CCL\{E_1, \ldots, E_n\} = \frac{1}{n}\sum_{k=1}^{n} CCL(E_k). \tag{5.10}$$

If $CCL\{E_1, \ldots, E_n\} = 0$, then all experts have full cardinal consensus with the collective opinion. Otherwise, the smaller $CCL\{E_1, \ldots, E_n\}$ value indicates the higher cardinal consensus level among $\{E_1, E_2, \ldots, E_n\}$.

Let $R^k = (r_1^k, r_2^k, \ldots\ldots, r_m^k)^T$, where r_i^k is the position of alternative X_i in R^{k*}. For example, if $pv^{k*} = (0.2, 0.5, 0.3)^T$, then $R^k = (3, 1, 2)^T$. Let $R^c = (r_1^c, r_2^c, \ldots, r_m^c)^T$, where r_i^c is the position of alternative X_i in R^{c*}. We define the ordinal consensus level (OCL) as Definition 5.2.

Definition 5.2 The ordinal consensus level for E_k is defined by

$$OCL(E_k) = \frac{1}{m^2} \sum_{i=1}^{m} \left| r_i^k - r_i^c \right|. \tag{5.11}$$

The ordinal consensus level among all the experts is defined by

$$OCL\{E_1, \ldots, E_n\} = \frac{1}{n} \sum_{k=1}^{n} OCL(E_k). \tag{5.12}$$

If $OCL\{E_1, \ldots, E_n\} = 0$, then all experts have full ordinal consensus with the collective opinion. Otherwise, the smaller $OCL\{E_1, \ldots, E_n\}$ value indicates the higher ordinal consensus level among $\{E_1, \ldots, E_n\}$.

(2) Feedback adjustment

Feedback adjustment aims at giving adjustment suggestions to help experts improve the consensus level. A lot of feedback adjustment methods have been proposed [20, 24, 25]. Here, we propose the novel feedback adjustment rules, which are associated with the individual preference representation structures, consist of two steps:

(i) Transforming the standardized collective preference vector pv^{c*} into the preference information that is described by the preference representation structure used by the individual expert. For example, if the expert E_k provided his/her preference information by the utility preference, then the standardized collective preference vector pv^{c*} is transformed into the preference information described by the utility preference. In this way, the original preference information associated with E_k and the transformed collective preference information associated with the pv^{c*} have the same preference representation structure.
(ii) The expert revise his/her preferences, according to the original individual preference information and the transformed collective preference information.

According to the formats of preference representation structures, four cases for feedback adjustment are considered.

Case A: $E_k \in E^U$

Let $U^k = (u_1^k, u_2^k, \ldots\ldots, u_m^k)^T$ be as earlier. Based on Eqs. (5.1) and (5.6), U^k is transformed into a standardized preference vector. By the inverse process of Eqs. (5.1) and (5.6), we transform $pv^{c*} = (pv_1^{c*}, pv_2^{c*}, \ldots\ldots, pv_m^{c*})^T$ into $U^{c,k} = (u_1^{c,k}, u_2^{c,k}, \ldots\ldots, u_m^{c,k})^T$ where

$$u_i^{c,k} = pv_i^{c*} \sum\nolimits_{i=1}^{m} u_i^k. \tag{5.13}$$

Let $\overline{U^k} = \left(\overline{u_1^k}, \overline{u_2^k}, \ldots\ldots, \overline{u_m^k}\right)^T$ be the adjusted utility preference provided by the expert E_k. When constructing $\overline{U^k} = \left(\overline{u_1^k}, \overline{u_2^k}, \ldots\ldots, \overline{u_m^k}\right)^T$, we suggest that

$$\overline{u_i^k} \in [\min(u_i^k, u_i^{c,k}), \max(u_i^k, u_i^{c,k})]. \tag{5.14}$$

Case B: $E_k \in E^R$

Let $R^{c,k} = (r_1^{c,k}, r_2^{c,k}, \ldots\ldots, r_m^{c,k})^T$ be the transformed collective preference information described by preference orderings. If pv_i^{c*} is the tth largest value in $\{pv_1^{c*}, pv_2^{c*}, \ldots\ldots, pv_m^{c*}\}$, then

$$r_i^{c,k} = t. \tag{5.15}$$

Let $R^k = (r_1^k, r_2^k, \ldots\ldots, r_m^k)^T$ be as earlier. Let $\overline{R^k} = \left(\overline{r_1^k}, \overline{r_2^k}, \ldots\ldots, \overline{r_m^k}\right)^T$ be the adjusted preference ordering provided by the expert E_k.

When constructing $\overline{R^k} = \left(\overline{r_1^k}, \overline{r_2^k}, \ldots\ldots, \overline{r_m^k}\right)^T$, we suggest that

$$\overline{r_i^k} \in [\min(r_i^k, r_i^{c,k}), \max(r_i^k, r_i^{c,k})]. \tag{5.16}$$

Case C: $E_k \in E^A$

Based on the approach presented in Fan et al. [16], we transform pv^{c*} into a multiplicative preference relation $A^{c,k} = \left(a_{ij}^{c,k}\right)_{m\times m}$, where

$$a_{ij}^{c,k} = \frac{pv_i^{c*}}{pv_j^{c*}}. \tag{5.17}$$

Let $A^k = (a_{ij}^k)_{m\times m}$ be as earlier. Let $\overline{A^k} = (\overline{a_{ij}^k})_{m\times m}$ be the adjusted multiplicative preference relation provided by the expert E_k. When constructing $\overline{A^k} = (\overline{a_{ij}^k})_{m\times m}$, we suggest that

$$\begin{cases} \overline{a_{ij}^{k}} \in \left[\min\left(a_{ij}^{k}, a_{ij}^{c,k}\right), \max\left(a_{ij}^{k}, a_{ij}^{c,k}\right)\right], i < j, \\ \overline{a_{ij}^{k}} = 1, \ i = j, \\ \overline{a_{ij}^{k}} = \frac{1}{\overline{a_{ji}^{k}}}, i > j. \end{cases} \tag{5.18}$$

Case D: $E_k \in E^D$

Based on the approach presented in Fan et al. [16], we transform pv^{c*} into an additive preference relation $D^{c,k} = (d_{ij}^{c,k})_{m \times m}$, where

$$d_{ij}^{c,k} = \frac{pv_i^{c*}}{pv_i^{c*} + pv_j^{c*}}. \tag{5.19}$$

Let $\overline{D^k} = (\overline{d_{ij}^k})_{m \times m}$ be the adjusted additive preference relation provided by expert E_k. When constructing $\overline{D^k} = (\overline{d_{ij}^k})_{m \times m}$, we suggest that

$$\begin{cases} \overline{d_{ij}^{k}} \in \left[\min\left(d_{ij}^{k}, d_{ij}^{c,k}\right), \max\left(d_{ij}^{k}, d_{ij}^{c,k}\right)\right], i < j, \\ \overline{d_{ij}^{k}} = 0.5, i = j, \\ \overline{d_{ij}^{k}} = 1 - \overline{d_{ji}^{k}}, i > j. \end{cases} \tag{5.20}$$

The detailed consensus process is presented in Algorithm 5.1.

Algorithm 5.1

Input: The original individual preference information $\{U^1, \ldots, U^{n_1}, R^{n_1+1}, \ldots, R^{n_2}, A^{n_2+1}, \ldots, A^{n_3}, D^{n_3+1}, \ldots, D^n\}$, and the predefined consensus level ε.

Output: The adjusted individual preference information $\left\{\overline{U^1}, \ldots, \overline{U^{n_1}}, \overline{R^{n_1+1}}, \ldots, \overline{R^{n_2}}, \overline{A^{n_2+1}}, \ldots, \overline{A^{n_3}}, \overline{D^{n_3+1}}, \ldots, \overline{D^n}\right\}$ and the standardized collective preference vector $\overline{pv^{c*}} = (\overline{pv_1^{c*}}, \overline{pv_2^{c*}}, \ldots, \overline{pv_m^{c*}})^T$.

Step1: Let $z = 0$. Let $U_z^k = (u_{1,z}^k, u_{2,z}^k, \ldots, u_{m,z}^k)^T = (u_1^k, u_2^k, \ldots, u_m^k)^T (k = 1, \ldots, n_1)$, $R_z^k = (r_{1,z}^k, r_{2,z}^k, \ldots, r_{m,z}^k)^T = (r_1^k, r_2^k, \ldots, r_m^k)^T (k = n_1 + 1, \ldots, n_2)$, $A_z^k = (a_{ij,z}^k)_{m \times m} = (a_{ij}^k)_{m \times m} (k = n_2 + 1, \ldots, n_3)$ and $D_z^k = (d_{ij,z}^k)_{m \times m} = (d_{ij}^k)_{m \times m} (k = n_3 + 1, \ldots, n)$.

Step 2: According to the formats of preference representation structures, four cases are considered to obtain the individual preference vectors $pv^{k,z} = (pv_1^{k,z}, pv_2^{k,z}, \ldots, pv_m^{k,z})^T (k = 1, 2, \ldots, n)$.

Case A: $E_k \in E^U$, i.e., $k = 1, 2, \ldots, n_1$. In this case, $pv_i^{k,z} = u_{i,z}^k$.

Case B: $E_k \in E^R$, i.e., $k = n_1 + 1, \ldots, n_2$. In this case, $pv_i^{k,z} = \frac{m - r_{i,z}^k}{m-1}$.

Case C: $E_k \in E^A$, i.e., $k = n_2 + 1, \ldots, n_3$. In this case,

$$pv_i^{k,z} = \frac{\left(\prod_{j=1}^{m} a_{ij,z}^k\right)^{1/m}}{\sum_{i=1}^{m}\left(\prod_{j=1}^{m} a_{ij,z}^k\right)^{1/m}}.$$

Case D: $E_k \in E^D$, i.e., $k = n_3 + 1, \ldots, n$. In this case, $pv_i^{k,z} = F_{Q^k}^{OWA}\left(d_{i1,z}^k, d_{i2,z}^k, \ldots, d_{im,z}^k\right)$.

Step 3: Based on Eq. (5.6), the individual preference vector $pv^{k,z}$ $(k = 1, 2, \ldots, n)$ is transformed into the standardized individual preference vector $pv^{k*,z} = (pv_1^{k*,z}, pv_2^{k*,z}, \ldots, pv_m^{k*,z})^T$, where $pv_i^{k*,z} = \frac{pv_i^{k,z}}{\sum_{i=1}^{m} pv_i^{k,z}}$. Next, Based on Eq. (5.7), the OWA operator and the fuzzy majority Q^c are applied to obtain the collective preference vector $pv^{c,z} = \left(pv_1^{c,z}, pv_2^{c,z}, \ldots, pv_m^{c,z}\right)^T$, where $pv_i^{c,z} = F_{Q^c}^{OWA}(pv_i^{1*,z}, pv_i^{2*,z}, \ldots, pv_i^{m*,z})$. Normalizing $pv^{c,z} = \left(pv_1^{c,z}, pv_2^{c,z}, \ldots, pv_m^{c,z}\right)^T$ based on Eq. (5.8) yields the standardized collective preference vector $pv^{c*,z} = (pv_1^{c*,z}, pv_2^{c*,z}, \ldots, pv_m^{c*,z})^T$, where $pv_i^{c*,z} = \frac{pv_i^{c,z}}{\sum_{i=1}^{m} pv_i^{c,z}}$.

Step 4: Using Definition 5.1 obtains $CCL\{E_1, \ldots, E_n\}$. If $CCL\{E_1, \ldots, E_n\} \leq \varepsilon$, then go to step 6; otherwise, continue with the next step.

Step 5: According to the formats of preference representation structures, four cases for feedback adjustment are considered.

Case A: $E_k \in E^U$. Let $U_z^{c,k} = (u_{1,z}^{c,k}, u_{2,z}^{c,k}, \ldots, u_{m,z}^{c,k})^T$, where $u_{i,z}^{c,k} = pv_i^{c*,z} \sum_{i=1}^{m} u_{i,z}^k$. Let $U_{z+1}^k = (u_{1,z+1}^k, u_{2,z+1}^k, \ldots, u_{m,z+1}^k)^T$ be the adjusted utility preference provided by the expert E_k. When constructing $U_{z+1}^k = (u_{1,z+1}^k, u_{2,z+1}^k, \ldots, u_{m,z+1}^k)^T$, we suggest that

$$u_{\mathrm{i},z+1}^k \in [\min(u_{i,z}^k, u_{i,z}^{c,k}), \max(u_{i,z}^k, u_{i,z}^{c,k})].$$

Case B: $E_k \in E^R$. Let $R_z^{c,k} = (r_{1,z}^{c,k}, r_{2,z}^{c,k}, \ldots, r_{m,z}^{c,k})^T$, where $r_{i,z}^{c,k} = t$ if $pv_i^{c*,z}$ is the tth largest value in $\{pv_1^{c*,z}, pv_2^{c*,z}, \ldots, pv_m^{c*,z}\}$. Let $R_{z+1}^k = (r_{1,z+1}^k, r_{2,z+1}^k, \ldots, r_{m,z+1}^k)^T$ be the adjusted preference ordering provided by the expert E_k. When constructing $R_{z+1}^k = (r_{1,z+1}^k, r_{2,z+1}^k, \ldots, r_{m,z+1}^k)^T$, we suggest that

$$r_{i,z+1}^k \in [\min(r_{i,z}^k, r_{i,z}^{c,k}), \max(r_{i,z}^k, r_{i,z}^{c,k})].$$

Case C: $E_k \in E^A$. Let $A_z^{c,k} = \left(a_{ij,z}^{c,k}\right)_{m \times m}$, where $a_{ij,z}^{c,k} = \frac{pv_i^{c*,z}}{pv_j^{c*,z}}$. Let $A_{z+1}^k = (a_{ij,z+1}^k)_{m \times m}$ be the adjusted multiplicative preference relation provided by expert E_k. When constructing $A_{z+1}^k = (a_{ij,z+1}^k)_{m \times m}$, we suggest that

$$\begin{cases} a^k_{ij,z+1} \in [\min(a^k_{ij,z}, a^{c,k}_{ij,z}), \max(a^k_{ij,z}, a^{c,k}_{ij,z})], i < j, \\ a^k_{ij,z+1} = 1, \quad i = j, \\ a^k_{ij,z+1} = 1/a^k_{ji,z+1}, \qquad i > j. \end{cases}$$

Case D: $E_k \in E^D$. Let $D^{c,k}_z = \left(d^{c,k}_{ij,z}\right)_{m\times m}$, where $d^{c,k}_{ij,z} = \frac{pv^{c*,z}_i}{pv^{c*,z}_i + pv^{c*,z}_j}$. Let $D^k_{z+1} = (d^k_{ij,z+1})_{m\times m}$ be the adjusted additive preference relation provided by the expert E_k. When constructing $D^k_{z+1} = (d^k_{ij,z+1})_{m\times m}$, we suggest that

$$\begin{cases} d^k_{ij,z+1} \in [\min(d^k_{ij,z}, d^{c,k}_{ij,z}), \max(d^k_{ij,z}, d^{c,k}_{ij,z})], i < j, \\ d^k_{ij,z+1} = 0.5, \; i = j, \\ d^k_{ij,z+1} = 1 - d^k_{ji,z+1}, i > j, \end{cases}$$

and $z = z + 1$. Then go to step 2.

Step 6: Let $\overline{U^k} = U^k_z (k = 1, 2, \ldots, n_1)$, $\overline{R^k} = r^k_z (k = n_1 + 1, \ldots, n_2)$, $\overline{A^k} = A^k_z (k = n_2 + 1, \ldots, n_3)$, $\overline{D^k} = D^k_z (k = n_3 + 1, \ldots, n)$ and $\overline{pv^{c*}} = pv^{c*,z}$.

Algorithm 5.1 is based on the cardinal consensus measure (i.e., Definition 5.1). In Algorithm 5.1, we replace Step 4 by Step 4′. We call the modified algorithm, Algorithm 5.2.

Step 4′: Using Definition 5.2 obtains $OCL\{E_1, \ldots, E_n\}$. If $OCL\{E_1, \ldots, E_n\} \leq \varepsilon$, then go to step 6; otherwise, continue with the next step.

(3) Example 5.2

We continue with Example 5.1, and use the direct consensus process to help improve the cardinal and ordinal consensus levels among the experts.

Applying Eqs. (5.10) and (5.12) obtains the cardinal and ordinal consensus levels among the experts, $CCL\{E_1, \ldots, E_8\} = 0.0767$ and $OCL\{E_1, \ldots, E_8\} = 0.2153$, respectively. Then, the proposed feedback adjustment rules are used to improve consensus levels among experts. According to the formats of preference representation structures, different feedback adjustment rules are considered.

Since $E_1, E_2 \in E^U$, using Eq. (5.13) transforms pv^{c*} into the preference information described by the utility preferences, associated with E_1 and E_2. They are

$$U^{c,1} = (0.4469, 0.5657, 0.5638, 0.3154, 0.2976, 0.2107)^T,$$

$$U^{c,2} = (0.5586, 0.7071, 0.7047, 0.3942, 0.3720, 0.2634)^T.$$

Let $SUG^k = (sug^k_1, sug^k_2, \ldots, sug^k_6)^T (k = 1, 2)$ denote the adjusted suggestions for the expert E_k, where $sug^k_i = [\min(u^k_i, u^{c,k}_i), \max(u^k_i, u^{c,k}_i)]$. SUG^1 and SUG^2 are as follows:

$$SUG^1 = ([0.3, 0.447], [0.2, 0.566], [0.564, 0.8], [0.315, 0.6], [0.298, 0.4], [0.1, 0.211])^T,$$

$$SUG^2 = ([0.3, 0.559], [0.707, 0.9], [0.4, 0.705], [0.2, 0.394], [0.372, 0.7], [0.263, 0.5])^T.$$

Let $\overline{U^k} = \left(\overline{u_1^k}, \overline{u_2^k}, \ldots, \overline{u_6^k}\right)^T$ $(k = 1, 2)$ be the adjusted utility preference provided by the expert E_k. When constructing $\overline{U^k} = \left(\overline{u_1^k}, \overline{u_2^k}, \ldots, \overline{u_6^k}\right)^T$ $(k = 1, 2)$, we suggest that $\overline{u_i^k} \in sug_i^k$. Without loss of generality, the adjusted utility preferences are

$$\overline{U^1} = (0.44, 0.3, 0.57, 0.4, 0.4, 0.15)^T,$$

$$\overline{U^2} = (0.55, 0.75, 0.4, 0.3, 0.65, 0.35)^T.$$

Since $E_3, E_4 \in E^R$, using Eq. (5.15) transforms pv^{c*} into the preference information described by the preference orderings, associated with E_3 and E_4. They are

$$R^{c,3} = (3, 1, 2, 4, 5, 6)^T, \ R^{c,4} = (3, 1, 2, 4, 5, 6)^T.$$

Let $SUG^k = (sug_1^k, \ldots, sug_6^k)^T$ $(k = 3, 4)$ denote the adjusted suggestion for the expert E_k, where $sug_i^k = [\min(r_i^k, r_i^{c,k}), \max(r_i^k, r_i^{c,k})]$. SUG^3 and SUG^4 are as follows:

$$SUG^3 = ([2, 3], [1, 1], [2, 3], [4, 6], [4, 5], [5, 6])^T,$$

$$SUG^4 = ([1, 3], [1, 3], [2, 4], [2, 4], [5, 6], [5, 6])^T.$$

Let $\overline{R^k} = \left(\overline{r_1^k}, \overline{r_2^k}, \ldots, \overline{r_6^k}\right)^T$ $(k = 3, 4)$ be the adjusted preference ordering provided by the expert E_k. When constructing $\overline{R^k} = \left(\overline{r_1^k}, \overline{r_2^k}, \ldots, \overline{r_6^k}\right)^T$, we suggest that $\overline{r_i^k} \in sug_i^k$. Without loss of generality, the adjusted preference orderings are

$$\overline{R^3} = (2, 1, 3, 5, 4, 6)^T, \ \overline{R^4} = (1, 2, 4, 3, 5, 6)^T.$$

Since $E_5, E_6 \in E^A$, using Eq. (5.17) transforms pv^{c*} into the preference information described by the multiplicative preference relations, associated with E_5 and E_6. They are

$$A^{c,5} = A^{c,6} = \begin{pmatrix} 1 & 0.79 & 0.79 & 1.42 & 1.5 & 2.12 \\ 1.27 & 1 & 1 & 1.79 & 1.9 & 2.68 \\ 1.26 & 1 & 1 & 1.79 & 1.89 & 2.68 \\ 0.71 & 0.56 & 0.56 & 1 & 1.06 & 1.5 \\ 0.67 & 0.53 & 0.53 & 0.94 & 1 & 1.41 \\ 0.47 & 0.37 & 0.37 & 0.67 & 0.71 & 1 \end{pmatrix}.$$

Let $SUG^k = (sug_{ij}^k)_{6\times 6} (k = 5, 6)$ denote the adjusted suggestions for the expert E_k, where $sug_{ij}^k = [\min(a_{ij}^k, a_{ij}^{k,c}),\ \max(a_{ij}^k, a_{ij}^{k,c})]$. SUG^5 and SUG^6 are as follows:

$$SUG^5 = \begin{pmatrix} [1,1] & [0.5,0.79] & [0.33,0.79] & [1.42,4] & [1.5,3] & [2.12,5] \\ [1.27,2] & [1,1] & [0.33,1] & [0.25,1.79] & [1.9,4] & [2.68,6] \\ [1.26,3] & [1,3] & [1,1] & [1.79,7] & [1.89,6] & [2.68,9] \\ [0.25,0.71] & [0.56,4] & [0.14,0.56] & [1,1] & [0.5,1.06] & [1.5,3] \\ [0.33,0.67] & [0.25,0.53] & [0.12,0.53] & [0.94,2] & [1,1] & [1.41,4] \\ [0.2,0.47] & [0.12,0.37] & [0.11,0.37] & [0.33,0.67] & [0.25,0.71] & [1,1] \end{pmatrix},$$

$$SUG^6 = \begin{pmatrix} [1,1] & [0.2,0.79] & [0.25,0.79] & [0.5,1.42] & [1.5,3] & [0.17,2.12] \\ [1.27,5] & [1,1] & [1,2] & [1.79,4] & [1.9,6] & [0.33,2.68] \\ [1.26,4] & [0.5,1] & [1,1] & [1.79,3] & [1.89,5] & [2.68,4] \\ [0.71,2] & [0.25,0.56] & [0.33,0.56] & [1,1] & [1.06,3] & [1.5,6] \\ [0.33,0.67] & [0.17,0.53] & [0.2,0.53] & [0.33,0.94] & [1,1] & [1.41,8] \\ [0.47,6] & [0.37,3] & [0.25,0.37] & [0.17,0.67] & [0.13,0.71] & [1,1] \end{pmatrix}.$$

Let $\overline{A^k} = (\overline{a_{ij}^k})_{6\times 6} (k = 5, 6)$ be the adjusted multiplicative preference relation provided by the expert E_k. When constructing $\overline{A^k} = (\overline{a_{ij}^k})_{6\times 6}$, we suggest that $\overline{a_{ij}^k} \in sug_{ij}^k$ for $i \le j$, $\overline{a_{ij}^k} = \frac{1}{\overline{a_{ji}^k}}$ for $i > j$. Without loss of generality, the adjusted multiplicative preference relations are

$$\overline{A^5} = \begin{pmatrix} 1 & 1/2 & 1/2 & 3 & 3 & 4 \\ 2 & 1 & 1/2 & 1/3 & 3 & 4 \\ 2 & 2 & 1 & 3 & 3 & 4 \\ 1/3 & 3 & 1/3 & 1 & 1/2 & 2 \\ 1/3 & 1/3 & 1/3 & 2 & 1 & 4 \\ 1/4 & 1/4 & 1/4 & 1/2 & 1/4 & 1 \end{pmatrix}, \quad \overline{A^6} = \begin{pmatrix} 1 & 1/4 & 1/2 & 1 & 3 & 1 \\ 4 & 1 & 2 & 3 & 3 & 2 \\ 2 & 1/2 & 1 & 2 & 3 & 3 \\ 1 & 1/3 & 1/2 & 1 & 2 & 4 \\ 1/3 & 1/3 & 1/3 & 1/2 & 1 & 7 \\ 1 & 1/2 & 1/3 & 1/4 & 1/7 & 1 \end{pmatrix}.$$

Since $E_7, E_8 \in E^D$, using Eq. (5.19) transforms pv^{c*} into the preference information described by the additive preference relations, associated with E_7 and E_8. They are

$$D^{c,7} = D^{c,8} = \begin{pmatrix} 0.5 & 0.44 & 0.44 & 0.59 & 0.6 & 0.68 \\ 0.56 & 0.5 & 0.5 & 0.64 & 0.66 & 0.73 \\ 0.56 & 0.5 & 0.5 & 0.64 & 0.65 & 0.73 \\ 0.41 & 0.36 & 0.36 & 0.5 & 0.51 & 0.6 \\ 0.4 & 0.34 & 0.35 & 0.49 & 0.5 & 0.59 \\ 0.32 & 0.27 & 0.27 & 0.4 & 0.41 & 0.5 \end{pmatrix}.$$

Let $SUG^k = (sug_{ij}^k)_{6\times 6} (k = 7, 8)$ denote the adjusted suggestions for the expert E_k, where $sug_{ij}^k = [\min(d_{ij}^k, d_{ij}^{k,c}),\ \max(d_{ij}^k, d_{ij}^{k,c})]$. SUG^7 and SUG^8 are as follows:

$$SUG^7 = \begin{pmatrix} [0.5, 0.5] & [0.44, 0.55] & [0.44, 0.45] & [0.25, 0.59] & [0.6, 0.7] & [0.3, 0.68] \\ [0.45, 0.56] & [0.5, 0.5] & [0.5, 0.7] & [0.64, 0.85] & [0.4, 0.66] & [0.73, 0.8] \\ [0.55, 0.56] & [0.3, 0.5] & [0.5, 0.5] & [0.64, 0.65] & [0.65, 0.7] & [0.6, 0.73] \\ [0.41, 0.75] & [0.15, 0.36] & [0.35, 0.36] & [0.5, 0.5] & [0.51, 0.95] & [0.6, 0.6] \\ [0.3, 0.4] & [0.35, 0.6] & [0.3, 0.35] & [0.05, 0.49] & [0.5, 0.5] & [0.59, 0.85] \\ [0.32, 0.7] & [0.2, 0.27] & [0.27, 0.4] & [0.4, 0.4] & [0.15, 0.42] & [0.5, 0.5] \end{pmatrix},$$

$$SUG^{(8)} = \begin{pmatrix} [0.5, 0.5] & [0.44, 0.7] & [0.44, 0.75] & [0.59, 0.95] & [0.6, 0.6] & [0.68, 0.85] \\ [0.3, 0.56] & [0.5, 0.5] & [0.5, 0.55] & [0.64, 0.8] & [0.4, 0.66] & [0.65, 0.73] \\ [0.25, 0.56] & [0.45, 0.5] & [0.5, 0.5] & [0.64, 0.7] & [0.6, 0.65] & [0.45, 0.73] \\ [0.05, 0.41] & [0.2, 0.36] & [0.3, 0.36] & [0.5, 0.5] & [0.51, 0.85] & [0.4, 0.6] \\ [0.4, 0.4] & [0.34, 0.6] & [0.35, 0.4] & [0.15, 0.49] & [0.5, 0.5] & [0.59, 0.75] \\ [0.15, 0.32] & [0.27, 0.35] & [0.27, 0.55] & [0.4, 0.6] & [0.25, 0.41] & [0.5, 0.5] \end{pmatrix}.$$

Let $\overline{P^k} = (\overline{p_{ij}^k})_{6\times 6}(k = 7, 8)$ be the adjusted additive preference relation provided by the expert E_k. When constructing $\overline{D^k} = (\overline{d_{ij}^k})_{6\times 6}$, we suggest that $\overline{d_{ij}^k} \in sug_{ij}^k$ for $i \leq j$ and $\overline{d_{ij}^k} = 1 - \overline{d_{ji}^k}$ for $i > j$. Without loss of generality, the adjusted additive preference relations are

$$\overline{D^7} = \begin{pmatrix} 0.5 & 0.55 & 0.45 & 0.5 & 0.7 & 0.55 \\ 0.45 & 0.5 & 0.6 & 0.7 & 0.55 & 0.75 \\ 0.55 & 0.4 & 0.5 & 0.645 & 0.66 & 0.62 \\ 0.5 & 0.3 & 0.355 & 0.5 & 0.52 & 0.6 \\ 0.3 & 0.45 & 0.34 & 0.48 & 0.5 & 0.85 \\ 0.45 & 0.25 & 0.38 & 0.4 & 0.15 & 0.5 \end{pmatrix},$$

$$\overline{D^8} = \begin{pmatrix} 0.5 & 0.55 & 0.75 & 0.8 & 0.6 & 0.8 \\ 0.45 & 0.5 & 0.54 & 0.7 & 0.4 & 0.68 \\ 0.25 & 0.46 & 0.5 & 0.642 & 0.6 & 0.45 \\ 0.2 & 0.3 & 0.358 & 0.5 & 0.6 & 0.55 \\ 0.4 & 0.6 & 0.4 & 0.4 & 0.5 & 0.75 \\ 0.2 & 0.32 & 0.55 & 0.45 & 0.25 & 0.5 \end{pmatrix}.$$

Again, using the proposed selection process derives a standardized collective preference vector,

$$\overline{pv^{c*}} = (0.2162, 0.2339, 0.2011, 0.1403, 0.1442, 0.0643)^T.$$

Using Definitions 5.1 and 5.2 obtains $CCL\{E_1, \ldots, E_8\} = 0.0514$ and $OCL\{E_1, \ldots, E_8\} = 0.1389$, respectively, which indicates that the consensus level among the experts has been obviously improved. According to $\overline{pv^{c*}}$, the ranking of the six alternatives is $X_2 \succ X_1 \succ X_3 \succ X_5 \succ X_4 \succ X_6$.

5.1.4 Properties of the Direct Model

Here, we discuss two properties of the direct consensus model: *internal consistency* and *pareto principle*.

(1) Internal consistency and Pareto principle

Definition 5.3 (Internal consistency [8, 9]). The internal consistency refers to the ranking among alternatives derived from the transformed preference representation structure is the same as that derived from the original preference representation structure.

Definition 5.4 (Pareto principle [2, 26]). Let X_i and X_j be two alternatives. If all experts prefer X_i to X_j, then the collective should be in favor of X_i.

Next, we propose the desirable properties of the direct consensus model as Properties 5.1 and 5.2.

Property 5.1 The direct consensus model can avoid internal inconsistency issue.

Proof In the direct consensus model, there only exists the transformation between the preference vectors and the standardized preference vectors. While, since $pv_i^{k*} = pv_i^k / \sum_{i=1}^m pv_i^k$, we have that $pv_i^{k*} \geq pv_j^{k*}$ under the condition that $pv_i^k \geq pv_j^k$. As a result, the direct consensus model can avoid internal inconsistency issue. This completes the proof of Property 5.1.

Property 5.2 $pv_i^{c*} \geq pv_j^{c*}$ under the condition that $pv_i^k \geq pv_j^k$ for $k = 1, 2, \ldots, n$.

Proof Since $pv_i^k \geq pv_j^k$, according to Property 5.1, $pv_i^{k*} \geq pv_j^{k*}$. Further, since $pv_i^c = F_{Q^k}^{OWA}(pv_i^{1*}, pv_i^{2*}, \ldots, pv_i^{n*})$ and $pv_j^c = F_{Q^c}^{OWA}(pv_j^{1*}, pv_j^{2*}, \ldots, pv_j^{n*})$ according to the property of the OWA operator, $pv_i^c \geq pv_j^c$. Similar to the proof of Property 5.1, we easily obtain that $pv_i^{c*} \geq pv_j^{c*}$. This completes the proof of Property 5.2.

Based on Property 5.2, we can obtain that the direct consensus model satisfies the Pareto principle of social choice theory.

(2) Example 5.3

We provide the following example to show that the selection process proposed in [7, 8, 20] does not satisfy internal consistency.

Let $X = \{X_1, \ldots, X_6\}$ be six alternatives. Let $A = (a_{ij})_{6\times 6}$ be a multiplicative preference relation on X:

$$A = \begin{pmatrix} 1 & 1 & 2 & 3 & 4 & 7 \\ 1 & 1 & 3 & 3 & 3 & 3 \\ 1/2 & 1/3 & 1 & 2 & 2 & 2 \\ 1/3 & 1/3 & 1/2 & 1 & 2 & 2 \\ 1/4 & 1/3 & 1/2 & 1/2 & 1 & 2 \\ 1/7 & 1/3 & 1/2 & 1/2 & 1/2 & 1 \end{pmatrix}.$$

The multiplicative preference relation $A = (a_{ij})_{6\times 6}$ is transformed into the additive preference relation $D = (d_{ij})_{6\times 6}$ using the transformation function [8], $d_{ij} = 0.5(1 + \log_9 a_{ij})$. D is listed below:

$$D = \begin{pmatrix} 0.5 & 0.5 & 0.6577 & 0.75 & 0.8155 & 0.9428 \\ 0.5 & 0.5 & 0.75 & 0.75 & 0.75 & 0.75 \\ 0.3423 & 0.25 & 0.5 & 0.6577 & 0.6577 & 0.6577 \\ 0.25 & 0.25 & 0.3423 & 0.5 & 0.6577 & 0.6577 \\ 0.1845 & 0.25 & 0.3423 & 0.3423 & 0.5 & 0.6577 \\ 0.0572 & 0.25 & 0.3423 & 0.3423 & 0.3423 & 0.5 \end{pmatrix}.$$

Based on Eq. (5.3), the preference vector, pv, is derived from $A = (a_{ij})_{6\times 6}$ i.e.,

$$pv = (0.3231, 0.2861, 0.1443, 0.107, 0.081, 0.0585)^T.$$

Using an OWA operator with the fuzzy quantifier *as many as possible* (i.e., the OWA operator with the weighting vector $(0, 0, 0, 1/3, 1/3, 1/3)^T$), the quantifier-guided choice degrees of alternatives acting over $D = (d_{ij})_{6\times 6}$, i.e., *QGDD*, is derived:

$$QGDD = (0.5526, 0.5833, 0.3641, 0.2808, 0.2589, 0.2165)^T.$$

From the values of pv, we find that alternative X_1 is better than X_2. However, alternative X_2 is better than X_1 according to *QGDD*, which contradicts the internal consistency.

In the direct consensus model, there only exists the transformation between the preference vectors and the standardized preference vectors. Let pv^* be the standardized preference vector associated with pv. Using Eq. (5.6) obtains pv^*:

$$pv^* = (0.3231, 0.2861, 0.1443, 0.107, 0.081, 0.0585)^T.$$

From pv and pv^*, we have that $pv_i^* \geq pv_j^*$ if $pv_i \geq pv_j (i, j = 1, 2, \ldots, 6)$, which satisfies the internal consistency.

(3) Example 5.4

We provide the following example to show that the selection process proposed in [8, 9, 20] does not satisfy Pareto principle.

Let $X = \{X_1, \ldots, X_6\}$ be six alternatives. Let $A = (a_{ij})_{6\times 6}$ and $D = (d_{ij})_{6\times 6}$ be a multiplicative preference relation and an additive preference relation on X, respectively. A and D are listed below:

$$A = \begin{pmatrix} 1 & 1 & 4 & 5 & 5 & 5 \\ 1 & 1 & 4 & 7 & 3 & 4 \\ 1/4 & 1/4 & 1 & 2 & 2 & 2 \\ 1/5 & 1/7 & 1/2 & 1 & 2 & 2 \\ 1/5 & 1/3 & 1/2 & 1/2 & 1 & 2 \\ 1/5 & 1/4 & 1/2 & 1/2 & 1/2 & 1 \end{pmatrix}, D = \begin{pmatrix} 0.5 & 0.53 & 0.56 & 0.56 & 0.6 & 0.6 \\ 0.47 & 0.5 & 0.8 & 0.6 & 0.8 & 0.9 \\ 0.44 & 0.2 & 0.5 & 0.6 & 0.7 & 0.55 \\ 0.44 & 0.4 & 0.4 & 0.5 & 0.6 & 0.6 \\ 0.4 & 0.2 & 0.3 & 0.4 & 0.5 & 0.55 \\ 0.4 & 0.1 & 0.45 & 0.4 & 0.45 & 0.5 \end{pmatrix}.$$

In the following, two kinds of selection processes are used to obtain the ranking of alternatives.

(i) The selection process presented in [7, 8, 20]

The selection process presented in [7, 8, 20] consists of three steps.

(a) Making the information uniform

The multiplicative preference relation $A = (a_{ij})_{6\times6}$ is transformed into the additive preference relation $\overline{D} = (\overline{d_{ij}})_{6\times6}$ using the transformation function [8], $\overline{d_{ij}} = 0.5(1 + \log_9 a_{ij})$. $\overline{D}$ is listed below:

$$\overline{D} = \begin{pmatrix} 0.5 & 0.5 & 0.8155 & 0.8662 & 0.8662 & 0.8662 \\ 0.5 & 0.5 & 0.8155 & 0.9428 & 0.75 & 0.8155 \\ 0.1845 & 0.1845 & 0.5 & 0.6577 & 0.6577 & 0.6577 \\ 0.1338 & 0.0572 & 0.3423 & 0.5 & 0.6577 & 0.6577 \\ 0.1338 & 0.25 & 0.3423 & 0.3423 & 0.5 & 0.6577 \\ 0.1338 & 0.1845 & 0.3423 & 0.3423 & 0.3423 & 0.5 \end{pmatrix}.$$

(b) Aggregating all the uniformed preference relations

Using the fuzzy majority criterion with the fuzzy linguistic quantifier *most* (i.e., the OWA operator with the weighting vector $(0.4, 0.6)^T$), the additive preference relations $\overline{D} = (\overline{d_{ij}})_{6\times6}$ and $D = (d_{ij})_{6\times6}$ are aggregated into a collective additive preference relation $D^c = (d^c_{ij})_{6\times6}$:

$$D^c = \begin{pmatrix} 0.5 & 0.512 & 0.6622 & 0.6825 & 0.7065 & 0.7065 \\ 0.482 & 0.5 & 0.8062 & 0.7371 & 0.77 & 0.8493 \\ 0.2867 & 0.1907 & 0.5 & 0.6231 & 0.6746 & 0.5931 \\ 0.2563 & 0.1943 & 0.3654 & 0.5 & 0.6231 & 0.6231 \\ 0.2403 & 0.2200 & 0.3169 & 0.3654 & 0.5 & 0.5931 \\ 0.2403 & 0.1338 & 0.3854 & 0.3654 & 0.3854 & 0.5 \end{pmatrix}.$$

(c) Ranking all the alternatives

Using an OWA operator with the fuzzy quantifier *as many as possible*, (i.e., the OWA operator with the weighting vector $(0, 0, 0, 1/3, 1/3, 1/3)^T$), the quantifier-guided choice degrees ($QGDD$) of alternatives acting over $\overline{D} = (\overline{d_{ij}})_{6\times6}$, $D = (d_{ij})_{6\times6}$ and $D^c = (d^c_{ij})_{6\times6}$ are obtained, respectively, i.e., $\overline{QGDD}$, $QGDD$ and $QGDD^c$:

$$\overline{QGDD} = (0.6052, 0.5833, 0.2897, 0.1777, 0.2420, 0.2202)^T,$$

$$QGDD = (0.5300, 0.5233, 0.3800, 0.4133, 0.3000, 0.3000)^T,$$

$$QGDD^c = (0.5581, 0.5730, 0.3258, 0.2720, 0.2591, 0.2465)^T.$$

Observing the values of $\overline{QGDD}$ and $QGDD$, we find that both experts consider that X_1 is the best alternative. However, from $QGDD^c$, we find that the best alternative is X_2, which violates Pareto principle.

(ii) Direct selection process

The direct selection process consists of two steps.

(a) Obtaining individual preference vectors

Based on Eq. (5.3), the preference vector $pv = (pv_1, \ldots, pv_6)^T$ is derived from $A = (a_{ij})_{6\times 6}$. pv is listed below:

$$pv = (0.3538, 0.3312, 0.1119, 0.0779, 0.0713, 0.0539)^T.$$

According to Eq. (5.4) with the fuzzy quantifier *as many as possible* (i.e., the OWA operator with the weighting vector $(0, 0, 0, 1/3, 1/3, 1/3)^T$), we can obtain the $\widetilde{QGDD}$ value from $D = (d_{ij})_{6\times 6}$. Then, using Eq. (5.5) obtains $\widetilde{pv} = (\widetilde{pv_1}, \ldots, \widetilde{pv_6})^T$:

$$\widetilde{pv} = (0.5300, 0.5233, 0.3800, 0.4133, 0.3000, 0.3000)^T.$$

(b) Obtaining the collective preference vector

Based on Eq. (5.6), pv and $\widetilde{pv}$ are transformed into standardized preference vectors respectively, i.e., pv^* and $\widetilde{pv^*}$:

$$pv^* = (0.3538, 0.3312, 0.1119, 0.0779, 0.0713, 0.0539)^T,$$

$$\widetilde{pv^*} = (0.2166, 0.2139, 0.1553, 0.1689, 0.1226, 0.1226)^T.$$

Using the fuzzy majority criterion with the fuzzy linguistic quantifier *most* (i.e., the OWA operator with the weighting vector $(0.4, 0.6)^T$), pv^* and $\widetilde{pv^*}$ are aggregated into a collective preference vector pv^c:

$$pv^c = (0.2715, 0.2608, 0.1293, 0.1143, 0.0918, 0.0814)^T.$$

Observing the values of pv and $\widetilde{pv}$, we find that both experts consider that X_1 is the best alternative. From pv^c, we find that the best alternative is also X_1, which satisfies Pareto principle.

5.2 Prospect Theory Based Consensus Model

The existing methods have made significant contributions to the GDM problems with heterogeneous preference representation structures. However, the experts' psychological behaviors are seldom considered in these methods. A lot of empirical evidences have shown that the experts' psychological behaviors would play an important role in decision analysis. The prospect theory is one of the most influential psychological behavior theories and is founded on a large number of empirical and experimental studies.

In this section, we take the experts' psychological behaviors into consideration, and propose a prospect theory based consensus model for GDM with heterogeneous preference representation structures.

5.2.1 Prospect Theory and Preference-Approval Structures

The basic knowledge regarding the prospect theory and preference-approval structures are introduced below.

(1) Prospect theory

The prospect theory has been initiated by Kahneman and Tversky [22], and it is a descriptive theory for forecasting individual actual decision behavior under risk [17]. Since the appearance of prospect theory, it has been regarded as one of the most influential behavioral decision theories.

Generally, the prospect theory is comprised of two modules: the editing phase and the evaluation phase. In the editing phase, outcomes of alternatives are coded as gains or losses relative to a reference point. If the value of the alternative is larger than the reference point, the part in excess can be regarded as gain; otherwise, the corresponding part can be regarded as loss. In the evaluation phase, the prospect values are evaluated by a prospect value function and a weighting function, and then the alternative with the highest prospect value is selected. The prospect theory involves three important principles:

(i) Reference dependence. The experts perceive the gains and losses according to a reference point. Thus, the prospect value function can be divided into the gain domain and the loss domain relative to the reference point.
(ii) Diminishing sensitivity. The experts exhibit risk-averse tendency for gains and risk-seeking tendency for losses. According to the principle of diminishing sensitivity, the prospect value function is concave in the loss domain and convex in the gain domain, i.e., the marginal value of both gains and losses is decreasing with the size.

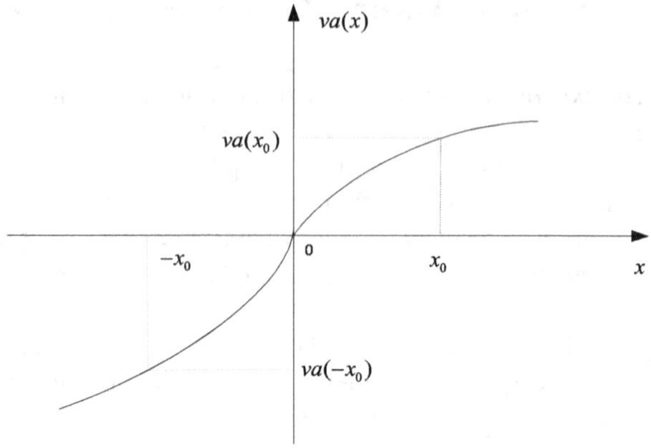

Fig. 5.2 The prospect value function

(iii) Loss aversion. The experts are more sensitive to losses than to equal gains [1]. In accordance with the principle of loss aversion, the prospect value function is steeper in the loss domain than in the gain domain.

In accordance with the above three principles, an S-shaped value function has been proposed in the prospect theory (see Fig. 5.2.). In Fig. 5.2, the original point is the reference point, and x denotes the gain ($x \geq 0$) or the loss ($x < 0$) of the outcome compared with the reference point. The prospect value function $v(x)$ is given by Kahneman and Tversky, and $va(x)$ denotes the function value for gain ($x \geq 0$) or loss ($x < 0$):

$$va(x) = \begin{cases} x^{\alpha}, x \geq 0 \\ -\lambda(-x)^{\beta}, x < 0 \end{cases}, \tag{5.21}$$

In this value function, α and β are the two parameters which determine the concavity and convexity of the function, respectively, and $0 \leq \alpha, \beta \leq 1$. λ is the coefficient of loss aversion, $\lambda > 1$.

(2) The preference-approval structures

In order to determine the reference points, the preference-approval structures proposed by Brams and Sanver [5] are used in this chapter. Some collective decision making models [3, 4, 27] have assumed that the experts take a common language when they evaluate alternatives, and these models aggregate labels such as approved and disapproved. Brams and Sanver suggested a framework that could be considered as a compromise between standard and non-standard models by combining the information of ranking and approval in a hybrid system which they called preference-approval. The preference-approval structure can be expressed as the following example:

$$a\ b\,|c\ d.$$

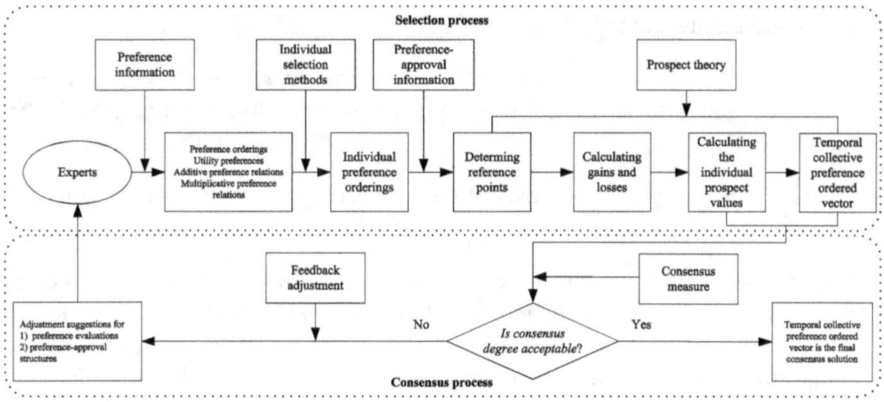

Fig. 5.3 The consensus framework based on prospect theory

The alternatives on the left of the cut-off line are approved by the expert, and on the right are disapproved. That is to say, a and b are approved, and c and d are disapproved in this structure.

5.2.2 Prospect Theory Based Consensus Framework

Let X, E, E^U, E^R, E^A and E^D be as earlier. We propose a novel consensus framework based on prospect theory, and the implementation of the novel consensus framework deals with a two-process procedure. The details of this framework are described in Fig. 5.3.

(1) Selection process

The use of the selection process yields the collective preference ordering. The selection process in our framework consists of a four-step procedure.

(i) Obtaining the individual preference orderings

In this step, the individual selection methods, associated with heterogeneous preference structures, are used to obtain individual preference orderings.

(ii) Determining the reference points

Considering the individual preference-approval information provided by the experts, and combining the obtained individual preference orderings, each expert's reference point over the positional order can be determined.

(iii) Calculating the gains and losses

In this step, the gains and losses for the positional orders of each alternative over the reference points are calculated. And a gain matrix and a loss matrix can be further obtained.

(iv) Calculating the prospect values of the alternatives and obtaining the selection outcome

By substituting the gains and losses into the prospect value function developed by Tversky and Kahneman [28], the individual prospect values of different alternatives are calculated. Further, the collective prospect values of each alternative are obtained by using simple additive weighting method. Finally, a collective ordering is obtained.

(2) Consensus process

The consensus process consists of consensus measure and feedback adjustment.

(i) Consensus measure

In this step, a consensus measure method based on the prospect values is proposed to measure the consensus level among the experts.

(ii) Feedback adjustment

When the consensus level among the experts does not reach the acceptable level, their opinions have to be adjusted. Feedback adjustments rules are introduced to provide the support for the experts adjusting their preference evaluations and preference-approval information.

The selection process and consensus process in the prospect theory based consensus model are called the selection process and consensus process with reference points, respectively.

5.2.3 Selection Process with Reference Points

The selection process with reference points deals with a four-step procedure: *obtaining the individual preference orderings*, *determining the reference points*, *calculating the gains and losses*, and *calculating the prospect values and obtaining the selection outcome*.

(1) Obtaining the individual preference orderings

Let $R^k = (r_1^k, r_2^k, \ldots, r_m^k)$ $(k = 1, 2, \ldots, n)$ be the preference ordering associated with expert E_k. To obtain R^k, four cases are considered:

Case A: $E_k \in E^U$

In this case, expert E_k provides his/her preference information on X by means of the utility preferences $U^k = (u_1^k, u_2^k, \ldots, u_m^k)^T$. Considering that larger value of u_i^k indicates the smaller positional order r_i^k. Therefore, the preference ordering R^k of the alternatives from best to worst is obtained by using utility preference.

Case B: $E_k \in E^R$

In this case, expert E_k provides his/her preference information on X by means of preference ordering. Therefore, the preference orderings R^k is a direct result of expert E_k's preference information over X.

Case C: $E_k \in E^A$

In this case, expert E_k provides his/her preference information on X by the multiplicative preference relations $A^k = (a_{ij}^k)_{m\times m}$. The preference value regarding alternative X_i is computed as $pv_i^k = \dfrac{\left(\prod_{j=1}^m a_{ij}^k\right)^{1/m}}{\sum_{i=1}^m \left(\prod_{j=1}^m a_{ij}^k\right)^{1/m}}$

The larger value of pv_i^k indicates the smaller positional order r_i^k. Therefore, we can obtain the preference ordering R^k according to pv_i^k.

Case D: $E_k \in E^D$.

In this case, expert E_k provides his/her preference information on X by means of the additive preference relations $D^k = (d_{ij}^k)_{m\times m}$. For the alternative X, the quantifier-guided dominance degree, is used to quantify the dominance that the alternative X has over all the others in a linguistic majority sense Q^k as follows: $QGDD_i^k = F_{Q^k}^{OWA}(d_{i1}^k, d_{i2}^k, \ldots, d_{im}^k)$.

The larger value of $QGDD_i^k$ indicates the smaller positional order r_i^k. Therefore, we can obtain the preference ordering R^k according to $QGDD_i^k$.

(2) Determining the reference points

Let the preference-approval structure provided by the expert E_k be expressed as (5.22):

$$PA^k(X) = X_{\sigma(1)}^k, X_{\sigma(2)}^k, \ldots, X_{\sigma(l)}^k \,\Big|\, X_{\sigma(l+1)}^k, X_{\sigma(l+2)}^k, \ldots, X_{\sigma(m)}^k \tag{5.22}$$

where $(\sigma(1), \sigma(2), \ldots, \sigma(m))$ is a permutation of $(1, 2, \ldots, m)$, and $X_{\sigma(i)}^k \in X$, $X_{\sigma(i)}^k \succ X_{\sigma(i+1)}^k$, i.e., if X_i is the jth largest based on the preference ordering of E_k, then $X_{\sigma(j)}^k = X_i^k$.

Then, based on the preference-approval structure $PA^k(X)$, we can determine the reference point of the expert E_k. Under the situation of considering the expert E_k's reference dependence behavior, if one alternative is approved, then expert E_k regards this alternative as gain; Otherwise, this alternative is thought as loss by expert E_k.

In Eq. (5.22), the last approved alternative is $X^k_{\sigma(l)}$ and the first disapproved alternative is $X^k_{\sigma(l+1)}$. Let rp^k be expert E_k's reference point on preference ordering. rp^k is given by

$$rp^k = \frac{2l+1}{2}, \ k = 1, 2, \ldots, n. \tag{5.23}$$

(3) Calculating the gains and losses

Let G^k_i and L^k_i be the gain and loss of the alternative X_i associated with the expert E_k, i.e.,

$$G^k_i = -(r^k_i - rp^k), \ r^k_i < rp^k, \tag{5.24}$$

$$L^k_i = -(r^k_i - rp^k), \ r^k_i \geq rp^k. \tag{5.25}$$

In Eqs. (5.24) and (5.25), if $r^k_i < rp^k$, then the expert E_k's gain on alternative X_i can be regarded as $rp^k - r^k_i$; if $r^k_i \geq rp^k$, then the expert E_k's loss on alternative X_i can be regarded as $r^k_i - rp^k$. Let $G = [G^k_i]_{n\times m}$ and $L = [L^k_i]_{n\times m}$ be the gain and loss matrices.

(4) Calculating the prospect values and obtaining the selection outcome

Let va^k_i be the prospect value of the positional order of alternative X_i over the reference point rp^k. Based on the idea of classical prospect theory, va^k_i is calculated by

$$va^k_i = \begin{cases} (G^k_i)^{\alpha_k} & r^k_i < rp^k \\ -\lambda_k (L^k_i)^{\beta_k} & r^k_i \geq rp^k \end{cases}, \ k = 1, 2, \ldots, n; \ i = 1, 2, \ldots, m. \tag{5.26}$$

where the parameter $\alpha_k (0 \leq \alpha_k \leq 1)$ represents expert E_k's sensitive degree on gain, the parameter $\beta_k (0 \leq \beta_k \leq 1)$ represents expert E_k's sensitive degree on loss and the parameter $\lambda_k > 1$ represents expert E_k's loss aversion degree. As for determining the three parameter values, some scholars have conducted the experiments (see [1, 18, 29–31]). Some available parameters are then determined. It is worth pointing out that the most influential and widely used available parameter values are the result determined by Tversky and Kahneman [28]. They suggest $\alpha_k = \beta_k = 0.88$ and $\lambda_k = 2.25$.

On the basis of obtaining the prospect values $va^1_i, va^2_i, \ldots, va^n_i$, the collective prospect value va^c_i of the alternative X_i can be determined by

$$va^c_i = \frac{1}{n} \sum_{k=1}^{n} va^k_i, \ i = 1, 2, \ldots, m. \tag{5.27}$$

Obviously, the higher value of va^c_i is, the alternative X_i is ranking higher. Therefore, a ranking order of all alternatives is obtained and a collective prospect values vector is obtained.

Due to the special structure of the prospect value function, the approved alternatives' prospect values are always non-negative while the disapproved alternatives are negative. Based on this rule, the collective preference-approval structure is easily obtained according to the collective prospect values. For example, the collective prospect values for a set of six alternatives are $va_1^c = -0.5$, $va_2^c = 1$, $va_3^c = 3$, $va_4^c = -3$, $va_5^c = 2$, $va_6^c = -1$, then the collective preference ordering is $X_3 \succ X_5 \succ X_2 \succ X_1 \succ X_6 \succ X_4$, and the collective preference-approval structure is $PA^c(X) = X_3, X_5, X_2 \,|X_1, X_6, X_4$.

5.2.4 Consensus Process with Reference Points

The consensus process with reference points consists of two steps: *consensus measure* and *feedback adjustment*.

(1) Consensus measure

In general, the consensus level for GDM problems is calculated as the distance between individual preference values and collective preference values [10]. We define the prospect value consensus level ($PVCL$) by measuring the distance between the individual prospect values and the collective prospect values, as Definition 5.5.

Definition 5.5 Let va_i^c and va_i^k be as earlier. The consensus level of the expert E_k is defined by

$$PVCL(E_k) = \sqrt{\frac{1}{m}\sum_{i=1}^{m}\left(\frac{va_i^k - va_i^c}{va(m) - va(-m)}\right)^2},\ k = 1, 2, \ldots, n. \tag{5.28}$$

The consensus level among all experts is

$$PVCL\{E_1, \ldots, E_n\} = \frac{1}{n}\sum_{k=1}^{n} PVCL(E_k). \tag{5.29}$$

The smaller $PVCL\{E_1, \ldots, E_n\}$ value shows the higher consensus level among all the experts. If $PVCL\{E_1, \ldots, E_n\} = 0$, then it means the full and unanimous agreement of all experts.

(2) Feedback adjustment

When the consensus level $PVCL\{E_1, \ldots, E_n\}$ does not reach the acceptable level, the opinions of the experts must be adjusted. The feedback adjustment aims at giving adjustment suggestions to help the experts improve the consensus level. We propose a two-step feedback adjustment process which will adjust both the preference evaluations and the preference-approval information. The rules of this feedback adjustment can be described as follows.

(i) Adjustment of the preference evaluations

Similar to Herrera-videma et al. [20], the opinions will be changed using the following three rules:

R.1. If $va_i^k > va_i^c$, then the expert E_k should decrease the preference evaluation of X_i;

R.2. If $va_i^k = va_i^c$, then the expert E_k should not change the preference evaluation of X_i;

R.3. If $va_i^k < va_i^c$, then the expert E_k should increase the preference evaluation of X_i;

Particularly, according to different formats of preference representation structures, four cases need to be considered.

Case A: $E_k \in E^U$

Let $\overline{U^k} = (\overline{u_1^k}, \overline{u_2^k}, \ldots, \overline{u_m^k})^T$ be the utility preference vector provided by expert E_k at the new round. For any alternative X_i, the following conditions are concerned.

(a) If $va_i^k > va_i^c$, then $\overline{u_i^k} < u_i^k$;
(b) If $va_i^k = va_i^c$, then $\overline{u_i^k} = u_i^k$;
(c) If $va_i^k < va_i^c$, then $\overline{u_i^k} > u_i^k$.

Case B: $E_k \in E^R$

Let $\overline{R^k} = (\overline{r_1^k}, \overline{r_2^k}, \ldots, \overline{r_m^k})^T$ be the preference ordering vector provided by expert E_k at the new round. For any alternative X_i, the following conditions are concerned.

(a) If $va_i^k > va_i^c$, then $\overline{r_i^k} > r_i^k$;
(b) If $va_i^k = va_i^c$, then $\overline{r_i^k} = r_i^k$;
(c) If $va_i^k < va_i^c$, then $\overline{r_i^k} < r_i^k$.

Case C: $E_k \in E^A$

Let $\overline{A} = (\overline{a_{ij}})_{m\times m}$ be the multiplicative preference relations provided by expert E_k at the new round, $t \in N$ and $t \geq 1$.

For any alternative X_i, the following conditions are concerned.

(a) If $va_i^k > va_i^c$, then $\overline{a_{ij}^k} \leq a_{ij}^k$, $j = i+1, i+2, \ldots, m$, $\overline{a_{ji}^k} = 1\big/\overline{a_{ij}^k}$ and $\exists l \in \{i+1, i+2, \ldots, m\}$, such that $\overline{a_{il}^k} < a_{il}^k$;

(b) If $va_i^k = va_i^c$, then $\overline{a_{ij}^k} = a_{ij}^k$, $j = i+1, i+2, \ldots, m$.

(c) If $va_i^k < va_i^c$, then $\overline{a_{ij}^k} \geq a_{ij}^k$, $j = i+1, i+2, \ldots, m$, $\overline{a_{ji}^k} = 1\big/\overline{a_{ij}^k}$ and $\exists l \in \{i+1, i+2, \ldots, m\}$, such that $\overline{a_{il}^k} > a_{il}^k$;

Case D: $E_k \in E^D$

Let $\overline{D^k} = (\overline{d_{ij}^k})_{m\times m}$ be the additive preference relations provided by expert E_k at the new round. For any alternative X_i, the following conditions are concerned.

(a) If $va_i^k > va_i^c$, then $\overline{d_{ij}^k} \le d_{ij}^k$, $j = i+1, i+2, \ldots, m$, $\overline{d_{ji}^k} = 1 - \overline{d_{ij}^k}$ and $\exists l \in \{i+1, i+2, \ldots, m\}$, such that $\overline{d_{il}^k} < d_{il}^k$;

(b) If $va_i^k = va_i^c$, then $\overline{d_{ij}^k} = d_{ij}^k$, $j = i+1, i+2, \ldots, m$.

(c) If $va_i^k < va_i^c$, then $\overline{d_{ij}^k} \ge d_{ij}^k$, $j = i+1, i+2, \ldots, m$, $\overline{d_{ji}^k} = 1 - \overline{d_{ij}^k}$ and $\exists l \in \{i+1, i+2, \ldots, m\}$, such that $\overline{d_{il}^k} > d_{il}^k$.

(ii) Adjustment of the preference-approval information

Secondly, the experts need to adjust their preference-approval information to update the reference points. The rules are easy to apply:

R.1. If $va_i^c \ge 0$, then put the alternative X_i into the approved set;

R.2. If $va_i^c < 0$, then put the alternative X_i into the disapproved set.

After the adjustments for preference evaluations and preference-approval, we use the selection process with reference points to obtain the new preference orderings. The processes will carry on until the consensus level reaches the acceptable level.

5.2.5 Numerical Analysis

Here, we use two examples to demonstrate the prospect theory based consensus model. Meanwhile, we make some discussions by using two experiments.

(1) Example 5.5

Let $E = \{E_1, E_2, \ldots, E_6\}$ be the set of six experts, and let $X = \{X_1, X_2, \ldots, X_4\}$ be the set of four alternatives. Specifically, the experts E_1 and E_2 provide their preference information by means of utility preferences U^1 and U^2, respectively. The experts E_3 and E_4 provide their preference information by means of preference orderings R^3 and R^4, respectively. The expert E_5 provides his/her preference information by means of multiplicative preference relation A^5. The expert E_6 provides his/her preference information by means of additive preference relation D^6. Their preferences are as follows:

$$U^1 = (0.5, 0.7, 1, 0.1)^T, \quad U^2 = (0.7, 0.9, 0.6, 0.3)^T,$$

$$R^3 = (3, 1, 4, 2)^T, \quad R^4 = (3, 2, 1, 4)^T,$$

$$A^5 = \begin{pmatrix} 1 & 5 & 1/3 & 4 \\ 1/5 & 1 & 2 & 6 \\ 3 & 1/2 & 1 & 1/8 \\ 1/4 & 1/6 & 8 & 1 \end{pmatrix}, \quad D^6 = \begin{pmatrix} 0.5 & 0.1 & 0.6 & 0.7 \\ 0.9 & 0.5 & 0.7 & 0.4 \\ 0.4 & 0.3 & 0.5 & 0.9 \\ 0.3 & 0.6 & 0.1 & 0.5 \end{pmatrix}.$$

(i) Selection process with reference points

(a) Obtaining individual preference orderings

Unify the heterogeneous preference structures into preference orderings by the individual selection methods.

Since $E_1, E_2 \in E^U$, the preference orderings for E_1 and E_2 are

$$R^1 = (3, 2, 1, 4)^T, \ R^2 = (2, 1, 3, 4)^T.$$

Since $E_5 \in E^A$, according to Eq. (5.3), the preference vector $pv^5 = (pv_1^5, .., pv_4^5)^T$ can be calculated. By comparing the values of pv^5, the individual preference orderings for E_5 is obtained as:

$$R^5 = (1, 2, 4, 3)^T.$$

Using an OWA operator with the fuzzy quantifier *as many as possible*, the QGDD of alternatives acting over D^6 are:

$$QGDD^6 = (0.3, 0.45, 0.35, 0.2)^T.$$

Therefore, the preference ordering for E_6 is

$$R^6 = (3, 1, 2, 4)^T.$$

(b) Determining the reference points

Based on the obtained individual preference orderings, the experts provide their preference-approval structures as follows:

$$PA^1(X) = X_3, X_2, X_1 | X_4, \ \ PA^2(X) = X_2, X_1 | X_3, X_4,$$

$$PA^3(X) = X_2 | X_4, X_1, X_3, \ \ PA^4(X) = X_3, X_2 | X_1, X_4,$$

$$PA^5(X) = X_1, X_2, X_4 | X_3, \ \ PA^6(X) = X_2, X_3, X_1 | X_4.$$

Based on the Eq. (5.23), each expert's reference point over positional order is obtained as:

$$rp^1 = 3.5, \ rp^2 = 2.5, \ rp^3 = 1.5, \ rp^4 = 2.5, \ rp^5 = 3.5, \ rp^6 = 3.5.$$

(c) Calculating the gains and losses

After obtaining the reference points, according to the Eqs. (5.24) and (5.25), the gain matrix $G = [G_i^k]_{6\times 4}$ and loss matrix $L = [L_i^k]_{6\times 4}$ are obtained as follows:

$$G = \begin{pmatrix} 0.5 & 1.5 & 2.5 & 0 \\ 0.5 & 1.5 & 0 & 0 \\ 0 & 0.5 & 0 & 0 \\ 0 & 0.5 & 1.5 & 0 \\ 2.5 & 1.5 & 0 & 0.5 \\ 0.5 & 2.5 & 1.5 & 0 \end{pmatrix}, \ L = \begin{pmatrix} 0 & 0 & 0 & -0.5 \\ 0 & 0 & -0.5 & -1.5 \\ -1.5 & 0 & -2.5 & -0.5 \\ -0.5 & 0 & 0 & -1.5 \\ 0 & 0 & -0.5 & 0 \\ 0 & 0 & 0 & -0.5 \end{pmatrix}.$$

(d) Calculating the prospect values and ranking the alternatives

Assume all the experts set the parameters α, β and λ as the experiment result conducted by Kahneman and Tversky [22], i.e., $\alpha = \beta = 0.88$, $\lambda = 2.25$.
Then, based on the Eq. (5.26), let $VA = (va_i^k)_{6\times 4}$ be the prospect values matrix:

$$VA = \begin{pmatrix} 0.543367 & 1.428763 & 2.239686 & -1.22258 \\ 0.543367 & 1.428763 & -1.22258 & -3.21472 \\ -3.21472 & 0.543367 & -5.03929 & -1.22258 \\ -1.22258 & 0.543367 & 1.428763 & -3.21472 \\ 2.239686 & 1.428763 & -1.22258 & 0.543367 \\ 0.543367 & 2.239686 & 1.428763 & -1.22258 \end{pmatrix}.$$

Further, by Eq. (5.27), the collective prospect values of the alternatives X_1, X_2, X_3, X_4 are obtained, respectively.

$$va_1^c = -0.094585, \ va_2^c = 1.26878, \ va_3^c = -0.39789, \ va_4^c = -1.5923.$$

Therefore, the collective preference ordering of the four alternatives is obtained

$$X_2 \succ X_1 \succ X_3 \succ X_4.$$

Then, the collective preference-approval structure is obtained:

$$PA^c(X) = X_2 \,|X_1, X_3, X_4.$$

(ii) Consensus process with reference points

The consensus process with reference points deals with a two-step procedure: *consensus measure* and *feedback adjustment*.

(a) Consensus measure

By Eqs. (5.28) and (5.29), the consensus level among all the experts are: $PVCL\{E_1, \ldots, E_6\} = 0.1056$.
Without loss of generality, we set that the acceptable consensus level is 0.07. Because $PVCL = 0.1056 > 0.07$, we use the feedback adjustment to improve the consensus level.

(b) Feedback adjustment

The experts adjust their preference evaluations according to the adjustment rules proposed in Sect. 5.2.4. Their new preference representation structures are as follows:

$$U^{1,1} = (0.4, 0.7, 0.6, 0.1), \quad U^{2,1} = (0.7, 0.8, 0.6, 0.4)$$

$$R^{3,1} = (2, 1, 3, 4), \quad R^{4,1} = (2, 1, 4, 3)$$

$$A^{5,1} = \begin{pmatrix} 1 & 1/3 & 1/6 & 4 \\ 3 & 1 & 1 & 7 \\ 6 & 1 & 1 & 1/2 \\ 1/4 & 1/7 & 2 & 1 \end{pmatrix}, \quad D^{6,1} = \begin{pmatrix} 0.5 & 0.2 & 0.8 & 0.7 \\ 0.8 & 0.5 & 0.8 & 0.3 \\ 0.2 & 0.2 & 0.5 & 0.8 \\ 0.3 & 0.7 & 0.2 & 0.5 \end{pmatrix}.$$

The new individual orderings of each expert are calculated as follows.

$$R^{1,1} = (3, 1, 2, 4), \quad R^{2,1} = (2, 1, 3, 4),$$

$$R^{3,1} = (2, 1, 3, 4), \quad R^{4,1} = (2, 1, 4, 3),$$

$$R^{5,1} = (3, 1, 2, 4), \quad R^{6,1} = (2, 1, 4, 3).$$

Meanwhile, according to the rules proposed in Sect. 5.2.4, the experts adjust their information to obtain new preference-approval structures as:

$$PA^{1,1}(X) = X_2|X_3, X_1, X_4, \quad PA^{2,1}(X) = X_2|X_1, X_3, X_4,$$

$$PA^{3,1}(X) = X_2|X_1, X_3, X_4, \quad PA^{4,1}(X) = X_2|X_1, X_4, X_3,$$

$$PA^{5,1}(X) = X_2|X_3, X_1, X_4, \quad PA^{6,1}(X) = X_2|X_1, X_4, X_3$$

Based on the Eq. (5.23), the updated reference points for all the experts are as follows:

$$rp^{1,1} = 1.5, \; rp^{2,1} = 1.5, \; rp^{3,1} = 1.5, \; rp^{4,1} = 1.5, \; rp^{5,1} = 1.5, \; rp^{6,1} = 1.5.$$

According to the Eqs. (5.24) and (5.25), the new gain matrix $G^1 = (G_i^{k,1})_{6\times 4}$ and loss matrix $L^1 = (L_i^{k,1})_{6\times 4}$ are obtained as follows:

$$G^1 = \begin{pmatrix} 0 & 0.5 & 0 & 0 \\ 0 & 0.5 & 0 & 0 \\ 0 & 0.5 & 0 & 0 \\ 0 & 0.5 & 0 & 0 \\ 0 & 0.5 & 0 & 0 \\ 0 & 0.5 & 0 & 0 \end{pmatrix}, \quad L^1 = \begin{pmatrix} -1.5 & 0 & -0.5 & -2.5 \\ -0.5 & 0 & -1.5 & -2.5 \\ -0.5 & 0 & -1.5 & -2.5 \\ -1.5 & 0 & -2.5 & -1.5 \\ -1.5 & 0 & -0.5 & -2.5 \\ -0.5 & 0 & -2.5 & -1.5 \end{pmatrix}.$$

By Eqs. (5.28) and (5.29), the new consensus level among all the experts is $PVCL\{E_1, \ldots, E_6\} = 0.0668$.

Comparing with the previous consensus level 0.1056, the consensus level among the experts is obviously improved. The final ordering of the four alternatives is $X_2 \succ X_1 \succ X_3 \succ X_4$.

(2) Example 5.6

We continue with Example 5.1, and use the prospect theory based consensus model to help experts reach a consensus.

(i) Selection process with reference points

(a) Obtaining individual preference orderings

Based on Example 5.1, we can obtain the individual preference orderings, which are listed below:

$$R^1 = (4,\ 5,\ 1,\ 2,\ 3,\ 6)^T,\ \ R^2 = (5,\ 1,\ 4,\ 6,\ 2,\ 3)^T,$$

$$R^3 = (2,\ 1,\ 3,\ 6,\ 4,\ 5)^T,\ \ R^4 = (1,\ 3,\ 4,\ 6,\ 2,\ 5)^T,$$

$$R^5 = (2,\ 3,\ 1,\ 4,\ 5,\ 6)^T,\ \ R^6 = (6,\ 2,\ 1,\ 3,\ 5,\ 4)^T,$$

$$R^7 = (4,\ 1,\ 2,\ 3,\ 5,\ 6)^T,\ \ R^8 = (1,\ 2,\ 3,\ 6,\ 4,\ 5)^T.$$

(b) Determining the reference points

Based on the obtained individual preference orderings, the experts provide their preference-approval structures as follows:

$$PA^1(X) = X_3, X_4|X_5, X_1, X_2, X_6,\ \ PA^2(X) = X_2, X_5|X_6, X_3, X_1, X_4,$$

$$PA^3(X) = X_2, X_1, X_3|X_5, X_6, X_4,\ \ PA^4(X) = X_1, X_4, X_2, X_3|X_6, X_5,$$

$$PA^5(X) = X_3, X_1, X_2, X_4|X_5, X_6,\ \ PA^6(X) = X_3, X_2, X_4|X_6, X_5, X_1,$$

$$PA^7(X) = X_2, X_3, X_4|X_1, X_5, X_6,\ \ PA^8(X) = X_1, X_2, X_3, X_5, X_6|X_4.$$

Based on the Eq. (5.23), each expert's reference point on positional order is obtained as:

$$rp^1 = 2.5,\ rp^2 = 2.5,\ rp^3 = 3.5,\ rp^4 = 4.5,$$

$$rp^5 = 4.5,\ rp^6 = 3.5,\ rp^7 = 3.5,\ rp^8 = 5.5.$$

(c) Calculating the gains and losses

After obtaining the reference points, according to the Eqs. (5.24) and (5.25), the gain matrix $G = [G_i^k]_{8\times6}$ and loss matrix $L = [L_i^k]_{8\times6}$ are obtained as follows:

$$G = \begin{pmatrix} 0 & 0 & 1.5 & 0.5 & 0 & 0 \\ 0 & 1.5 & 0 & 0 & 0.5 & 0 \\ 1.5 & 2.5 & 0.5 & 0 & 0 & 0 \\ 3.5 & 1.5 & 0.5 & 2.5 & 0 & 0 \\ 2.5 & 1.5 & 3.5 & 0.5 & 0 & 0 \\ 0 & 1.5 & 2.5 & 0.5 & 0 & 0 \\ 0 & 2.5 & 1.5 & 0.5 & 0 & 0 \\ 4.5 & 3.5 & 2.5 & 0 & 1.5 & 0.5 \end{pmatrix}, \quad L = \begin{pmatrix} -1.5 & -2.5 & 0 & 0 & -0.5 & -3.5 \\ -2.5 & 0 & -1.5 & -3.5 & 0 & -0.5 \\ 0 & 0 & 0 & -2.5 & -0.5 & -1.5 \\ 0 & 0 & 0 & 0 & -1.5 & -0.5 \\ 0 & 0 & 0 & 0 & -0.5 & -1.5 \\ -2.5 & 0 & 0 & 0 & -1.5 & -0.5 \\ -0.5 & 0 & 0 & 0 & -1.5 & -2.5 \\ 0 & 0 & 0 & -0.5 & 0 & 0 \end{pmatrix}.$$

(d) Calculating the prospect values and ranking the alternatives

Assume all the experts set the parameters α, β and λ as the experiment result conducted by Kahneman and Tversky [22], i.e., $\alpha = \beta = 0.88$, $\lambda = 2.25$.

Then, based on the Eq. (5.26), let $VA = (va_i^k)_{8\times6}$ be the prospect values matrix:

$$VA = \begin{pmatrix} -3.215 & -5.039 & 1.429 & 0.543 & -1.223 & -6.776 \\ -5.039 & 1.429 & -3.215 & -6.779 & 0.543 & -1.223 \\ 1.429 & 2.24 & 0.543 & -5.039 & -1.223 & -3.215 \\ 3.011 & 1.429 & 0.543 & 2.240 & -3.215 & -1.226 \\ 2.240 & 1.429 & 3.011 & 0.543 & -1.223 & -3.215 \\ -5.039 & 1.429 & 2.240 & 0.543 & -3.215 & -1.223 \\ -1.223 & 2.24 & 1.429 & 0.543 & -3.215 & -5.039 \\ 3.757 & 3.011 & 2.240 & -1.223 & 1.429 & 0.543 \end{pmatrix}.$$

Further, by Eq. (5.27), the collective prospect values of the alternatives are obtained as

$$va_1^c = -0.50988, \; va_2^c = 1.020826, \; va_3^c = 1.02755,$$

$$va_4^c = -1.07807, \; va_5^c = -1.41747, \; va_6^c = -2.67112.$$

Therefore, the collective preference ordering of the six alternatives is obtained:

$$X_3 \succ X_2 \succ X_1 \succ X_4 \succ X_5 \succ X_6.$$

Then, the collective preference-approval structure is obtained:

$$PA^c(X) = X_3, X_2 \,|X_1, X_4, X_5, X_6.$$

(ii) Consensus process with reference points

The consensus process deals with a two-step procedure: consensus measure and feedback adjustment.

(a) Consensus measure

By Eqs. (5.28) and (5.29), the consensus level among all the experts is $PVCL\{E_1, \ldots, E_6\} = 0.1502$.
Without loss of generality, we set that the acceptable consensus level is 0.05. Because $PVCL\{E_1, \ldots, E_6\} = 0.1502 > 0.05$, we use the feedback adjustment to improve the consensus level.

(b) Feedback adjustment

The experts adjust their preference evaluations according to the adjustment rules proposed in Sect. 5.2.4. Their new preference representation structures are as follows:

$$U^{1,1} = (0.6, 0.9, 0.8, 0.5, 0.4, 0.3),\ \ U^{2,1} = (0.5, 0.8, 0.6, 0.7, 0.4, 0.3),$$

$$R^{3,1} = (3, 2, 1, 4, 5, 6),\ \ R^{4,1} = (2, 3, 1, 4, 5, 6),$$

$$A^{5,1} = \begin{pmatrix} 1 & 1/5 & 1/4 & 3 & 1/2 & 7 \\ 5 & 1 & 1/2 & 1/2 & 3 & 4 \\ 4 & 2 & 1 & 5 & 3 & 2 \\ 1/3 & 2 & 1/5 & 1 & 1/4 & 2 \\ 2 & 1/3 & 1/3 & 4 & 1 & 2 \\ 1/7 & 1/4 & 1/2 & 1/2 & 1/2 & 1 \end{pmatrix},\ A^{6,1} = \begin{pmatrix} 1 & 1/2 & 1/2 & 2 & 5 & 2 \\ 2 & 1 & 3 & 6 & 3 & 1/2 \\ 2 & 1/3 & 1 & 2 & 3 & 5 \\ 1/2 & 1/6 & 1/2 & 1 & 1/2 & 5 \\ 1/5 & 1/3 & 1/3 & 1/2 & 1 & 9 \\ 1/2 & 2 & 1/5 & 1/5 & 1/9 & 1 \end{pmatrix},$$

$$D^{7,1} = \begin{pmatrix} 0.5 & 0.6 & 0.55 & 0.4 & 0.8 & 0.5 \\ 0.4 & 0.5 & 0.6 & 0.8 & 0.3 & 0.6 \\ 0.45 & 0.4 & 0.5 & 0.5 & 0.6 & 0.55 \\ 0.6 & 0.2 & 0.5 & 0.5 & 0.7 & 0.4 \\ 0.2 & 0.7 & 0.4 & 0.3 & 0.5 & 0.95 \\ 0.5 & 0.4 & 0.45 & 0.6 & 0.05 & 0.5 \end{pmatrix},\ D^{8,1} = \begin{pmatrix} 0.5 & 0.6 & 0.5 & 0.6 & 0.55 & 0.75 \\ 0.4 & 0.5 & 0.5 & 0.6 & 0.6 & 0.7 \\ 0.5 & 0.5 & 0.5 & 0.5 & 0.8 & 0.7 \\ 0.4 & 0.4 & 0.5 & 0.5 & 0.95 & 0.65 \\ 0.45 & 0.4 & 0.2 & 0.5 & 0.5 & 0.8 \\ 0.25 & 0.3 & 0.3 & 0.35 & 0.2 & 0.5 \end{pmatrix}.$$

The new individual orderings of each expert are calculated as follows.

$$R^{1,1} = (3, 1, 2, 4, 5, 6),\ \ R^{2,1} = (4, 1, 3, 2, 5, 6),$$

$$R^{3,1} = (3, 2, 1, 4, 6, 5),\ \ R^{4,1} = (2, 3, 1, 4, 5, 6),$$

$$R^{5,1} = (4, 2, 1, 5, 3, 6),\ \ R^{6,1} = (4, 1, 2, 4, 5, 6),$$

$$R^{7,1} = (1, 2, 3, 4, 6, 5),\ \ R^{8,1} = (1, 2, 3, 4, 5, 6).$$

According to the rules proposed in Sect. 5.2.4, the experts adjust their information to obtain new preference-approval structures as:

$$PA^{1,1}(X) = X_2, X_3|X_1, X_4, X_5, X_6, \; PA^{2,1}(X) = X_2, X_4, X_3|X_1, X_5, X_6,$$

$$PA^{3,1}(X) = X_3, X_2|X_1, X_4, X_6, X_5, \; PA^{4,1}(X) = X_3, X_1, X_2|X_4, X_5, X_6,$$

$$PA^{5,1}(X) = X_3, X_2|X_5, X_1, X_4, X_6, \; PA^{6,1}(X) = X_2, X_3|X_1, X_4, X_5, X_6,$$

$$PA^{7,1}(X) = X_1, X_2, X_3|X_4, X_6, X_5, \; PA^{8,1}(X) = X_1, X_2, X_3|X_4, X_5, X_6.$$

Based on the Eq. (5.23), the updated reference points for all the experts are as follows:

$$rp^{1,1} = 2.5, \; rp^{2,1} = 3.5, \; rp^{3,1} = 2.5, \; rp^{4,1} = 3.5,$$

$$rp^{5,1} = 2.5, \; rp^{6,1} = 2.5, \; rp^{7,1} = 3.5, \; rp^{8,1} = 3.5.$$

According to the Eqs. (5.24) and (5.25), the new gain matrix $G^1 = [G_i^{k,1}]_{8\times 6}$ and loss matrix $L^1 = [L_i^{k,1}]_{8\times 6}$ are obtained as follows:

$$G^1 = \begin{pmatrix} 0 & 1.5 & 0.5 & 0 & 0 & 0 \\ 0 & 2.5 & 0.5 & 1.5 & 0 & 0 \\ 0 & 0.5 & 1.5 & 0 & 0 & 0 \\ 1.5 & 0.5 & 2.5 & 0 & 0 & 0 \\ 0 & 0.5 & 1.5 & 0 & 0 & 0 \\ 0 & 1.5 & 0.5 & 0 & 0 & 0 \\ 2.5 & 1.5 & 0.5 & 0 & 0 & 0 \\ 1.5 & 1.5 & 0.5 & 0 & 0 & 0 \end{pmatrix}, \; L^1 = \begin{pmatrix} -0.5 & 0 & 0 & -1.5 & -2.5 & -3.5 \\ -0.5 & 0 & 0 & 0 & -1.5 & -2.5 \\ -0.5 & 0 & 0 & -1.5 & -3.5 & -2.5 \\ 0 & 0 & 0 & -0.5 & -1.5 & -2.5 \\ -1.5 & 0 & 0 & -2.5 & -0.5 & -3.5 \\ -0.5 & 0 & 0 & -1.5 & -2.5 & -3.5 \\ 0 & 0 & 0 & -0.5 & -2.5 & -1.5 \\ 0 & 0 & 0 & -0.5 & -1.5 & -2.5 \end{pmatrix}.$$

By Eqs. (5.28) and (5.29), the new consensus level among all the experts is obtained as $PVCL\{E_1, \ldots, E_8\} = 0.0843$.

Since the acceptable consensus level is 0.05 and $PVCL\{E_1, \ldots, E_8\} = 0.0843 > 0.05$. Obviously, one more turn of feedback adjustment is needed.

(iii) One more turn of feedback adjustment

According to the preference evaluation rules proposed in Sect. 5.2.4, the new preference evaluations are represented as follows:

$$U^{1,2} = (0.6, 0.8, 0.9, 0.5, 0.4, 0.3), \; U^{2,2} = (0.7, 0.8, 0.9, 0.5, 0.4, 0.3),$$

$$R^{3,2} = (4, 2, 1, 3, 5, 6), \; R^{4,2} = (4, 2, 1, 3, 5, 6),$$

$$A^{5,2} = \begin{pmatrix} 1 & 1/5 & 1/4 & 3 & 1/2 & 7 \\ 5 & 1 & 1/2 & 1/2 & 3 & 4 \\ 4 & 2 & 1 & 5 & 3 & 2 \\ 1/3 & 2 & 1/5 & 1 & 4 & 2 \\ 2 & 1/3 & 1/3 & 1/4 & 1 & 2 \\ 1/7 & 1/4 & 1/2 & 1/2 & 1/2 & 1 \end{pmatrix}, \; A^{6,2} = \begin{pmatrix} 1 & 1/2 & 1/2 & 2 & 5 & 2 \\ 2 & 1 & 1/3 & 6 & 3 & 1/2 \\ 2 & 3 & 1 & 2 & 3 & 5 \\ 1/2 & 1/6 & 1/2 & 1 & 1/2 & 5 \\ 1/5 & 1/3 & 1/3 & 1/2 & 1 & 9 \\ 1/2 & 2 & 1/5 & 1/5 & 1/9 & 1 \end{pmatrix},$$

$$D^{7,2} = \begin{pmatrix} 0.5 & 0.3 & 0.4 & 0.9 & 0.8 & 0.4 \\ 0.7 & 0.5 & 0.2 & 0.7 & 0.3 & 0.6 \\ 0.6 & 0.8 & 0.5 & 0.5 & 0.6 & 0.55 \\ 0.1 & 0.3 & 0.5 & 0.5 & 0.7 & 0.6 \\ 0.2 & 0.7 & 0.4 & 0.3 & 0.5 & 0.95 \\ 0.6 & 0.4 & 0.45 & 0.4 & 0.05 & 0.5 \end{pmatrix}, \quad D^{8,2} = \begin{pmatrix} 0.5 & 0.4 & 0.2 & 0.6 & 0.55 & 0.75 \\ 0.6 & 0.5 & 0.5 & 0.6 & 0.6 & 0.7 \\ 0.8 & 0.5 & 0.5 & 0.5 & 0.8 & 0.7 \\ 0.4 & 0.4 & 0.5 & 0.5 & 0.95 & 0.65 \\ 0.45 & 0.4 & 0.2 & 0.5 & 0.5 & 0.8 \\ 0.25 & 0.3 & 0.3 & 0.35 & 0.2 & 0.5 \end{pmatrix}.$$

The new individual orderings of each expert are updated as follows:

$$R^{1,2} = (3, 2, 1, 4, 5, 6), \; R^{2,2} = (3, 2, 1, 4, 5, 6),$$

$$R^{3,2} = (4, 2, 1, 3, 5, 6), \; R^{4,2} = (4, 2, 1, 3, 5, 6),$$

$$R^{5,2} = (4, 2, 1, 3, 5, 6), \; R^{6,2} = (3, 2, 1, 4, 5, 6),$$

$$R^{7,2} = (3, 1, 2, 4, 5, 6), \; R^{8,2} = (3, 2, 1, 4, 5, 6).$$

According to the rules proposed in Sect. 5.2.4, the experts adjust their information to obtain new preference-approval structures as:

$$PA^{1,2}(X) = X_3, X_2|X_1, X_4, X_5, X_6, \; PA^{2,2}(X) = X_3, X_2|X_1, X_4, X_5, X_6,$$

$$PA^{3,2}(X) = X_3, X_2|X_4, X_1, X_5, X_6, \; PA^{4,2}(X) = X_3, X_2|X_4, X_1, X_5, X_6,$$

$$PA^{5,2}(X) = X_3, X_2|X_4, X_1, X_5, X_6, \; PA^{6,2}(X) = X_3, X_2|X_1, X_4, X_5, X_6,$$

$$PA^{7,2}(X) = X_2, X_3|X_1, X_4, X_5, X_6, \; PA^{8,2}(X) = X_3, X_2|X_1, X_4, X_5, X_6.$$

Based on the Eq. (5.23), the updated reference points for all the experts are as follows:

$$rp^{1,2} = 2.5, \; rp^{2,2} = 2.5, \; rp^{3,2} = 2.5, \; rp^{4,2} = 2.5,$$

$$rp^{5,2} = 2.5, \; rp^{6,2} = 2.5, \; rp^{7,2} = 2.5, \; rp^{8,2} = 2.5.$$

According to the Eqs. (5.24) and (5.25), the new gain matrix $G^2 = [G_i^{k,2}]_{8\times 6}$ and loss matrix $L^2 = [L_i^{k,2}]_{8\times 6}$ are obtained as follows:

$$G^2 = \begin{pmatrix} 0 & 0.5 & 1.5 & 0 & 0 & 0 \\ 0 & 0.5 & 0.5 & 0 & 0 & 0 \\ 0 & 0.5 & 1.5 & 0 & 0 & 0 \\ 0 & 0.5 & 1.5 & 0 & 0 & 0 \\ 0 & 0.5 & 1.5 & 0 & 0 & 0 \\ 0 & 0.5 & 1.5 & 0 & 0 & 0 \\ 0 & 1.5 & 0.5 & 0 & 0 & 0 \\ 0 & 0.5 & 1.5 & 0 & 0 & 0 \end{pmatrix}, \quad L^2 = \begin{pmatrix} -0.5 & 0 & 0 & -1.5 & -2.5 & -3.5 \\ -0.5 & 0 & 0 & -1.5 & -2.5 & -3.5 \\ -1.5 & 0 & 0 & -0.5 & -2.5 & -3.5 \\ -1.5 & 0 & 0 & -0.5 & -2.5 & -3.5 \\ -1.5 & 0 & 0 & -0.5 & -2.5 & -3.5 \\ -0.5 & 0 & 0 & -1.5 & -2.5 & -3.5 \\ -0.5 & 0 & 0 & -1.5 & -2.5 & -3.5 \\ -0.5 & 0 & 0 & -1.5 & -2.5 & -3.5 \end{pmatrix}.$$

By Eqs. (5.28)–(5.29), the new consensus level among all the experts is obtained as $PVCL\{E_1, \ldots, E_8\} = 0.036$.

Compared with the previous consensus level 0.0843, the consensus level among the experts is obviously improved. The final ordering of the six alternatives is $X_2 \succ X_3 \succ X_1 \succ X_4 \succ X_5 \succ X_6$.

(3) Discussion

In the following, we propose Experiments 5.1 and 5.2 based on Examples 5.5 and 5.6 to show the advantages of the prospect theory based consensus model.

(i) Experiment 5.1

In Experiment 5.1, we set different preference-approval structures (i.e. different reference points) in Examples 5.5 and 5.6, and then use the selection process with reference points to obtain the selection outcomes. The experimental results are listed in Tables 5.1 and 5.2.

Table 5.1 The experimental results based on Example 5.5 in Experiment 5.1

Preference-approval structures	Selection outcomes	$PVCL$
$PA^1(X) = X_2 \vert X_4, X_1, X_3,\ PA^2(X) = X_3, X_2 \vert X_1, X_4$	$X_2 \succ X_1 \succ X_3 \succ X_4$	0.1056
$PA^3(X) = X_3, X_2, X_1 \vert X_4,\ PA^4(X) = X_2, X_1 \vert X_3, X_4$		
$PA^5(X) = X_2, X_3, X_1 \vert X_4,\ PA^6(X) = X_1, X_2, X_4 \vert X_3$		
$PA^1(X) = X_2, X_4, X_1 \vert X_3,\ PA^2(X) = X_3 \vert X_2, X_1, X_4$	$X_2 \succ X_3 \succ X_1 \succ X_4$	0.1287
$PA^3(X) = X_3 \vert X_2, X_1, X_4,\ PA^4(X) = X_2, X_1, X_3 \vert X_4$		
$PA^5(X) = X_2, X_3 \vert X_1, X_4,\ PA^6(X) = X_1 \vert X_2, X_4, X_3$		

Table 5.2 The experimental results based on Example 5.6 in Experiment 5.1

Preference-approval structures	Selection outcomes	$PVCL$
$PA^1(X) = X_3, X_4 \vert X_5, X_1, X_2, X_6,$	$X_3 \succ X_2 \succ X_1 \succ X_4 \succ X_5 \succ X_6$	0.1502
$PA^2(X) = X_2, X_5 \vert X_6, X_3, X_1, X_4,$		
$PA^3(X) = X_2 \vert X_1, X_3 \vert X_5, X_6, X_4,$		
$PA^4(X) = X_1, X_4, X_2, X_3 \vert X_6, X_5,$		
$PA^5(X) = X_3, X_1, X_2, X_4 \vert X_5, X_6,$		
$PA^6(X) = X_3, X_2, X_4 \vert X_6, X_5, X_1,$		
$PA^7(X) = X_2, X_3, X_4 \vert X_1, X_5, X_6,$		
$PA^8(X) = X_1, X_2, X_3, X_5, X_6 \vert X_4.$		
$PA^1(X) = X_3, X_4, X_5, X_1, X_2 \vert X_6,$	$X_2 \succ X_3 \succ X_1 \succ X_4 \succ X_5 \succ X_6$	0.1762
$PA^2(X) = X_2 \vert X_5, X_6, X_3, X_1, X_4,$		
$PA^3(X) = X_2 \vert X_1, X_3 \vert X_5, X_6, X_4,$		
$PA^4(X) = X_1, X_4, X_2 \vert X_3, X_6, X_5,$		
$PA^5(X) = X_3, X_1, X_2 \vert X_4, X_5, X_6,$		
$PA^6(X) = X_3, X_2 \vert X_4, X_6, X_5, X_1$		
$PA^7(X) = X_2 \vert X_3, X_4, X_1, X_5, X_6,$		
$PA^8(X) = X_1, X_2 \vert X_3, X_5, X_6, X_4.$		

Table 5.3 The experimental results based on Example 5.5 in Experiment 5.2

	Adjusting both	$PVCL$	Adjusting only preference evaluations	$PVCL$
Round 1	$PA^1(X) = X_2 \| X_1, X_3, X_4$	0.0668	$PA^1(X) = X_2 \| X_1, X_3, X_4$	0.0904
	$PA^2(X) = X_2 \| X_1, X_4, X_3$		$PA^2(X) = X_2, X_1 \| X_4, X_3$	
	$PA^3(X) = X_2 \| X_3, X_1, X_4$		$PA^3(X) = X_2, X_3, X_1 \| X_4$	
	$PA^4(X) = X_2 \| X_1, X_3, X_4$		$PA^4(X) = X_2, X_1 \| X_3, X_4$	
	$PA^5(X) = X_2 \| X_1, X_4, X_3$		$PA^5(X) = X_2, X_1, X_4 \| X_3$	
	$PA^6(X) = X_2 \| X_3, X_1, X_4$		$PA^6(X) = X_2, X_3, X_1 \| X_4$	

Table 5.4 The experimental results based on Example 5.6 in Experiment 5.2

	Adjusting both	$PVCL$	Adjusting only preference evaluations	$PVCL$
Round 1	$PA(X^1) = X_2, X_3 \| X_1, X_4, X_5, X_6$	0.0843	$PA^1(X) = X_2, X_3 \| X_1, X_4, X_5, X_6$	0.0998
	$PA^2(X) = X_2, X_4, X_3 \| X_1, X_5, X_6$		$PA^2(X) = X_2, X_4 \| X_3, X_1, X_5, X_6$	
	$PA^3(X) = X_3, X_2 \| X_1, X_4, X_6, X_5$		$PA^3(X) = X_3, X_2, X_1 \| X_4, X_6, X_5$	
	$PA^4(X) = X_3, X_1, X_2 \| X_4, X_5, X_6$		$PA^4(X) = X_3, X_1, X_2 \| X_4, X_5, X_6$	
	$PA^5(X) = X_3, X_2 \| X_5, X_1, X_4, X_6$		$PA^5(X) = X_3, X_2, X_5, X_1 \| X_4, X_6$	
	$PA^6(X) = X_2, X_3 \| X_1, X_4, X_5, X_6$		$PA^6(X) = X_2, X_3, X_1, X_4 \| X_5, X_6$	
	$PA^7(X) = X_1, X_2, X_3 \| X_4, X_6, X_5$		$PA^7(X) = X_1, X_2, X_3 \| X_4, X_6, X_5$	
	$PA^8(X) = X_1, X_2, X_3 \| X_4, X_5, X_6$		$PA^8(X) = X_1, X_2, X_3, X_4, X_5 \| X_6$	
Round 2	$PA^1(X) = X_3, X_2 \| X_4, X_1, X_5, X_6$	0.036	$PA^1(X) = X_3, X_2 \| X_1, X_4, X_5, X_6$	0.0815
	$PA^2(X) = X_3, X_2 \| X_1, X_4, X_5, X_6$		$PA^2(X) = X_3, X_2 \| X_1, X_4, X_5, X_6$	
	$PA^3(X) = X_3, X_2 \| X_4, X_1, X_5, X_6$		$PA^3(X) = X_3, X_2, X_4 \| X_1, X_5, X_6$	
	$PA^4(X) = X_3, X_1, X_2 \| X_4, X_5, X_6$		$PA^4(X) = X_3, X_2, X_4, X_1 \| X_5, X_6$	
	$PA^5(X) = X_3, X_2 \| X_4, X_1, X_5, X_6$		$PA^5(X) = X_3, X_2, X_4, X_1 \| X_5, X_6$	
	$PA^6(X) = X_3, X_2 \| X_1, X_4, X_5, X_6$		$PA^6(X) = X_3, X_2, X_1 \| X_4, X_5, X_6$	
	$PA^7(X) = X_2, X_3 \| X_1, X_4, X_5, X_6$		$PA^7(X) = X_2, X_3, X_1 \| X_4, X_5, X_6$	
	$PA^8(X) = X_3, X_2 \| X_1, X_4, X_5, X_6$		$PA^8(X) = X_3, X_2, X_1, X_4, X_5 \| X_6$	

From Experiment 5.1, we find that the use of different reference points will yield different outputs of the selection process in GDM.

(ii) Experiment 5.2

In Experiment 5.2, we consider two cases:

Case A: In Case A, the experts adjust both the preference evaluations and the preference-approval information.

Case B: In Case B, the experts only adjust the preference evaluations.

The experimental results based on Examples 5.5 and 5.6 are listed in Tables 5.3 and 5.4, respectively.

As we can see from Tables 5.3 and 5.4, compared with only adjusting the preference evaluations, adjusting both the preference evaluations and the preference-approval information can accelerate the pace of consensus reaching.

5.3 Consensus with Minimum Adjustments Under Prospect Theory

In this section, in the prospect theory framework, we further propose a minimum adjustments consensus model in GDM with heterogeneous preference representation structures.

5.3.1 Minimum Adjustments with Reference Points

Let $\overline{R^k} = (\overline{r_1^k}, \overline{r_2^k}, \ldots, \overline{r_m^k})$ $(k = 1, 2, \ldots, n)$ be the adjusted value of the preference ordering associated with R^k, and let $\overline{rp^k}$ $(k = 1, 2, \ldots, n)$ be the adjusted value of the reference point associated with rp^k.

Using Eq. (5.26) obtains the prospect value $\overline{va_i^k}$ $(k = 1, 2, \ldots, n;\ i = 1, 2, \ldots, m)$ from $\overline{R^k}$ and $\overline{rp^k}$. Employing Eq. (5.27) yields the collective prospect value, i.e., $\overline{va_i^c} = \frac{1}{n} \sum\limits_{k=1}^{n} \overline{va_i^k}$ $(i = 1, 2, \ldots, m)$. Then, the consensus level regarding the adjusted values of the preference orderings and the adjusted values of the reference points can be calculated as follows:

$$\overline{PVCL}\{E_1, \ldots, E_n\} = \frac{1}{nm} \sum_{k=1}^{n} \sum_{i=1}^{m} \left| \frac{\overline{va_i^k} - \overline{va_i^c}}{va(m) - va(-m)} \right|. \tag{5.30}$$

Naturally, we not only want to minimize the number of the adjusted values of the individual preference orderings, but also hope to minimize the number of the adjusted values of the reference points, in the consensus building based on prospect theory, i.e.,

$$min \sum_{k=1}^{n} \sum_{i=1}^{m} y_{ik} + \sum_{k=1}^{n} h_k \tag{5.31}$$

where y_{ik} and h_k count the number of the adjusted values of the individual preference orderings and reference points, respectively, i.e.,

$$y_{ik} = \begin{cases} 1, \ r_i^k \neq \overline{r_i^k} \\ 0, \ r_i^k = \overline{r_i^k} \end{cases}, \quad k = 1, 2, \ldots, n; \ i = 1, 2, \ldots, m, \tag{5.32}$$

and

$$h_k = \begin{cases} 1, \ rp^k \neq \overline{rp^k} \\ 0, \ rp^k = \overline{rp^k} \end{cases}, \quad k = 1, 2, \ldots, n. \tag{5.33}$$

Meanwhile, the consensus level among experts is acceptable, i.e.,

$$\overline{PVCL}\{E_1, \ldots, E_n\} \leq \varepsilon \tag{5.34}$$

where ε is the established consensus threshold.

And each expert should provide the strict individual orderings, i.e.,

$$\overline{r_i^k} \neq \overline{r_j^k}, \ i \neq j; \ i, j = 1, 2, \ldots, m; k = 1, 2, \ldots, n. \tag{5.35}$$

Based on (5.31)–(5.35), the consensus model with minimum adjustments is proposed using an optimization-based model:

$$\begin{cases} min \sum\limits_{k=1}^{n} \sum\limits_{i=1}^{m} y_{ik} + \sum\limits_{k=1}^{n} h_k \\ s.t. \begin{cases} \overline{r_i^k} \neq \overline{r_j^k}, \ i \neq j; \ i, j = 1, 2, \ldots, m; k = 1, 2, \ldots, n \\ \overline{r_i^k} \in \{1, 2, \ldots, m\}, \ i = 1, 2, \ldots, m; \ k = 1, 2, \ldots, n \\ \overline{va_i^k} = \begin{cases} \left(\overline{rp^k} - \overline{r_i^k}\right)^{\alpha_k}, & \overline{r_i^k} < \overline{rp^k} \\ -\lambda_k \left(\overline{r_i^k} - \overline{rp^k}\right)^{\beta_k}, & \overline{r_i^k} \geq \overline{rp^k} \end{cases}, \ i = 1, 2, \ldots, m; \ k = 1, 2, \ldots, n \\ \overline{va_i^c} = \frac{1}{n} \sum\limits_{k=1}^{n} \overline{va_i^k}, \ i = 1, 2, \ldots, n \\ \frac{1}{mn} \sum\limits_{k=1}^{n} \sum\limits_{i=1}^{m} \left| \frac{\overline{va_i^k} - \overline{va_i^c}}{va(m) - va(-m)} \right| \leq \varepsilon \\ y_{ik} = \begin{cases} 1, \ r_i^k \neq \overline{r_i^k} \\ 0, \ r_i^k = \overline{r_i^k} \end{cases}, \quad i = 1, 2, \ldots, m; \ k = 1, 2, \ldots, n \\ h_k = \begin{cases} 1, \ rp^k \neq \overline{rp^k} \\ 0, \ rp^k = \overline{rp^k} \end{cases}, \quad k = 1, 2, \ldots, n \end{cases} \end{cases} \tag{5.36}$$

In model (5.36), $\overline{r_i^k}(i = 1, 2, \ldots, m; k = 1, 2, \ldots, n)$ and $\overline{rp^k}(k = 1, 2, \ldots, n)$ are decision variables. Solving model (5.36) obtains the optimal solution $\overline{r_i^{k*}}$ $(i = 1, 2, \ldots, m;\ k = 1, 2, \ldots, n)$ and $\overline{rp^{k*}}(k = 1, 2, \ldots, n)$.

5.3.2 Comparison Analysis

In the following, we provide a comparison analysis to show the advantages of the prospect theory based minimum adjustments consensus model (i.e., model (5.36)).

(1) Example 5.7

We continue with Example 5.5. Based on the selection process of Example 5.5, we obtain the individual preference orderings R^k $(k = 1, 2, \ldots, 6)$ and the reference points rp^k $(k = 1, 2, \ldots, 6)$.

Let $\varepsilon = 0.05$. Taking R^k and rp^k $(k = 1, 2, \ldots, 6)$ as inputs of model (5.36), we can obtain that the values of the adjusted preference orderings $\overline{R^k}$ $(k = 1, 2, \ldots, 6)$ and the values of the adjusted reference points $\overline{rp^k}$ $(k = 1, 2, \ldots, 6)$. $\overline{R^k}$ and $\overline{rp^k}$ $(k = 1, 2, \ldots, 6)$ are listed below:

$$\overline{R^1} = (3, 2, 1, 4)^T,\ \overline{R^2} = (2, 1, 3, 4)^T,$$

$$\overline{R^3} = (3, 1, 2, 4)^T,\ \overline{R^4} = (3, 2, 1, 4)^T,$$

$$\overline{R^5} = (1, 2, 3, 4)^T,\ \overline{R^6} = (3, 2, 1, 4)^T.$$

$$\overline{rp^1} = 3.5,\ \overline{rp^2} = 3.5,\ \overline{rp^3} = 3.5,\ \overline{rp^4} = 3.5,\ \overline{rp^5} = 3.5,\ \overline{rp^6} = 3.5.$$

Meanwhile, we obtain the adjusted preference-approval structures from $\overline{R^k}$ and $\overline{rp^k}$ $(k = 1, 2, \ldots, 6)$, which are listed below:

$$PA^1(X) = X_3, X_2, X_1|X_4,\ PA^2(X) = X_2, X_1, X_3|X_4,$$

$$PA^3(X) = X_2, X_3, X_1|X_4,\ PA^4(X) = X_3, X_2, X_1|X_4,$$

$$PA^5(X) = X_2, X_1, X_3|X_4,\ PA^6(X) = X_3, X_2, X_1|X_4.$$

Using Definition 5.5 obtains the consensus level among experts, $PVCL\{E_1, \ldots, E_6\} = 0.0396$, which indicates the consensus level is obviously improved. Further, we can obtain the collective ranking of alternative from $\overline{R^k}$ and $\overline{rp^k}$ $(k = 1, 2, \ldots, 6)$, i.e., $X_3 \succ X_2 \succ X_1 \succ X_4$.

(2) Example 5.8

We continue with the Example 5.6. Based on the selection process of Example 5.6, we obtain the individual preference orderings R^k $(k = 1, 2, \ldots, 8)$ and the reference points rp^k $(k = 1, 2, \ldots, 8)$.

Let $\varepsilon = 0.05$. Taking R^k and rp^k $(k = 1, 2, \ldots, 8)$ as inputs of model (5.36), we can obtain the adjusted preference orderings $\overline{R^k}$ $(k = 1, 2, \ldots, 8)$ and the adjusted reference points $\overline{rp^k}$ $(k = 1, 2, \ldots, 8)$. $\overline{R^k}$ and $\overline{rp^k}$ $(k = 1, 2, \ldots, 8)$ are listed below:

$$\overline{R^1} = (4, 5, 1, 2, 3, 6),\ \overline{R^2} = (5, 1, 4, 3, 2, 6),$$

$$\overline{R^3} = (2, 1, 3, 5, 4, 6),\ \overline{R^4} = (1, 3, 4, 2, 5, 6),$$

$$\overline{R^5} = (2, 3, 1, 4, 5, 6),\ \overline{R^6} = (4, 2, 1, 3, 5, 6),$$

$$\overline{R^7} = (4, 1, 2, 3, 5, 6),\ \overline{R^8} = (1, 2, 3, 5, 4, 6).$$

$$rp^1 = 5.5, rp^2 = 5.5, rp^3 = 5.5, rp^4 = 5.5,$$

$$rp^5 = 5.5, rp^6 = 5.5, rp^7 = 5.5, rp^8 = 5.5,$$

Meanwhile, we obtain the adjusted preference-approval structures from $\overline{R^k}$ and $\overline{rp^k}$ $(k = 1, 2, \ldots, 8)$, which are listed below:

$$PA^1(X) = X_3, X_4, X_5, X_1, X_2|X_6,\ PA^2(X) = X_2, X_5, X_4, X_3, X_1|X_6,$$

$$PA^3(X) = X_2, X_1, X_3, X_5, |X_4, X_6,\ PA^4(X) = X_1, X_4, X_2, X_3, X_5|X_6,$$

$$PA^5(X) = X_3, X_1, X_2, X_4, X_5|X_6,\ PA^6(X) = X_3, X_2, X_4, X_5, X_1|X_6,$$

$$PA^7(X) = X_2, X_3, X_4, X_1, X_5|X_6,\ PA^8(X) = X_1, X_2, X_3, X_5, X_4|X_6.$$

Using Definition 5.5 yields the consensus level among experts, $PVCL\{E_1, \ldots, E_6\} = 0.0396$, which indicates the consensus level is obviously improved. Further, we can obtain the collective ranking of alternative from $\overline{R^k}$ and $\overline{rp^k}$ $(k = 1, 2, \ldots, 8)$, i.e., $X_2 \succ X_3 \succ X_1 \succ X_4 \succ X_5 \succ X_6$.

(3) Comparison results

Let $z_1 = \sum_{k=1}^{n} \sum_{i=1}^{m} y_{ik} + \sum_{k=1}^{n} h_k$, which counts the total number of adjusted values of the individual preference-approval structures and preference orderings. Let $z_2 = \sum_{k=1}^{n} \sum_{i=1}^{m} |r_i^k - \overline{r_i^k}| + \sum_{k=1}^{n} |rp^k - \overline{rp^k}|$, which measures the adjustment amounts of the individual preference-approval structures and preference orderings.

Table 5.5 The comparison results between Examples 5.5 and 5.7

	z_1	z_2	$\overline{PVCL}$
Example 5.5	20	28	0.0668
Example 5.7	7	10	0.0396

Table 5.6 The comparison results between Examples 5.6 and 5.8

	z_1	z_2	$\overline{PVCL}$
Example 5.6	72	108	0.036
Example 5.8	17	30	0.0499

Let $\overline{PVCL}$ be as before, and $\varepsilon = 0.05$. We use the values for z_1, z_2 and $\overline{PVCL}$ as the criteria to obtain the comparative results, which are listed in Tables 5.5 and 5.6.

Tables 5.5 and 5.6 show that model (5.36) needs less z_1 (the number of the adjusted values of individual preference-approval structures and preference orderings) and z_2 (the adjustment amounts of the individual preference-approval structures and preference orderings) than the prospect theory based consensus model.

References

1. M. Abdellaoui, H. Bleichrodt, C. Paraschiv, Loss aversion under prospect theory: a parameter-free measurement. Manage. Sci. **53**, 1659–1674 (2007)
2. K.J. Arrow, *Social Choice and Individual Values* (Wiley, New York, 1963)
3. M.L. Balinski, R. Laraki, *Majority Judgment: Measuring, Ranking and Electing* (The MIT Press, Cambridge, 2010)
4. S.J. Brams, P.C. Fishburn, *Approval Voting* (Springer, 2007)
5. S.J. Brams, M.R. Sanver, *Voting Systems that Combine Approval and Preference, The Mathematics of Preference, Choice and Order* (Springer, Berlin, 2009)
6. X. Chen, H.J. Zhang, Y.C. Dong, The fusion process with heterogeneous preference structures in group decision making: a survey. Inf. Fusion **24**, 72–83 (2015)
7. F. Chiclana, F. Herrera, E. Herrera-Viedma, Integrating three representation models in fuzzy multipurpose decision making based on additive preference relations. Fuzzy Sets Syst. **97**, 33–48 (1998)
8. F. Chiclana, F. Herrera, E. Herrera-Viedma, Integrating multiplicative preference relations in a multipurpose decision-making model based on additive preference relations. Fuzzy Sets Syst. **122**, 277–291 (2001)
9. F. Chiclana, F. Herrera, E. Herrera-Viedma, A note on the internal consistency of various preference representations. Fuzzy Sets Syst. **131**, 75–78 (2002)
10. F. Chiclana, F. Mata, L. Martínez, E. Herrera-Viedma, S. Alonso, Integration of a consistency control module within a consensus decision making model. Int. J. Uncertainty Fuzziness Knowl. Based Syst. **16**, 35–53 (2008)
11. Y.C. Dong, H.Y. Li, Y.F. Xu, On reciprocity indexes in the aggregation of fuzzy preference relations using the OWA operator. Fuzzy Sets Syst. **159**, 185–192 (2008)
12. Y.C. Dong, N. Luo, H.M. Liang, Consensus building in multiperson decision making with heterogeneous preference representation structures: A perspective based on prospect theory. Appl. Soft Comput. **35**, 898–910 (2015)

13. Y.C. Dong, Y.F. Xu, S. Yu, Linguistic multiperson decision making based on the use of multiple preference relations. Fuzzy Sets Syst. **160**, 603–623 (2009)
14. Y.C. Dong, H.J. Zhang, Multiperson decision making with different preference representation structures: a direct consensus framework and its properties. Knowl. Based Syst. **58**, 45–57 (2014)
15. Z.P. Fan, J. Ma, Y.P. Jiang, Y.H. Sun, L. Ma, A goal programming approach to group decision making based on multiplicative preference relations and fuzzy preference relations. Eur. J. Oper. Res. **174**, 311–321 (2006)
16. Z.P. Fan, S.H. Xiao, G.F. Hu, An optimization method for integrating two kinds of preference information in group decision-making. Comput. Ind. Eng. **46**, 329–335 (2004)
17. Z.P. Fan, X. Zhang, F.D. Chen, Y. Liu, Multiple attribute decision making considering aspiration-levels: a method based on prospect theory. Comput. Ind. Eng. **65**, 341–350 (2013)
18. X.D. He, X.Y. Zhou, Portfolio choice under cumulative prospect theory: an analytical treatment. Manage. Sci. **57**, 315–331 (2011)
19. F. Herrera, E. Herrera-Viedma, J.L. Verdegay, Direct approach processes in group decision making using linguistic OWA operators. Fuzzy Sets Syst. **79**, 175–190 (1996)
20. E. Herrera-Viedma, F. Herrera, F. Chiclana, A consensus model for multiperson decision making with different preference structures. IEEE Trans. Syst. Man Cybern. Part A Syst. Hum. **32**, 394–402 (2002)
21. Y.P. Jiang, Z.P. Fan, J. Ma, A method for group decision making with multigranularity linguistic assessment information. Inf. Sci. **178**, 1098–1109 (2008)
22. D. Kahneman, A. Tversky, Prospect theory: an analysis of decision under risk, Econometrica J. Econometric Soc. 263-291 (1979)
23. J. Ma, Z.P. Fan, Y.P. Jiang, J.Y. Mao, An optimization approach to multiperson decision making based on different formats of preference information. IEEE Trans. Syst. Man Cybern. Part A Syst. Hum. **36**, 876–889 (2006)
24. I. Palomares, L. Martínez, F. Herrera, A consensus model to detect and manage non-cooperative behaviors in large scale group decision making. IEEE Trans. Fuzzy Syst. **22**, 516–530 (2014)
25. I.J. Pérez, F.J. Cabrerizo, S. Alonso, E. Herrera-Viedma, A new consensus model for group decision making problems with non-homogeneous experts. IEEE Trans. Syst. Man Cybern. Syst. **44**, 494–498 (2014)
26. A. Sen, *Collective Choice and Social Welfare* (Holdenday, San Francisco, CA, 1970)
27. W.D. Smith, *On Balinski and Laraki's Majority Judgement Median-based Range-like Voting Scheme* (2007)
28. A. Tversky, D. Kahneman, Advances in prospect theory: cumulative representation of uncertainty. J. Risk Uncertainty **5**, 297–323 (1992)
29. P.P. Wakker, *Prospect Theory: For Risk and Ambiguity* (Cambridge University Press, Cambridge, 2010)
30. G. Wu, R. Gonzalez, Curvature of the probability weighting function. Manage. Sci. **42**, 1676–1690 (1996)
31. H.L. Xu, J. Zhou, W. Xu, A decision-making rule for modeling travelers' route choice behavior based on cumulative prospect theory. Transp. Res. Part C **19**, 218–228 (2011)

Chapter 6
Consensus in Multiple Attribute Decision Making

We present two multiple attribute consensus rules with minimum adjustments: *the distance-based consensus rule* and *the count-based consensus rule*. The distance-based consensus rule is to minimize the distance between the original opinions and adjusted opinions, and the count-based consensus rule seeks to minimize the number of adjusted preference values. Based on the distance-based and count-based consensus rules, we develop an interactive consensus reaching process for MAGDM.

6.1 Consensus Problem with Multiple Attributes

The basic knowledge regarding the multiple attribute decision matrix and the consensus problem with multiple attributes is presented as follows.

(1) Multiple attribute decision making

Consider a MAGDM problem. Let $X = \{X_1, X_2, \ldots, X_m\}$ and $E = \{E_1, E_2, \ldots, E_n\}$ be as before. Let $w = (w_1, w_2, \ldots, w_n)^T$ be the associated weight vector of experts, where $w_k \geq 0 (k = 1, 2, \ldots, n)$ and $\sum_{k=1}^{n} w_k = 1$. Let $C = \{C_1, C_2, \ldots, C_l\}$ be the set of predefined attributes, and $\lambda = (\lambda_1, \lambda_2, \ldots, \lambda_l)^T$ be the associated weight vector of the attributes, where $\lambda_j \geq 0 (j = 1, 2, \ldots, l)$ and $\sum_{j=1}^{l} \lambda_j = 1$. Then, let $PM^k = (pm_{ij}^k)_{m \times l} (k = 1, 2, \ldots, n)$ be the decision matrix given by the expert $E_k \in E$, where pm_{ij}^k represents the preference value for alternative $X_i \in X$ with respect to the attribute $C_j \in C$.

Y. Dong and J. Xu, *Consensus Building in Group Decision Making*,
DOI 10.1007/978-981-287-892-2_6

The process of solving a MAGDM problem includes three steps:

(i) Normalization of the individual decision matrix

In MAGDM problems, attributes are classified into two categories: benefit attributes and cost attributes. The expert's decision matrix $PM^k = (pm_{ij}^k)_{m\times l}$ is normalized into a corresponding standardized individual decision matrix $V^k = (v_{ij}^k)_{m\times l}$, where

$$v_{ij}^k = \begin{cases} \dfrac{pm_{ij}^k - \min\limits_{1\le i\le m} pm_{ij}^k}{\max\limits_{1\le i\le m} pm_{ij}^k - \min\limits_{1\le i\le m} pm_{ij}^k}, & \text{for benefit attribute } C_j \in C \\ \dfrac{\max\limits_{1\le i\le m} pm_{ij}^k - pm_{ij}^k}{\max\limits_{1\le i\le m} pm_{ij}^k - \min\limits_{1\le i\le m} pm_{ij}^k}, & \text{for cost attribute } C_j \in C \end{cases}. \tag{6.1}$$

(ii) Aggregation of the standardized individual decision matrix

We use the OWA operator to aggregate individual opinions and obtain the group decision matrix, $V^c = (v_{ij}^c)_{m\times l}$, where

$$v_{ij}^c = F_w^{OWA}(v_{ij}^1, v_{ij}^2, \ldots, v_{ij}^n), \quad i = 1, 2, \ldots, m;\ j = 1, 2, \ldots, l. \tag{6.2}$$

(iii) Selection of alternatives

Using the WA operator to aggregate all the elements in the ith row of V^c, we can obtain the evaluation value of the alternative X_i, $EV(i)$, i.e.,

$$EV(i) = \sum_{j=1}^{l} \lambda_j v_{ij}^c, \quad i = 1, 2, \ldots, m. \tag{6.3}$$

Thus, experts select the alternative(s) with higher evaluation value.

(2) Measuring consensus and adjustment amounts

The consensus measure and adjustment amounts measure methods in consensus based MAGDM are introduced below.

(i) Consensus measure

Using Manhattan distance, we define the consensus measure of MAGDM as Definition 6.1.

Definition 6.1 Let $V^k = (v_{ij}^k)_{m\times l}(k = 1, 2, \ldots, n)$ be the standardized individual decision matrix provided by expert E_k, and $V^c = (v_{ij}^c)_{m\times l}$ be the group decision matrix obtained by aggregating experts' opinions with an OWA operator. Then, the consensus measure is defined as follows:

$$CL\{V^1, V^2, \ldots, V^n\} = \frac{1}{nml}\sum_{k=1}^{n} d(V^k, V^c) \quad (6.4)$$

where $d(V^k, V^c)$ is Manhattan distance between V^k and V^c, i.e.,

$$d(V^k, V^c) = \sum_{i=1}^{m}\sum_{j=1}^{l} |v_{ij}^k - v_{ij}^c| \;\; k = 1, 2, \ldots, n. \quad (6.5)$$

If $CL\{V^1, V^2, \ldots, V^n\} = 0$, then all the experts have full and unanimous consensus with the collective opinion. Otherwise, the smaller $CL\{V^1, V^2, \ldots, V^n\}$ value indicates the higher consensus level among all the experts.

(ii) Measuring adjustment amounts

As described in Eq. (1.8), the core problem in consensus models is to minimize the adjustments between individual original opinions and adjusted opinions. In general, the measure of adjustment amounts is done by measuring the distance between individual original opinions and adjusted opinions. Let $V = \{V^1, V^2, \ldots, V^n\}$ be the set of standardized individual decision matrices provided by experts, and $\overline{V} = \left\{\overline{V^1}, \overline{V^2}, \ldots, \overline{V^n}\right\}$ be the set of adjusted decision matrices of experts. The adjustment amounts based on Manhattan distance between V and $\overline{V}$ is presented as Eq. (6.6):

$$AD(V, \overline{V}) = \frac{1}{ml}\sum\nolimits_{k=1}^{n} d(V^k, \overline{V^k}). \quad (6.6)$$

Ben-Arieh and Easton [1] have defined the concept of minimum-cost consensus, which seeks to minimize the cost of reaching consensus. The measure of adjustment amounts between V and $\overline{V}$ can be considered as a special case of consensus cost, where the cost of changing each expert's opinion 1 unit distance is the same.

However, experts often expect to minimize the number of adjusted preference values when reaching consensus [16]. Thus, we propose a new measure for adjustment amounts between V and $\overline{V}$ as Eq. (6.7):

$$NAD(V, \overline{V}) = \sum_{k=1}^{n}\sum_{i=1}^{m}\sum_{j=1}^{l} x_{ij}^k, \quad (6.7)$$

where x_{ij}^k counts the number of adjusted preference values, i.e.,

$$x_{ij}^k = \begin{cases} 0, & if\ \overline{v_{ij}^k} = v_{ij}^k \\ 1, & if\ \overline{v_{ij}^k} \neq v_{ij}^k \end{cases}. \quad (6.8)$$

The *NAD* value counts the number of adjusted preference values. If $NAD(V, \overline{V}) = 0$, all the experts don't adjust their preferences. Otherwise, the bigger $NAD(V, \overline{V})$ value indicates more adjustment amounts between V and $\overline{V}$.

A large number of consensus models have been proposed for MAGDM problems (e.g., [2–5, 7, 9, 11–13]). In the following, based on minimum adjustment amounts, we propose two novel multiple attribute consensus rules, and develop an interactive consensus reaching process with minimum adjustments for MAGDM problems.

6.2 Multiple Attribute Consensus Rules

This section proposes two multiple attribute consensus rules: *distance-based consensus rule* and *count-based consensus rule*.

6.2.1 Distance-Based Consensus Rule

Let $\overline{V^k} = \left(\overline{v_{ij}^k}\right)_{m\times l}$ $(k = 1, 2, \ldots, n)$ be the adjusted decision matrix of expert E_k, and let $\overline{V^c} = \left(\overline{v_{ij}^c}\right)_{m\times l}$ denote the collective decision matrix, which is obtained by aggregating the adjusted decision matrices with an OWA operator, i.e.,

$$\overline{v_{ij}^c} = F_w^{OWA}\left(\overline{v_{ij}^1}, \overline{v_{ij}^2}, \ldots, \overline{v_{ij}^n}\right) \; i = 1, 2, \ldots, m; \; j = 1, 2, \ldots, l. \tag{6.9}$$

Based on Eq. (6.6), minimizing the distance between the original opinions and adjusted opinions can be described as Eq. (6.10):

$$min\frac{1}{ml}\sum_{k=1}^{n} d(V^k, \overline{V^k}). \tag{6.10}$$

Simultaneously, it is natural that $\overline{V^k}(k = 1, 2, \ldots, n)^T$ has acceptable consensus level, i.e.,

$$\frac{1}{nml}\sum_{k=1}^{n} d(\overline{V^k}, \overline{V^c}) \leq \varepsilon \tag{6.11}$$

where ε is the established consensus threshold.

As a result, according to Eqs. (6.9)–(6.11), the distance-based consensus rule can be constructed as follows:

$$\begin{cases} min \frac{1}{ml} \sum_{k=1}^{n} d(V^k, \overline{V^k}) \\ s.t. \begin{cases} \frac{1}{nml} \sum_{k=1}^{n} d(\overline{V^k}, \overline{V^c}) \leq \varepsilon \\ \overline{v_{ij}^c} = F_w^{OWA}(\overline{v_{ij}^1}, \overline{v_{ij}^2}, \ldots, \overline{v_{ij}^n})\ i = 1, 2, \ldots, m;\ j = 1, 2, \ldots, l \end{cases} \end{cases} \tag{6.12}$$

where $\overline{V^k}(k = 1, 2, \ldots, n)$ and $\overline{V^c}$ are the decision variables in model (6.12). In model (6.12), the consensus level needs to reach the given consensus threshold ε. Denote model (6.12) as $P_{6.1}$.

To solve the optimization problem of nonlinear programming, we need to make some mathematical derivations. We denote $\{\sigma_{ij}(1), \sigma_{ij}(2), \ldots, \sigma_{ij}(n)\}$ as the permutation of $\{1, 2, \ldots, n\}$ such that $v_{ij}^{\sigma_{ij}(k)} \geq v_{ij}^{\sigma_{ij}(k+1)}$ (i.e., $v_{ij}^{\sigma_{ij}(k)}$ is the kth largest variable in $\{v_{ij}^1, v_{ij}^2, \ldots, v_{ij}^n\}$). Then, we introduce a new model as follows:

$$\begin{cases} min \frac{1}{ml} \sum_{k=1}^{n} d(V^k, \overline{V^k}) \\ s.t. \begin{cases} \frac{1}{nml} \sum_{k=1}^{n} d(\overline{V^k}, \overline{V^c}) \leq \varepsilon \\ \overline{v_{ij}^c} = \sum_{k=1}^{n} w_k \overline{v_{ij}^{\sigma_{ij}(k)}},\ i = 1, \ldots, m;\ j = 1, \ldots, l \\ \overline{v_{ij}^{\sigma_{ij}(k)}} - \overline{v_{ij}^{\sigma_{ij}(k+1)}} \geq 0\ i = 1, \ldots, m;\ j = 1, \ldots, l;\ k = 1, \ldots, n-1 \end{cases} \end{cases} \tag{6.13}$$

where $\overline{V^k}(k = 1, 2, \ldots, n)$ and $\overline{V^c}$ are the decision variables in model (6.13). Denote model (6.13) as $P_{6.2}$. Moreover, let $\Omega_{6.1}$ and $\Omega_{6.2}$ be the feasible sets corresponding to $P_{6.1}$ and $P_{6.2}$. Then, to provide a linkage of $P_{6.2}$ to $P_{6.1}$, Lemma 6.1 is introduced.

Lemma 6.1 *Let* $\{V^{*1}, V^{*2}, \ldots, V^{*n}, V^{*c}\}$ *be the optimal solution to* $P_{6.1}$. *If* $v_{xy}^{*p} > v_{xy}^{*q}$ *and* $v_{xy}^{p} < v_{xy}^{q}$, *then* $\left\{\overline{\overline{V^1}}, \overline{\overline{V^2}}, \ldots, \overline{\overline{V^n}}, V^{*c}\right\}$ *is also the optimal solution to* $P_{6.1}$, *where*

$$\overline{\overline{v_{ij}^k}} = \begin{cases} v_{ij}^{*p}, & if\ k = q,\ i = x,\ j = y \\ v_{ij}^{*q}, & if\ k = p,\ i = x,\ j = y. \\ v_{ij}^{*k}, & otherwise \end{cases}$$

Proof Since

$$\overline{\overline{v_{ij}^k}} = \begin{cases} v_{ij}^{*p}, & k = q,\ i = x,\ j = y \\ v_{ij}^{*q}, & k = p,\ i = x,\ j = y. \\ v_{ij}^{*k}, & otherwise \end{cases} \tag{6.14}$$

Obviously, we can obtain that

$$v_{ij}^{*c} = F_w^{OWA}(v_{ij}^{*1}, v_{ij}^{*2}, \ldots, v_{ij}^{*n}) = F_w^{OWA}(\overline{\overline{v_{ij}^1}}, \overline{\overline{v_{ij}^2}}, \ldots, \overline{\overline{v_{ij}^n}}), \tag{6.15}$$

$$\frac{1}{nml}\sum_{k=1}^{n} d(\overline{\overline{V^k}}, V^{*c}) = \frac{1}{nml}\sum_{k=1}^{n}\sum_{i=1}^{m}\sum_{j=1}^{l}\left|\overline{\overline{v_{ij}^k}} - v_{ij}^{*c}\right| = \frac{1}{nml}\sum_{k=1}^{n}\sum_{i=1}^{m}\sum_{j=1}^{l}\left|v_{ij}^{*k} - v_{ij}^{*c}\right| \le \varepsilon. \tag{6.16}$$

It is shown by Eqs. (6.15) and (6.16) that $\left\{\overline{\overline{V^1}}, \overline{\overline{V^2}}, \ldots, \overline{\overline{V^n}}, V^{*c}\right\} \in \Omega_{6.1}$. Consequently,

$$\min_{\left\{\overline{V^1},\overline{V^2},\ldots,\overline{V^n},\overline{V^c}\right\}\in\Omega_{6.1}} \frac{1}{ml}\sum_{k=1}^{n} d(V^k, \overline{V^k}) \le \frac{1}{ml}\sum_{k=1}^{n} d(V^k, \overline{\overline{V^k}}). \tag{6.17}$$

Since $\left\{V^{*1}, V^{*2}, \ldots, V^{*n}, V^{*c}\right\}$ is the optimal solution to $P_{6.1}$.

$$\frac{1}{ml}\sum_{k=1}^{n} d(V^k, V^{*k}) = \min_{\left\{\overline{V^1},\overline{V^2},\ldots,\overline{V^n},\overline{V^c}\right\}\in\Omega_{6.1}} \frac{1}{ml}\sum_{k=1}^{n} d(V^k, \overline{V^k}). \tag{6.18}$$

The following can be obtained based on Eqs. (6.14) and (6.18):

$$\begin{aligned}
&\tfrac{1}{ml}\sum_{k=1}^{n} d(V^k, \overline{\overline{V^k}}) - \min_{\left\{\overline{V^1},\overline{V^2},\ldots,\overline{V^n},\overline{V^c}\right\}\in\Omega_{6.1}} \tfrac{1}{ml}\sum_{k=1}^{n} d(V^k, \overline{V^k}) \\
&= \tfrac{1}{ml}\sum_{k=1}^{n} d(V^k, \overline{\overline{V^k}}) - \tfrac{1}{ml}\sum_{k=1}^{n} d(V^k, V^{*k}) \\
&= \tfrac{1}{ml}\left(\left|v_{xy}^p - \overline{\overline{v_{xy}^p}}\right| + \left|v_{xy}^q - \overline{\overline{v_{xy}^q}}\right| - \left|v_{xy}^p - v_{xy}^{*p}\right| - \left|v_{xy}^q - v_{xy}^{*q}\right|\right) \\
&= \tfrac{1}{ml}\left(\left|v_{xy}^p - v_{xy}^{*q}\right| + \left|v_{xy}^q - v_{xy}^{*p}\right| - \left|v_{xy}^p - v_{xy}^{*p}\right| - \left|v_{xy}^q - v_{xy}^{*q}\right|\right).
\end{aligned} \tag{6.19}$$

Since $v_{xy}^{*p} > r_{xy}^{*q}$ and $v_{xy}^p < r_{xy}^q$, according to Lemma 2.2, the following can be obtained:

$$\frac{1}{ml}\sum_{k=1}^{n} d(V^k, \overline{\overline{V^k}}) - \min_{\left\{\overline{V^1},\overline{V^2},\ldots,\overline{V^n},\overline{V^c}\right\}\in\Omega_{6.1}} \frac{1}{ml}\sum_{k=1}^{n} d(V^k, \overline{V^k}) \le 0 \tag{6.20}$$

Based on Eqs. (6.17) and (6.20), we can obtain that:

$$\frac{1}{ml}\sum_{k=1}^{n} d(V^k, \overline{\overline{V^k}}) = \min_{\left\{\overline{V^1},\overline{V^2},\ldots,\overline{V^n},\overline{V^c}\right\}\in\Omega_{6.1}} \frac{1}{ml}\sum_{k=1}^{n} d(V^k, \overline{V^k}).$$

Therefore, $\left\{\overline{\overline{V^1}}, \overline{\overline{V^2}}, \ldots, \overline{\overline{V^n}}, V^{*c}\right\}$ is the optimal solution to $P_{6.1}$. This completes the proof of Lemma 6.1.

Based on Lemmas 2.2 and 6.1, we can obtain Lemma 6.2.

Lemma 6.2 *If* $\left\{\overline{V^{*1}}, \overline{V^{*2}}, \ldots, \overline{V^{*n}}, \overline{V^{*c}}\right\}$ *is the optimal solution to* $P_{6.2}$, *then* $\left\{\overline{V^{*1}}, \overline{V^{*2}}, \ldots, \overline{V^{*n}}, \overline{V^{*c}}\right\}$ *is also the optimal solution to* $P_{6.1}$.

Proof Let $\left\{\overline{\overline{V^1}}, \overline{\overline{V^2}}, \ldots, \overline{\overline{V^n}}, \overline{\overline{V^c}}\right\}$ be an optimal solution to $P_{6.1}$. Denote $\{\phi_{ij}(1), \phi_{ij}(2), \ldots, \phi_{ij}(n)\}$ as the permutation of $\{1, 2, \ldots, n\}$ such that $v_{ij}^{\phi_{ij}(k)} \geq v_{ij}^{\phi_{ij}(k+1)}$ (i.e., $v_{ij}^{\phi_{ij}(k)}$ is the kth largest variable in $\left\{v_{ij}^1, v_{ij}^2, \ldots, v_{ij}^n\right\}$). Firstly, we construct a new decision matrix $\underline{\underline{V^k}} = \left(\underline{\underline{v_{ij}^k}}\right)_{m\times l}$, where $\left\{\underline{\underline{v_{ij}^1}}, \underline{\underline{v_{ij}^2}}, \ldots \underline{\underline{v_{ij}^n}}\right\}$ is the permutation of $\left\{\overline{\overline{v_{ij}^1}}, \overline{\overline{v_{ij}^2}}, \ldots \overline{\overline{v_{ij}^n}}\right\}$ such that $\underline{\underline{v_{ij}^{\phi_{ij}(k)}}} \geq \underline{\underline{v_{ij}^{\phi_{ij}(k+1)}}}$. Then, based on Lemma 6.1, $\left\{\underline{\underline{V^1}}, \underline{\underline{V^2}}, \ldots, \underline{\underline{V^n}}, \overline{\overline{V^c}}\right\}$ is also the optimal solution to $P_{6.1}$.

Since $\Omega_{6.2} \subseteq \Omega_{6.1}$, we have that

$$\begin{aligned}\frac{1}{ml}\sum_{k=1}^{n} d\left(V^k, \underline{\underline{V^k}}\right) &= \min_{\left\{\overline{V^1}, \overline{V^2}, \ldots, \overline{V^n}, \overline{V^c}\right\} \in \Omega_{6.1}} \frac{1}{ml}\sum_{k=1}^{n} d(V^k, \overline{V^k}) \\ &\leq \min_{\left\{\overline{V^1}, \overline{V^2}, \ldots, \overline{V^n}, \overline{V^c}\right\} \in \Omega_{6.2}} \frac{1}{ml}\sum_{k=1}^{n} d(V^k, \overline{V^k}) \\ &= \frac{1}{ml}\sum_{k=1}^{n} d\left(V^k, \overline{V^{*k}}\right)\end{aligned} \tag{6.21}$$

Since $v_{ij}^{\phi_{ij}(k)} \geq v_{ij}^{\phi_{ij}(k+1)}$ and $\underline{\underline{v_{ij}^{\phi_{ij}(k)}}} \geq \underline{\underline{v_{ij}^{\phi_{ij}(k+1)}}}$, it follows that $\{\underline{\underline{V^1}}, \underline{\underline{V^2}}, \ldots, \underline{\underline{V^n}}, \overline{\overline{V^c}}\} \in \Omega_{6.2}$. We have that

$$\frac{1}{ml}\sum_{k=1}^{n} d\left(V^k, \underline{\underline{V^k}}\right) \geq \min_{\left\{\overline{V^1}, \overline{V^2}, \ldots, \overline{V^n}, \overline{V^c}\right\} \in \Omega_{6.2}} \frac{1}{ml}\sum_{k=1}^{n} d(V^k, \overline{V^k}) = \frac{1}{ml}\sum_{k=1}^{n} d\left(V^k, \overline{V^{*k}}\right) \tag{6.22}$$

Based on Eqs. (6.21) and (6.22), we can obtain that

$$\frac{1}{ml}\sum_{k=1}^{n} d\left(V^k, \underline{\underline{V^k}}\right) = \frac{1}{ml}\sum_{k=1}^{n} d\left(V^k, \overline{V^{*k}}\right)$$

$$\min_{\left\{\overline{V^1}, \overline{V^2}, \ldots, \overline{V^n}, \overline{V^c}\right\} \in \Omega_{6.1}} \frac{1}{ml}\sum_{k=1}^{n} d(V^k, \overline{V^k}) = \frac{1}{ml}\sum_{k=1}^{n} d\left(V^k, \overline{V^{*k}}\right) \tag{6.23}$$

Since $\Omega_{6.2} \subseteq \Omega_{6.1}$, $\left\{\overline{V^{*1}}, \overline{V^{*2}}, \ldots, \overline{V^{*n}}, \overline{V^{*c}}\right\}$ is also the optimal solution to $P_{6.1}$. This completes the proof of Lemma 6.2.

Theorem 6.1 *$P_{6.2}$ can be equivalently transformed into the following linear programming model:*

$$\begin{cases} \min \frac{1}{ml} \sum_{k=1}^{n} \sum_{i=1}^{m} \sum_{i=1}^{l} c_{ijk} & (a) \\ s.t. \begin{cases} b_{ijk} = v_i^k - \overline{v_i^k}, \quad i = 1, \ldots, m; j = 1, \ldots, l; k = 1, \ldots, n & (b) \\ b_{ijk} \le c_{ijk}, \quad i = 1, \ldots, m; j = 1, \ldots, l; k = 1, \ldots, n & (c) \\ -b_{ijk} \le c_{ijk}, \quad i = 1, \ldots, m; j = 1, \ldots, l; k = 1, \ldots, n & (d) \\ \frac{1}{mnl} \sum_{k=1}^{n} \sum_{i=1}^{m} \sum_{i=1}^{l} f_{ijk} \le \varepsilon & (e) \\ d_{ijk} = \overline{v_{ij}^k} - \overline{v_{ij}^c}, \quad i = 1, \ldots, m; j = 1, \ldots, l; k = 1, \ldots, n & (f) \\ d_{ijk} \le f_{ijk}; i = 1, \ldots, m; j = 1, \ldots, l; k = 1, \ldots, n & (g) \\ -d_{ijk} \le f_{ijk}, \quad i = 1, \ldots, m; j = 1, \ldots, l; k = 1, \ldots, n & (h) \\ \overline{v_{ij}^c} = \sum_{k=1}^{n} w_k \overline{v_{ij}^{\sigma_{ij}^k}}, \quad i = 1, \ldots, m; j = 1, \ldots, l & (i) \\ \overline{v_{ij}^{\sigma_{ij}^k}} - \overline{v_{ij}^{\sigma_{ij}^{k+1}}} \ge 0, \quad i = 1, \ldots, m; j = 1, \ldots, l; k = 1, \ldots, n-1 & (j) \end{cases} \end{cases} \tag{6.24}$$

where, $b_{ijk} = v_{ij}^k - \overline{v_{ij}^k}$, $c_{ijk} = |b_{ijk}|$, $d_{ijk} = \overline{v_{ij}^k} - \overline{v_{ij}^c}$, $f_{ijk} = |d_{ijk}|$.

Proof In the model (6.24), constraints (*b*)–(*d*) guarantee that $\left|v_{ij}^k - \overline{v_{ij}^k}\right| \le c_{ijk}$. According to the objective function of model (6.24), any feasible solution with $c_{ijk} > \left|v_{ij}^k - \overline{v_{ij}^k}\right|$ is not the optimal solution to model (6.24). Thus, constraints (*b*)–(*d*) guarantee that $c_{ijk} = \left|v_{ij}^k - \overline{v_{ij}^k}\right|$. Constraints (*e*)–(*g*) guarantee that $\frac{1}{nml} \sum_{k=1}^{n} d(\overline{V^k}, \overline{V^c}) \le \varepsilon$. Therefore, $P_{6.2}$ can be equivalently transformed into the model (6.24). Thus, this completes the proof of Theorem 6.1.

Denote model (6.24) as $P_{6.3}$. Based on Theorem 6.1, the optimal solution to $P_{6.2}$ can be obtained by solving $P_{6.3}$. As a result, based on Lemma 6.2 and Theorem 6.1, the optimal adjusted decision matrices in the distance-based consensus rule can be obtained by solving $P_{6.3}$.

6.2.2 Count-Based Consensus Rule

Based on Eqs. (6.7) and (6.8), the count-based consensus rule seeks to minimize the number of adjusted preference values, i.e.,

$$min\sum_{k=1}^{n}\sum_{i=1}^{m}\sum_{j=1}^{l}x_{ij}^{k} \tag{6.25}$$

where x_{ij}^{k} counts the number of adjusted preference values, i.e.,

$$x_{ij}^{k}=\begin{cases}0, & if\ \overline{v_{ij}^{k}}=v_{ij}^{k}\\ 1, & if\ \overline{v_{ij}^{k}}\neq v_{ij}^{k}\end{cases}. \tag{6.26}$$

As a result, according to Eqs. (6.9), (6.11), (6.25) and (6.26), the count-based consensus rule can be constructed as follows:

$$\begin{cases}min\sum\limits_{k=1}^{n}\sum\limits_{i=1}^{m}\sum\limits_{j=1}^{l}x_{ij}^{k}\\ s.t.\begin{cases}\frac{1}{nml}\sum\limits_{k=1}^{n}d(\overline{V^{k}},\overline{V^{c}})\leq\varepsilon\\ \overline{v_{ij}^{c}}=F_{w}^{OWA}(\overline{v_{ij}^{1}},\overline{v_{ij}^{2}},\ldots,\overline{v_{ij}^{n}}),\ i=1,\ldots,m;\ j=1,\ldots,l\\ x_{ij}^{k}=\begin{cases}0, & if\ \overline{v_{ij}^{k}}=v_{ij}^{k}\\ 1, & if\ \overline{v_{ij}^{k}}\neq v_{ij}^{k}\end{cases},\ k=1,\ldots,n,\ i=1,\ldots,m;\ j=1,\ldots,l\end{cases}\end{cases} \tag{6.27}$$

where $\overline{V^{k}}(k=1,2,\ldots,n)$ and $\overline{V^{c}}$ are the decision variables in model (6.27). Denote model (6.27) as $P_{6.4}$. $P_{6.4}$ can be equivalently transformed into the following programming problem:

$$\begin{cases}min\sum\limits_{k=1}^{n}\sum\limits_{i=1}^{m}\sum\limits_{j=1}^{l}x_{ij}^{k}\\ s.t.\begin{cases}\frac{1}{nml}\sum\limits_{k=1}^{n}d(\overline{V^{k}},\overline{V^{c}})\leq\varepsilon\\ \overline{v_{ij}^{c}}=F_{w}^{OWA}(\overline{v_{ij}^{1}},\overline{v_{ij}^{2}},\ldots,\overline{v_{ij}^{n}}),\ \ i=1,\ldots,m;\ j=1,\ldots,l\\ (v_{ij}^{k}-\overline{v_{ij}^{k}})(1-x_{ij}^{k})=0,\ \ i=1,\ldots,m;\ j=1,\ldots,l;\ k=1,\ldots,n\\ x_{ij}^{k}\in\{0,1\},\ \ i=1,\ldots,m;\ j=1,\ldots,l;\ k=1,\ldots,n\end{cases}\end{cases} \tag{6.28}$$

Denote model (6.28) as $P_{6.5}$. Since $(v_{ij}^{k}-\overline{v_{ij}^{k}})(1-x_{ij}^{k})=0$, we can obtain that: If $v_{ij}^{k}\neq\overline{v_{ij}^{k}}$, $x_{ij}^{k}=1$. If $v_{ij}^{k}=\overline{v_{ij}^{k}}$, $x_{ij}^{k}=0$ or 1. However, it is obvious that $x_{ij}^{k}=0$ can minimize the objective function when $v_{ij}^{k}=\overline{v_{ij}^{k}}$. Thus, the optimal solutions to $P_{6.4}$ and $P_{6.5}$ are uniform. To facilitate the solving process of $P_{6.5}$, Lemma 6.3 is introduced.

Lemma 6.3 *$Y=\{y_1,y_2,\ldots,y_n\}$ is a set of real numbers. $\{y_{(1)},y_{(2)},\ldots,y_{(n)}\}$ is a permutation of Y such that $y_{(1)}\geq y_{(2)},\ldots,\geq y_{(n)}$. If z_i satisfies the following constraints*

$$\begin{cases} z_i \le y_i + M \cdot A_{ij}, & i,j = 1,2,\ldots,n \\ z_i \ge y_i - M \cdot B_{ij}, & i,j = 1,2,\ldots,n \\ \sum_{j=1}^{n} A_{ij} \le n - i, & i = 1,2,\ldots,n \\ \sum_{j=1}^{n} B_{ij} \le i - 1, & i = 1,2,\ldots,n \\ A_{ij}, B_{ij} \in \{0,1\}, & i,j = 1,2,\ldots,n \end{cases} \tag{6.29}$$

where M is $+\infty$, then we can obtain that $z_i = y_{(i)}$.

Proof Based on the research in Ogryczak and Śliwiński [8], it is obvious that $z_i \le y_j + M \cdot A_{ij}$ and $\sum_{j=1}^{n} A_{ij} \le n - i$ guarantee that the maximum value of z_i is the ith largest element in $\{y_1, y_2, \ldots, y_n\}$. Similarly, $z_i \ge y_j - M \cdot B_{ij}$ and $\sum_{j=1}^{n} B_{ij} \le i - 1$ guarantee that the minimum value of z_i is the ith largest element in $\{y_1, y_2, \ldots, y_n\}$. Thus, constraint (6.29) guarantees that z_i is the ith largest element in $\{y_1, y_2, \ldots, y_n\}$. Thus, this completes the proof of Lemma 6.3.

Then, based on Lemmas 2.6 and 6.3, Theorem 6.2 is introduced.

Theorem 6.2 *$P_{6.5}$ can be equivalently transformed into the following mixed 0-1 linear programming model:*

$$\begin{cases} \min \sum_{k=1}^{n} \sum_{i=1}^{m} \sum_{j=1}^{l} x_{ij}^{k} & (a) \\ s.t. \begin{cases} \frac{1}{nml} \sum_{k=1}^{n} \sum_{i=1}^{m} \sum_{j=1}^{l} f_{ijk} \le \varepsilon & (b) \\ d_{ijk} = \overline{v_{ij}^{k}} - \overline{v_{ij}^{c}}, \quad i = 1,\ldots,m;\ j = 1,\ldots,l;\ k = 1,\ldots,n & (c) \\ d_{ijk} \le f_{ijk}, \quad i = 1,\ldots,m;\ j = 1,\ldots,l;\ k = 1,\ldots,n & (d) \\ -d_{ijk} \le f_{ijk}, \quad i = 1,\ldots,m;\ j = 1,\ldots,l;\ k = 1,\ldots,n & (e) \\ \overline{v_{ij}^{(k)}} \le \overline{v_{ij}^{s}} + M \cdot A_{ijk}^{s}, \quad i = 1,\ldots,m;\ j = 1,\ldots,l;\ k,s = 1,\ldots,n & (f) \\ \overline{v_{ij}^{(k)}} \ge \overline{v_{ij}^{s}} - M \cdot B_{ijk}^{s}, \quad i = 1,\ldots,m;\ j = 1,\ldots,l;\ k,s = 1,\ldots,n & (g) \\ \sum_{s=1}^{T} A_{ijk}^{s} \le n - k, \quad i = 1,\ldots,m;\ j = 1,\ldots,l;\ k = 1,\ldots,n & (h) \\ \sum_{s=1}^{T} B_{ijk}^{s} \le k - 1, \quad i = 1,\ldots,m;\ j = 1,\ldots,l;\ k = 1,\ldots,n & (i) \\ \overline{v_{ij}^{c}} = \sum_{k=1}^{n} w_k \overline{v_{ij}^{(k)}}, \quad i = 1,\ldots,m;\ j = 1,\ldots,l & (j) \\ v_{ij}^{k} - \overline{v_{ij}^{k}} - v_{ij}^{k} x_{ij}^{k} + z_{ij}^{k} = 0, \quad i = 1,\ldots,m;\ j = 1,\ldots,l;\ k = 1,\ldots,n & (k) \\ 0 \le z_{ij}^{k} \le x_{ij}^{k}, \quad i = 1,\ldots,m;\ j = 1,\ldots,l;\ k = 1,\ldots,n & (l) \\ \overline{v_{ij}^{k}} + x_{ij}^{k} - 1 \le z_{ij}^{k} \le \overline{v_{ij}^{k}}, \quad i = 1,\ldots,m;\ j = 1,\ldots,l;\ k = 1,\ldots,n & (m) \\ A_{ijk}^{s}, B_{ijk}^{s}, x_{ij}^{k} \in \{0,1\}, \quad i = 1,\ldots,m; j = 1,\ldots,l; k,s = 1,\ldots,n & (n) \end{cases} \end{cases} \tag{6.30}$$

where M is $+\infty$, $d_{ijk} = \overline{v_{ij}^{k}} - \overline{v_{ij}^{c}}$ and $f_{ijk} = |d_{ijk}|$.

Proof In model (6.30), constraints (*b*)–(*e*) guarantee that $\frac{1}{nml}\sum_{k=1}^{n} d(\overline{V^k}, \overline{V^c}) \leq \varepsilon$. Based on Lemma 6.3, constraints (*f*)–(*i*) guarantee that $\overline{v_{ij}^{(k)}}$ is the *k*th largest element in $\left\{\overline{v_{ij}^1}, \overline{v_{ij}^2}, \ldots, \overline{v_{ij}^n}\right\}$. Thus, constraints (*f*)–(*j*) guarantee that $\overline{v_{ij}^c} = F_w^{OWA}(\overline{v_{ij}^1}, \overline{v_{ij}^2}, \ldots, \overline{v_{ij}^n})$. Based on Lemma 2.6, constraints (*k*)–(*m*) guarantee that $(v_{ij}^k - \overline{v_{ij}^k})(1 - x_{ij}^k) = 0$. Therefore, $P_{6.5}$ can be equivalently transformed into the model (6.30). Thus, this completes the proof of Theorem 6.2.

Based on Theorem 6.2, the optimal solution to $P_{6.5}$ can be obtained by solving the mixed 0-1 programming model (6.30). Denote model (6.30) as $P_{6.6}$. Then, the distance-based consensus rule and the count-based consensus rule are respectively transformed into the linear programming model and the mixed 0-1 linear programming model, which are easier to solve by the software packages such as CPLEX and MATLAB.

6.3 Multiple Attribute Consensus Reaching Process

Based on the distance-based consensus rule and the count-based consensus rule, this section proposes an interactive consensus reaching process for MAGDM problems.

6.3.1 The Interactive Consensus Reaching Process

Based on the distance-based consensus rule and the count-based consensus rule, we propose an interactive consensus reaching process for MAGDM problems, which is described as Fig. 6.1.

The core idea of the consensus reaching process is to return the optimal adjusted decision matrix $\overline{V^k}$, which is obtained from the distance-based consensus rule or the count-based consensus rule, to the expert E_k to reconsider constructing a new decision matrix $V^{k'} = (v_{ij}^{k'})_{m\times l}$. When constructing $V^{k'}$, we suggest that

$$v_{ij}^{k'} \in [min\{v_{ij}^k, \overline{v_{ij}^k}\}, max\{v_{ij}^k, \overline{v_{ij}^k}\}].$$

Specifically, we firstly normalize the individual decision matrix into a standardized individual decision matrix $V^k(k = 1, 2, \ldots, n)$. Then, the OWA operator is used to aggregate individual decision matrices $V^k(k = 1, 2, \ldots, n)$ into the collective decision matrix V^c. Next, based on the proposed consensus measurement (i.e., Definition 6.1), the consensus level among all the experts is measured. Finally, if the consensus level among all the experts is unacceptable, the adjusted suggestions are provided based on the optimal adjusted decision matrix obtained by distance-based consensus rule or the count-based consensus rule. This procedure is followed until

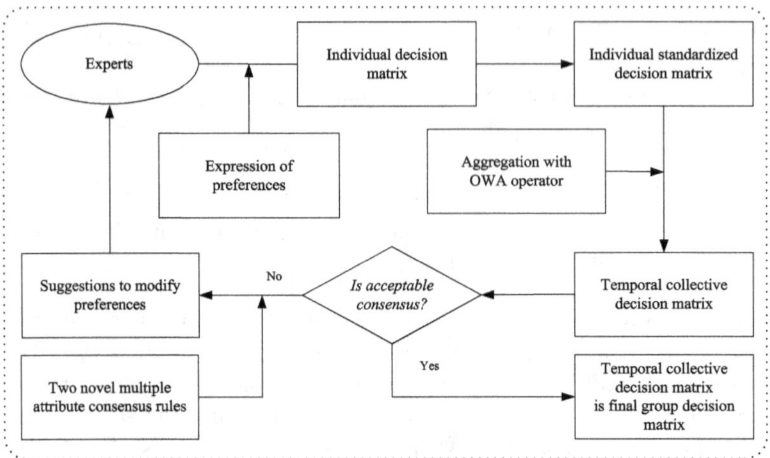

Fig. 6.1 Consensus reaching process based on the distance-based and count-based consensus rules

the individual decision matrices with acceptable consensus level are obtained. The details of the consensus reaching process with the distance-based consensus rule are depicted as Algorithm 6.1.

Algorithm 6.1

Input: The standardized individual decision matrices $V^k(k = 1, 2, \ldots, n)$, the consensus threshold ε, and the associated weight vector of experts w.

Output: The adjusted individual decision matrices $\overline{V^k}(k = 1, 2, \ldots, n)$, the collective decision matrix $\overline{V^c}$, and the number of the iterations z.

Step 1: Let $z = 0$ and $V_k^z = (v_{ijk}^z)_{m\times l} = (v_{ij}^k)_{m\times l}$.

Step 2: Calculate the collective decision matrix $V_c^z = (v_{ijc}^z)_{m\times l}$, where $v_{ijc}^z = F_w^{OWA}(v_{ij1}^z, v_{ij2}^z, \ldots, v_{ijn}^z)$, and the consensus measure $CL^z\{E_1, \ldots, E_n\} = \frac{1}{nml}\sum_{k=1}^{n} d(V_k^z, V_c^z)$. If $CL^z\{E_1, \ldots, E_n\} \le \varepsilon$, then go to Step 4. Otherwise, continue with the next step.

Step 3: Let $V_k^z(k = 1, 2, \ldots, n)$ be the original individual decision matrices in the distance-based consensus rule. Then, utilizing the distance-based consensus rule (i.e., $P_{6.3}$) obtains the optimal adjusted individual decision matrices $\overline{V_k^z}(k = 1, 2, \ldots, n)$. When constructing the adjusted individual decision matrix $V_k^{z+1} = (v_{ijk}^{z+1})_{m\times l}$, we suggest that $v_{ijk}^{z+1} \in [min\{v_{ijk}^z, \overline{v_{ijk}^z}\}, max\{v_{ijk}^z, \overline{v_{ijk}^z}\}]$. Then, let $z = z + 1$, and go to Step 2.

Step 4: Let $\overline{V^k} = V_k^z(k = 1, 2, \ldots, n)$ and $\overline{V^c} = V_c^z$. Output adjusted individual decision matrices $\overline{V^k}(k = 1, 2, \ldots, n)$, the collective decision matrix $\overline{V^c}$ and the number of the iterations z.

Algorithm 6.1 is based on the distance-based consensus rule. Similarly, we may use the count-based consensus rule in the consensus reaching process. In Algorithm 6.1, we replace Step 3 by Step 3*, and then obtain a new algorithm, Algorithm 6.2.

Step 3*: Let $V_k^z(k=1,2,\ldots,n)$ be the original individual decision matrices in the count-based consensus rule. Then, utilizing the count-based consensus rule (i.e., $P_{6.6}$) obtains the optimal adjusted individual decision matrices $\overline{V_k^z}(k=1,2,\ldots,n)$. When constructing the adjusted individual decision matrix $V_k^{z+1}=(v_{ijk}^{z+1})_{m\times l}$, we suggest that $v_{ijk}^{z+1}\in[min\{v_{ijk}^z,\overline{v_{ijk}^z}\},max\{v_{ijk}^z,\overline{v_{ijk}^z}\}]$. Then, let $z=z+1$, and go to Step 2.

6.3.2 Convergence Analysis

To explore the convergence of the above consensus reaching processes, we propose several properties as Lemmas 6.4–6.6.

Let DV_z be the minimum distance between the original opinions and adjusted opinions obtained by the distance-based consensus rule in the zth iteration of Algorithm 6.1, i.e., $DV_z=\frac{1}{ml}\sum_{k=1}^n d(V_k^z,\overline{V_k^z})$.

Lemma 6.4 *In the consensus reaching process with the distance-based consensus rule (i.e., Algorithm 6.1),* $DV_z=\frac{1}{ml}\sum_{k=1}^n d(V_k^z,V_k^{z+1})+DV_{z+1}$.

Proof From Step 3 of Algorithm 6.1, we have that

$$v_{ijk}^{z+1}\in[\min\{v_{ijk}^z,\overline{v_{ijk}^z}\},\max\{v_{ijk}^z,\overline{v_{ijk}^z}\}]. \tag{6.31}$$

Without loss of generality, we obtain that

$$v_{ijk}^{z+1}=\alpha_{ijk}^z v_{ijk}^z+(1-\alpha_{ijk}^z)\overline{v_{ijk}^z},\ (0\le\alpha_{ijk}^z\le 1). \tag{6.32}$$

Then, we can obtain that

$$\sum_{k=1}^n d(V_k^z,\overline{V_k^z})=\sum_{k=1}^n d(V_k^z,V_k^{z+1})+\sum_{k=1}^n d(V_k^{z+1},\overline{V_k^z}). \tag{6.33}$$

Since $\overline{V_k^{z+1}}(k=1,2,\ldots,n)$ is the optimal solution obtained by the distance-based consensus rule in the $(z+1)$th iteration of Algorithm 6.1, we can obtain that

$$\frac{1}{ml}\sum_{k=1}^n d(V_k^{z+1},\overline{V_k^z})\ge\frac{1}{ml}\sum_{k=1}^n d(V_k^{z+1},\overline{V_k^{z+1}}).$$

Then, it follows that

$\frac{1}{ml}\sum_{k=1}^{n} d(V_k^z, \overline{V_k^z}) = \frac{1}{ml}\sum_{k=1}^{n} d(V_k^z, V_k^{z+1}) + \frac{1}{ml}\sum_{k=1}^{n} d(V_k^{z+1}, \overline{V_k^z}) \geq \frac{1}{ml}\sum_{k=1}^{n} d(V_k^z, V_k^{z+1}) +$
$\frac{1}{ml}\sum_{k=1}^{n} d(V_k^{z+1}, \overline{V_k^{z+1}})$

$$DV_z \geq \frac{1}{ml}\sum_{k=1}^{n} d(V_k^z, V_k^{z+1}) + DV_{z+1} \tag{6.34}$$

Since $\overline{V_k^z}(k = 1, 2, \ldots, n)$ is the optimal solution obtained by the distance-based consensus rule in the zth iteration of Algorithm 6.1, we have

$$\begin{aligned} DV_z &= \frac{1}{ml}\sum_{k=1}^{n}\sum_{i=1}^{m}\sum_{j=1}^{l}\left|v_{ijk}^z - \overline{v_{ijk}^z}\right| \leq \frac{1}{ml}\sum_{k=1}^{n}\sum_{i=1}^{m}\sum_{j=1}^{z}\left|v_{ijk}^z - \overline{v_{ijk}^{z+1}}\right| \\ &= \frac{1}{ml}\sum_{k=1}^{n}\sum_{i=1}^{m}\sum_{j=1}^{z}\left|v_{ijk}^z - v_{ijk}^{z+1} + v_{ijk}^{z+1} - \overline{v_{ijk}^{z+1}}\right| \\ &\leq \frac{1}{ml}\sum_{k=1}^{n}\sum_{i=1}^{m}\sum_{j=1}^{l}\left|v_{ijk}^z - v_{ijk}^{z+1}\right| + \frac{1}{ml}\sum_{k=1}^{n}\sum_{i=1}^{m}\sum_{j=1}^{l}\left|v_{ijk}^{z+1} - \overline{v_{ijk}^{z+1}}\right| \\ &= \frac{1}{ml}\sum_{k=1}^{n} d(V_k^z, V_k^{z+1}) + DV_{z+1}. \end{aligned} \tag{6.35}$$

Then, based on Eqs. (6.34) and (6.35), we have that

$$DV_z = \frac{1}{ml}\sum_{k=1}^{n} d(V_k^z, V_k^{z+1}) + DV_{z+1}. \tag{6.36}$$

Thus, this completes the proof of Lemma 6.4.

Based on Lemma 6.4, a desirable property of the consensus reaching process with the distance-based consensus rule is presented as Lemma 6.5.

Lemma 6.5 *In the consensus reaching process with the distance-based consensus rule (i.e., Algorithm 6.1),* $\lim_{z\to\infty} DV_z = 0$.

Proof Based on Lemma 6.4, we obtain that $\{DV_z\}$ is monotonous and bounded. Thus, according to the existence of limit for a sequence, we can have that

$$\lim_{z\to\infty} DV_z \geq 0. \tag{6.37}$$

According to Lemma 6.4, we have that

$$DV_z = \frac{1}{ml}\sum_{k=1}^{n} d(V_k^z, V_k^{z+1}) + DV_{z+1}. \tag{6.38}$$

Let $\lim_{z \to \infty} DV_z = A$, then, we can obtain that

$$\forall \varepsilon > 0, \text{ if } z > N, |DV_z - DV_{z+1}| \le \varepsilon.$$

Since $DV_z = \frac{1}{ml}\sum_{k=1}^{n} d(V_k^z, V_k^{z+1}) + DV_{z+1}$, we can have that

$$\frac{1}{ml}\sum_{k=1}^{n} d(V_k^z, V_k^{z+1}) \le \varepsilon, (z > N). \tag{6.39}$$

Since $\frac{1}{ml}\sum_{k=1}^{n} d(V_k^z, V_k^{z+1}) \in (0, DV_z]$, the following inequality can be obtained

$$DV_z \le \varepsilon, (z > N).$$

Since $\inf\{DV_z\} = \lim_{z \to \infty} DV_z = A$, we have that

$$0 \le A \le \varepsilon.$$

Since ε is arbitrarily small, we can obtain that

$$\lim_{z \to \infty} DV_z = A = 0. \tag{6.40}$$

Thus, this completes the proof of Lemma 6.5.

Let NV_z be the minimum number of adjusted preference values obtained by the count-based consensus rule in the zth iteration of Algorithm 6.2, i.e., $NV_z = \sum_{k=1}^{n}\sum_{i=1}^{m}\sum_{j=1}^{l} x_{ijk}^z$.

Lemma 6.6 *In the consensus reaching process with the count-based consensus rule (i.e., Algorithm 6.2),* $NV_{z+1} \le NV_z$.

Proof Let $\left\{\overline{\overline{V_1^z}}, \overline{\overline{V_2^z}}, \ldots, \overline{\overline{V_n^z}}, \overline{\overline{V_c^z}}\right\}$ be the optimal adjusted individual decision matrices obtained by the count-based consensus rule ($P_{6.6}$) in the zth iteration. Then, according to Algorithm 6.2, $\left\{\overline{\overline{V_1^z}}, \overline{\overline{V_2^z}}, \ldots, \overline{\overline{V_n^z}}, \overline{\overline{V_c^z}}\right\}$ is also a feasible solution in the $(z+1)$th iteration. If the solution to $P_{6.6}$ is $\left\{\overline{\overline{V_1^z}}, \overline{\overline{V_2^z}}, \ldots, \overline{\overline{V_n^z}}, \overline{\overline{V_c^z}}\right\}$ in the $(z+1)$th iteration, let $\overline{NV_{z+1}}$ be the value of the objective function in the $(z+1)$th iteration.

Then, we can obtain that

$$\overline{NV_{z+1}} \geq \min_{\left\{\overline{V_1^{z+1}},\overline{V_2^{z+1}},\ldots,\overline{V_n^{z+1}},\overline{V_c^{z+1}}\right\}} \sum_{k=1}^{n}\sum_{i=1}^{m}\sum_{j=1}^{l} x_{ij}^k = NV_{z+1}. \tag{6.41}$$

Obviously, according to Algorithm 6.2, we have

$$\overline{NV_{z+1}} \leq NV_z. \tag{6.42}$$

Based on Eqs. (6.41) and (6.42), we can obtain that

$$NV_{z+1} \leq NV_z.$$

Thus, this completes the proof of Lemma 6.6.

Based on Lemmas 6.5 and 6.6, we have Theorem 6.3.

Theorem 6.3 *Let* $\{CL_1^z\}$ *be the consensus level sequence in Algorithm 6.1, and let* $\{CL_2^z\}$ *be the consensus level sequence in Algorithm 6.2. Then,* $\lim_{z\to\infty} CL_t^z \leq \varepsilon$ *for* $t = 1, 2$.

Proof In Algorithm 6.1, based on Lemma 6.5, $\lim_{z\to\infty} DV_z = 0$. Then, we can obtain that

$$\lim_{z\to\infty} \frac{1}{ml} \sum_{k=1}^{n}\sum_{i=1}^{m}\sum_{j=1}^{l} \left|\overline{v_{ijk}^z} - v_{ijk}^z\right| = 0.$$

Consequently,

$$\lim_{z\to\infty} \overline{v_{ijk}^z} = \lim_{z\to\infty} v_{ijk}^z. \tag{6.43}$$

Then, we have that

$$\lim_{z\to\infty} CL_1^z = \lim_{z\to\infty} \frac{1}{nml} \sum_{k=1}^{n}\sum_{i=1}^{m}\sum_{j=1}^{l} \left|v_{ijk}^z - v_{ijc}^z\right| = \lim_{z\to\infty} \frac{1}{nml} \sum_{k=1}^{n}\sum_{i=1}^{m}\sum_{j=1}^{l} \left|\overline{v_{ijk}^z} - \overline{v_{ijc}^z}\right| \leq \varepsilon. \tag{6.44}$$

In Algorithm 6.2, based on Lemma 6.5, we can obtain that

$$\lim_{z\to\infty} NV_z \geq 0.$$

Assume that $\lim_{z\to\infty} NV_z = NV_\infty > 0$. Since $\{NV_z\}$ is a sequence of nonnegative integer, without loss of generality, suppose that

$$NV_z = NV_\infty \ (z \geq Z). \tag{6.45}$$

Let $\left\{\overline{\overline{V_1^z}}, \overline{\overline{V_2^z}}, \ldots, \overline{\overline{V_n^z}}, \overline{\overline{V_c^z}}\right\}$ be the optimal adjusted individual decision matrices, which are obtained by the count-based consensus rule ($P_{6.6}$) in the zth iteration. Then, according to Algorithm 6.2, $\left\{\overline{\overline{V_1^z}}, \overline{\overline{V_2^z}}, \ldots, \overline{\overline{V_n^z}}, \overline{\overline{V_c^z}}\right\}$ is also a feasible solution in the $(z+1)$th iteration. In the $(z+1)$th iteration, if the solution to $P_{6.6}$ is $\left\{\overline{\overline{V_1^z}}, \overline{\overline{V_2^z}}, \ldots, \overline{\overline{V_n^z}}, \overline{\overline{V_c^z}}\right\}$, let $\overline{NV_{z+1}}$ be the value of the objective function in the $(z+1)$th iteration.

According to Eqs. (6.41) and (6.42), we have that

$$NV_{z+1} \leq \overline{NV_{z+1}} \leq NV_z. \tag{6.46}$$

Then, according to Eqs. (6.45) and (6.46), we can obtain that

$$\overline{NV_{z+1}} = NV_{z+1} = NV_\infty \ (z \geq Z). \tag{6.47}$$

Thus, when $z \geq Z$, $\left\{\overline{\overline{V_1^z}}, \overline{\overline{V_2^z}}, \ldots, \overline{\overline{V_n^z}}, \overline{\overline{V_c^z}}\right\}$ is the optimal solution to $P_{6.6}$ in the $(z+1)$th iteration.

Then, when $z \geq Z$, we can reasonably suppose that the consensus reaching process gives the same adjustment advice as in the zth iteration. With the increase of the number of iterations, all the opinion values of experts tend to the optimal solution $\left\{\overline{\overline{V_1^Z}}, \overline{\overline{V_2^Z}}, \ldots, \overline{\overline{V_n^Z}}, \overline{\overline{V_c^Z}}\right\}$, and the number of adjusted preference values tends to 0. This violates the assumption that $\lim_{z\to\infty} NV_z = NV_\infty > 0$. Thus, we can obtain that

$$\lim_{z\to\infty} NV_z = 0.$$

Then, we have that

$$\lim_{z\to\infty} \overline{v_{ijk}^z} = \lim_{z\to\infty} v_{ijk}^z.$$

Thus, we can obtain that

$$\lim_{z\to\infty} CL_2^z = \lim_{z\to\infty} \frac{1}{nml} \sum_{k=1}^{n} \sum_{i=1}^{m} \sum_{j=1}^{l} \left| v_{ijk}^z - v_{ijc}^z \right| = \lim_{z\to\infty} \frac{1}{nml} \sum_{k=1}^{n} \sum_{i=1}^{m} \sum_{j=1}^{l} \left| \overline{v_{ijk}^z} - \overline{v_{ijc}^z} \right| \leq \varepsilon. \tag{6.48}$$

Based on Eqs. (6.44) and (6.48), we have that $\lim_{z\to\infty} CL_t^z \leq \varepsilon$ for $t = 1, 2$. This completes the proof of Theorem 6.3.

Based on Theorem 6.3, Algorithms 6.1 and 6.2 are convergent.

6.3.3 Mixing Use of Multiple Attribute Consensus Rules

In the following, we propose the mixing use of the distance-based consensus rule and the count-based consensus rule. Firstly, we define a control coefficient, p, to decide which consensus rule is selected in each round of iteration, where

$$p = \frac{CL - \varepsilon}{CL} \tag{6.49}$$

The control coefficient p reflects the difference between the consensus level and the consensus threshold. The smaller p value indicates the higher consensus level among all the experts.

According to the actual situation, the experts establish the threshold $\theta \in [0, 1]$ for p. If $p > \theta$, the consensus level among all experts is low, and a high number of changes of opinions might be necessary for reaching consensus. Then, the consensus reaching process uses the distance-based consensus rule to generate adjustment advice. As the consensus level increases, less and less experts might need to change their opinions. If $p \leq \theta$, the consensus reaching process selects the count-based consensus rule, which seeks to reach consensus with minimum number of adjusted preference values, to generate adjustment advice.

Obviously, when $\theta = 0$, the consensus reaching process with mixing consensus rules reduces to the consensus reaching process with the distance-based consensus rule. When $\theta = 1$, the consensus reaching process with mixing consensus rules reduces to the consensus reaching process with the count-based consensus rule.

In Algorithm 6.1, we add a parameter θ in the input, and replace Step 3 by Step $3^{\#}$. Then, we can obtain a new algorithm, Algorithm 6.3.

Step $3^{\#}$: Let $V_k^z(k = 1, 2, \ldots, n)$ be the original individual decision matrices in the distance-based ans count-based consensus rules, and $p^z = \frac{CL^z - \varepsilon}{CL^z}$. If $p^z > \theta$, utilizing the distance-based consensus rule (i.e., $P_{6.3}$) obtains the optimal adjusted individual decision matrices $\overline{V_k^z}(k = 1, 2, \ldots, n)$. If $p^l \leq \theta$, utilizing the count-based consensus rule (i.e., $P_{6.6}$) obtains the optimal adjusted individual decision matrices $\overline{V_k^z}(k = 1, 2, \ldots, n)$. When constructing the adjusted individual decision matrix $V_k^{z+1} = (v_{ijk}^{z+1})_{m \times l}$, we suggest that $v_{ijk}^{z+1} \in [min\{v_{ijk}^z, \overline{v_{ijk}^z}\}, max\{v_{ijk}^z, \overline{v_{ijk}^z}\}]$. Then, let $z = z + 1$, and go to Step 2.

In the consensus reaching process, the distance-based consensus rule and the count-based consensus rule can be used flexibly to generate the adjustment suggestions that experts use as a reference to modify their individual opinions. Let p be the control coefficient in Algorithm 6.3, and let θ be the threshold for p. Figure 6.2 shows the use of the distance-based consensus rule and the count-based consensus rule in the feedback processes of Algorithms 6.1–6.3.

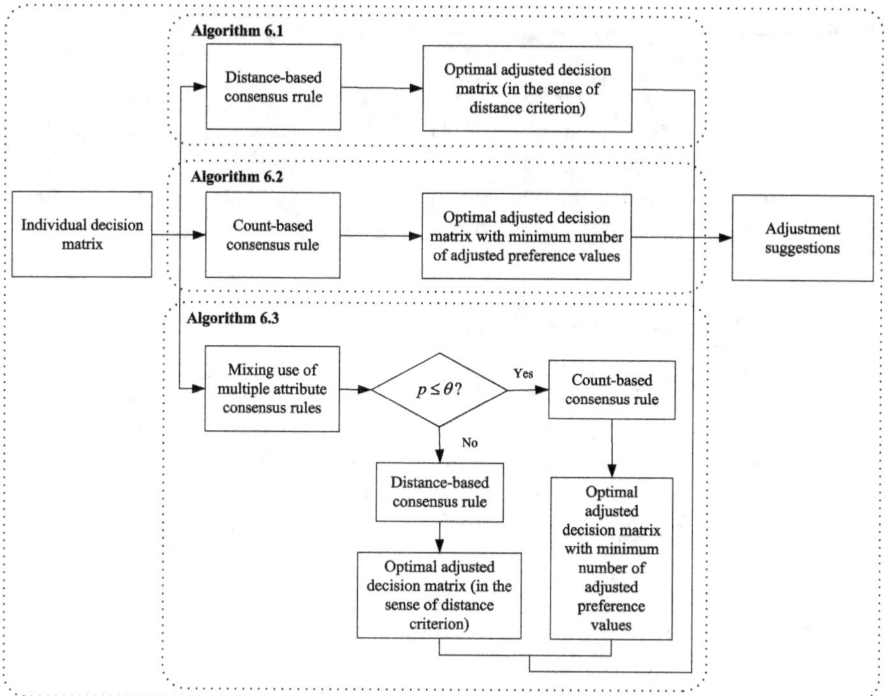

Fig. 6.2 The use of the distance-based and count-based consensus rules in the feedback process

6.4 Numerical and Comparison Analysis

In this section, we use a numerical analysis to demonstrate the proposed consensus models (i.e., Algorithms 6.1–6.3). Moreover, we conduct a comparison analysis to show the advantages of the proposed consensus rules with minimum adjustments.

6.4.1 Numerical Analysis

Here, we expound the implementation of the proposed consensus reaching process with the numerical example used in Xu [10] and Yoon [15]. In this example, the alternatives $X_i (i = 1, 2, 3, 4, 5)$ are evaluated by three experts $E_k (k = 1, 2, 3)$, and each expert evaluates the alternatives based on eight different attributes $C_i (i = 1, 2, \ldots, 8)$. The standardized individual decision matrices $V_k^0 (k = 1, 2, 3)$ are listed in Tables 6.1, 6.2 and 6.3. For a detailed description of the original individual decision matrices, please see Xu [10] and Yoon [15].

In the following, we use Algorithm 6.3 to help experts reach a consensus. Let the associated weight vector of experts be $w = (0.2, 0.5, 0.3)^T$ and the

Table 6.1 Standardized individual decision matrix V_1^0

	C_1	C_2	C_3	C_4	C_5	C_6	C_7	C_8
X_1	0.5000	0.0000	1.0000	1.0000	0.2000	1.0000	0.0000	0.7500
X_2	1.0000	0.5000	0.0000	0.0000	0.0000	0.0000	1.0000	0.0000
X_3	0.5000	0.5000	0.2500	0.1430	0.8000	0.5000	1.0000	0.2500
X_4	0.0000	1.0000	0.7500	0.8750	1.0000	0.7500	0.7500	0.7500
X_5	0.2500	0.0000	0.5000	0.4290	0.4000	1.0000	0.2500	1.0000

Table 6.2 Standardized individual decision matrix V_2^0

	C_1	C_2	C_3	C_4	C_5	C_6	C_7	C_8
X_1	0.0000	0.3330	0.6670	1.0000	0.0000	1.0000	0.3330	0.0000
X_2	1.0000	0.6670	0.3330	0.0000	0.5000	0.0000	0.5000	0.5000
X_3	0.0000	1.0000	0.0000	0.1890	1.0000	0.3750	0.5000	0.7500
X_4	0.3330	0.6670	0.6670	0.8650	1.0000	0.5360	1.0000	0.5000
X_5	0.6670	0.0000	1.0000	0.5410	0.6670	0.7140	0.0000	1.0000

Table 6.3 Standardized individual decision matrix V_3^0

	C_1	C_2	C_3	C_4	C_5	C_6	C_7	C_8
X_1	1.0000	0.3330	0.8000	1.0000	0.5000	0.8820	0.0000	0.0000
X_2	0.7500	0.0000	0.0000	0.0860	0.0000	0.0000	0.8000	0.5000
X_3	0.2500	0.6670	0.2000	0.0000	1.0000	0.6470	1.0000	0.2500
X_4	0.0000	0.3330	1.0000	0.7710	1.0000	0.9410	0.4000	0.7500
X_5	0.5000	1.0000	0.8000	0.4290	1.0000	1.0000	0.2000	1.0000

Table 6.4 Collective decision matrix V_c^0

	C_1	C_2	C_3	C_4	C_5	C_6	C_7	C_8
X_1	0.4500	0.2331	0.8001	1.0000	0.2000	0.9646	0.0666	0.1500
X_2	0.9250	0.3834	0.0666	0.0172	0.1000	0.0000	0.7500	0.3500
X_3	0.2250	0.6835	0.1500	0.1093	0.9400	0.4919	0.8500	0.3500
X_4	0.0666	0.6334	0.7751	0.8388	1.0000	0.7240	0.6950	0.6750
X_5	0.4584	0.2000	0.7500	0.4514	0.6535	0.9142	0.1500	1.0000

consensus threshold $\varepsilon = 0.05$. We set the threshold for the control coefficient to be $\theta = 0.3$. Moreover, let the associated weight vector of the attributes be $\lambda = (0.10, 0.08, 0.12, 0.13, 0.17, 0.15, 0.11, 0.14)^T$.

(1) In the first iteration, utilize the OWA operator to fuse standardized individual decision matrices $V_k^0 (k = 1, 2, 3)$ into the collective decision matrix V_c^0 (see Table 6.4).

Since the consensus measure $CL\{E_1, E_2, E_3\} = 0.143 > 0.05$ and the control coefficient $p = 0.6503 > 0.3$, we apply the distance-based consensus rule (i.e., $P_{6.3}$) to calculate the optimal individual decision matrices $\overline{V_k^0}(k = 1, 2, 3)$. Then, we return $\overline{V_k^0}$ to expert E_k to reconsider constructing a new decision matrix $V_k^1 = (v_{ijk}^1)_{m\times l}$. When constructing V_k^1, we suggest that $v_{ijk}^1 \in [min\{v_{ijk}^0, \overline{v_{ijk}^0}\}, max\{v_{ijk}^0, \overline{v_{ijk}^0}\}]$. Without loss of generality, based on the adjustment suggestion, experts give the adjusted individual decision matrices $V_k^1(k = 1, 2, 3)$ as follows. (See Tables 6.5, 6.6 and 6.7).

(2) In the second iteration, utilize the OWA operator to fuse standardized individual decision matrices $V_k^1(k = 1, 2, 3)$ into the collective decision matrix V_c^1 (see Table 6.8).

Since the consensus measure $CL\{E_1, E_2, E_3\} = 0.0593 > 0.05$ and the control coefficient $p = 0.1569 < 0.3$, we apply the count-based consensus rule (i.e., $P_{6.6}$) to obtain the optimal individual decision matrices $\overline{V_k^1}(k = 1, 2, 3)$. Then, we return $\overline{V_k^1}$

Table 6.5 Adjusted individual decision matrix V_1^1

	C_1	C_2	C_3	C_4	C_5	C_6	C_7	C_8
X_1	0.5000	0.2997	0.9996	1.0000	0.2000	1.0000	0.0000	0.0750
X_2	1.0000	0.5000	0.0000	0.0000	0.0000	0.0000	1.0000	0.4500
X_3	0.5000	0.6011	0.2500	0.1430	0.9800	0.5000	1.0000	0.2500
X_4	0.0000	1.0000	0.7500	0.8750	1.0000	0.7500	0.7500	0.7500
X_5	0.3748	0.0000	0.6500	0.4290	0.4405	1.0000	0.2500	1.0000

Table 6.6 Adjusted individual decision matrix V_2^1

	C_1	C_2	C_3	C_4	C_5	C_6	C_7	C_8
X_1	0.1500	0.3330	0.6670	1.0000	0.0000	1.0000	0.0333	0.0000
X_2	1.0000	0.6670	0.0333	0.0000	0.0500	0.0000	0.6500	0.5000
X_3	0.0750	0.7741	0.1500	0.1890	1.0000	0.3993	0.9500	0.3000
X_4	0.0333	0.6670	0.6670	0.8650	1.0000	0.6140	1.0000	0.7250
X_5	0.6670	0.0000	1.0000	0.4402	0.6670	0.9714	0.1500	1.0000

Table 6.7 Adjusted individual decision matrix V_3^1

	C_1	C_2	C_3	C_4	C_5	C_6	C_7	C_8
X_1	1.0000	0.3330	0.8000	1.0000	0.5000	0.9882	0.0000	0.0000
X_2	0.9750	0.3498	0.0000	0.0086	0.0000	0.0000	0.8000	0.5000
X_3	0.2500	0.6670	0.2000	0.1011	1.0000	0.6470	1.0000	0.2500
X_4	0.0000	0.4338	0.8871	0.8496	1.0000	0.9410	0.5650	0.7500
X_5	0.5000	0.1000	0.8000	0.4290	1.0000	1.0000	0.2000	1.0000

Table 6.8 Collective decision matrix V_c^1

	C_1	C_2	C_3	C_4	C_5	C_6	C_7	C_8
X_1	0.4950	0.3230	0.8000	1.0000	0.2000	0.9965	0.0067	0.0150
X_2	0.9925	0.4883	0.0067	0.0017	0.0100	0.0000	0.7950	0.4850
X_3	0.2475	0.6686	0.1950	0.1396	0.9940	0.4992	0.9850	0.2600
X_4	0.0067	0.6636	0.7525	0.8624	1.0000	0.7474	0.7445	0.7425
X_5	0.4958	0.0200	0.7950	0.4312	0.6657	0.9914	0.1950	1.0000

Table 6.9 Adjusted individual decision matrix V_1^2

	C_1	C_2	C_3	C_4	C_5	C_6	C_7	C_8
X_1	0.9500	0.2997	0.9996	1.0000	0.2000	1.0000	0.0000	0.0750
X_2	1.0000	0.5000	0.0000	0.0000	0.0000	0.0000	1.0000	0.4500
X_3	0.5000	0.6011	0.2500	0.1430	0.9800	0.5000	1.0000	0.2500
X_4	0.0000	1.0000	0.7500	0.8750	1.0000	0.7500	0.7500	0.7500
X_5	0.3748	0.0000	0.6500	0.4290	0.4405	1.0000	0.2500	1.0000

Table 6.10 Adjusted individual's decision matrix V_2^2

	C_1	C_2	C_3	C_4	C_5	C_6	C_7	C_8
X_1	0.9500	0.3330	0.6670	1.0000	0.0000	1.0000	0.0333	0.0000
X_2	1.0000	0.6670	0.0000	0.0000	0.0500	0.0000	0.6500	0.5000
X_3	0.0750	0.7741	0.1500	0.1890	1.0000	0.3993	0.9500	0.3000
X_4	0.0333	0.6670	0.6670	0.8650	1.0000	0.6140	1.0000	0.7250
X_5	0.6670	0.0000	1.0000	0.4402	0.6670	0.9714	0.1500	1.0000

Table 6.11 Adjusted individual's decision matrix V_3^2

	C_1	C_2	C_3	C_4	C_5	C_6	C_7	C_8
X_1	1.0000	0.3330	0.8000	1.0000	0.0500	0.9882	0.0000	0.0000
X_2	0.9750	0.3498	0.0000	0.0086	0.0000	0.0000	0.8000	0.5000
X_3	0.2500	0.6670	0.2000	0.1011	1.0000	0.6470	1.0000	0.2500
X_4	0.0000	0.4338	0.8871	0.8496	1.0000	0.9410	0.5650	0.7500
X_5	0.5000	0.1000	0.8000	0.4290	1.0000	1.0000	0.2000	1.0000

to expert E_k to reconsider constructing a new decision matrix $V_k^2 = (v_{ijk}^2)_{m \times l}$. When constructing V_k^2, we suggest that $v_{ijk}^2 \in [min\{v_{ijk}^1, \overline{v_{ijk}^1}\}, max\{v_{ijk}^1, \overline{v_{ijk}^1}\}]$. Without loss of generality, based on the adjustment suggestion, experts give the adjusted individual decision matrices $V_k^2 (k = 1, 2, 3)$ as follows. (See Tables 6.9–6.11)

Table 6.12 Collective decision matrix V_c^2

	C_1	C_2	C_3	C_4	C_5	C_6	C_7	C_8
X_1	0.9600	0.3230	0.8000	1.0000	0.0650	0.9965	0.0067	0.0150
X_2	0.9925	0.4883	0.0000	0.0017	0.0100	0.0000	0.7950	0.4850
X_3	0.2475	0.6686	0.1950	0.1396	0.9940	0.4992	0.9850	0.2600
X_4	0.0067	0.6636	0.7525	0.8624	1.0000	0.7474	0.7445	0.7425
X_5	0.4958	0.0200	0.7950	0.4312	0.6657	0.9914	0.1950	1.0000

(3) In the third iteration, utilize the OWA operator to fuse standardized individual decision matrices $V_k^2(k = 1, 2, 3)$ into the collective decision matrix V_c^2 (see Table 6.12). Calculate the consensus measure $CL\{E_1, E_2, E_3\} = 0.05 \leq 0.05$, and Algorithm 6.3 ends. Denote $V_k^2(k = 1, 2, 3)$ as the adjusted decision matrices using Algorithm 6.3.

Based on Eq. (6.3), we calculate the evaluation values $EV(i)(i = 1, 2, 3, 4, 5)$ of the alternatives $X_i(i = 1, 2, 3, 4, 5)$:

$$EV(1) = 0.5112, EV(2) = 0.2956, EV(3) = 0.5084,$$

$$EV(4) = 0.7241, EV(5) = 0.6260.$$

Then, we sort all the alternatives according to the evaluation values: $X_4 \succ X_5 \succ X_1 \succ X_3 \succ X_2$. Thus, the best alternative is X_4.

6.4.2 Comparison Analysis

In the following, we compare the multiple attribute consensus model based on distance-based and count-based consensus rules with the multiple attribute consensus model based on IR and DR.

(1) Multiple attribute consensus model based on IR and DR

Based on IR and DR introduced in Chap. 1, two consensus reaching models for MAGDM problems are designed:

Multiple attribute consensus model A (MACM A): in each round of iteration, based on DR, all the experts move their opinions to the collective opinion.

Multiple attribute consensus model B (MACM B): in each round of iteration, based on IR, we identify the expert whose opinion has the biggest difference from the collective opinion and should be changed. Based on DR, we adjust his/her opinion.

Let z be the number of the iterations. Then, MACM A is described as follows (see Algorithm 6.4).

Algorithm 6.4

Input: The standardized individual decision matrices $V^k(k = 1, 2, \ldots, n)$, the consensus threshold ε, the maximum number of iterations z, the associated weight vector of experts w.

Output: The adjusted individual decision matrices $\overline{V^k}(k = 1, 2, \ldots, n)$, the collective decision matrix $\overline{V^c}$, the number of the iterations z.

Step 1: Set $z = 0$ and $V_k^z = V^k(k = 1, 2, \ldots, n)$.

Step 2: Calculate the collective decision matrix $V_c^z = (v_{ijc}^z)_{m\times l}$, where $v_{ijc}^z = F_w^{OWA}(v_{ij1}^z, v_{ij2}^z, \ldots, v_{ijn}^z)$. Then, calculate the consensus measure $CL^z = \frac{1}{nml}\sum_{k=1}^{n} d(V_k^z, V_c^z)$. If $CL^z \leq \varepsilon$ or $z \geq Z$, go to Step 4. Otherwise, go to the next step.

Step 3: When constructing the adjusted decision matrix $V_k^{z+1} = (v_{ijk}^{z+1})_{m\times l}$, we suggest that $v_{ijk}^{z+1} \in [\min\{v_{ijk}^z, v_{ijc}^z\}, \max\{v_{ijk}^z, v_{ijc}^z\}](i = 1, 2, \ldots, m;\ j = 1, 2, \ldots, l;\ k = 1, 2, \ldots, n)$. Then, let $z = z + 1$, and go to Step 2.

Step 4: Let $\overline{V^k} = V_k^z(k = 1, 2, \ldots, n)$ and $\overline{V^c} = V_c^z$. Output the adjusted individual decision matrices $\overline{V^k}(k = 1, 2, \ldots, n)$, the group decision matrix $\overline{V^c}$ and the number of the iterations z.

In MACM A, we replace Step 3 by Step 3′, and then obtain MACM B (i.e., Algorithm 6.5).

Step 3′: Without loss of generality, suppose that $d(V_q^z, V_c^z) = \max_k \{d(V_k^z, V_c^z)\}$. Then, when constructing the adjusted decision matrix $V_k^{z+1} = (v_{ijk}^{z+1})_{m\times l}$, we suggest that

$$\begin{cases} v_{ijk}^{z+1} \in [\min\{v_{ijk}^z, v_{ijc}^z\}, \max\{v_{ijk}^z, v_{ijc}^z\}], & k = q \\ v_{ijk}^{z+1} = v_{ijk}^z, & k \neq q \end{cases}$$

Then, let $z = z + 1$, and go to Step 2.

(2) Parameter setting and data generation

To facilitate the comparison analysis, we simplify Algorithms 6.1–6.5 into an automatic consensus process by introducing an adjustment coefficient, β. In Algorithms 6.1–6.3, we replace $v_{ijk}^{z+1} \in [min\{v_{ijk}^z, \overline{v_{ijk}^z}\}, max\{v_{ijk}^z, \overline{v_{ijk}^z}\}]$ by $v_{ijk}^{z+1} = \beta v_{ijk}^z + (1-\beta)\overline{v_{ijk}^z}$. In Algorithms 6.4 and 6.5, we replace $v_{ijk}^{z+1} \in [min\{v_{ijk}^z, v_{ijc}^z\}, max\{v_{ijk}^z, v_{ijc}^z\}]$ by $v_{ijk}^{z+1} = \beta v_{ijk}^z + (1-\beta)v_{ijc}^z$.

In the following, we make three comparison analyses, i.e., Comparison analysis 6.1, Comparison analysis 6.2 and Comparison analysis 6.3. In Comparison analysis 6.1, we use the numerical example presented in Sect. 6.4.1. Comparison analyses 6.2 and 6.3 are based on the numerical examples used in Yu and Lai [14], and Herrera and Herrera-Viedma [6], respectively. Tables 6.13 and 6.14 show the standardized individual decision matrices in Comparison analysis 6.2 and Comparison analysis 6.3, respectively.

Table 6.13 Standardized individual decision matrices in Comparison analysis 6.2

	E_1			E_2			E_3		
	C_1	C_2	C_3	C_1	C_2	C_3	C_1	C_2	C_3
X_1	0.0000	0.2222	1.0000	0.7500	0.9091	1.0000	0.0000	0.7143	1.0000
X_2	0.3333	0.0000	0.2727	1.0000	1.0000	0.4000	0.4483	1.0000	0.8214
X_3	0.2222	0.2222	0.6364	0.5000	0.6818	1.0000	0.2759	0.0000	0.0000
X_4	1.0000	1.0000	0.0000	0.0000	0.0000	0.0000	0.6897	0.8571	0.4286
X_5	0.0556	0.3333	1.0000	0.2500	0.4545	1.0000	1.0000	0.9286	0.1786

Table 6.14 Standardized individual decision matrices in Comparison analysis 6.3

	E_1				E_2				E_3			
	C_1	C_2	C_3	C_4	C_1	C_2	C_3	C_4	C_1	C_2	C_3	C_4
X_1	0.81	0.00	1.00	0.14	0.66	1.00	0.71	0.23	0.44	0.49	0.28	0.50
X_2	0.91	0.28	0.97	0.00	0.00	0.74	1.00	0.69	0.38	0.00	1.00	1.00
X_3	0.00	0.55	1.00	0.92	0.85	0.39	0.28	0.00	0.77	0.65	0.66	0.00
X_4	1.00	0.96	0.49	0.79	1.00	0.66	0.00	0.95	1.00	0.71	0.00	0.59
X_5	0.63	1.00	0.00	1.00	0.68	0.00	0.97	1.00	0.00	1.00	0.90	0.22

(3) Comparison results

In the comparison analysis, under different adjustment coefficients β, we apply Algorithms 6.1–6.5 to the three comparison analyses. Then, we make a comparison analysis based on two criteria: the distance between individual original opinions and adjusted opinions and the number of adjusted preference values.

In Comparison analysis 6.1, let the associated weight vector of experts be $w = (0.3285, 0.3394, 0.3321)^T$, and let the consensus threshold $\varepsilon = 0.2$. Table 6.15 shows the comparison results regarding the distance between individual original opinions and adjusted opinions under different adjustment coefficients β in Comparison analysis 6.1. Table 6.16 shows the comparison results regarding the number of adjusted preference values under different adjustment coefficients β in Comparison analysis 6.1.

In Comparison analysis 6.2, let the associated weight vector of decision makers be $w = (0.1, 0.6, 0.3)^T$, and let the consensus threshold $\varepsilon = 0.1$. Then, Table 6.17 shows the comparison results regarding the distance between individual original opinions and adjusted opinions under different adjustment coefficients β in Comparison analysis 6.2. Table 6.18 shows the comparison results regarding the number of adjusted preference values under different adjustment coefficients β in Comparison analysis 6.2.

In Comparison analysis 6.3, let the associated weight vector of experts be $w = (0.1, 0.6, 0.3)^T$ and let the consensus threshold $\varepsilon = 0.1$. Then, Table 6.19 displays the comparison results regarding the distance between individual original opinions and

Table 6.15 The comparison results regarding the distance between individual original opinions and adjusted opinions in Comparison analysis 6.1

β	Algorithms 6.1	Algorithms 6.2	Algorithms 6.3		Algorithms 6.4	Algorithms 6.5
			$\theta = 0.2$	$\theta = 0.3$		
0.1	0.2243	0.3413	0.2466	0.2457	0.3862	0.3316
0.2	0.2243	0.3290	0.2453	0.2599	0.3433	0.3004
0.3	0.2243	0.3203	0.2471	0.2471	0.3003	0.3120
0.4	0.2243	0.3317	0.2376	0.2562	0.3604	0.2794
0.5	0.2243	0.3257	0.2481	0.2481	0.3218	0.3044
0.6	0.2243	0.3280	0.2427	0.2595	0.3364	0.2871
0.7	0.2243	0.3365	0.2479	0.2529	0.2819	0.2909
0.8	0.2243	0.3394	0.2498	0.2595	0.2885	0.2840
0.9	0.2243	0.3232	0.2461	0.2688	0.2795	0.2783

Table 6.16 The comparison results regarding the number of adjusted preference values in Comparison analysis 6.1

β	Algorithms 6.1	Algorithms 6.2	Algorithms 6.3		Algorithms 6.4	Algorithms 6.5
			$\theta = 0.2$	$\theta = 0.3$		
0.1	179	32	42	40	107	108
0.2	214	36	74	45	108	108
0.3	285	46	77	77	107	144
0.4	357	57	111	83	214	144
0.5	464	74	116	116	214	216
0.6	607	101	158	133	321	252
0.7	819	147	233	208	321	360
0.8	1282	232	356	306	535	540
0.9	2702	473	782	633	1070	1080

adjusted opinions under different adjustment coefficients β in Comparison analysis 6.3. Table 6.20 displays the comparison results regarding the number of adjusted preference values under different adjustment coefficients β in Comparison analysis 6.3.

From Tables 6.15–6.20, we have made the following observations:

(i) In the existing studies, the distance between individual original opinions and adjusted opinions is used to measure the adjustment amounts in the consensus process. Tables 6.15, 6.17 and 6.19 show that the consensus reaching process with the distance-based consensus rule (i.e., Algorithm 6.1) needs less adjustment amounts than MACM A (i.e., Algorithm 6.4) and MACM B (i.e., Algorithm 6.5) in the sense of distance criterion. However, on the other hand,

Table 6.17 The comparison results regarding the distance between individual original opinions and adjusted opinions in Comparison analysis 6.2

β	Algorithms 6.1	Algorithms 6.2	Algorithms 6.3		Algorithms 6.4	Algorithms 6.5
			$\theta = 0.05$	$\theta = 0.1$		
0.1	0.1813	0.1845	0.2232	0.2232	0.7578	0.2721
0.2	0.1813	0.2133	0.1969	0.1850	0.6736	0.2419
0.3	0.1813	0.1867	0.2116	0.2116	0.5894	0.3739
0.4	0.1813	0.2057	0.1997	0.1923	0.5052	0.3223
0.5	0.1813	0.1863	0.1836	0.1973	0.4210	0.2722
0.6	0.1813	0.2074	0.1892	0.1929	0.3368	0.3104
0.7	0.1813	0.1833	0.1861	0.1843	0.2526	0.3026
0.8	0.1813	0.1926	0.1822	0.1919	0.3031	0.2525
0.9	0.1813	0.1885	0.1843	0.1814	0.2896	0.2463

Table 6.18 The comparison results regarding the number of adjusted preference values in Comparison analysis 6.2

β	Algorithms 6.1	Algorithms 6.2	Algorithms 6.3		Algorithms 6.4	Algorithms 6.5
			$\theta = 0.05$	$\theta = 0.1$		
0.1	11	5	6	6	45	15
0.2	13	5	10	6	45	15
0.3	21	5	10	10	45	30
0.4	20	7	12	10	45	30
0.5	40	8	14	12	45	30
0.6	63	12	19	16	45	45
0.7	98	12	33	23	45	60
0.8	153	23	53	36	90	75
0.9	365	43	110	75	180	150

Tables 6.16, 6.18 and 6.20 also show that Algorithm 6.1 sometimes adjusts more number of preference values than MACM A and MACM B.

(ii) When using the number of adjusted preference values to measure the adjustment amounts, Tables 6.16, 6.18 and 6.20 show that the consensus reaching process with the count-based consensus rule (i.e., Algorithm 6.2) adjusts less number of preference values than MACM A (i.e., Algorithm 6.4) and MACM B (i.e., Algorithm 6.5). Simultaneously, Tables 6.15, 6.17 and 6.19 show that Algorithm 6.2 needs less adjustment amounts than MACM A and MACM B in the sense of distance criterion, for most cases.

(iii) The consensus reaching process with mixing consensus rules (i.e., Algorithm 6.3) not only needs obviously less adjustment amounts than MACM A and MACM B in the sense of distance criterion, but also adjusts less number of preference values.

Table 6.19 The comparison results regarding the distance of adjusted preference values in Comparison analysis 6.3

β	Algorithms 6.1	Algorithms 6.2	Algorithms 6.3		Algorithms 6.4	Algorithms 6.5
			$\theta = 0.05$	$\theta = 0.1$		
0.1	0.0965	0.1314	0.1219	0.1219	0.6529	0.2976
0.2	0.0965	0.1364	0.1084	0.1084	0.5803	0.2646
0.3	0.0965	0.1295	0.1151	0.1030	0.5078	0.4015
0.4	0.0965	0.1110	0.1075	0.1077	0.4352	0.3465
0.5	0.0965	0.1110	0.1076	0.1030	0.3627	0.2908
0.6	0.0965	0.1060	0.1096	0.1051	0.2902	0.3226
0.7	0.0965	0.1034	0.1111	0.1085	0.2176	0.2514
0.8	0.0965	0.1086	0.1012	0.1020	0.1451	0.2624
0.9	0.0965	0.1014	0.1006	0.1046	0.1378	0.2344

Table 6.20 The comparison results regarding the number of adjusted preference values in Comparison analysis 6.3

β	Algorithms 6.1	Algorithms 6.2	Algorithms 6.3		Algorithms 6.4	Algorithms 6.5
			$\theta = 0.05$	$\theta = 0.1$		
0.1	15	3	7	7	56	19
0.2	21	4	7	7	57	19
0.3	24	4	10	8	57	38
0.4	38	4	11	8	57	38
0.5	37	5	12	9	56	38
0.6	36	6	14	13	57	57
0.7	43	8	19	15	57	57
0.8	63	14	27	20	56	95
0.9	334	29	75	46	112	171

References

1. D. Ben-Arieh, T. Easton, Multi-criteria group consensus under linear cost opinion elasticity. Decis. Support Syst. **43**, 713–721 (2007)
2. C. Fu, M. Huhns, S.L. Yang, A consensus framework for multiple attribute group decision analysis in an evidential reasoning context. Inf. Fusion **17**, 22–35 (2014)
3. C. Fu, S.L. Yang, The group consensus based evidential reasoning approach for multiple attributive group decision analysis. Eur. J. Oper. Res. **206**, 601–608 (2010)
4. C. Fu, S.L. Yang, An evidential reasoning based consensus model for multiple attribute group decision analysis problems with interval-valued group consensus requirements. Eur. J. Oper. Res. **223**, 167–176 (2012)
5. D. Guha, D. Chakraborty, Fuzzy multi attribute group decision making method to achieve consensus under the consideration of degrees of confidence of experts' opinions. Comput. Ind. Eng. **60**, 493–504 (2011)

6. F. Herrera, E. Herrera-Viedma, Linguistic decision analysis: steps for solving decision problems under linguistic information. Fuzzy Sets Syst. **115**, 67–82 (2000)
7. Z.M. Li, M. Liechty, J.P. Xu, B. Lev, A fuzzy multi-criteria group decision making method for individual research output evaluation with maximum consensus. Knowl.-Based Syst. **56**, 253–263 (2014)
8. W. Ogryczak, T. Śliwiński, On solving linear programs with the ordered weighted averaging objective. Eur. J. Oper. Res. **148**, 80–91 (2003)
9. R.O. Parreiras, P.Y. Ekel, J.S.C. Martini, R.M. Palhares, A flexible consensus scheme for multicriteria group decision making under linguistic assessments. Inf. Sci. **180**, 1075–1089 (2010)
10. Z.S. Xu, An automatic approach to reaching consensus in multiple attribute group decision making. Comput. Ind. Eng. **56**, 1369–1374 (2009)
11. J.P. Xu, Z.B. Wu, A discrete consensus support model for multiple attribute group decision making. Knowl.-Based Syst. **24**, 1196–1202 (2011)
12. J.P. Xu, Z.B. Wu, Y. Zhang, A consensus based method for multi-criteria group decision making under uncertain linguistic setting. Group Decis. Negot. **23**, 127–148 (2014)
13. Y.J. Xu, W.C. Zhang, H.M. Wang, A conflict-eliminating approach for emergency group decision of unconventional incidents. Knowl.-Based Syst. **83**, 92–104 (2015)
14. L. Yu, K.K. Lai, A distance-based group decision-making methodology for multi-person multi-criteria emergency decision support. Decis. Support Syst. **51**, 307–315 (2011)
15. K. Yoon, The propagation of errors in multiple-attribute decision analysis: a practical approach. J. Oper. Res. soc. **40**, 681–686 (1989)
16. B.W. Zhang, Y.C. Dong, Y.F. Xu, Multiple attribute consensus rules with minimum adjustments to support consensus reaching. Knowl.-Based Syst. **67**, 35–48 (2014)

www.ingramcontent.com/pod-product-compliance
Lightning Source LLC
LaVergne TN
LVHW052320200926
848481LV00002B/623

* 9 7 8 9 8 1 1 0 1 2 8 3 9 *